THE FLAMING HEART

MARIO PRAZ, born in Rome in 1896, lived in Switzerland until his father's death four years later. He then moved to Florence, his mother's family home, where he received his education. After abandoning the study of law, he took his "laurea in lettere" (Litt. D.) in 1920. He secured a scholarship from the Italian Ministry of Education and was engaged in research work at the British Museum in 1923; for the following eight years he was Senior Lecturer in Italian at Liverpool. He became Professor of Italian Studies in Manchester in 1932, and since 1934 has been a professor of English in Rome. He has traveled widely in Europe, visiting the United States once. His journey in Spain led to the publication of *Unromantic Spain* (1929). Other works in English are *Machiavelli and the Elizabethans* (1928), *The Romantic Agony* (1933), *Studies in Seventeenth Century Imagery* (I, 1939, II, 1948), and *The Hero in Eclipse in Victorian Fiction* (1956). He is editor of the *English Miscellany*. His more recent publications have been essays and travel pieces.

THE FLAMING HEART:

Essays on Crashaw, Machiavelli, and Other Studies in the Relations between Italian and English Literature from Chaucer to T. S. Eliot by Mario Praz

The Norton Library
W · W · NORTON & COMPANY · INC · NEW YORK

W. W. Norton & Company, Inc. also publishes *The Norton Anthology of English Literature,* edited by M. H. Abrams et al; *The Norton Anthology of Poetry,* edited by Arthur M. Eastman et al; *World Masterpieces,* edited by Maynard Mack et al; *The Norton Reader,* edited by Arthur M. Eastman et al; *The Norton Facsimile of the First Folio of Shakespeare,* prepared by Charlton Hinman; and the Norton Critical Editions.

Library of Congress Cataloging in Publication Data

Praz, Mario, 1896–
    The flaming heart.

    (The Norton library)
    1. Literature, Comparative—English and Italian.
2. Literature, Comparative—Italian and English.
I. Title.
[PR129.I8P7   1973]   820'.9   72-10369
ISBN 0-393-00669-7

ACKNOWLEDGEMENTS

Some of the essays in this volume have been issued separately. "Chaucer and the Great Italian Writers of the Trecento" appeared in *The Monthly Criterion* for 1927. ' "The Politic Brain": Machiavelli and the Elizabethans' was my Annual Italian Lecture to the British Academy for 1928. 'Shakespeare's Italy' was printed in *Shakespeare Survey*, vii, and 'Donne's Relation to the Poetry of His Time' in *A Garland for John Donne*, edited by Theodore Spencer (Harvard University Press, 1931). The essay on Eliot and Dante appeared in *The Southern Review*, ii, 3 (1937). There are considerable additions to all these essays in the present edition. To the several publishers I wish to make grateful acknowledgement for permitting the present reprint. The Introduction is a partial English version of an essay ('Rapporti tra la letteratura italiana e la letteratura inglese') published in the fourth volume (*Letterature comparate*) of *Problemi ed orientamenti critici di lingua e di letteratura italiana* edited by A. Momigliana (Milan, 1948). The following essays appear for the first time in English in this volume: 'Ben Jonson's Italy' (first published in *Rivista italiana del dramma*, November 15, 1937), 'The Flaming Heart: Richard Crashaw and the Baroque' (first published in *Secentismo e marinismo in Inghilterra*, Florence, 1925), 'Ariosto in England' (first published in *Il Veltro*, June–July 1957), 'Tasso in England' (first published in the volume *Torquato Tasso, Celebrazioni Ferraresi 1954*, Milan, 1957), and 'Petrarch in England', which appears here for the first time in any form.

MARIO PRAZ

Rome, November 1957

CONTENTS

THE FLAMING HEART

Introduction: Literary Relations between Italy and England from Chaucer to the Present

LITERARY relations between England and Italy do not form a homogeneous picture, in so far as the interchanges did not take place at the same time. The direction of the influence was reversed when England's position shifted from the fringe to the centre of Western culture. Hence the Italian ignorance of even first-rate literary works from that marginal province of European culture to which pre-eighteenth century England belonged, and the English ignorance of Italian literary works as soon as, from the end of that century, Italy's position became to a great extent peripheral. Of course, in this latter case ignorance was not absolute, because the increasing number of channels of cultural influence nowadays permits the rapid diffusion of any work possessing a certain amount of originality and appeal. Italian influence in England, after an isolated wave in the second half of the fourteenth century (with Chaucer), spread into every field of culture and fashion during the Renaissance, and gradually died out during the seventeenth century after a last surge with Milton, which in its intensity presents, in the phase of decline, a parallel case to the fourteenth-century wave which preceded the full tide. On the other hand English influence in Italy has no such clean-cut course: Italy felt it for the most part indirectly, through the medium of Paris, and the imitation of English works and points of view was sporadic and provincial, never affecting the creations of genius, as had been the case with Chaucer, Shakespeare, and Milton.

No general survey of the Italian influence on English literature has appeared since 1902, when Lewis Einstein published *The Italian Renaissance in England* (Columbia University Press). Arturo Farinelli in a long review in the *Giornale storico della letteratura italiana* (xliii) pointed out the gaps in Einstein's book; a detailed research into the influence of the social customs of the Italian Renaissance in English literature can be found in T. F. Crane's *Italian Social Customs of the XVI Century and their Influence on the Literature of Europe* (New Haven, 1920), and a number of further studies on various aspects of that influence have made it desirable that a comprehensive work on the subject should be available to the general student. In 1934 R. Marshall's *Italy in English Literature, 1755–1815* appeared in New York, to which the author promised to add two more volumes for the periods 1642–1755 and 1815–1900; but this plan was apparently abandoned; so that even when Professor A. Lytton Sells's recent *Italian Influence on English Poetry* (Indiana University Press, 1955), is concluded, we shall not possess a complete study of all the aspects of the Italian influence in England. Mr. Marshall's work provided an amount of new material which, though often of merely marginal importance, showed that he had based his book on first-hand information. This is not the case with Professor Sells, who has only aimed at collecting the results of other people's studies 'in a form accessible to the student and the cultured reader,' so that his book is mainly useful as a preliminary approach to a wide and complex subject. How wide and complex, may be guessed from the present book, which is meant to illustrate some of the salient aspects and phases of that influence in detail, without setting out to give a complete picture. In the following pages I shall try, however, to enable the reader to see those episodes in their proper place in the whole.

Chaucer's Italian adventure is a special case, a curious cultural development of an influence which was chiefly financial and commercial. The banking system had been first introduced into England by Sienese, then, after the middle of the thirteenth century, by Florentine merchants; Venice appeared on the scene at the beginning of the fourteeth century. Italian words became Anglicized in the language of merchants and sailors; but there was as yet no trace of literary influence. Then in 1372–73 Chaucer journeyed to Italy to discuss with the Genoese government the establishment of a trading port in England for Genoese merchants, and to conduct in Florence certain secret business of the King's, very likely the negotiation of a loan with the Florentine bankers. We do not know whom he met in Florence, but since this young diplomat from a family of merchants was also a scholar and a man of letters, he managed to alternate the meetings with Florentine bankers with the purchase of some of the literary works which enjoyed great esteem at the time, and brought back home, together with the report of his cautious negotiations, manuscripts of Dante, Petrarch, and Boccaccio. Thus an episode of mercantile history, which at best would have been consigned to a footnote in the history of trade, found its way into literary history, where it stood out in strong relief, for Chaucer's mission changed the course of English poetry, which until then had been solely beholden to French models.

Only what is related can be assimilated: never in the course of history has a totally different culture intervened in the development of another culture or in the career of an artist. Well may the Squire of the *Canterbury Tales* tell of Cambuscan, king of Tartary; there is no more reason to talk of Oriental influence in such a case than when we see Mongolian pigtails in the frescoes of the Spanish Chapel in Florence, or scraps of Chinese materials in fourteenth-century paintings, or of Turkish carpets in Italian, Spanish or Flemish masters of the end of the fifteenth and beginning of the sixteenth century. Picturesque hints of this kind do not in the least mean that the artist's vision or the form of his works is affected. Now mediaeval culture was uniform throughout Europe; Chaucer's Latin classics were those which had exerted a strong influence on the minor Renaissance of the twelfth century, whose study was recommended by the current poetics (Matthiew de Vendôme, Geoffroi de Vinsauf); the works Chaucer translated were the most popular ones in the Western world, the *Roman de la Rose,* Boethius' *De Consolatione,*

Albertano da Brescia's *Liber Consolationis et Consilii,* and Pope Innocent's *De Contemptu Mundi.* Chaucer and the great Italian writers of the Trecento spoke different languages, but had a common culture, and it is easy to understand why, in a period in which there were no well-defined limits between works of imagination and works of learning, Chaucer could annex the great Italian poets to his own cultural patrimony in the same way in which he had appropriated the works of the feeble imitators of the *Roman de la Rose* (Machaut, Froissart). What is still more relevant is that the borrowings were not confined to the contents of the works: the common linguistic foundations (thanks to the strong French—and therefore Latin—influence on the English language) made it possible also to influence the form.

Chaucer's example encouraged Gower to write in English, whereas before he used to write in Latin and in French. But although Gower appears to have known Italian, or at least Dante (he quotes from *Inferno* xiii, 64–66, and xiv, 79), he does not imitate the Italians. And one has to wait until the Renaissance to speak again of Italian influence on English literature. The effects of the first phase of Italian Renaissance, or humanism, as it is called, on literary works in the vernacular, were, however, slow in making themselves felt in England. The example set by Wyatt and Surrey, who in the first half of the sixteenth century imported the Petrarchan sonnet (already tinged with Serafino's conceits) from Italy, had no following. Neither was another of Surrey's innovations quick in bearing fruits: the introduction of blank verse into English poetry, after the example of the *endecasillabo sciolto* used by Cardinal Ippolito de' Medici in his rendering of the Second Book of the *Aeneid* (1539). This heroic verse, used by Chaucer in the *Canterbury Tales,* but deprived of its rhyme, was destined to become the metre of the drama and the epic poem, a perfect instrument in the hands of Shakespeare and Milton. Wyatt's and Surrey's verses appeared posthumously, in 1557, and Watson and Sidney, the fathers of the Elizabethan sonnet, who wrote at the end of the century, did not derive from them, but from the Franco-Italian tradition which had established itself with the Pléiade, the names of whose poets, Ronsard, Du Bellay, Desportes, had become no less famous than the Italian ones. The pattern of the fourteen-line sonnet came from Italy, whereas the habit of grouping a series of sonnets under the fictitious name of a beloved lady (Drayton's *Idea*, Daniel's *Delia*, etc.) came from France. Themes, language, and conceits belong to the common stock of the sonneteers; the Platonic and pastoral *motifs* are Italian, the allusion to the flight of years and the decay of beauty, French; the 'kisses' and the amorous compliments derive from the humanist poets (Pontanus, Johannes Secundus, Marullus). Petrarchism in Sidney's sonnets frequently bears a French stamp, and also the anti-Petrarchism of certain of his lines is of French inspiration (Du Bellay's ode *Contre les Pétrarquistes*).

Italian influence on the form of English literary works is limited to the collections of sonnets, to Spenser's poem, and to euphuism, but the cultural influence in the wide sense of the word has an enormous range, starting from the foundation of classical studies in England laid by Thomas Linacre and William Grocyn on their return from Italy about 1490. Castiglione's *Cortegiano* and Machiavelli's *Principe* had already found disciples at the court of Henry VIII; towards the end of the sixteenth century the text-books of the new era became widely known thanks to the translators. The *Cortegiano*, translated by Sir Thomas Hoby, led to the establishment of the English notion of a 'gentleman', equally accomplished in arms and letters—*tam Marti quam Mercurio*—and accustomed to dissimulate his skill under an elegant carelessness (*sprezzatura*); Robert Paterson translated the *Galateo* (1576), Pettie the first three books of Guazzo's *Civil Conversazione* (1581; the fourth book was translated into English by Bartholomew Young in 1586). The Platonism of the Florentine Academy spread also to England, together with its parlour adaptations: disquisitions on the nature of love, problems and paradoxes, and the related subtleties of devices and emblems. Samuel Daniel translated Giovio's *Dialogo delle imprese* (*The worthy tract of Paulus Iovius*, 1585), and Geoffrey Whitney derived his *Choice of Emblems* (1586) mostly from Alciat. George Chapman utilised Florentine Neoplatonism and the Italian mythologists in his poems and dramas, Spenser derived his *Fowre Hymnes* from Benivieni, and Greene and Lyly imitated

Italian courtesy-books. Italian society was a model for Europe and Shakespeare in *Richard II* (ii, 1) spoke of

> proud Italy,
> Whose manners still our tardy apish nation
> Limps after in base imitation.

Everything from fencing and horsemanship to poetry and music, was 'Italianate'. An event of the greatest importance for the development of English poetry and music was the publication in 1588 of *Musica Transalpina*, a collection of madrigals translated from the Italian; while towards the end of the sixteenth century the first group of musical terms was introduced from Italy.[1] Translations were not always made directly from the Italian; frequently a French version or imitation acted as the medium; thus Bandello, who supplied themes to the Elizabethan dramatists, was done into English by Painter (*The Palace of Pleasure*, 1566) and by Fenton (*Tragical Discourses*, 1567) through the medium of Belleforest's French text.[2] And if a few could could read Machiavelli in the original, translations of his chief work remained unpublished, and most people knew him through Gentillet's travesty, which was done into English by Simon Patericke, so that it was easy for him to become the symbol of whatever vice the Protestants saw in Southern Europe. Also Italian critical theories found followers in England: theorists like Minturno and Scaliger were echoed by Sidney in his *Apologie for Poetrie*.

The spreading of the knowledge of the Italian language and Italian manners in England owed much to Giovanni Florio, whose principal title to fame is, however, the transla-

[1] See my study on 'The Italian Element in English' in *Essays and Studies by Members of the English Association*, Vol. xi, reprinted in *Ricerche anglo-italiane*, Rome, 1944.

[2] This does not mean that the Italian text was unknown in England. Webster probably knew Bandello also in the original since the story of the Egyptian thief (found in Herodotus) from which he took the suggestion for Ferdinand's trick of the dead man's hand (*Duchess of Malfi*, iv, 1, 35 ff.), immediately precedes that of the Duchess of Malfi (respectively i, 25 and i, 26), and, unlike this, is not included in Painter's *Palace of Pleasure*, nor is it given by Fenton. A *catalogue raisonné* of *Elizabethan Translations from Italian* was published by Mary Augusta Scott, Boston and New York, 1916.

tion of Montaigne's *Essays* (1603); and it was from Montaigne, indeed, and from Seneca that the Elizabethan dramatists drew their philosophical background. Florio was probably also the first translator into English of the *Decameron*.[3] He became well known as a teacher of Italian in Oxford and London. Italian was the second modern language to produce a crop of teaching manuals (French had been the first). The year 1550 saw William Thomas's grammar, a compilation from Italian manuals followed by a dictionary intended to assist readers of Italian classics; Thomas thought that Italian was taking a place in education beside Latin and Greek. But the real pioneers of the study of Italian in England were the refugees, above all Michelangelo Florio and his son Giovanni, as we have seen. Giovanni's method could not fail to procure him a large public. In his two volumes *First Fruits* (1578) and *Second Fruits* (1591), which he made attractive by modelling them on Italian treatises of manners, he set forth his Puritan point of view, which was calculated to overcome the objections of those who attributed a corrupting influence to Italian culture (like Roger Ascham in his celebrated *Scholemaster*, 1570). His teaching aimed at storing the pupils' minds with ready-made phrases, proverbs, etc., allowing them to show off in the smart set to which they belonged: a fault which was not so much typical of the author as of his period, and it can hardly even be called a fault, because polite conversation was then only beginning, and could not avoid a certain mechanical formality and stiffness; dialogue consisted to a large extent of compliments and puns, as may be seen from so many scenes in Shakespeare's plays. Therefore Florio, to supplement his *Fruits*, published a *Giardino di Ricreatione nel quale crescono fronde, fiori e frutti, vaghe* [sic], *leggiadri, e soavi, sotto nome di sei mila Proverbij, e piacevoli riboboli Italiani, colti e scelti da Giovanni Florio, non solo utili, ma dilettevoli per ogni spirito vago della nobil lingua Italiana* (London, 1591); thus, thanks to a few idiomatic sentences inserted at the right moment, or a more or less aptly quoted

[3] See Herbert G. Wright, *The First English Translation of the Decameron*, Upsala, 1953, and *Boccaccio in England from Chaucer to Tennyson*, University of London, The Athlone Press, 1957, p. 191.

proverb, a gentleman or a gentlewoman could give the impression of a deep acquaintance with Italian; and not only courtiers and gentlemen availed themselves of such repertories, but playwrights also, like Shakespeare and Jonson, made use of Florio's volumes. Florio compiled, moreover, a famous dictionary, *A Worlde of Wordes, Or Most copious, and exact Dictionarie in Italian and English* (1598), reprinted in 1611 as *Queen Anna's New World of Words*, and in 1659 enriched with the English-Italian section by another teacher of Italian in London, Giovanni Torriano. Florio, though the most conspicuous, was not the sole author of handbooks for the study of Italian: there were those of Scipione Lentulo translated by Henry Grantham, of the Frenchman Desainsliens, known as Claudius Hollyband, and *The Passenger* by Benvenuto. No education could be considered complete without a knowledge of Italian, and Milton, who knew the language well enough to be able to compose a few plausible sonnets in it, maintained in his *Tractate on Education* (1644) that boys, besides the prescribed subjects, might easily learn Italian in their spare time.

The habit of English gentlemen of completing their education with a journey to Italy dates from the Renaissance. It was a habit at which Protestant rigorists looked askance; Ascham, as we have already said, denounced the corruption of papal Rome, and Italianate propensities; George Gascoigne, after having introduced several literary innovations from Italy, repudiated the new profane and ostentatious customs in *The Steele Glass* (1576), and Thomas Nash in *The Unfortunate Traveller* (1594) gave a highly coloured picture of Italian splendours and crimes. John Lyly, in his famous novel, *Euphues, or the Anatomy of Wit* (1579), described the adventures of a young Athenian in corrupt Naples (that is, of an Oxford student in the corrupt Italianate society of London, which Lyly accused of irreligion and immorality). However, while condemning Italian customs, Lyly let himself become imbued with that deeper Italianism that was the influence on style. That artificial sentence structure characterized by alliterations, antitheses, and every sort of rhetorical device, which took the name of euphuism from the title of his novel, originated in the writers of the silver age, and had been adapted to a vernacular language by Boccaccio in his *Filocolo*. It is noticeable that Watson also, in his *Hekatompathia* (1582), while translating and imitating Serafino Aquilano's sonnets, came naturally to write in a euphuistic style. Lyly's style deserves an attention which is out of all proportion to the contents of his works, because of the influence it had on English prose, and not only that of his time: its cadences were to be echoed not only by Robert Greene, but by Sir Thomas Browne, and, much later, by De Quincey. On the other hand the predilection for strange similes derived from the ancient natural historians (chiefly Pliny) and Alciat's *Emblems* gives a peculiar colour, both mediaeval and manneristic, to Lyly's pages. A hastening of the *tempo* by means of elliptical fore-shortening was in due course to transform this style into the metaphysical wit Donne brought into fashion.

Lyly followed the Italian models closely, and imitated their courtly atmosphere, also in his mythological and pastoral plays (among which *Endymion*, 1588, is the best): by adopting for the stage the type of Neoplatonic and courtly dialogue he had derived from Italy, and introducing light and graceful poems into his plays, in the manner of the *Decameron*, Lyly paved the way to Shakespeare's comedies.

Sir Philip Sidney was in Italy in 1573–74, studied at Padua and lived in Venice, where he knew Tintoretto and sat to Paolo Veronese for his portrait (which cannot be traced); on Languet's advice he avoided Rome for fear of being corrupted by the atmosphere of the papal court: his dream was to make English poetry comparable with the poetry of Italy, and by his example and patronage he greatly encouraged English letters: his pastoral-political novel, the *Arcadia*, which owes little more than the title to Sannazaro, was for many a mine of thoughts and conceits; his *Astrophel and Stella* greatly promoted the vogue for the sonnet; and his *Apologie for Poetrie* gave the quintessence of Italian literary criticism. Giordano Bruno dedicated the *Spaccio* and the *Eroici furori* to him. The philosophical discussions reported in the *Cena delle ceneri* took place in the house of Sidney's friend and biographer, Sir Fulke Greville (Bruno's Folco Grivello). Nevertheless it is far from easy to trace Bruno's ideas in Greville's writings, or, for that matter, in Sidney's or those of any other contemporary English writer, although according to some the Italian philosopher is hinted at in the character of Berowne (or Biron) in Shakespeare's *Love's Labour's Lost*.

On the other hand, one of the most obvious cases of Italian influence, Spenser's *Faerie Queene*, is not so simple as it may at first appear. Certainly the list of Spenser's borrowings from Ariosto and Tasso is impressive; and without Ariosto's *ottava* the Spenserian stanza would never have been born, to which, however, the final Alexandrine gives a dreaming air, a plaintive, reverberating cadence. And Spenser was the first in England, in 1590, to call one of the divisions of a long poem a *canto*. But for all the precise parallels of passages one can muster, and all the indisputable derivations of characters and episodes, Spenser's resemblance to Ariosto is only superficial, as we shall see. In a sense Spenser, compared with Ariosto, marked a return to the ideals of the Middle Ages, just as Chaucer did in respect to Boccaccio in his *rifacimento* of the *Filostrato*, and both in this respect and in his taste for pageants and allegories, he offers a striking resemblance to the Italian mannerist painters, with whom he has in common also a contrast between the vividness of painstakingly reproduced details and an unreal, arbitrarily constructed space.

Renaissance tragedy has its starting point in Seneca also in England; but Seneca was an Italian rediscovery. His reputation as an author of tragedies had died down during the Middle Ages, but the second half of the thirteenth century saw the beginnings of a revival; in the course of time Giraldi Cinthio became its authoritative supporter in the *Discorso intorno al comporre delle comedie e delle tragedie:* 'In almost all his tragedies he excelled (so far as I can judge) whatever was written by the Greeks in wisdom, gravity, decorum, stateliness, and sententiousness.' This opinion finds a close parallel in the visual arts, for which the model of the new classicism was Roman art, chiefly of the period of the Antonines, rather than Greek art, which was practically unknown in its genuine monuments.

The point of view of the Italian critics prevailed also in France, and when the English critics, who echoed those of the Continent, sought for a name to indicate perfection in the tragic art, their choice naturally fell on Seneca. The Senecan type of tragedy which became prevalent was fixed once for all in Italy by Giraldi Cinthio (who came to the fore in 1541 with *Orbecche*), in France by Étienne Jodelle (1552), and in England by Thomas Kyd (1586). Sensationalism was the kind of theatrical appeal which attracted Cinthio to Seneca: the themes of the *Thyestes* and the *Medea*, the cruelty of a diabolical tyrant and the fury of a wronged woman, lent themselves to the presentation of horrors: for Giraldi Cinthio interpreted as 'horror' the φόβος Aristotle demanded from tragedy. In fact Cinthio had much in common with the Elizabethan dramatists, except a quality without which all the rest was of little avail, that is, a spark of genius.

Italy was a guide to England in acquainting her with Seneca. Nor was it merely a case of bookish influence. Italian actors toured in England in 1572, 1574, and 1578, and from 1582 on we have evidence that the most typical aspect of the Italian drama was known on the English stage. Even when those actors had no Senecan dramas in their repertory, they offered all the same an example of stage technique. Then we have English dramas modelled on, or actually translated from, Italian ones; e.g., Gascoigne's *Jocasta* was an English rendering of Dolce's *Giocasta*, which in its turn had been translated from Euripides; Alabaster's Latin drama, *Roxana*, followed Groto's *Dalida* closely, and the prologue of Dolce's *Didone* served as a model to the prologue of *Gismond of Salerne*. It is noteworthy that whereas throughout the whole Elizabethan period there are only four plays directly copied from the Italian, three of them appeared between 1564 and 1568, that is, during the formative period which coincides with the establishment of the Senecan influence. Moreover the authors of those English Senecan tragedies belonged to that part of society which advocated an Italian journey as a part of the making of a gentleman, and in fact *Gorboduc*, the only tragedy of the first group of Senecan dramas which has not an Italian model, is in part the work of an author who had travelled in Italy. Moreover the Italian *intermezzi* gave suggestions for the transformation of that courtly entertainment, the mask, and Stephen Gosson, in *Plays confuted in five actions* (1581), bears witness that Italian actors frequently appeared on the English stage to perform Italian plays, also in Italian. They acted both the popular *commedia dell'arte* and the literary drama of Latin origin. The strolling players in *Hamlet* stage a *commedia dell'arte*. It has been shown that Shakespeare had Italian scenarios in mind when he wrote *The Tempest;* the scenes between Stephano and Trinculo (this latter name being probably derived from a Neapolitan drinking song, according to Croce) seem to be actual translations from some Neapolitan farce. Also the figures of the two clowns, Launce and Speed, in *The Two Gentlemen of Verona,* spring from the zanies of the *commedia dell'arte.*

Italian words and phrases occur frequently in the Elizabethan dramatists, who, with the exception of Shakespeare—whose balance confirms his genius—saw Italy through the dark spectacles of religious prejudice and sensationalism, seeking there that exotic thrill which the Italian sixteenth-century authors (Giraldi Cinthio and Speroni) found in Oriental stories. A fictitious Machiavelli, mostly taken from Gentillet's travesty, helped to give the principle of evil a dramatic mask, and lift the presentation of the Devil from the rudimentary puppet of the mediaeval stage to the fascinating complexity of Iago and Bosola. This type of superhuman villain, appearing now and again on the Elizabethan stage, is none other than Seneca's perfidious tyrant brought up to date by an infusion of Machiavellian cynicism.

However even when the source of the plot of an Elizabethan drama is a *novella* or a more or less legendary Italian story—to cite only the chief blood-and-thunder tragedies with an Italianate background: *The Spanish Tragedy,* a mixture of Italian and Spanish elements; Marlowe's *Jew of Malta* (1589); Marston's *Antonio and Mellida* (1599) and *The Insatiate Countess* (about 1610); Middleton's *Women Beware Women* (1612); Tourneur's *Revenger's Tragedy* (1607) and *Atheist's Tragedy* (1611); Webster's *White Devil* (1612) and *The Duchess of Malfi* (about 1613–14); Middleton's and Rowley's *Changeling* (1623); Ford's *'Tis Pity She's a Whore* —even when the text of the story found in Fenton or Painter is followed closely enough, we must always bear in mind that if in such cases we talk of Italian influence, it is in a different degree than when we talk of it apropos of Chaucer. With the same Senecan starting point, the Italian dramas of the Renaissance and those of Elizabethan England could hardly be more different, and the difference can be summed up briefly: the former are stillborn, the latter throb with life. Here, in the midst of disconnected and confused chatter, or bombastic rant, we are suddenly struck by a cry which thrills us as if it came from a close friend; as if in a monster covered with strange scales or exotic feathers we were suddenly to discover the appealing look of a brother. Bloodthirsty plots, barbaric roars, fragments of Roman Seneca inserted in between the gargoyles of a Gothic cathedral—and then those plain sentences with their terrible precision, that *de te fabula* which takes us by surprise: 'Cover her face; mine eyes dazzle; she died young. . . .' We find nothing like this in the Italian plays of the Cinquecento, empty shells of second-hand rhetoric which does not even shine with those formal beauties that redeem so many commonplace sonnets of the Italian followers of Petrarch. Any comparison seems then superfluous; and even if phrases and images of Groto's *Adriana* (1578) seem to echo in *Romeo and Juliet* (mostly those which were the stock-in-trade of the Petrarchan school), even if there are a few coincidences between Orlando Pescetti's *Cesare* (1594) and Shakespeare's *Julius Caesar*, we feel that to talk of influence in such cases would amount to stultifying source-hunting, and mean not seeing the wood for the trees. Only in Ben Jonson's *Volpone* do we find the Venetian local colour rendered with such exactness that a search for his source of information appears rewarding.

As for Shakespeare, if we want to talk of Italian influence, we must abandon his major works and direct our attention to the scenes of *The Tempest* in the manner of the *commedia dell'arte*, we must look at the witty conversations in the comedies, where the characters talk according to an etiquette and a taste which Castiglione had taught in his *Cortegiano*, and make puns of the kind illustrated in that manual of the fashionable world,[4] and we must also consider the licentious atmosphere and Alexandrian conceits of *Venus and Adonis*

---

[4] See my essay on 'Shakespeare, il Castiglione e le facezie,' in *Machiavelli in Inghilterra, ed altri saggi*, Rome, 1942. Many among the *facezie* quoted by Castiglione find a counterpart in Shakespeare.

and *The Rape of Lucrece,* which, like Marino's *Adone,* do not soar much above the average taste of the period.

In the passage *To the Reader* prefixed to Robert Southwell's *St. Peter's Complaint* some critics have seen an allusion to the profaneness of *Venus and Adonis.* But Southwell, a Jesuit poet, who had lived in Rome from 1578 to 1586, had begun the translation of Tansillo's *Lacrime di San Pietro* even before his imprisonment in London,[5] and possibly the passage does not mean more than its words import, that is, an antithesis between Christ's thorn and Venus's rose, this latter being a symbol of the erotic Muse in general. The lines of this Catholic martyr strike the first notes of that flamboyant baroque which found a conspicuous, if somewhat isolated, champion in England in Richard Crashaw (who in the latter part of his life repaired to Rome and was secretary to Cardinal Pallotta and died at Loreto). Crashaw learned much from Marino, in addition to what he imitated from the Jesuit poets in Latin.

A different kind of *concettismo* is illustrated by Donne's metaphysical wit, which owes little to Italian poets except, possibly, for his famous simile of the compasses in *A Valediction: forbidding Mourning,* which is found in one of Guarini's madrigals.[6] But Donne was acquainted with the chief Italian poets, and when he described the union of lovers in *The Extasie,* he did it in a way which reminds us of one of Petrarch's sonnets ('Quando giunge per gli occhi al cor profondo . . .') and according to the recipe of the Italian Neoplatonists.

During the course of the seventeenth century we watch the progressive decline of the Italian influence. The Italian poets, who had a wide circulation in Elizabeth's time, were later read only by a restricted circle of courtiers and scholars. Already the translations and imitations by William Drummond of Hawthornden (from Marino, and from many other

[5] See my study on 'Robert Southwell's "Saint Peter's Complaint" and its Italian Source' in *Ricerche anglo-italiane, op. cit.*

[6] Con voi sempre son io Agitato ma fermo, E se'l meno v'involo, il più vi lasso; Son simile al compasso, Ch'un piede in voi, quasi mio centro, i'fermo, L'altro patisce di fortuna i giri, Ma non può far, che intorno a voi non giri.

Italian poets of whom, both great and small, his library was full, such as Luigi Groto, Ludovico Paterno, Lelio Capilupi, Maurizio Moro, etc.), published in 1616 and 1627, betrayed the fashion of a bygone age. The vogue for the sonnet had long been dead, dying soon after its climax in 1609 when Shakespeare's sonnets were published. However, Drummond was not forgotten. His poems were published in 1656 with a preface by Milton's nephew, Edward Phillips, who was under Milton's influence and possibly echoed some of his opinions in his plagiarised encyclopaedia, the *Theatrum Poetarum* (1675), in which the Italian poets are allotted a considerable share.

The so-called 'Cavalier poets' were occasionally inspired by the Italians, but were acquainted also with French and Spanish poets; we find a belated group of Italianate gentlemen round Thomas Stanley, who had been a pupil of the son of Edward Fairfax, Tasso's translator. Stanley, who had travelled much abroad, translated Petrarch, Tasso, Guarini, Marino, and minor writers like Preti, Casone, and Gatti. Richard Lovelace, a friend and relative of Stanley's, introduced into English poetry, in imitation of Achillini, the praise of women with physical defects and the theme of the whipped courtesan. Edward Sherburne, another friend of Stanley's, travelled in Italy and in other parts of the Continent in the period 1654–59. A translator and imitator of Marino and his Italian and French followers, Sherburne divided his 1651 collection of poems (*Salmacis, Lyrian and Sylvia*) into sections (*Erotica, Ludicra, Ethica, Sacra*) modelled on those in Marino's *Rime* (*Amorose, Morali, Sacre, etc.*). Philip Ayres (1638–1712) is also linked to Stanley's circle, and his *Lyric Poems made in imitation of the Italians* (1687) faintly echoed the fashion of the beginning of the century: like Lovelace, he also translated Achillini's *Bellissima Mendica*, and other verse of Marino and the Marinists.[7]

[7] See my study on 'Stanley, Sherburne and Ayres as Translators and Imitators of Italian, Spanish and French Poets,' in *Ricerche anglo-italiane, op. cit.* Both this study and the one on Southwell cited above originally appeared in *The Modern Language Review*, Vols. xx (1925) and xix (1924) respectively. See also Galbraith M. Crump, 'A Thomas Stanley Ms.' in *The Times Literary Supplement*, July 26, 1957, p. 457. Prof. Edward Wilson and Prof. E. R. Vincent have prepared an edition of that Ms.

The last of the metaphysical poets, and the least representative of them (although Dr. Johnson chose him as typical of the school), Abraham Cowley, introduced into England the Pindaric ode and the heroic poem modelled on Tasso. He combined Tasso with suggestions from Crashaw's version of Marino's *Sospetto d'Erode* for his own Infernal Council. And with those poets, and a list of Dante quotations from the works of Sir Thomas Browne,[8] we should close this survey of the seventeenth century with a less impressive record of Italian influence than the sixteenth, were it not for Milton, who brings a long tradition of Italian influence in England to a glorious conclusion.

Milton first studied the Greek and Latin poets, chiefly Ovid; but as soon as, acting on his father's advice, he had learned French and Italian, he found that above the Latin poets, who occasionally spoke 'unworthy things of themselves or unchaste of those names which before they had extolled,' he 'preferred the two famous renowners of° Beatrice and Laura, who never write but honour of them to whom they devote their verse, displaying sublime and pure thoughts, without transgression.' Dante and Petrarch made him aware of the spiritual deficiency of the pagans. The results of Milton's new allegiance are to be seen in the *Sonnet to a Nightingale* and more directly in those early sonnets, both English and Italian, whose date can be assigned with a fair degree of certainty to 1630. Mr John Smart showed that in 1629 Milton purchased a copy of the 1565 edition of the sonnets of Giovanni della Casa; and the sonnet form Milton adopted when he revived this short poem was not the Elizabethan one, but that which Della Casa invented, characterized by run-on, instead of the Petrarchan end-stop, lines.

When, in 1638, Milton travelled to Italy, he was already an accomplished Italian scholar. In Florence he attended meetings of the Academy of the Svogliati, where he read Latin verse. One cannot imagine anything more uncongenial to Milton's tastes than the *milieu* of mediocre Florentine writers with whom he consorted; one of them, Antonio Malatesti, mischievously ridiculed Milton's severe chastity by dedicating

[8] See my study on 'Sir Thomas Browne' in *English Studies*, xi, 5 (1929), collected in *Studi e svaghi inglesi*, Florence, 1937.

to him a collection of licentious verse, *La Tina, Equivoci rusticali*. According to his own statement in the *Areopagitica*, he visited Galileo, at the time a prisoner of the Inquisition; this visit, which might have taken place in the spring of 1639, has been called in question, but not conclusively disproved.[9] In Naples Milton met a more congenial personage than the Florentine literati, the pompous G. B. Manso, Marquis of Villa, who posed as a protector of letters, and had been the patron of both Tasso and Marino. To him Milton addressed some Latin lines in which he expressed the desire to find such a friend as would pay honour to him as Manso had paid honour to the poet Marino, and revealed the intention of writing an epic poem on a national theme in the manner of the *Aeneid* and the *Gerusalemme*. From Tasso's *Discorsi* Milton derived not only a suggestion for the theme of his intended epos (Arthur), but chiefly, as we shall see, precepts for writing a heroic poem. Manso must have called Milton's attention to Marino's *Strage degli Innocenti*, which he remembered for an important detail, the conception of Satan. Among the many sources which have been suggested for *Paradise Lost*, we find mention of G. B. Andreini's mystery play (*sacra rappresentazione*) *Adamo*, Milan, 1613, and of *L'Adamo Caduto*, a tragedy by Serafino della Salandra, Cosenza, 1647: the claim of this latter, maintained by a Neapolitan writer, Francesco Zicari, in 1845, in our own time found a conspicuous supporter in Norman Douglas, who discussed the source in *Old Calabria*; but, apart from the fact that certain resemblances may be due to the utilisation of the same Biblical sources, we find no mention of Della Salandra (whereas we find mention of Andreini) in Phillips's *Theatrum Poetarum*, which, as we have seen, reflects Milton's culture.

Italian influence on English literature declines from about the middle of the seventeenth century and regains some strength only in the romantic period. In the long interval we find the Italian impressions of English travellers, the influence of the Italian opera on music, and of Italian art on the vogue for the picturesque which preceded romanticism (the Italian

[9] See S. B. Liljegren, *Studies in Milton*, Lund, 1918; A. B. Gilbert, 'Milton and Galileo,' in *Studies in Philology*, xix (1922), and Liljegren's rejoinder in *Anglia Beiblatt*, xxxiv (1923).

landscape became fashionable about 1770 for its 'picturesque' aspects admired in the paintings of Salvator Rosa, Poussin and Claude: the English garden-designers were urged to imitate the 'horrid graces' of 'savage Salvator,' and to 'create new Tivolis,' since the waterfalls of Terni and Tivoli threw people into ecstasies), but in no case can one speak of a close relation between the two literatures, except for the influence of Boccalini's *Ragguagli di Parnaso* and of the French version (*L'Espion du Grand Seigneur*, 1684–87?) of a book by Giovanni Paolo Marana whose Italian text has not been preserved. Professor J. B. Robertson [10] remarked that 'even Dryden makes no parade of his knowledge of Italian sources, although this was undoubtedly considerable': at any rate in three of his *Fables* he gave, in Joseph Warton's words, 'high poetical improvements' of three of Boccaccio's tales, deriving the plots (*Sigismonda and Guiscardo* from *Decameron*, Giorn. iv, nov. 1, *Theodore and Honoria* from Giorn. i, nov. 8, and *Cymon and Iphigenia* from Giorn. v, nov. 1) without being in the least affected by the style. If we compare the enormous vogue for Machiavelli abroad with the lack of interest in another great Italian thinker, Vico, we realise how far the diffusion of a writer is helped not only by his genius, but also (one could almost say: first of all) by the fashion his country is enjoying among foreigners at the time. In Machiavelli's time Italy was in the limelight; in Vico's she was little more than a geographical expression. One has to wait until Joyce's *Finnegans Wake* to speak of Vico's influence on English literature.

After the mid-seventeenth century the esteem for the Italian people had been declining in England, and it is mostly contempt that we find in Addison's *Remarks on Several Parts of Italy* (1705). Those were the years in which the English became fully aware of their strength and wisdom; the more they felt they were the true heirs not only of the republican virtues, but also of the imperial glories of ancient Rome, the more they were ready to condemn the degenerate Italians, ignorant, superstitious, slavish, hiding their immorality under the veneer of a decayed beauty. They were shocked at the idea of having once gone to school to Italy, and now they

[10] *Studies in the Genesis of Romantic Theory in the Eighteenth Century*, Cambridge University Press, 1923, p. 245.

repudiated her with scorn. Addison calls the best contemporary Italian writers pedants (*Spectator*, no. 5), follows Boileau in his contempt for Tasso, and shows little acquaintance with Italian literature, except for Boccalini's *Ragguagli di Parnaso*; his remarks on the pleasures of imagination and good taste, according to Professor Robertson,[11] indicate that he must have looked into Muratori's *Della perfetta poesia italiana*.

Before the English, who with the rise of the middle class had become imbued with Puritan ideas, could consider Italy with equanimity, it was necessary first of all to redeem the character of the Italians. The typical Italian was for them a caricature of the legendary Machiavelli who had been the butt of the Elizabethan stage: a diabolical apologist of the crimes of princes. Much was done towards dispelling this sinister memory of the past by the live presence in England of an Italian in whose character the English were surprised to find a vigour and an integrity akin to those which they claimed as their own. Giuseppe Baretti did much to spread the knowledge of Italian prestige thanks to the personal respect he gained from Doctor Johnson and his circle. The contact with a man of character was worth many eloquent vindications for an empirical race like the English. And an eloquent vindication, coming from Baretti, was calculated to carry weight. This vindication was *An Account of the Manners and Customs of Italy* which Baretti brought out in rejoinder to Samuel Sharp's slanderous *Letters from Italy*. Baretti showed the Italians as possessing all the affections proper to a feeling heart. Neither did they lack manly virtues. Just then the attention of all Europeans who were inspired by the new democratic spirit was concentrated on Corsica; Rousseau planned a democratic constitution for the island, and Johnson's friend, Boswell, travelled to Corsica and defined Pasquale Paoli's government as 'the best that hath ever existed in the democratical form.' It was as if ancient republican Rome was coming back to life. Corsica was the seed of that English enthusiasm for Italian independence which sprang up during the nineteenth century.

[11] *Op. cit.*, pp. 246–249.

The reawakened interest in Italy in the second half of the eighteenth century is also witnessed by a number of translations from Italian epic and lyric poems: as a rule these translations were very mediocre and remained in manuscript or had a very limited circulation; William Huggins's version of the *Orlando Furioso* is no exception, although that eccentric gentleman generously rewarded Baretti for helping him to put it to rights. As for the poets, or rather versifiers (some of whom, by the end of the eighteenth century, gathered in Florence round Robert Merry, and styled themselves 'Della Cruscans' in sign of protest against the Grand Duke's suppression of that Academy in 1783, which in their opinion had dealt a severe blow at Italian poetry, and published in 1785 *The Florence Miscellany*), they frequently exhorted the Italians to independence in many a *canzone* modelled on Petrarch or Guidi, but there were also some who dug up the old scandals of the Borgias and the Medicis.

These scandals, with their customary sinister background, enjoyed a spell of belated popularity with the 'tales of terror,' for which Horace Walpole had given a recipe in his *Castle of Otranto* (1765: which pretended to be a translation from the Italian), a recipe Mrs. Radcliffe was to improve by the end of the century thanks to extensive borrowings of picturesque descriptions of Italian landscapes taken from travel books and of the portrait of the wicked Machiavellian from Elizabethan dramas. Italy, that for the Elizabethans was a magnificent, if somewhat sinister, court, shining with beauty and passion and steeped in the warm colours of the Venetian school, had now come down to the rank of a *genre* painting: a picturesque landscape with blasted trees in the foreground, villages perched up on rocky hills and a grim Gothic castle in the distance, and, by way of human figures, a group of banditti armed with long stilettoes: a darksome Gothic vision as against the classical one of old. For, as is well known, one sees only what one *wants* to see. What we say here about the interpretation of the character of a whole nation is true also in the case of a single author.

The study of an author's fortune, particularly abroad, inevitably points to one conclusion: that an author is popular in so far as he lends himself to be interpreted in the terms of a current vogue or a prevalent tendency of the age. The case of Dante is typical. For Chaucer, the scholarly bourgeois poet of fourteenth-century England, Dante was a learned man, a sage, the author of a line which kept humming in his ears, with the characteristic change to 'pity' instead of 'love': 'For pitee renneth sone in gentil herte'; he was the poet who more than any other had touched the supreme chords of human pity and sympathy in the Ugolino episode. In the period of the tale of terror and the craze for the picturesque, the English discovered a different Dante: the same Ugolino episode was seen from another angle: a delicious horror prevailed over melting pity. Dante's reputation in England during the Age of Reason had not fared much better than in France, where he was the butt of Voltaire's sarcasm. As late as 1782 Horace Walpole wrote in the spirit of Voltaire: 'Dante was extravagant, absurd, disgusting, in short a Methodist parson in Bedlam.' By this time, however, the new romantic sensibility was changing the direction of taste; Gray had opened his *Elegy* with a line inspired by Dante, and the episode of Count Ugolino was found to possess all the thrill of a tale of terror, with its gruesome death of innocent creatures *in a Gothic dungeon.* For it is through the thin wedge of the debased taste for the terrific that Dante's work penetrated again into English culture. In 1772, or even earlier, Sir Joshua Reynolds painted the arresting picture which was exhibited at the Royal Academy in 1773 with the title, *Count Hugolino and his Children in the Dungeon, as Described by Dante, in the Thirty-third Canto of the Inferno.* Dante had been mentioned in the same breath with Michelangelo by theorists of the fine arts, among others by the painter Jonathan Richardson, who as early as 1719 had published his version of the Ugolino episode, 'the first *avowed* translation from Dante in English literature,' says P. Toynbee in his survey of Dante's record in England. Michelangelo, according to Algarotti, whose *Essay on Painting* had appeared in English in 1764, made drawings for the whole *Commedia,* and, according to Richardson, composed a bas-relief of Ugolino sitting among his children. Now Reynolds worshipped Michelangelo as his master; and, by way of an experiment in 'history' painting, chose his subject from Dante's poem. If Reynolds did not actually start the vogue for Dante with his picture, he certainly contributed much to enlarging and intensifying the growing interest in Dante: he also set a new theme for painters, which Fuseli, Blake and Flaxman took up later on. The taste for the terrible as well as for the picturesque was amply gratified by Dante: Thomas Warton and William Hayley appreciated the dark 'Salvator Rosa' aspect of the poet. Praising Reynolds's painting of Ugolino, the poetaster and laureate Hayley wrote:

> Thy Ugolino gives the heart to thrill,
> With Pity's tender throbs, and Horror's icy chill.

And when another minor poet, Kirk White, addressed a poem to Fuseli, he invoked the 'genius of horror and romantic awe' to confer on Fuseli the wand once wielded by Dante, as on the man of all other moderns best qualified to express its 'shuddering images.' Dante meant much to Fuseli, although strangely enough he spoke of him seldom; no doubt Blake's interest in Dante was stirred by Fuseli. It is not however of Fuseli or Blake, but rather of Flaxman that we are reminded when reading nowadays Cary's translation of the *Commedia*, which first appeared complete in 1814, and was proclaimed by Wordsworth 'a great national work,' and praised by Coleridge as 'Dante's English Duplicate and reincarnation': the *Quarterly Review* in 1821 expressed its gratitude to Mr Cary 'for having opened to us the wild and romantic recesses of Dante's vision.' It was, however, no longer the terrific, but rather the lyrical, strain of Dante which appealed to the romantics. While in Fuseli's time the Dante = Michelangelo equation seemed natural, Shelley dismissed it with disgust: if in Michelangelo 'we find some of the gross and strong outlines which are employed in the few most distasteful passages of the "Inferno", where shall we find your Francesca . . . and all the exquisite tenderness, and sensibility, and ideal beauty, in which Dante excelled all poets except Shakespeare?' The influence of the gentler aspects of Dante, the Dante of the angelic hosts instead of the Dante of the demons, is evident in the *Epipsychidion* and in the exultant choruses of that earthly Paradise which occupies the greatest portion of *Prometheus Unbound*. Petrarch's *Trionfi* were little more than an external model for *The Triumph of Life*; actually the spirit of the poem is Dantesque through and through; under the stimulus of the *Commedia*, Shelley came very near formal excellence and acquired a new plastic force in his images.

The revival of Dante took place at the same time with a movement which tended to interpret Italian history in a new light. The lives of Lorenzo de' Medici and Leo X by that gifted son of a Liverpool gardener and innkeeper, William Roscoe, did much to dispel the traditional view of Italian history as a succession of gruesome, though picturesque, crimes; then, at the beginning of the nineteenth century, came Sismondi's famous *Histoire des républiques italiennes,* which enjoyed great popularity in England. Roscoe pictured Leo X and Julius II as patriots, and 'sought to invalidate' the dreadful imputations which tarnished the name of Lucrezia Borgia; Sismondi saw the Italy of the communes as a democratic paradise, an age of enlightenment, at a time when the rest of Europe was overrun by ignorance and tyranny. The republican spirit redeemed the revolts and violent deeds of which Italian history was full; henceforward the poets, Landor and Byron among the first, derived a new inspiration from Italian history. The rebellious Este princes, in Landor's *Ferrante and Giulio,* advocate the ideals of the French Revolution; Landor rehabilitated Giovanna of Naples, Shelley Beatrice Cenci, Browning Pompilia Comparini. These tragic figures of women whom the English poets try to clear from obloquy seem almost to symbolise what happened to Italy's fame in England; while the fanatical Protestants of the sixteenth and seventeenth centuries identified Italy with the Whore of Babylon, the great English poets of the nineteenth century saw her as an incarnation of Freedom triumphing over Tyranny: the 'mystic rose' of Swinburne's *Song of Italy,* 'ingrained with blood, impearled with tears of all the world'.

From the beginning of the nineteenth century English writers drew inspiration not so much from Italian literature as from the Italian landscape, art, and people. Wordsworth (who translated several of Chiabrera's epitaphs and some of Michelangelo's sonnets) recorded in verse his Italian journeys of 1790, 1820, and 1837; Rogers dedicated a poem to Italy; Byron left a sentimental guide of his pilgrimage; Shelley composed his best poems in some of the most beautiful spots of Italy: *Prometheus Unbound* on the terraces of Villa Cappuccini at Este and in the Baths of Caracalla, the *Cenci* at Villa Valsovano at Leghorn, some of his finest lyrics in the Cascine of Florence, in the pine-woods of Versilia, on the San Giuliano meadows near Pisa, among the Euganean Hills, and *The Triumph of Life* in a boat on the Gulf of Spezia. But these facts are less relevant for our subject than the following: that the *Divine Comedy*, read in the original, inspired Blake's famous series of illustrations, that the Francesca episode made such an impression on Keats that we find a trace of it in a passage of *La Belle Dame sans Merci*,[1] and that the fifth story of the Fourth Day of the *Decameron* suggested *Isabella: or, The Pot of Basil;* that Byron nearly identified himself with Dante, the patriot-poet, political martyr, and exile, in *The Prophecy of Dante* (a passionate monologue which seems rather to anticipate a number of nineteenth-century romantic pieces by Tennyson (*Ulysses, Tithonus*), Browning, and even Swinburne (*Anactoria*), than to paraphrase such autobiographical passages as Byron could find in Dante), and looked to Alfieri as to a model for *Marino Faliero,* and to the Italian mock-heroic poets (Pulci, Casti) for *Beppo* and *Don Juan*; or that Shelley, as we have seen, wrote *The Triumph of Life* in the same metre as the *Commedia,* and intended it to be

a wonder worthy of the rhyme
Of him who[m] from the lowest depths of hell,
    Through every paradise and through all glory,
    Love led serene, and who returned to tell
The words of hate and awe; the wondrous story
    How all things are transfigured except Love . . .

In these latter cases Italy has not only suggested the subject or the background, but the very form of the poems. For this same reason the work of James Thomson, the translator and follower of Leopardi, is even more interesting, from our point of view, than that of Robert Browning, who certainly discovered fundamental aspects of Italian life and landscape,

---

[1] See however E. C. Pettet, *On the Poetry of Keats*, Cambridge University Press, 1957, p. 32n.

but has nothing Italian in his manner of writing or of looking at things. Italy was a source of infinite wonder for the sharp eyes of the poet who plunged into the coloured and sonorous atmosphere of the South with the same gusto he ascribes (in *Two in the Campagna*) to the beetles groping among the honey-meal of a flower. Take for instance *The Englishman in Italy* with the subtitle 'Piano di Sorrento': who, before Browning, had observed so much, nay, discovered so much, in the Neapolitan landscape? He found in Italy, more frequently than elsewhere, characters who were completely rounded figures, gifted with such a cohesion of life and passion as to be art already. Many of these Italian portraits of Browning's are deservedly famous: Galuppi, Fra Lippo Lippi, Andrea del Sarto, the Bishop of Saint Praxed, the humanist of *A Grammarian's Funeral*.[1] . . . Also the protagonists of the longer poems are Italians: in *Sordello, Pippa Passes,* and *The Ring and the Book*; he conjures up also the figures of minor men of letters, such as Daniello Bartoli, or minor painters, such as Pacchiarotto and Francesco Furini (the first and the third, in *Parleyings with Certain People of Importance in their Day,* 1887, the second in *Of Pacchiarotto, and how he worked in Distemper,* 1876, a humorous version of an anecdote told by Vasari). We find historical, or semi-historical, Italian characters in *King Victor and King Charles,* in *My Last Duchess,* in *The Statue and the Bust,* in *Cristina and Monaldeschi,* and so on. Landor, too, had introduced Italian personages into his *Imaginary Conversations,* and even written one in Italian (the conversation between Savonarola and the Prior of Saint Mark's).

But in all these cases we cannot speak of influence of the Italian literature: the foreign artists create their characters afresh, on the basis, true, of historical sources, and coming in this way much closer to reality than ancient painters when they put exotic or historical figures into their pictures, but after all we must admit that neither the point of view nor the style of those writers is modified by a literary influence, as they were in the case of so many of the Elizabethans. There-

[1] Some characteristics of the Grammarian's are taken from Strömer's Latin letter on the death of Erasmus; no one of the many commentators on Browning seems to have noticed this.

fore, excepting the case of Dante Gabriel Rossetti, who was deeply impressed by the *Vita Nuova* and by the early Italian poets he translated, and that of T. S. Eliot, whose relation to Dante forms the subject of the last of the present studies, we need not dwell on the works of the English writers of the last century and of our time who in one way or another have drawn inspiration from Italy: neither on Tennyson's *Lady of Shalott,* suggested, but only just suggested, by the cxixth story of the *Novellino* (because the essential elements of the poem, the mirror, the magical web, the spell, the tragical death of the lady, are not in the Italian text), nor on the echoes of Dante in Swinburne's poems (for instance of the fifth Canto of the *Inferno* in *Laus Veneris,* and in *Tristram of Lyonesse*), nor on certain curious resemblances between Francis Thompson's *Hound of Heaven* and Silvio Pellico's *Dio amore;* nor on Meredith's novel inspired by the Risorgimento (*Vittoria*); nor on D. H. Lawrence's admiration for Verga (some of whose stories he translated), nor again on Lawrence's or Aldous Huxley's descriptions of Italian landscapes and milieux (e.g., Lawrence's *Twilight in Italy*), nor on the many essays inspired by Italian scenery and art in Vernon Lee, in Osbert and Sacheverell Sitwell, nor on a number of works of fiction which have Italy as a background (Percy Lubbock's *Roman Pictures,* Norman Douglas's *Siren Land* and *South Wind,* E. M. Forster's *Where Angels Fear to Tread* and *A Room with a View,* etc.). In many of the writers we have just mentioned Italian themes are found side by side with others inspired by other countries: Browning, for instance, in his dramatic monologues has also German, French and Russian characters; Swinburne, singer of Italy as he is, is specially beholden to French models; Forster has India as well as Italy as a background of his novels; Huxley and the Sitwells have been inspired by many countries. Thus, even if we find remarkable traces of Italian influence in modern authors, we never come across that shaping of a whole culture as in the golden period which extends from Chaucer to Milton.

Chaucer and the Great Italian
Writers of the Trecento

I

WHEN the Canterbury pilgrims reach Boughton-under-Blean, two new characters—you will remember—join themselves to the pious and merry company: the Canon and his Yeoman. The dapple-grey hackney of the Canon is sweating wonderfully, and so is the Canon himself, whose forehead drips 'as a stillatorie'.[1] The newcomer, still breathless from the rush, greets the pilgrims, and asks to be permitted to ride in such a merry company. Then the Yeoman proceeds to praise his master's skill, wisdom and discretion: his master is an altogether excellent man, greater than a clerk, able to turn upsidedown the road upon which they are riding, and pave it all in silver and gold. The Host wonders why a lord of such a high prudence is so shabbily dressed, and the Yeoman reveals then a sad state of affairs: his master is *too* wise, his wit is overgreat; and what is overdone proves to be a vice. His very subtlety cankers his undertakings, so that he is constantly missing his conclusion.

In the course of my readings with a view to the present essay, the character of the sweating, slovenly, overskilful, half-deceiving, half-deceived Canon-alchemist was persis-

[1] The quotations of Chaucer are from the "Student's Cambridge Edition" ed. F. N. Robinson, Oxford University Press, 1934.

In order to make references as brief as possible, I have omitted such titles as Prof, Dr, Mr, before the names of Chaucer students.

Full bibliographical references will be found at the end of this essay.

tently recalled to my mind by the sisyphean efforts of the scholars of two continents, bent on throwing additional light, as they call it, on the wondrous mysteries in which the career and writings of Chaucer supremely abound. The parallel between the source-hunter and the gold-hunter can be aptly drawn, almost to a nicety. One need not go very far in looking up Chauceriana in either German or American philological reviews, to become convinced that most source-hunters possess to an extreme degree the Canon's ability to turn upside down the road upon which they are riding, and, no less than the painstaking baffled Alchemist, they fall short of paving it again with silver and gold. I cannot resist indulging a somewhat extravagant fancy: if Chaucer could only have guessed the treatment he was going to receive at the hands of modern scholars, what a magnificent satire would he have made upon his future commentators! To be sure, he would have added another character to the immortal gallery of the pilgrims: the character of the source-hunter.

Like an alchemist racking his own brain to discover the hidden virtues of the metals, and to invent unheard-of formulae out of which the philosophers' stone may be produced as by miracle, the source-hunter is devising complexes of Macrobius, and Dante, and Claudian, and Alanus de Insulis, and *Roman de la Rose,* and, pleased with his final concoction, he identifies it with gold, i.e., Chaucer. And then, suddenly, 'the pot to-breketh, and farewell! al is go!' A rival source-hunter has countermined the elaborate fabric, and lo! the wondrous work is blown up. The 'little additional light' results in much unnecessary darkness, and the mystery is as thick as ever. The rival alchemists are at loggerheads, commentaries are piled upon commentaries, as Pelion on Ossa, the sky is dimmed with smoke, the air poisonous with smell of brimstone, the fighters level at each other's heads formulae and figures—formidable-looking references to dissertations and articles scattered in scores of periodicals—and meanwhile, as Aldous Huxley puts it,[2] 'year by year the sediment of muddy comment and criticism thickens round the great man's bones: the sediment sets firm: what was once a living organism is turned into a fossil.'

[2] The *London Mercury,* June, 1920 (Vol. ii, No. 8), p. 179.

I am going to give only one instance of priceless petti-
fogging interpretation, because it may serve as a convenient
introduction to my study of Italian influence on Chaucer.
A contributor to *The Nation* for October 20, 1904, conjectured
that the nineteen ladies following the God of Love in the
Prologue to the *Legend of Good Women* were suggested by
the hundred and forty and four thousand sealed out of every
tribe of the children of Israel, and the 'tras of wemen' by the
great multitude which no man could number standing before
the throne and before the Lamb in the seventh chapter of
the Apocalypse! J. L. Lowes, on the other hand, is quite justified in seeing in Chaucer's procession of ladies another instance of the endlessly recurring convention, in the poems of
the Court of Love *genre,* of the band of lovers about the God
of Love, and proceeds to point out an accidental parallel in
Dante (*Purgatorio,* xxxii, line 38 ff.). Now the suggestion
for the 'tras of wemen' comes actually from Dante, as I am
going to show, and it is strange that the source should have
escaped Lowes, who has gone deeper than anyone else in the
study of Dante's influence on Chaucer. The passage in the
Prologue (Text G, line 188 ff.) of the *Legend* runs thus:

> And after hem (i.e., the God of Love) come
>   of wemen swich a tras
> That, syn that God Adam had mad of erthe,
> The thridde part of wemen, ne the ferthe,
> Ne wende I not by possibilite
> Hadden evere in this wyde world ybe.

In the Ante-Hell Dante meets the spirits of the pusillanimous:
they are preceded by a banner,

> E dietro le venia sì lunga tratta
> Di gente, ch'io non averei creduto
> Che morte tanta n'avesse disfatta.
>   (*Inf.,* iii, 55–57)

[And behind it came so long a train of people, that I could
never have conceived that so many had been undone by
death.]

Further on, in the same Canto, is mentioned Adam's sinful
offspring, *il mal seme d'Adamo.* The mention of Adam, to-

gether with the use of the word *tras,* is a conclusive test. The word *tras* is used only here by Chaucer in the sense of 'train of people,' and is obviously a close rendering of *tratta.* Moreover, the whole line 188 echoes line 55 in *Inferno,* iii, and the word *tras,* as well as *tratta,* occurs in rhyme. One could even push the investigation a little further, and guess why Chaucer was reminded of that passage in Dante. A few lines back Chaucer describes the appearance of the God of Love (Prologue, Text G, lines 163–165, 168):

> For sikerly his face shon so bryghte,
> That with the glem astoned was the syghte;
> A furlong-wey I myghte hym not beholde.
>
> . . . .
>
> And aungellych hys winges gan he sprede.

The appearance of the God of Love has been modelled on the appearance of the angel in the Second Canto of *Purgatorio* (lines 37–39, 34.):

> Poi, come più e più verso noi venne
> L'uccel divino, più chiaro appariva;
> Per che l'occhio da presso nol sostenne
>
> . . . .
>
> Vedi come l'ha dritte verso il cielo.

[Anon, as the bird of heaven came ever towards us, he was more bright, so that, when near, mine eyes were overpowered. . . . Mark how he raised his wings towards heaven.]

And the skylark (line 141 ff.) had heralded the approach of the God of Love thus:

> 'I se,' quod she, 'the myghty god of Love!
> Lo! yond he cometh, I se his wynges sprede—'

in the same way as Virgil had announced to Dante the coming of the angel (line 26 ff.):

> Mentre che i primi bianchi apparser ali:
> Allor che ben conobbe il galeotto,
> Gridò: 'Fa, fa che le ginocchia cali:
> Ecco l'angel di Dio . . .

[. . . while the first white features revealed themselves as wings: when he clearly recognized the pilot, he cried: 'See, see thou bend thy knees, behold the angel of God. . . .'] [3]

Now the angel appears first to Dante and Virgil in the form of a light approaching over the sea with such speed, that no bird's flight could rival its motion (line 16 ff.):

> . . . m'apparve . . .
> Un lume per lo mar venir sì ratto,
> Che 'l mover suo nessun volar pareggia.

The speed of approach of the vessel of saved souls piloted by the angel has reminded Chaucer at once of another speedy approaching of spirits, precisely in that Canto of the *Inferno* which, containing the description of Charon's boat ferrying the lost souls into Hell, is a counterpart of the second Canto of the *Purgatorio*. The spirits of the cowards appear in the wake of

> . . . una insegna
> Che girando correva tanto ratta,
> Che d'ogni posa mi parea indegna.
> (*Inf.*, iii, 52–54)

Possibly line 17 of *Purgatorio*, ii, has brought about the association of ideas. That line runs:

> Un lume per lo mar venir sì *ratto*.

Such a line is apt to recall instantaneously to one's mind *Inferno*, iii, 53:

> Che girando correva tanto *ratta*.

Both sense and sound are closely related in these two lines. Finally the two 'fyry dartes, as the gleedes rede,' which Love holds in hand, are his *insegna*, and they are red as glow-

---

[3] Version G of the Prologue is much closer to Dante's lines than F, which runs (lines 232–233): 'Therewith me thoghte his face shoon so bryghte   That wel unnethes myghte I him beholde'. This divergence constitutes a strong evidence against the hypothesis of the priority of the F version.

ing embers, because the light approaching over the sea, in the *Purgatorio*, was at first like the planet Mars, when, at dawn, it glimmers red in the west above the sea-level: 'Per li grossi vapor Marte rosseggia' (*Purg.*, ii, 14).

The case of derivation I have just examined is safely established, as I was saying, by the use of the word *tras* corresponding in meaning, sound, and position to the Dantesque word *tratta*. If one wished indeed to formulate rules about Chaucer's borrowings, the first one should be: in most of the cases where Chaucer is following a source, he betrays himself, so to say, by the use of some word closely modelled on some of the foreign words of the text he has either before his mind or before his eyes. Very often, in *Troilus and Criseyde*, he takes his rhyme-words over from the Italian original, the *Filostrato*.[4] Apart from the exceedingly frequent case of *Troie* rhyming with either *joye* or *anoye*, in the final couplet of a stanza, to be parallelled in Boccaccio's frequent rhyme of *Troia* with *gioia* and *noia* in the same position, you find there *descerne-eterne-werne* (Tr., iii, st. 2), where the *Filostrato* has, in the corresponding stanza (iii, st. 75), *discerno-eterno*; *martire-desire* (iv, st. 117), to reproduce *desiri-martiri* (*Fil.*, iv, st. 96); *sentement-argument* (iv, st. 169), echoing Boccaccio's *sentimento-argomento* (*Fil.*, iv, st. 119); *Diomede-(blede)* (v, st. 3) modelled on *Diomede- (diede-vede)* (*Fil.*, v, st. 1); and most remarkable of all, *Monesteo-Rupheo* (iv, st. 8), taken over bodily from Boccaccio's stanza 3 of Book iv.[5] I call· this last case very remarkable indeed, because one would expect Chaucer to give to proper names the endings used in English. But, in the field of proper names, consistency is the last thing to be expected from him: a proper name, chiefly a classical one, appeals to him like a spell, a magic

[4] The borrowing of rhymes is, of course, not confined to *Troilus*. So for instance the rhyme, *Anne-Osanne*, in *Canterbury Tales* B, 641–642, and G, 69–70, is a reminiscence of Dante's *Anna Osanna* (*Par.*, xxxii, 133–135).

[5] In a few cases the Italian rhyme impresses Chaucer as mere spelling and sound, quite apart from the meaning. So in *Troilus*, v, st. 131, *pace-face-deface* is suggested by *fallace-face* (from the verb *fare*, to make) —*piace* in *Filostrato*, vi, st. 20. Perhaps Dante's rhyme (*Inferno*, xxvii, 119–123) *come-chiome-o me*, has suggested Chaucer's *Rome-tó me* (*Canterbury Tales*, A, 671–672).

formula, and apparently he does not dare to subject it to the common laws of language. This point ought to be kept in mind when I shall speak of Chaucer's use of authorities. In another passage of *Troilus* (v, line 1806) Chaucer spells *Achille* as he found it spelt in the parallel Italian stanza (*Fil.*, viii, st. 27), in the *House of Fame* (line 458) he uses the form *Lavyna* (Lavinia), probably from Dante's *Lavina* (*Purg.*, xvii, 37), and in the same poem Marsyas is spelt *Marcia* (line 1229) and made feminine, very likely through a confusion engendered by Dante's mention of Marcia, Cato's wife. Moreover, throughout his translation of Boethius Chaucer employs the form *Boece* from the French translation, and, in the *Clerk's Prologue and Tale*, the forms *Padowe* (Padua), *Ytaille* (Italy) and *Frounceys Petrak*, which also point to the use of the French version of the Griselda story.[6] Apart from the borrowing of rhymes [7] Chaucer's use of words modelled on foreign ones he has found in his sources could be abundantly illustrated. Sometimes his candour goes so far as to borrow the foreign word, and then to devote one or more lines to the explanation of it, as when, after copying from Boccaccio the learned word *ambage* (*Fil.*, vi, st. 17) he proceeds thus (*Tr.*, v, st. 129):

> And but if Calkas lede us with ambages,
> That is to seyn, with double wordes slye,
> Swiche as men clepen a word with two visages.

But this passage falls rather under the heading, 'display of learning', of which I shall have to speak later on. The word

[6] In fact for the *Clerk's Tale* Chaucer used an anonymous French prose translation of Petrarch's Latin version and the revised draft of this latter as it left Petrarch's hand shortly before his death in 1374.

[7] Even where no definite source has been traced, Chaucer's use of foreign words shows at once in what language we should expect to find his original. Thus in *Troilus* (ii, st. 124), we find the word *verre*, used only here by Chaucer for 'glas', rhyming with *werre* (war). Such two words rhyme together only in French: *verre-guerre*. Accordingly, the version of the proverb Chaucer has in mind ought to be a French one. The quotation occurs in Antigone's song, which bears a general resemblance to Guillaume de Machaut's *Paradis d'amour* (see Kittredge, *Modern Language Notes*, xxv, 158).

ambages is used only once by Chaucer, in connexion with Boccaccio's *ambage*: such is often the case with foreign words he borrows. They are transferred into English with just as much alteration in spelling as is deemed sufficient to naturalize them; but they lack vitality, they do not occur again, independent of their source. Such is the case with *poeplissh* (*appetit*) = popular, used in *Tr.*, iv, 1677, to translate Boccaccio's (*appetito*) *popolesco* (*Fil.*, iv, st. 165), of *palestral* (*pleyes*) (*Tr.*, v, 304), rendering Boccaccio's *palestral* (*gioco*) (*Teseide*, vii, st. 27), of *erratik* (*sterres*) (*Tr.*, v, 1812), corresponding to (*stelle*) *erratiche* in *Teseida*, xi, st. 1, of *affect*, a characteristically Dantesque word, used only in *Troilus*, iii, 1393, in a passage inspired by Dante, and of *revoken* used in the sense of 'to recall' only in *Troilus*, iii, 1118.

As in the other instances, *revoken* is here the sign-manual of the author from whom Chaucer derives the entire passage; and the author, in the present case, which, so far as I know, has escaped notice, is Boccaccio. The use of that word, which is the Italian *rivocare* slightly disguised, gives evidence that the episode of Troilus's fainting at the sight of Criseyde crying, in Book iii, is nothing else but a transferred episode of the Italian poem, Book iv, when Troilus faints at learning that the Trojans are willing to give up Criseyde to the Greeks. In stanza 160 of the English poem Pandarus and Criseyde try to revive Troilus:

> Therwith his pous and paumes of his hondes
> They gan to frote, and wete his temples tweyne;
>
> . . . .
>
> Hym to *revoken* she did al hire peyne.

In stanza 19 of Book iv of the *Filostrato*, Priam and his other sons try to recall to life Troilus:

> . . . e ciascun si procaccia
> Di confortarlo, e le sue forze morte,
> Ora i polsi fregando, ed or la faccia
> Bagnandogli sovente . . .
> . . . s'ingegnavan *rivocare*.

[And each one of them tries to comfort him, and now by rubbing his wrists, now by wetting his face, they were trying to *revoke* his dead spirits.]

Once the source is established, it is easy to find out other parallels in the same passage.

Of course in Book iv, when Chaucer's Troilus learns that Criseyde must be delivered to the Greeks, he is sensible enough not to faint as in Boccaccio: he had already made use of his fainting propensities in Book iii, and he had been left nothing to spare for the next opportunity. Still, this is not entirely correct: something had been spared in Book iii, and now has come the moment to use it up. Troilus at line 235 of Book iv appears:

> Ful lik a ded ymage, pale and wan

precisely as Boccaccio's fainting Troilus (iv, st. 20):

> E'l viso suo pallido, smorto . . .
> . . . e più morta parea
> Che viva cosa.

[And his face pale, wan . . . seemed more a dead thing than a living one.]

This last case illustrates well a curious practice of Chaucer's, which is usually described as his wonderful economy. Illustrations of the peculiar way Chaucer has of making use of his sources are so well-known and abundant that I must content myself with reminding the reader only of the most remarkable ones. So in the *Knight's Tale* the soaring of Arcite's soul to heaven is not described, because Boccaccio's description of that journey had been already used with respect to the death of Troilus; in the *Second Nun's Tale* the *Invocatio ad Mariam* is taken from Dante, *Paradiso*, xxxiii, 1–9, but Dante's lines following the ninth, though no less worth imitating, are left out because they had already been used in *Troilus*, iii, 1262 ff., in a prayer to Venus, and the translation of Dante's l.16 ('La tua benignità non pur soccorre'), which occurs in both of Chaucer's passages, is differently worded in each case.[8] No doubt Chaucer must have been an excellent con-

[8] See Koeppel, 'Chauceriana,' in *Anglia* xiii, p. 229.

troller, since he knew so well how to husband his literary resources. No waste with him: to use a very homely and indecorous simile, I should say that he knew how to use the dripping, after he had roasted in an English fashion the foreign meat. Whenever, for instance, in *Troilus* he leaves out a passage of the *Filostrato*, you may be sure that the passage will be turned to account in another connexion: you almost imagine him pronouncing Pandarus's words in Shakespeare's *Troilus and Cressida*: 'Let us cast away nothing, for we may live to have need of such a verse; we see it, we see it!' In the second book of *Troilus* Chaucer does not relate the lovers' letters *in extenso*: is he going then to waste those letters? Not he. The time for them to be exploited comes only in Book v, when Criseyde writes to Troilus her last letter. 'The letter of Criseyde has no counterpart in *Filostrato*'—runs the remark of the commentator. No counterpart in the corresponding passage of the story, but one has only to look up the letters in the *Filostrato*, Book ii, to recognize at once the model of Criseyde's last letter. Criseyde's beginning in *Troilus*, v (st. 228), is:

> How myght a wight in torment and in drede
> And heleles, yow sende as yet gladnesse?

This is a close rendering of *Filostrato*, ii, st. 96 (Troilus's letter):

> Come può quegli che in affanno è posto,
> In pianto grave e in istato molesto
>
> . . . .
> Ad alcun dar salute?
> [How might one who is dwelling with sorrow, heavy crying and troublesome plight . . . send gladness to anyone?]

And the closing line of the stanza:

> Yow neyther sende ich herte may nor hele

is echoing

> Qui da me salutata non sarai.

Next stanza (229) is modelled on a passage of Criseyde's letter in Book ii of the *Filostrato* (st. 122):

> Youre lettres ful, the papir al ypleynted,
> Conceyved hath myn hertes pietee.
> I have ek seyn with teris al depeynted
> Youre lettre
>
> . . . .
>
> I' ho avute. . . .
> Piene la carte della tua scrittura;
> Nelle quai lessi la tua vita grama
> Non senza doglia . . .
> . . . e benché sian fregiate
> Di lacrime, pur l'ho assai mirate.

[I have received your papers full of your writing, in which I read of your miserable life not without compassion . . . and although they are decorated (*depeynted*) with tears, still I have admired them very much.]

Finally, the conclusion of Criseyde's letter is derived from stanza 126 of the same book of the *Filostrato*.

Two other passages in *Troilus* are of great interest as illustrations of Chaucer's sense of economy. In the *Filostrato*, Book vii, st. 23–24, Troilus dreams of a boar which tramples down Criseyde, then tears out her heart with its tusks (*grifo*, i.e., snout: Root, in his note to *Troilus*, v, 1233–1243, translates it by 'claws', obviously misled by *grifo* resembling in sound French *griffe*, and entirely overlooking the fact that a boar is not favoured with claws). Criseyde, in Boccaccio, seems not to consider the treatment she receives at the hands (Root's 'claws'!) of the boar as a pain, but rather as a pleasure. Had Freud known of this dream, he would have quoted it as a striking illustration of his theories. But let us see now the use Chaucer has made of this dream. He has split it up into two. On one hand he draws upon it for Criseyde's dream in Book ii (st. 133): Criseyde dreams that her heart is being torn out by an eagle which replaces it in her breast with its own heart: 'of which she nought agroos, ne nothyng smerte.' On the other hand, in Book v, st. 177–178, in the passage corresponding to *Filostrato*, vii, st. 23–24,

Troilus dreams of a boar 'with tuskes grete' which is kissing Criseyde. Obviously Chaucer has distributed the different elements of the one dream he found in Boccaccio into the two dreams of his poem. But why an eagle in the first case? Was the eagle suggested by *grifo*, by the same mistake into which Root has fallen? The use by Chaucer of the word *claws* seems to countenance this view. But another explanation occurs to me. *Grifo*, in Italian, means not only 'snout', but also 'griffin', and Chaucer must have been reminded of Dante's *grifo* in the mystic pageant which takes place in the Earthly Paradise (*Purg.*, xxix, 108, and foll. Cantos). The griffin or *grifone* or *grifo* has a double nature of eagle and lion: part of its limbs, in Dante, are white. Chaucer's eagle is 'fethered whit as bon'. Moreover, in *Purgatorio*, xxxii, where the allegorical pageantry is still going on, an eagle rushes down with the speed of a thunderbolt on the mystic tree, tears off its bark, flowers and fresh leaves, and smites the triumphal chariot with its full force: then it leaves the chariot covered with its own plumage. The chariot undergoes a wonderful transformation. Finally, in another Canto of the *Purgatorio* (ix) Dante dreams of another eagle, which also comes down with the speed of a thunderbolt, and snatches Dante up to the region of fire: an episode Chaucer exploits in his *House of Fame*, as is well known. Similar cases of associations of ideas in Chaucer seem to point to the fact that the eagle has stolen into Criseyde's dream through a process not unlike the one here described.

To conclude about economy, Chaucer is so averse to repetition that he does not even allow Boccaccio to repeat himself. In Book iv of the *Filostrato* (st. 120 ff.), Troilus, believing Criseyde to be dead, unsheathes his sword in order to kill himself. In the parallel passage in *Troilus* (iv, st. 170) also Troilus 'his swerd anon out of his shethe he twighte, hymself to slen'. So far, so good. But Boccaccio's Troilus is reckless, and in Book vii (st. 33), on being aware of Criseyde's disloyalty, runs to a knife and tries to smite his own breast with it. This will not do for Chaucer, and his Troilus wisely avoids the monotony which would ensue from attempting suicide a second time, when confronted with Criseyde's falsehood. *Non bis in idem* seems to have been Chaucer's motto.

The most interesting fact emerging from the study of

Chaucer's economy is the deliberate, conscious use he makes of his sources. He succeeds in avoiding repetition to such an extent as to lead one to postulate on his part either a prodigious memory, or a constant consultation of his authorities. Very likely the latter supposition hits the mark. As in the case of the Clerk's tale, where no doubt can be entertained, so in most of the other cases of imitation Chaucer had the foreign text before his eyes. To some of the foreign writers he had recourse every now and then, but others, who were always within his reach, supplied him with an inexhaustible mine of expressions and suggestions. Amongst these latter are to be ranked first of all the two great epitomes of the poetry of the Middle Ages: the *Roman de la Rose* and the *Divina Commedia*. It is the merit of Professor J. L. Lowes to have shown for the first time how deep, widespread and constant was the influence of Dante upon Chaucer. While drawing on other sources, Chaucer now and then combines them with passages from those two masterpieces of the Middle Ages. For him, the least hint is sufficient to establish at once a connexion between the text which forms his immediate source and quotations from either the *Roman de la Rose* or the *Divina Commedia*: possibly he was so conversant with these two works as to have them always in the back of his mind: a fact which seems to suggest, if it does not necessarily imply, that he had them by heart.

In the same way as a hint from Machaut or Deschamps (for instance in the case of the *Book of the Duchess*) is sufficient to awake immediately in Chaucer's mind the memory of lines from the *Roman de la Rose*,[9] so, while imitating

[9] *The Book of the Duchess*, a naive *pastiche* of several French poems, offers a typical illustration of the manner in which associations work in Chaucer's mind. The sources of that poem have been chiefly studied by Kittredge (*Englische Studien*, xxvi, pp. 321-336; *Modern Philology*, vii, pp. 465-483; PMLA, xxx, pp. 1-24). For instance when the poet has succeeded in falling asleep according to the recipe found in Froissart's *Paradys d'Amours*— (in my *Geoffrey Chaucer e i Racconti di Canterbury*, Rome, Edizioni italiane, 1947—reprinted as G. Chaucer, *The Canterbury Tales*, ed. by M. Praz, Bari, Adriatica Editrice, 1957—I have shown in detail how Froissart's line 23 ff. sent Chaucer to similar lines, 571 ff., of Machaut's *Fonteinne Amoureuse*, and hence to the *Ovide moralisé*)—he develops the scene of the May

Boccaccio, he perceives at once whenever the Italian author
is reminiscent of Dante, and avails himself of the opportunity
for drawing on the better poet. Lowes has given several
instances of this proceeding, to which Ten Brink had already
called attention. I will give only one example, the significance
of which reaches beyond the particular passage in question.
In the *Filostrato*, when Troilus learns that Criseyde must be
given up to the Greeks, he falls as dead. Boccaccio makes use
of the Virgilian simile (iv, st. 18):

> Qual, poscia ch'è dall'aratro intaccato
> Ne' campi il giglio, per soverchio sole
> Casca ed appassa, e 'l bel color cangiato
> Pallido fassi. . . .

[As in the fields the lily, after it has been cut into by the
plough, falls and withers through too much sun, and its
fair colour, changed, turns pale . . .]

---

morning introduced by Froissart at 38 ff.: 'En mon dormant
me fu vis lors/Que jou estoie en un beau bois . . .' This is
enough to recall the May morning of the *Roman de la Rose*,
so that lines 300–320 of the Chaucerian poem are a mosaic
of passages of Guillaume de Lorris. Similarly further on (387 ff.)
Chaucer comes across a little dog, as in his model, which at this
point is Machaut's *Jugement dou Roy de Behaingne*: the *chiennet*
of this poem reminds him of the *petit chiennet* of the *Dit dou
Lyon* by the same French poet; accordingly Chaucer's little dog
behaves like the lion Machaut had likened to the *petit chiennet*.
The lion had led Machaut to a wilderness 'parmi ronces, parmi
orties'; the little dog leads Chaucer to a 'floury grene' which turns
out to be nothing else but Froissart's 'beau bois' mentioned above,
and again Froissart's description recalls the *Roman de la Rose*,
which becomes the model of lines 402–442 of the English poem.
The passage 1056–1057: 'Thogh I had had al the beaute/That
ever had Alcipyades' provides another instance. The principal
source of this passage is Machaut's *Remede de Fortune* (107 ff.);
and since this poem mentions 'la biauté qu'ot Absalon', Chaucer
is immediately reminded of 'Alcipiades/Qui de beautez avait
adès' of the *Roman de la Rose* (8944). Apropos of sources of
The Book of the Duchess it has not been noticed that the poet's
situation described in lines 345 ff. (he finds himself in a room,
suddenly hears an outside noise of men, horses and dogs going
to a hunt) is the result of a contamination of a passage from
Machaut's *Jugement dou Roy de Navarre* (459ff.) with a passage (905 ff.) from Froissart's *Paradys d'Amours*. *The Book of
the Duchess* is an ideal playground for source-hunters.

The simile is one of the most widespread commonplaces in Western literatures: Byron also employs it when the shipwrecked Don Juan faints on the shore of the Greek island. Chaucer, as I have shown above, had already exploited the fainting of Troilus in Book iii, and he does not repeat it here. Troilus here only becomes like a dead image, pale and wan. But the floral simile, which Boccaccio has taken from Virgil, recalls to his mind another simile derived also from decaying vegetation, a simile used by Dante in that third Canto of the *Inferno,* on which Chaucer has drawn several times: a Canto, moreover, at the end of which Dante is overpowered by a sudden earthquake and falls astounded like one mastered by sleep: not unlike Boccaccio's Troilus. Chaucer replaces the simile given in the *Filostrato* by the Dantesque one:

> Come d'autunno si levan le foglie
> L'una appresso dell'altra, infin che il ramo
> Vede a la terra tutte le sue spoglie . . .
>
> (*Inf.,* iii, 112–114)

> And as in wynter leves ben beraft,
> Ech after other, til the tree be bare,
> So that ther nys but bark and braunche ilaft . . .
>
> (*Tr.,* iv, st. 33)

Now Dante's lines, in their turn, are modelled on a passage of Virgil's *Aeneid.* This instance is very characteristic of the relations between the several poets concerned. What Virgil is to Dante, Dante is to Chaucer. Chaucer is an individual illustration of a phenomenon which was to become general in the Renaissance, when the legacy of the classical world was handed over to Europe through the medium of Italy.

Another instance of the manner in which many trains of thought led up to Dante in Chaucer's mind is provided by the proem to the *Parliament of Fowls.* Chaucer paraphrases there a portion of a book called *Tullyus of the Drem of Scipioun* (line 31), i.e., Cicero's *Somnium Scipionis.* It is the very passage Boccaccio had paraphrased in the first three stanzas of Book xi of the *Teseida,* which Chaucer was later to translate and insert into Book v of *Troilus.* Chaucer, then, has

traced Boccaccio's passage to its Latin source. But this is not
all. Cicero says that the souls of those who have indulged in
bodily pleasures, once they have come out of their bodies,
are seized by a hurricane which hurls them for centuries
round the earth: 'corporibus elapsi circa terram ipsam volu-
tantur, etc.' Now this is the very passage which is behind the
fifth canto of Dante's *Inferno*:

> La bufera infernal, che mai non resta,
> Mena li spirti con la sua rapina:
> Voltando e percotendo li molesta.

[The hurricane of hell which never abates harries the
spirits along in its fury, vexes them with whirling and
beating.]

Chaucer renders Cicero's passage faithfully enough: that
passage ends by saying that the souls of the lustful will come
back to heaven after having been tormented by the hurricane
for many centuries: 'nec hunc in locum, nisi multis exagitati
saeculis, revertuntur'. Chaucer writes (lines 83–84):

> Than shul they come into this blysful place,
> To which to comen God the sende his grace.

Is this Cicero? No, it is Dante. What has happened? The Latin
passage has at once reminded Chaucer of Dante's hurricane
of hell, and, at the same time, of Francesca's propitiatory
words:

> Se fosse amico il re dell' universo,
> Noi pregheremmo lui della tua pace . . .

[Were the world's King our friend, we would entreat him
for thy peace . . .]

Is it the idea of peace conjured up here, that immediately
after caused Chaucer to recall the beginning of Canto ii of
the *Inferno*? For the poet, soon after the line: 'To which to
comen God the sende his grace . . .', continues:

> The day gan faylen, and the derke nyght,
> That reveth bestes from here besynesse,
> Berafte me my bok for lak of lyght:

which is an almost literal rendering of Dante's:

> Lo giorno se n'andava, e l'aere bruno
> Toglieva li animai che sono in terra
> Alle fatiche loro; ed io sol uno . . .

[The day was going, and the darkened air was taking from their toil the animals that are on the earth; I only alone . . .]

Now, in the same way as Boccaccio had sent Chaucer to Cicero, Dante sends him to Claudian. For Chaucer goes on (99 ff.):

> The wery huntere, slepynge in his bed,
> To wode ayeyn his mynde goth anon;
> The juge dremeth how his plees been sped;

and so, in Chaucer's lines, we see various conditions of men continue their day's work while dreaming, exactly as in a passage from Claudian:

> Venator cum fessa toro sua membra reponit,
> Mens tamen ad silvas et sua lustra redit, etc.

But the link with the preceding lines must have been the beginning of *Paradise*, Canto xi, recalled to Chaucer's mind by the beginning of *Inferno*, Canto ii:

> Chi dietro a iura, e chi ad aforismi
> Sen giva, e chi seguendo sacerdozio,
>
> . . . .
>
> E chi rubare, e chi civil negozio,
> Chi nel diletto de la carne involto
> S'affaticava, e chi si dava a l'ozio,
> Quando, da tutte queste cose sciolto,
> Con Beatrice m'era suso in cielo . . .

[One was following after law, and one aphorisms, one was pursuing priesthood . . . and another plunder, and another civil business, and one, tangled in the pleasures of the flesh, was toiling, and one abandoned him to ease; the whilst, from all these things released, with Beatrice was I up in heaven . . .]

Not Beatrice, but Scipio Africanus appears at Chaucer's side in a dream. And Scipio tells the poet:

> Thow hast the so wel born
> In lokynge of myn olde bok totorn . . .
> That sumdel of thy labour wolde I quyte.

Dante told Virgil:

> Vagliami 'l lungo studio e 'l grande amore
> Che m'ha fatto cercar lo tuo volume.
> Tu se' lo mio maestro e 'l mio autore . . .

[May the long study and great love stand me in good stead, which made me peruse thy book. Thou art my master and my author . . .]

Chaucer, then, assigns to Scipio the role Virgil had in the *Commedia*.

The last stanza of the proem of *The Parliament of Fowls* contains an invocation to Cytherea which has been related to that which opens the second canto of Boccaccio's *Amorosa Visione*. But Chaucer goes back to Dante also in this case:

> Cytherea! thow blysful lady swete,
> That with thy fyrbrond dauntest whom the lest:

this is the Cytherea of the twenty-seventh canto of the *Purgatory*, 'who seemeth ever burning with the fire of love.' Many other passages of the *Commedia* are rehearsed in *The Parliament of Fowls*; the following, not noticed so far, is very typical. It has been known for a long time that the description of the garden in lines 183–259 is taken from Book vii of the *Teseida*; but it has escaped notice that Chaucer has transplanted into Boccaccio's garden flowers gathered in Dante's garden of the *Purgatory*. In Boccaccio's garden there are lively and clear fountains, *fonti vive e chiare*, but no river; the scene 'upon a ryver, in a grene mede' is that of Canto xxviii of the *Purgatory*. In Boccaccio the garden is full of every spring flower, *ogni fior novello*, but it is only in the *Purgatory* that we find the model for the 'floures white, blewe, yelwe, and rede' (1.186): 'volsesi in su i vermigli ad in su i gialli/fioretti'

(11.55–56: 'she turned upon the red and upon the yellow flowerets'). The passage (201 ff.):

> Therewith a wynd, unnethe it myghte be lesse,
> Made in the leves grene a noyse softe
> Accordaunt to the foules song alofte,

has no counterpart in Boccaccio; but the following lines of Dante (*Purgatory*, xxviii, 7–18) clearly show from what quarter the wind was blowing:

> Un'aura dolce, sanza mutamento
> Avere in sé, mi feria per la fronte
> Non di più colpo che soave vento:
> Per cui le fronte, tremolando pronte
>
> . . . .
>
> Non però dal loro esser dritto sparte
> Tanto, che li augelletti per le cime
> Lasciasser d'operare ogni lor arte;
>   . . . le foglie
> Che tenevan bordone a le sue rime.

[A sweet breeze, itself without change, was striking on my brow with no greater force than a gentle wind, and trembling to the touch of it, the branches . . . yet not so far bent aside from their erect state, that the little birds in the tops ceased to practise their every art; . . . the leaves, which were murmuring the burden to their songs.]

Once we have realised the importance of the *Commedia* as a permanent source of inspiration for Chaucer, to be put on the same level as the *Roman de la Rose* in this respect, we may ask ourselves whether the English poet assimilated the spirit of Dante's poem in the same way he had assimilated the spirit of Guillaume de Lorris and Jean de Meun's poem. The very formulation of this question reveals an impossibility. Chaucer was able to assimilate the spirit of the French poem thanks to the affinities of origin and social condition which bound him to the authors of the *Roman de la Rose*. But what had the bourgeois Chaucer in common with that disdainful aristocrat, Dante? Let us represent to ourselves the aspect of each of the two poets as it is described by themselves or others. Could we imagine a greater contrast? 'This Dante,' wrote Giovanni Villani, 'because of his learning was somewhat presumptuous, reserved and haughty, and almost like a surly philosopher, knew not well how to converse with laymen.' [10] Chaucer causes the Host in the Prologue to *Sir Thopas* to address him in this manner:

> 'What man artow?' quod he;
> 'Thou lookest as thou woldest fynde an hare,
> For evere upon the ground I se thee stare.

> 'Approche neer, and looke up murily.
> Now war yow, sires, and lat this man have place!
> He in the waast is shape as wel as I;
> This were a popet in an arm t'enbrace
> For any womman, smal and fair of face.
> He semeth elvyssh by his contenaunce,
> For unto no wight dooth he daliaunce.' [11]

The silent Dante described by Villani is a proud man; the silent Chaucer described in these words of the Host is a person habitually shy.

It is, howevever, the comparison of Chaucer's imitations with Dante's original passages which brings out the deep spiritual difference between the two poets. We have seen how Chaucer, having before him Boccaccio's *Amorosa Visione* for his *Parliament of Fowls*, was led back to Dante for his

[10] 'Questo Dante per suo saver fu alquanto presuntuoso, schifo e sdegnoso, e quasi a guisa di Filosofo mal grazioso, non ben sapeva conversare co'laici.'

[11] Some critics have thought that this description refers chiefly to the special circumstance: the impression produced in Chaucer by the moving tale of the Prioress (cf. Thomas Knott's article in *Modern Philology*, viii, pp. 135–139), as Chaucer's behaviour appears very different in the general Prologue to the Tales. However, he may actually have been shy by nature, as he certainly was 'rounde of shap' (*Lenvoy a Scogan*, 31). If Chaucer's behaviour was only caused by the moving story of Hugh of Lincoln, we might think of 'chinai 'l viso, e tanto il tenni basso,/fin che 'l poeta mi disse: Che pense?' [I bent my face down, and kept it so for such a long time, that the Poet asked me: What musest thou?] of Canto v of the *Inferno*, after Dante has heard Francesca's moving words.

invocation to Cytherea. At the beginning of the narration, Scipio leads the poet to the entrance of a garden; there are two inscriptions on the gate. The scene follows the *Amorosa Visione* down to the *scritta che pareva d'oro*, which corresponds to Chaucer's 'these vers of gold' (141). But the model of Chaucer's inscription is the famous one above the gate of Dante's Hell:

> Per me si va ne la città dolente,
> Per me si va ne l'eterno dolore,
>
> .   .   .   .
>
> Queste parole di colore oscuro
> Vid' io scritte al sommo d'una porta . . .

[Through me the way is to the City of Woe, through me the way into eternal pain. . . . These words, of a dim colour, I saw written above the lintel of a gateway . . .]

Chaucer repeats the pattern of the terrible inscription, but fills it with the light contents of French allegorical poems, whose spirit continued to dominate him:

> 'Thorgh me men gon into that blysful place
> Of hertes hele and dedly woundes cure;
> Thorgh me men gon unto the welle of grace,
> There grene and lusty May shal evere endure.
> This is the wey to al good aventure.
> Be glad, thow redere, and thy sorwe of-caste:
> Al open am I—passe in, and sped thee faste!'

> 'Thorgh me men gon,' than spak that other side,
> 'Unto the mortal strokes of the spere
> Of which Disdayn and Daunger is the gyde,
> Ther nevere tre shal fruyt ne leves bere. . . .'

> These vers of gold and blak inwriten were,
> Of whiche I gan astoned to beholde . . .

If we read the line 'Be glad, thow redere, and thy sorwe of-caste' next to the terrible 'Lasciate ogni speranza, voi ch'entrate,' Chaucer's lightsome treatment may appear to us a palinode, or even a parody of the passage in Dante.

The House of Fame, in which critics have tried to recognise that mysterious *Dante in ynglyssh* of Lydgate's list in the Prologue to *The Fall of Princes,* may seem to us also a parody of the *Commedia.* As a matter of fact, one of the first to study Dante's influence on Chaucer, Rambeau, went so far in the way of finding parallels between the *Divina Commedia* and *The House of Fame* that, since then, it has been a sign of good taste among safe critics to underrate Dante's influence on that poem. In times closer to us, Froissart's *Temple D'Onnour* has been set up by Brusendorff as having stronger claims than the *Divina Commedia* to the paternity of *The House of Fame.* Other critics, impressed by the undeniable diversity of spirit between *The House of Fame* and Dante's masterpiece, have suggested the possibility that what Chaucer was aiming at was some sort of travesty, or parody, of the *Divina Commedia.* The impression of an ironical intent is conveyed to modern readers chiefly by the metre of the poem, and the awkwardness of some of Chaucer's turns of phrase. Who would recognise a serious imitation of Virgil in the lines (143 ff.): 'I wol now singen, yif I kan,/The armes . . .'? It is Virgil interpreted by a mediaeval minstrel; but Chaucer was himself also a mediaeval minstrel, though he knew how to make fun of minstrels, when he liked, as in *Sir Thopas.*[12] Lowes [13] found the quintessence of the humour of the *House of Fame* in the second book:

in the irresistible contrast between the bland loquáciousness of the eagle, during the flight through the air, and the chastened monosyllables of the poet. Nothing could be more consummately done than Chaucer's replies, as if a breath too much might work disaster, to the preternaturally

[12] See C. S. Lewis's just remarks on the critics' tendency to see a humorous intention whenever Chaucer writes badly, in *The Allegory of Love,* Oxford University Press, 1936, pp. 163 and 171: 'The conception of the "mocking" Chaucer must not be so used as to render it impossible for us to say Chaucer ever wrote ill—which is what follows if everything that cannot please as poetry is immediately set down as humour. And what will be very funny if it is meant to be serious, may often be very feeble as a deliberate joke.'

[13] PMLA, xx, p. 859.

cheerful flow of conversation which the edifying bird keeps up: 'And I answerde, and seyde, "Yis." ' . . . ' "Wel," quod I' . . . 'I seyde, "Nay" ' . . . ' "What," quod I.'

Chaucer's eagle behaves like Virgil at the end of his first lesson on free will (*Purgatory*, xviii, 1 ff.):

> Posto avea fine al suo ragionamento
> L'alto dottore, ed attento guardava
> Ne la mia vista s'io parea contento.

[The lofty Teacher had put an end to his argument, and was looking intent in my face, if I seemed satisfied.]

Did Chaucer, like one of us to-day, see the humour of certain dissertations Virgil, Beatrice, and some of the saints lavish on Dante? Is Chaucer's 'Yis' really meant to be humorous, or is it only a counterpart of Dante's 'si' in *Purgatory*, xxxi, 13 ff., from which humour and irony are of course completely absent?

> Confusione e paura insieme miste
> Mi pinsero un tal 'si' fuor de la bocca,
> Al quale intender fuor mestier le viste.

[Confusion and fear, together mingled, drove forth from my mouth a 'Yes' such that to understand it the eyes were needed.]

Actually Chaucer has been led to a situation which to us appears rather comical by a chain of associations similar to those we have examined already. From the trite theme of the dream, so common with the school of the *Roman de la Rose*, Chaucer has passed on to Dante's dream at the beginning of Canto ix of the *Purgatory*. There Dante, frightened, is warned by Virgil on his waking up: 'Non aver tema' [Do not be afraid]; and Virgil explains to him how Lucia (the eagle of the dream) has borne him away from the little vale of the Princes, and placed him near to the gate of Purgatory proper. This being carried by the eagle's talons reminds Chaucer of a similar journey, on Geryon's back (*Inferno*, xvii). Dante had also been greatly terrified in that case, but fear of cutting a poor figure in Virgil's eyes had restrained him from manifesting his apprehension: 'Ma vergogna mi fé le sue minacce'. 'Maggior paura non credo che fosse . . .' [I do think there was not a greater fear . . .]

> For-whi it was to gret affray.
> Thus I longe in hys clawes lay,
> Til at the laste he to me spak
> In mannes vois, and seyde, 'Awak!
> And be not agast so, for shame!'

On the other hand the identification of the eagle with Lucia, and the theme of fear, could not fail to refer Chaucer to Canto ii of the *Inferno*, and to Virgil's exhortations contained in it:

Dunque che è? perché, perché ristai?
Perché tanta viltà nel cuore allette?
[What is it then? why dost thou hesitate? why nourishest thou such fear in thy heart?]

Once Chaucer has this Canto ii before his mind, he lifts from it the passage 'Io non Enea, io non Paolo sono', which becomes 'I neyther am Ennok, ne Elye . . .', as well as the lines:

Da questa tema acciò che tu ti solve,
Dirotti perch'io venni e quel ch'io 'ntesi . . .
[In order that thou mayst be freed from this fear, I will tell you why I came and what I heard . . .]

which become in Chaucer (600 ff.):

> 'But er I bere the moche ferre,
> I wol the telle what I am,
> And whider thou shalt, and why I cam
> To do thys, so that thou take
> Good herte, and not for fere quake.'

After studying such parallel passages, one wonders whether whatever humour we seem to detect in Chaucer's situation is intentional. It is, after all, possible that Chaucer really meant *The House of Fame* to be a sort of Dantesque journey through the realm of allegory, and tried to assimilate from the *Commedia* what was accessible to his spirit. A first great difference from Dante's journey is this: Dante speaks of his journey as of an actual one, has no recourse to the hackneyed mediaeval theme of the dream. To Dante his pilgrimage to the other world was no fiction, but a reality greater than any mundane reality. But the boldness of Dante's conception was not calculated to appeal to the bourgeois Chaucer. Does he not make certain typical disclosures on this point? We read in the Prologue to the *Legend of Good Women*:

> A thousand sythes have I herd men telle
> That there is joye in hevene and peyne in helle,
> And I acorde wel that it be so;
> But natheles, this wot I wel also,
> That ther is non that dwelleth in this contre,
> That eyther hath in helle or hevene ybe.

And in the *Canterbury Tales* (A2809 ff.):

> His spirit chaunged hous and wente ther,
> As I cam nevere, I kan nat tellen wher.
> Therfor I stynte, I nam no divinistre;
> Of soules fynde I nat in this registre,
> Ne me ne list thilke opinions to telle
> Of hem, though that they writen wher they dwelle.

In a way Dante must have appeared 'a divinistre' to Chaucer, since he talked of places and things of which he could not know anything. Perhaps the phrase 'there is non that dwelleth in this contre,' though it can be traced ultimately to a Biblical tag (*Liber Sapientiae*, ii, 1: 'non est qui agnitus sit reversus ab inferis'), contains a covert allusion to Dante. Any speculation on the other world must have seemed unreal to Chaucer. That is why, beginning the *House of Fame* as a dream, he inserts into it the part imitated from Dante at the point in which Dante speaks of a dream of his, in the ninth canto of the *Purgatory*:

> Vinto dal sonno, in su l'erba inchinai . . .
> . . . .
> In sogno mi parea veder sospesa
> Un'aguglia nel ciel con penne d'oro . . .

[Vanquished by sleep, I sank down on the grass . . . In a dream methought I saw an eagle poised in the sky, with plumes of gold . . .]

While the powerful vision of ultramundane kingdoms had no appeal for Chaucer's mind, which was anything but that of a 'divinistre', so that, in order to introduce a similar vision, he knew no better than to have recourse to the traditional device of the dream, there was another aspect of Dante's poem to which he must have felt equally irresponsive: the political aspect, the ardent hope of a social as well as a spiritual salvation. The placid London bourgeois could hardly sympathise with Dante's holy prophetic wrath against coward emperors and degenerated popes. Still political revolutions were not lacking in England in Chaucer's time, and they affected the poet's welfare too; but they do not seem to have left any direct trace in his works, although, of course, we may infer from them what was the state of society.[14] Dante had rightly said (*Paradise*, xxiii, 67–69):

Non è pileggio da picciola barca
Quel che fendendo va l'ardita prora,
Né da nocchier ch'a se medesmo parca.

['Tis no fit voyage for a little boat, this which my daring prow pursues as it cleaves the main, nor for a pilot who spares himself.]

Chaucer was no little boat: but he was a merchantman. His attitude towards Dante's sublimity finds an exact parallel in the position of another bourgeois poet—Horace—when confronted with Pindar (*Carmina*, iii, 3):

Non hoc iocosae conveniet lyrae—
Quo, Musa, tendis? desine pervicax
Referre sermones deorum et
Magna modis tenuare parvis.

[14] Apropos of R. P. Blackmur's remark: 'If *Piers Plowman* dealt with the class struggle, *The Canterbury Tales* did not,' S. E. Hyman writes (*The Armed Vision*, New York, 1948, p. 247): 'Actually, of course, *The Canterbury Tales* deal more patently with the class struggle than the great majority of literary works, from the decay of feudalism between Knight and Squire in the Prologue to the sharp class alignments in most of the tales.'

Nowhere can the difference of stature between Dante and Chaucer be better gauged than in reading side by side with Dante's powerful lines the English version of the episode of Count Ugolino. The *Monk's Tale* is not a tale proper, but rather a collection of brief 'tragedies' from Lucifer's fall to the death of Bernabò Visconti, duke of Milan. The style of at least one of these tragedies, that of Peter the Cruel, king of Spain, is a deliberate attempt at imitating Dante, even in the manner of indicating people through their coats of arms (Cf. *Inferno*, xxvii, 49–50, and *Purgatory*, viii, 79–80), but this is all; on the whole Chaucer ignores Dante's original framework and reverts to a traditional type of mediaeval composition; for in a sense the *Divina Commedia*, particularly the *Inferno*, may be considered as a series of brief tragedies, the stories of the various souls which they themselves narrate to Dante; but Chaucer makes nothing of Dante's novelty of treatment, and the *Monk's Tale* has the very indicative title *De Casibus Virorum Illustrium*. For Chaucer, Ugolino's tragedy is essentially a tragedy of death by starvation: his attention is concentrated solely on the manner of death.[15] Chaucer says that the prisoners had so little meat and drink, that it was hardly sufficient, and besides, it was very poor and bad. Chaucer is not content with hints, like Dante; he enters into details. After translating Dante's 'Oure flessh thou yaf us, take oure flessh us fro,' he adds: 'and ete ynogh'. And instead of the terrible pauses and silences and implications of Dante, you find the wailing of human beings in distress. For Dante the tragedy of Ugolino is not merely a tragedy inherent in a peculiar manner of death, namely, death by starvation; its import is much greater. The tragedy reaches such a high pitch in Dante because it is seen against the background of public events, because treachery, and revenge, and persecution, are there as themes of a Greek chorus. Chaucer slurs over Ugo-

[15] For a more detailed analysis of the Ugolino episode in Chaucer see my essay, 'Chaucer e i grandi trecentisti italiani' in *Machiavelli in Inghilterra*, pp. 41 ff. Considerations of the same kind as mine, which appeared for the first time in *The Monthly Criterion*, 1927, no. 1, have been made also by T. H. Spencer in *Speculum*, ix (1934), pp. 295–301 ('The Story of Ugolino in Dante and Chaucer'). Spencer had not seen my study.

lino's dream, in which the Count imagines himself and his children as a wolf and its cubs, hunted down with hue and cry, and, of course, does not translate the famous invective against Pisa—'vituperio de le genti' ['ah, Pisa, thou offence to the whole people']—with the apocalyptic vision of divine revenge which follows. What in Dante is magnified into a cosmic tragedy, in Chaucer becomes the forerunner of the pathetic genre painting of the nineteenth century (one is reminded of Dickens). It may be alleged that it is not Chaucer, but the Monk, who speaks. But would Chaucer, if he had been aware of the real nature of the Ugolino episode, have allowed one of his characters to spoil it as the Monk does? Rather we should say that here we come across the same barrier of incomprehension which caused the author of the *House of Fame* to translate the first lines of the *Aeneid* in a manner which to us sounds like a minstrel's parody. Moreover, the keynote of the Monk's tale of Ugolino is pity. Now a line of Dante which kept recurring to Chaucer's mind is the celebrated one: 'Amor, che a cor gentil ratto s'apprende . . .' A line modelled on this is found five times in Chaucer's works, but instead of 'love' we read 'pity':

For pitee renneth sone in gentil herte.

Pity, a warm feeling of human sympathy, is one of Chaucer's characteristics, the central theme of the story of Griselda as well as that of Troilus, of the story of Ugolino's children as well as of that of the boy killed by the Jews. The sublimer side of Dante's genius failed to find an echo in Chaucer's soul, but whatever is human and touching in the *Commedia* found a ready response in the bourgeois poet.

This brief survey of Dante's influence on Chaucer would not be complete without a glance at the metrical form. No doubt Chaucer owed much to Boccaccio, but Boccaccio's fluid, occasionally slack, *endecasillabo* was bound to impress the English poet less than Dante's hammered, virile verse, so rich in cadences.

Following Dante's example, Chaucer was the first to give backbone and resilience to the English decasyllabic. It is enough to read certain lines of Chaucer to notice immediately their Dantesque rhythm. The *Monk's Tale* offers several illustrations. Thus the line:

> O Lucifer, brightest of angels alle
> > (*Monk's Tale*, 3194)

recalls the rhythm of:

> O Buondelmonte, quanto mal fuggisti.
> > (*Paradise*, xvi, 140)

Compare also:

> Out of miserie, in which that thou art falle
> > (*Monk's Tale*, 3196)

with:

> Ne la miseria, dove tu mi vedi
> > (*Inferno*, xxiv, 134)

> Ne la miseria; e ciò sa 'l tuo dottore.
> > (*Inferno*, v, 123)

And:

> Of which he was so proud and ek so fayn
> That in vengeance he al his herte sette
> > (*Monk's Tale*, 3931–3932)

with:

> E li 'nfiammati infiammar sì Augusto,
> Che' lieti onor tornaro in tristi lutti.
> > (*Inferno*, xiii, 68–69)

The pattern of:

> Upon a tree he was, as that hym thoughte
> > (*Monk's Tale*, 3933)

is traceable to:

> de le palpebre mie, così mi parve.
> > (*Paradise*, xxx, 89)

Translation goes hand in hand with reproduction of rhythm
in the following couples:

> Oure flessh thou yaf us, take oure flessh us fro
> > (*Monk's Tale*, 3641)

> Queste misere carni, e tu le spoglia.
> > (*Inferno*, xxxiii, 63)

> His lustes were as lawe in his decree
> > (*Monk's Tale*, 3667)

> Che libito fe' licito in sua legge.
> > (*Inferno*, v, 56)

I have said that Chaucer treated the *Commedia* as an
encyclopaedia, deriving continuous suggestions from it. This
influence has, however, a fragmentary character: it does not
extend beyond comparatively short passages, as if Chaucer
loosened a line or a group of lines from their *legame musaico*
in Dante and used them as precious stones in his own
mosaic.[16] Another influence, of a more general character, will

---

[16] The first traces of Italian influence on Chaucer seem to
occur in *The Complaint unto Pity* and in *A Complaint to his
Lady:* the former represents the first experiment in the seven-
line stanza, and betrays Dante's model in the general design of
the *Bill of Complaint* (cf. *Paradise*, xxxiii) and in the phrase
'Herenus quene' (line 92); the latter is apparently the first and
last attempt of Chaucer at reproducing the *terzina,* possibly under
the impression of a first reading of the *Commedia*. As for the
Complaint unto Pity, there is a similarity between lines 57 ff. and
Saint Bernard's prayer to the Virgin in *Paradise* xxxiii. 'Humblest
of herte, highest of reverence' seems to echo 'umile e alta più
che creatura'; 'benygne flour', 'benygne creature' remind us of the
phrasing of Dante's passage (line 16: 'la tua benignità'; 2: 'umile
. . . più che creatura'; 9: 'questo fiore'); 'coroune of vertues alle'
may be compared with lines 19–21; 'ye ben annexed ever unto
Bounte' with lines 20–21; 'in te s'aduna/quantunque in creatura
è di bontade'; 'let som strem of youre lyght on me be sene' with
lines 10–11; 78–79 with 14–15 in Dante. The parallel seems to
gain in probability if we compare the *Bill of Complaint* with the
Second Nun's Prologue (*Invocatio ad Mariam*) and with
Troilus's prayer to Venus (*Troilus*, iii, 1261 ff.), where imitation
of *Paradise* xxxiii is evident; and with the *Prioress's Prologue* in

be discussed further on, apropos of the idea of the *Canterbury Tales*.

II

Chaucer, like most mediaeval minds, had an immoderate craving for what was deemed then the supreme achievement of learning, namely a multifarious command of quotations:

> For out of olde feldes, as men seyth,
> Cometh al this newe corn from yer to yere,
> And out of olde bokes, in good feyth,
> Cometh al this newe science that men lere.
>
> *(Parl. of Fowls*, 22 ff.)

Old books; the 'wise clerkes that ben dede' (*Troilus*, iii, line 292): these he reveres in his heart, to them he gives 'lust and credence' (*Legend of Good Women*, G-Prol., 31–32). They are shrines to which Chaucer goes for worship, as soon as he is released each day from his official duties; he goes home, and there, as dumb as any stone, sits at a book, till his eyesight is fully dazed (*House of Fame*, line 655 ff.). Dante and Petrarch were similarly keen on 'wise clerkes that ben dede', but they never fell into the grotesque, parvenu-like crudity of some of Chaucer's displays of erudition.

---

which the same passage from the *Paradise* seems to have been before Chaucer's mind through the intermediary of his own imitation in the *Invocatio ad Mariam*. Compare for instance lines 82–84 of the *Complaint* with *Troilus*, iii, 1265 ff.; line 94 with *Prioress's Prologue*, 1269 and 71ff. of the *Invocatio*. The passage imitated from the *Paradise* in the *Invocatio* was once considered the first trace of Dante's influence (see, however, C. Brown, 'The Prologue of Chaucer's Lyf of Saint Cecile', in *Modern Philology*, ix, pp. 1–16). Another reminiscence of another prayer from Dante (*Inferno*, ii, 103 ff.: 'Beatrice, loda di Dio vera,/Ché non soccorri quei che t'amò tanto . . . Non odi tu la pieta del suo pianto') may be seen in lines 92–93: 'Have mercy on me . . . That yow have sought so tendirly and yore.' A few lines before we read in Dante: 'Lucia, nimica di ciascun crudele'. We may, however, suspect also a French source in the *Complaint*, as the expression (line 70): 'Beaute, *apertenant* to Grace' seems to betray.

When Troilus gives the instructions for his funeral, he asks that his ashes be conserved

> In a vessell, that men clepeth an urne,
>
> (*Troilus*, v, 1. 311)

and informs Pandarus that the last two nights he had been warned of his approaching end by the owl 'which that hette Escaphilo' (*ibid.*, 319). Criseyde swears a solemn oath (iv, st. 221) on 'Satiry and Fawny more and lesse', and very sensibly informs whoever might be ignorant of it that those strange creatures 'halve goddes ben of wildernesse', as she, or rather Chaucer, had read in Boccaccio's *Genealogia Deorum: Faunos . . . et Satyros, nemorum dicebant deos.* Despondent Troilus, in the *Filostrato* (v, st. 17):

> . . . bestemmiava il giorno che fu nato,
>
> E gli dei e le dee e la natura.

But Chaucer's Troilus delights in letting us know how proficient he is in classical mythology (v, st. 30):

> He corseth Jove, Appollo, and ek Cupide,
>
> He corseth Ceres, Bacus, and Cipride,
>
> His burthe, hymself, his fate, and ek nature. . . .

Now Chaucer is in real earnest while parading such an amount of sound lore. Whenever he can supplement the source he has in hand for the moment with additional information derived from other sources, he does not let slip the opportunity. To add a new mythological name to a list, to adduce a new proverb in support of a statement, meant for him to follow the golden rules of Matthieu de Vendôme's and Geoffroi de Vinsauf's traditional rhetoric; to amplify, according to the mistaken decorative taste which prevailed also in the fashions of the period,[17] was to adorn. He little bothered whether the

[17] The period of the Middle Ages in which Chaucer lived was in a way an overripe and decadent one: its Gothic is flamboyant Gothic, in which structure has been subordinated to decoration: it aims at the exquisiteness of a crystal lace. This is the period of the great unfinished cathedrals; *The Canterbury Tales* is itself like an unfinished cathedral. Feudalism, ripened to the stage of fruition of the goods which had cost centuries of hard work, was dissolving into tournaments and pageants, had become more fond

mythological information was reliable or not, whether the proverb was so vulgar as to clash with the loftiness of the argument: the very fact of there being a classical name or a proverb conferred upon those purple patches an indisputable glamour.

When fully aware of this fact, one is apt to be very cautious before accepting modern views on Chaucer's sense of humour. In cases like the preceding ones Chaucer appears quaint to us, but he did not mean it, not in the least. When he causes the Franklin to speak of Marcus Tullius Cithero, he is not blundering on purpose, in order to make the Franklin appear really ignorant, as a benevolent critic was pleased to think. The Franklin is a very learned person, as he is going to show further on by his collection of stories of chaste women borrowed from St. Jerome (one feels that Dorigen could proceed to such didactic lengths as Dame Prudence: see *Canterbury Tales,* F, 1457–58). Confusion between Cithero and Cicero can be easily ascribed to phonetic influence.

---

of painted devices than of actual deeds. It was a brilliant, stylized epoch, which puts one in mind of the figures of a pack of cards. A typical painter of this period is, for instance, Altichiero da Verona, of whom B. Berenson writes (*The Italian Painters of the Renaissance,* Oxford University Press, 1932, pa. 226): 'But with these qualities Altichiero combines many faults of those later Trecento painters . . . He has their exaggerated love of costume and finery, their delight in trivial detail, their preoccupation with local colour. . . . The accessories absorb him, so that the humorous trivialities which life foists upon the sublimest events, at his hands sometimes receive more tender care than the principal figures. . . . Altichiero reduces the Crucifixion to something not far removed from a market scene, and the spectator is in danger of forgetting the Figure on the Cross by having his attention drawn to a dog lapping water from a ditch, a handsome matron leading a wilful child, or an old woman wiping her nose. The artist is so . little heedful of the highest artistic economy that he constantly abandons it for the passing fashions of the day. One of these fashions was a delight in contemporary costume, and Altichiero clothes his figures accordingly, bartering impressiveness for frippery.' See also p. 230: 'In him (Pisanello), art-evolution produced a painter most happily fitted to hold up an idealizing mirror to a parallel product of social evolution, the sunset of Chivalry.' On certain aspects of this phase of the Middle Ages see J. Huizinga's well-known book, *The Waning of the Middle Ages.*

Chaucer wants quotations and classical reminiscences to adorn his sentences, and authorities to ennoble the plots of his stories. The smile of Ariosto, referring for fun to the authority of Turpino, does not curl the lips of Chaucer, while he mentions Suetonius and other worthies in passages where they have no reason whatever to be produced; not even Agaton or the fabulous Zanzis are conjured up by the English poet as a freak of humour.

The older an authority is, the more venerable and worth quoting: the same principle which leads Chaucer to replace Boccaccio's lines by Dante's, when he recognises the ultimate source, prompts him, in the Knight's tale, to attribute to Statius, rather than to Boccaccio, statements which he actually finds made by Boccaccio, and appeal to Livy as the author he follows for the Virginia story, though he is really following the account in the *Roman de la Rose*. Occasionally, when the modernity of the source defies direct reference, he has recourse to some vague statement. So Dante's (since he is the authority vainly sought after by Root): [18]

> Né creator né creatura mai
> . . . fu sanza amore,
> O naturale, o d'animo. . . .

is referred to by Pandarus as the saying of 'wyse lered' (*Troilus*, I, st. 140):

> For this have I herd seyd of wyse lered,
> Was nevere man or womman yet bigete
> That was unapt to suffren loves hete,
> Celestial, or elles love of kynde.

But more frequently a ficticious authority is preferred to a vague one. So, in Book iv (st. 60), Pandarus is prevented by obvious chronological reasons from giving Ovid as the authority for 'the newe love out chaceth ofte the olde', and, quite naturally, he quotes the mysterious Zanzis as his source. Sandras's candour went so far as to suggest to emend *Zanzis*

[18] *The Book of Troilus and Criseyde* ed. R. K. Root, Princeton University Press, 1926, p. 429, 'I have not been able to discover who are the "wyse lered" on whose authority the Italian lines [the passage from *Filostrato*] are expanded.'

into *Naso,* as being *certainement la véritable leçon!* But Chaucer, for all his references to Seynt Venus, the Palladion service, and the tale of Wade, had enough historical sense to know that a Trojan was hardly in a position to quote Ovid, and he preferred to refer to a precise, though unwarrantable, authority, rather than to a vague one. So Froissart's *ce dist li escripture* becomes *Agaton* in the *Legend of Good Women* (G-Prol., 514) (probably because Plato's *Symposium,* which tells the story of Alcestis referred to by Chaucer in this passage, was known as *Agathonis Convivium.*) [19] Boccaccio, in the *Teseida* (i, st. 2), is speaking of

> . . . una storia antica
> Tanto negli anni riposta e nascosa
> Che latino autor non par ne dica,
> Per quel ch'io sento, in libro alcuna cosa.

[An old story so hidden and concealed in the past, that no Latin author, for what I know, seems to mention it in any book.]

But Chaucer does not like to rely solely on oral tradition, and he actually boasts to have found what Boccaccio had been unable to find (*Anelida and Arcite,* st. 2): 'This olde storie, *in Latyn* which I fynde.'

To Boccaccio, they say, Chaucer is indebted more than to anybody else; his silence with reference to that Italian author is positively unfair. First of all, it ought to be proved that Chaucer knew that Boccaccio was the author of the works he was exploiting—and we shall see shortly that this surmise is not so preposterous as it sounds; but even granted, for the moment, that he was fully aware of that authorship, we must remember that in the *Teseida* and the *Filostrato* Boccaccio, in his turn, confesses himself under obligation to old sources. And Chaucer's practice—we have seen—was always to have recourse to the older source as to the more authoritative. Boccaccio acted merely as a link between Chaucer and the old

[19] See Hales's article in *Modern Language Quarterly,* i, 5 ff. As for *Zanzis,* one has conjectured a corruption of *Zeuxis* (Zeuxis, the Greek painter, appears as *Zanzis* in the *Physician's Tale*) and a reference to Zeuxis, courtier of Philip of Macedon, who appears in the romance of Alexander. See Kittredge, *Chaucer's Lollius,* cited below.

source, on the authority of which the story ultimately relied. The artistic merit of Boccaccio's account has nothing to do with what was the real point with Chaucer: authority. The facts were not Boccaccio's invention—Chaucer believed—and the facts were everything to him, theoretically.[20] In practice he was drawing heavily on Boccaccio's artistic achievement, but in Chaucer's time the aesthetic truth that 'form is everything' was far from being discovered.

What are Boccaccio's sources for the *Teseida*? Chaucer assumed them to be Statius and 'Corynne': under this latter name he may have meant Ovid's *Amores*.[21] Then he, quite naturally, omits reference to the immediate and recent source, and goes straight for the fountainhead: 'First folowe I Stace, and after him Corynne' (*Anelida and Arcite*, 1.21). Also, in the *Filostrato* Boccaccio was the mouthpiece of earlier historians, he was following *antiche storie*, as he says in his proem: some ancient author, then, was ultimately responsible for the account of the story—so Chaucer assumed—no less

[20] To become convinced of the power of authoritative tradition over the mediaeval mind one has but to think of the iconographical formulae which controlled the fine arts until the Renaissance. While one artist was copying from another, for instance, the scene of the descent from the cross, he must have felt not that he was falling under a personal obligation to his model, but rather that he was merely accepting at the hands of the other artist a ritual, fixed convention. Should he have been asked on whose authority he was grouping the figures in that particular way rather than in another, he would probably have replied: on the authority of the Holy Scriptures. As to the mediaeval idea of artistic activity and its various phases, see H. H. Glunz, *Die Literarästhetik des europäischen Mittelalters: Wolfram–Rosenroman–Chaucer–Dante*, Bochum-Langendreer, 1937.

[21] See E. F. Shannon in *Chaucer and the Roman Poets*, Cambridge, Mass., 1929: referring to a passage of Dominicus Marius Niger's (*flor. c.* 1490) preface to the Frankfort edition of Ovid, 1601, from which it would appear that the title *Amores* had been lost and the work was quoted as *sine titulo* or as *Elegiae* and *Corinna* (Ovid's mistress, to whom many of the elegies are addressed). However D. Bush in *Speculum*, iv, 1929, pp. 106–107, doubts that Chaucer could have known of Ovid's *Amores*, and thinks he might have derived the reference to Corynne from a catalogue like the one which we read in Lydgate's *Troy Book*, a catalogue which to all appearances was a traditional one: in it are mentioned actually *Stace of Thebes* and *Corynne*.

here than in the cases of Benoit and Guido, where repeated appeals were found to the authority of Dares and Dictys. Now, possibly in the *Polycraticus* of John of Salisbury,[22] Chaucer had read a line of Horace which he understood as pointing to a certain Lollius, as to the 'greatest of writers of the Trojan war' (*Trojani belli scriptorem, Maxime Lolli*). Obviously. Lollius was the source for the account of the Troilus and Criseyde story: he was the chief authority.[23] If the *Filostrato* was merely the transcript of a Latin text, Chaucer could well disregard the fact of the Italian link and affirm that he was translating 'out of Latyn' (ii, 1.14). He even insists on the antiquity of the book in a passage (st. 4) which is akin to what Dante says in the First Treatise of the *Convivio* (v) and in the Second (xiii), and is to be traced ultimately to Horace's *Ars Poetica* ('Multa renascentur, etc.'). That 'Lollius' is not at all meant for a joke, as Ariosto's Turpino, is made certain by his being mentioned along with other Greek and Latin writers who have treated of the Trojan war as one of the 'bearers up of Troy' in the *House of Fame*, 1468. Since the *House of Fame* is presumably anterior to *Troilus*, Chaucer had no reason whatever for introducing there a fictitious name. Much has been written to little purpose, on the mysterious 'Trophe' Lydgate (*Fall of Princes*) gives as the source of *Troilus and Criseyde*; it is also mentioned as the name of a writer in the *Monk's Tale*; but whether Guido delle Colonne or another author is hiding in that obscure allusion, one fact is certain, that a joke here is surely out of the question.

To come back to why Chaucer does not mention Boccaccio, there is the double possibility that Boccaccio's works reached Chaucer either as anonymous or under the name of Petrarch.

[22] See *Notes and Queries*, 9th S., iii: note by E. A. Axon.

[23] Whenever a writer is a recognised authority on a subject, the instinctive tendency is to attribute to him every statement relating to that subject. The wildest of the French romances—Tyrwhitt remarks—are commonly said by the authors to be translated from some old Latin chronicle of St Denys. Close to this is the case of ascribing to an author opinions agreeing with his doctrines. So in the *Parson's Tale* the allusions to Seneca (Dante's *Seneca morale*) are numerous, and sentences from other authors are frequently attributed to him.

Rajna pointed out that sixteen out of twenty manuscripts of the *Filostrato* known to him bear no author's name. On the other hand, the English poet might have ascribed the *Filostrato* to Petrarch. This supposition seems to find support in the fact that Louis de Beauveau, the French translator of the *Filostrato,* who got hold of the book at a time (in the first half of the fifteenth century) and in a place (the 'comptour' of the King of Sicily) where its real authorship ought to have been known, declares that the *Filostrato fut composé par ung poethe Florentin nommé Petrearque.* If Chaucer had only imitated the *Filostrato,* either of the two hypotheses just mentioned might have strong probabilities in its favour. But Chaucer was acquainted also with three at least of Boccaccio's Latin works, with the *Teseida,* with the *Filocolo,* and with the *Amorosa Visione* (leaving aside the rather improbable borrowings from the *Corbaccio,* the *Ruffianella,* and the *Ameto*). One of these works, the *De Claris Mulieribus,* seems indeed to have been known to Chaucer as Petrarch's.[24] Relating the story of Zenobia, which derives from that Latin compilation, the Monk says (*Canterbury Tales,* B., 3515–16):

> Lat hym unto my maister Petrak go,
> That writ ynough of this, I undertake.

If silence about the Italian author in the cases of the *Teseida* and the *Filostrato* can somehow be explained through Chaucer's desire to refer to older and more authoritative sources, surely the same explanation would hardly fit the case of the story of Zenobia. 'Maister Petrak' was certainly a higher authority than Boccaccio, but we surmise that Chaucer would have conjured up a more ancient worthy had he really wanted to find for the old story an authority more suitable than Boccaccio.

If Chaucer had never gone to Italy, the slow and happy-go-lucky kind of transmission of books usual in the Middle Ages might account for such a thoroughgoing error of attribution on Chaucer's part. But we know that Chaucer went to

[24] Possibly—as Kittredge has suggested—through a confusion caused in Chaucer's memory by the similarity of the title with Petrarch's *De Viris Illustribus.*

Italy, and visited Florence in that year, 1373, in the autumn of which Boccaccio was to take up the very honorific appointment of commentator on the *Divina Commedia*. When Chaucer went to Florence, very likely Boccaccio was living in retirement at Certaldo, but it seems extremely improbable that the English envoy should not have heard of Boccaccio's renown.

But if Chaucer's failing to become acquainted with the real authorship of the works of which he made such a large use appears almost incredible, on the other hand he seems to have ignored the *Decameron*. Chaucer's disputed knowledge (or rather, ignorance) of the *Decameron* represents the climax in that wonderous series of mysteries in which his career and writings supremely abound.

The Italian writer Sacchetti, about 1392, was feeling encouraged to write a book of *novelle* because of the great success of the *Decameron*, which, he says, was not only well known in Italy, but also in France and England, and done in those languages: *infino in Francia e in Inghilterra l'hanno ridotto alla lor lingua*. Even if what we know about the diffusion of the *Decameron* abroad—as Farnham and Wright have shown—cannot be made to agree with Sacchetti,[25] who possibly was speaking of France and England by hearsay, still Sacchetti's words hold good in so far as Italy is concerned. L. Bruni, A. Loschi, F. Beroaldo, had given translations of *novelle* out of the *Decameron*. A poem in *terza rima* written in the first half of the fifteenth century, possibly by Giovanni da Prato, represents to us the whole of Italy under the spell of Boccaccio's hundred tales: *delle qual tutta Italia n'è repleta*. For all this Boccaccio's closest friend, Petrarch, in a well-known letter (*Seniles*, xvii, 3) written as late as 1373, tells Boccaccio how the *Decameron* has come by some accident (*nescio unde vel qualiter*) into his hands. Petrarch's tone is what at first we should call extremely patronising: 'Your book, which in your youth, as I think, you published in our mother

[25] The first English translation of the *Decameron* appeared in 1620; Herbert G. Wright (*The First English Translation of the Decameron*, in the series of *Essays and Studies on English Language and Literature*, ed. by S. B. Liljegren, Upsala, 1953) ascribes it to Giovanni Florio.

tongue . . .' One feels at once that Petrarch purposely looks down on the book, written in the language of the uneducated folk, by an irresponsible young man. We must not forget that the author Petrarch was addressing here was the convert who had repudiated the *Decameron* and now wrote only in Latin; so that partiality towards that juvenile work could hardly have been expected from the friend who pretended to slight his own *nugellas vulgares,* and had warmly encouraged Boccaccio to persevere in his new mode of life. 'I cannot say I have read it'—goes on Petrarch. 'It is a big book (*magnus valde*), written in prose for the use of the people (*ad vulgus et soluta scriptus oratione*), and I have little time, etc. I have only run it over (*excucurri eum, et festini viatoris in morem, hinc atque hinc circumspiciens nec subsistens*). I have been delighted with my cursory reading; the occasional immodesty of the book finds some excuse in your age, at the time you wrote it, in the style, the language, the very levity of the argument and of the intended readers. Amidst many levities I have marked some things of graver tone.' He goes on saying that the concluding story (Griselda's) has charmed him so much that he has learnt it by heart, to repeat it to his friends; then, thinking that also those who had no Italian might have been delighted with it, he has done the story into Latin.

From the letter it appears as if Petrarch felt as some grave don of to-day would feel in the presence of detective stories and popular novels: one cannot help having a glance at them, since they are found lying about in the house, but the shorter the time dedicated to the reading of them, the better. The category of readers for which the *Decameron* chiefly catered was poles asunder from the grave sphere in which Petrarch moved; and it is easy to understand why the author of the *Africa* hardly took any notice of the *Decameron* until 1373, if we observe what is happening round us, in a world in which publicity is infinitely greater. If Chaucer, during his Italian sojourns (?1368, 1373 and 1378), was only in touch with grave persons, he would have had very few chances of hearing of the success of the popular book. It is furthermore to be observed, with Lounsbury, that if Chaucer had been acquainted with the *Decameron,* it is certainly a matter of legitimate surprise why he should have taken the tale of

Griselda from Petrarch's Latin version, and a French translation of it, instead of Boccaccio's Italian original.[26]

Let us now turn to the *Canterbury Tales,* and see what internal evidence can be elicited in favour of Chaucer's acquaintance with the *Decameron.* Whereas indebtedness to the *Decameron* was once admitted with a light heart (for instance by Tyrwhitt and Warton), alleged parallels have since proved inconsistent on a closer scrutiny. The only story derived from the *Decameron* has reached Chaucer through the medium of Petrarch. The *Franklin's Tale,* which is similar to *Decameron* x, 5, is rather to be compared with the earlier version of that story in the *Filocolo.* The Pardoner's prologue is a satire on the monks who impose upon the credulity of the people with imaginary sacred relics; so is Boccaccio's tale of Frate Cipolla (vi, 10); but surely that kind of imposition was only too common in everyday life, and to infer interdependence in that case would be no more warrantable than to trace Chaucer's account of the Physician to Petrarch's hatred of doctors as instanced in his letters and in his invective *contra medicum quendam,* and the Yeoman's attack against the alchemists and their art to the dialogue *De Alchimia* in Petrarch's *De remediis utriusque fortunae.* Briefly, even Rajna who emphatically upholds the thesis of acquaintance with the *Decameron,* readily admits that none of the Canterbury tales appears to be a direct emanation from the Italian collection of *novelle.* As to verbal parallels, the only one which has been produced so far is to be found in the Reeve's prologue (A, 3878–79), where the proverb 'to have an hoor heed and a grene tayl, as hath a leek' is supposed (by Chiarini, for instance) to echo Boccaccio's *perché il porro abbia il capo bianco . . . la coda è verde* (Introduction to Day iv): as if the quotation of a proverb could be traced to a definite source.

Rajna's contention that Chaucer must have been acquainted with the *Decameron* rests upon two arguments, one derived from Petrarch's letter to Boccaccio accompanying the Latin

[26] See J. B. Severs, 'The Clerk's Tale', in *Sources and Analogues of Chaucer's Canterbury Tales,* University of Chicago Press, 1941, and *The Literary Relationships of Chaucer's 'Clerkes Tale',* Yale University Press, 1942.

translation of the Griselda story, the other from the character of the plan or framework of the *Canterbury Tales*. If Chaucer had read Petrarch's letter, he would have known who was the real author of the story and—Rajna argues—he would have been naturally impelled to get hold of the book containing the original. I am not quite sure of this consequence, since Petrarch does not show in his letter such appreciation of the entire work as to awake the curiosity of cultivated people. But did the manuscript of the *De Fide Uxoria* Chaucer had before his eyes actually contain that letter, as usual? [27] Did Chaucer read that letter?

The only evidence in favour—I am afraid—recoils disastrously on, and makes havoc of, the laborious fabric of arguments devised in support of Chaucer's meeting with Petrarch. Curiously enough, this fact has so far escaped the notice of the critics. As we have seen, Petrarch in his letter to Boccaccio, says that he learnt the tale by heart, and used to repeat it to his friends, much to their delight. Now Chaucer's Clerk of Oxford actually maintains that he has learned the tale of Padua from the very lips of Petrarch. Further on, anyhow, he proceeds to describe *the text* of the *De Fide Uxoria*, giving, first of all, a survey of the 'prohemye' about the situation of Saluces. Until now the way the clerk came to learn the Griselda story had seemed a reflex of a momentous event in Chaucer's life, namely, his meeting with Petrarch: it could merely be a reflex of Chaucer's reading the passage in Petrarch's letter about his habit of repeating the tale to his friends.

The Clerk's account of how he got hold of the story is so awkward as to bring evidence of its being an invention of the poet:

> But forth to tellen of this worthy man,
> That taughte me this tale, as I bigan,
> I seye that first with heigh style he enditeth,
> Er he the body of his tale *writeth,*
> A prohemye. . . .

[27] There is, however, no trace of this introductory letter in the following MSS., all dating from the fifteenth century: MS. 275, Corpus Christi College, Cambridge; MSS. 82, 178, 259, University Library, Utrecht.

The Clerk's words are as transparent as a child's lie. In brief, what he says amounts to this: Petrarch *told* me at Padua this story, and first of all he *writes* a proem to it. . . . Strange to say, the inconsistency of this account has failed to strike the poet, first, and his industrious critics, afterwards, until, as late as 1906, Hendrickson called attention to it.[28]

Even if we suppose that Chaucer was not prompted by Petrarch's letter to invent the episode of the Clerk's meeting with the Italian poet, we can imagine that fiction to have been brought about in another way. The tale itself, as in other cases—I shall have to expound this point in a moment— may have suggested by reflex the character of the story-teller: this process which we notice in most of Chaucer's stories would have been rendered easier in the case of the Griselda story by the presence of a figure so congenial to it as that of the worthy clerk Fraunceys Petrak. Natually, Petrarch could not be introduced in person as one of the Canterbury pilgrims, but a double of him, another clerk, an Englishman, could easily be imagined or actually found.[29] As a mediaeval student,

---

[28] See also E. K. Sisam, Introduction to *The Clerkes Tale*, Oxford, 1923. Another time Chaucer forgets to be consequent to his fiction. In the *Second Nun's Tale*, the words: 'Yet preye I yow that reden what I write' (G, 78), are inadvertently put into the mouth of a supposedly oral story-teller. The whole passage, as line 62 shows ('unworthy *sone* of Eve'), was never properly revised to suit it for the collection. The Man of Law's statement (*Canterbury Tales*, B, 132–133), of having learnt from a merchant the tale of Constance, which is in fact taken from Nicholas Trivet's chronicle, and Pandarus's affirmation (*Troilus*, i, st. 94) of having seen Oenone's letter to Paris (derived from Ovid's *Heroides*), are illustrative of the same kind of fiction as that instanced in the Clerk's getting the tale from the very lips of Petrarch. In the *House of Fame*, apropos of the story of Dido and Aeneas, Chaucer says (313–314) that he dreamt it all, and will not allege any other author. But later he forgets that the story has been imagined as painted on the walls of the temple, in a dream, and says (ix, 29): 'the book seyth.'

[29] In a letter published in *The Times Literary Supplement* for May 5, 1932, M. E. Richardson thinks that the model of the Clerk may have been Mestre Waulthier Dissy, a contemporary who was known to the Court *milieux* (see also the same magazine, May 19, 1932). As for the identification of the pilgrims with historical persons, see further in the present study.

he would be expected to visit the famous University of Padua, in the same way as Chaucer's Knight naturally did not miss any of the most remarkable contemporary fights against the infidels; and in Padua he would get the story from the very lips of its author, who was known to be associated with that place (like Livy, Petrarch was sometimes called Patavinus).

Much has been written pro and con the possibility of Chaucer's having met Petrarch: it is all divagation. In 1898 a battle royal on the subject was fought in the columns of the *Athenæum* between Ch. H. Bromby and St. Clair Baddeley. To say that some of their arguments were not apposite, would be unjust, but after having broken their best spears in the first encounter, the two champions proceeded to belabour each other's ribs with pinpricks, until they ultimately were reduced to discuss the point whether Petrarch was likely to be scared by Venetian troops fighting against Padua. The fight was between Padua and Venice—Mr. Baddeley argued—but Arquà, where Petrarch lived, lies in another direction, therefore, Venetian soldiers were not expected to come near it, though, strange to say, a Venetian captain was absurd enough to camp close by . . . The dispute could have gone on until doomsday, had not the Editor of the review been so cruel as to put an untimely end to it, by declaring: 'We cannot insert any more letters on this subject.' But the battle only shifted its centre: it was heard rumbling for some time in the distant papers of Italy. No doubt if Chaucer's journey abroad in 1368 was to Italy in the retinue of Prince Lionel, he might have met Petrarch at the Milan wedding of that prince with the daughter of Bernabò Visconti. The wedding took place on May 28, and the document empowering Chaucer to go abroad is dated July 17: it is however possible that he had already attended the marriage and then, immediately on his return home, had been sent abroad on another mission.

To conclude about Chaucer's acquaintance with the *Decameron* through Petrarch's prefatory letter, even if Chaucer had read that letter, he would have taken it at its face value, and found in it but little inducement to read what was represented there as a juvenile work, indeed a trifle, the only part of which worth knowing had been preserved in Petrarch's Latin version.

The second argument produced by Rajna concerns the framework of the story. Boccaccio arrived at his general plan only by degrees, one stage being represented by the *Filocolo*, and before him we have nothing properly similar in Europe. The *Libro dei Sette Savi* does not introduce a company of people telling stories in turns for mere pastime. But as soon as the *Decameron* had been published, all the collections of the same kind, and many of those of different kind, proved to be derived, either immediately or mediately, from Boccaccio's. The only exception would be the *Canterbury Tales*. The same phenomenon as the one which had taken place in Italy—strange to say—only a short time afterwards would have happened in a country which was so different from Italy and so much less mature. On the other hand—Rajna argues, repeating an old argument [30]—it cannot be maintained that Chaucer found the idea of the frame ready-made in what was happening round him, because the situation of a tale being told to a company of thirty people riding in a long and noisy row is not of those that can be found in real life. The loudspeaker had not yet been invented in Chaucer's time. Surely no great genius is needed to replace Boccaccio's sitting company by a moving one, since the Lucca writer Giovanni Sercambi, who is indebted to the *Decameron*, imagines his tales as being told, in part, along the road, to relieve the travellers from the monotony of the journey, as in the *Canterbury Tales*. Of course it is not impossible that Chaucer might have known Sercambi's collection, presumably—if one finds courage enough to maintain this dependence—during his 1378 mission to Italy: but the service Sercambi renders to us, is, according to Rajna, mainly to show by analogy what took place when Chaucer was confronted with the plan of the *Decameron*.

On the other hand, the case of independent invention would not be so unique. One could cite the *Dialogus Miraculorum* by Caesarius of Heisterbach (about 1230), whose frame has the form of a dialogue in which the novices try to find explanations for present circumstances, and the master explains them by telling stories from the past. Now this is exactly what happens in the famous collection of Indian tales

[30] See the *Edinburgh Review*, xlii (1826, p. 180).

Jātaka (third century B.C.), in which the Buddah first tells a story from the present, followed by a story from the past which explains to his followers the reasons of the circumstances of the present story. But this collection of Indian tales became known in Europe only in the last century. As for Boccaccio, it is not probable either that he derived the idea of the frame-story from the East; he did not know Arabic, and the *Arabian Nights* became known in Europe only at the beginning of the eighteenth century.

One important fact is overlooked by Rajna: the date, when the idea of forming a continuous series of tales was first entertained by Chaucer. This date is a late one; it is agreed to place it from 1386 or 1387 onwards. If Chaucer had at all to become acquainted with the *Decameron,* it stands to reason to suppose that he should have heard of it or seen it in connexion with his missions to Italy: not later, then, than in 1378, because the probability of his coming across that book is considerably less in the succeeding period of unbroken residence in England. But if Chaucer became acquainted with the *Decameron* in the seventies, is it not strange that he should not have been affected by it in the least for the years immediately following; that he should not have drawn from that collection the plot of any of his own stories, and, most of all, that he should have continued to compose the works that were to form the various parts of the future collection, as independent units, no less isolated each from the other than was the translation of Boethius's treatise from *Troilus and Criseyde?* To say that the influence of the *Decameron* remained latent and dormant for so many years, and then, late in the eighties, it dawned upon Chaucer in the shape of a profoundly altered idea of a narrative framework, is tantamount to attributing to Chaucer's mind the merit of the plan of the tales.

At a given moment, Chaucer found in his stock a plurality of short writings, his own translations and adaptations of works of widely divergent character, in prose and in verse: he found there a tale of womanly loyalty such as Griselda's, a confession of feminine wantonness such as the monologue of the *Wife of Bath,* a pious rhymed legend of Saint Cecile, a moral prose treatise on the advantages of prudence, a chivalric poem derived from Boccaccio's *Teseida,* a story of

Constance's trials adapted from Nicholas Trivet. . . . As soon as Chaucer began to survey these works simultaneously, as soon as he summoned them up together before the tribunal of his mind, his keen dramatic genius must have been aware of the amazing variety of contrasts they offered when thus envisaged side by side. Each one of them spoke with a different voice, with a different *tempo*. Each one possessed a character, an individuality, of its own. Here was such a romance as would have delighted a knight and a courtier; there was a tale which had been told by a worthy clerk in Italy; there again a chapter of the Golden Legend, fit to be perused by a refined nun.

It is generally maintained that the tales were used by Chaucer in such a way as to help set off the different characters of the pilgrims. *Les contes dont il disposait*—writes Legouis—*étaient disparates. Tant mieux! Il en profita, grâce à une habile distribution, pour caractériser les conteurs. Il choisit pour chacun l'histoire qui convenait à sa caste et à son caractère.* I think we are much nearer the truth, much more trustworthy in reconstructing what must actually have taken place in Chaucer's mind, when we imagine that a first group of characters sprang up from the stories themselves, as Chaucer contemplated them with his powerful dramatic imagination.[31] The plan of the *Canterbury Tales*—in my opinion—was not brought about through a juxtaposition of a framework—a company of story-tellers—and a body of tales already extant, but gradually took shape as Chaucer was envisaging his scattered writings as units endowed each of them with a peculiar character, coloured with a different experience; while he was contrasting them dramatically, personifying them as so many living beings. Such a projection of a story into the character of a story-teller, such an embodiment of the spirit of each work in a concrete person, is the nucleus of Chaucer's masterpiece, the sudden intuition of dramatic genius bringing light and order into a chaos of heterogeneous matter. The characters of the story-tellers form the central feature of

[31] This idea has been taken up, without acknowledging the source, by D. S. Brewer, *Chaucer*, London, 1953, p. 128. 'We may guess that his characters were first the product, so to speak, of the tales they were to tell.'

Chaucer's idea. Had he taken the hint for the frame from the *Decameron,* he would have represented his story-tellers as people belonging to the same class, bound to show a uniformity of taste and language, as Boccaccio's story-tellers do only too strikingly (in Boccaccio, the story-tellers are little more than shadows, the real speaker being always and solely Boccaccio himself).

As a next stage, we may imagine Chaucer bringing the characters together. In what occasion were people belonging to different strata of society, 'alien of end and of aim,' likely to be met together? It is at this point that Italian influence may have interfered: not Boccaccio's influence, but Dante's.

All stations of life, all kinds of character, from the lowest to the highest, appear and talk to Dante, bent on his pilgrimage through the realms of the dead. Loathsome, poignant, noble, celestial apparitions, they talk to him each one in a suitable style: demons speak the language of demons, brutes, like Nembrot, utter mere gibberish, angels, like Gabriel, sing with a voice sweeter than any human melody: between these extremes, 'each from the other heaven-high, hell-deep removed', all the modes and shades of human souls find expression in Dante's drama.

A pilgrimage to the other world, we have seen, was not among Chaucer's possibilities. He clings to the dear everyday world, and brings down to the homely plan of common sense the situations he finds in his models. The relation between Philosophy and Boethius, between Dame Prudence and Melibeus, is mirrored by Chaucer in his treatment of the relation between Pandarus and Troilus. Though trained in the school of French allegory, the English bourgeois poet was for the concrete, and, not unlike Sancho Panza, he understood in terms of common sense the quixotic visions of philosophers and divines. 'I . . . mervaile . . . that hee in that mistie time could see so clearly'—runs Sidney's appreciation. No pilgrimage to the kingdoms of the other world for the man who was no 'divinistre'; but an earthly pilgrimage to the shrine of the national saint. On this pilgrimage there were no demons or angels to be met, but all varieties of human folk; and Chaucer cared only for the humans. There was God's plenty, for him, in a company of pilgrims. Thus, in a far deeper and broader sense than the one meant by Lydgate, Chaucer succeeded in being 'Dante in ynglyssh', a human instead of a divine Dante, resuming, like the Florentine, the Middle Ages in the compass of a dramatic epos.

This analogy with Dante becomes stronger if we can be persuaded to identify the pilgrims with real persons with whom Chaucer can be shown to have had definite personal contacts, in the way suggested by J. M. Manly. The idea of grouping historical persons in an imagined experience—since Manly does not accept the theory that Chaucer related the circumstances of an actual pilgrimage—that idea of mixing history and fiction, is eminently Dante's idea. While Dante surveyed contemporary society for a universal aim, and having posterity in view, Chaucer would have confined himself to treat in a humorous, satirical manner people and events which were familiar to a relatively limited section of society, the group of courtiers, gentlemen, clergymen, professional men, public officials and merchants of the London of his time. Dante summoned persons who had left their mark on history, before the tribunal of men and of God, and only rarely allowed himself to consider private people and local worthies from a humorous point of view, as in the Belacqua episode (*Purgatory*, iv). On a lower, bourgeois level, Chaucer would have been rehearsing local gossip concerning popular, though not influential, figures. However, if we keep in mind Chaucer's habit of contaminating various sources, it stands to reason to surmise that the characters of the pilgrims are composed of elements of various origin, observed in a number of individuals, not necessarily always from real life, but also from literature. This may explain why it has been possible to find in historical documents several persons who more or less fit the characteristics of Chaucer's pilgrims. The Knight, for instance, corresponds with certain members of the Scrope and Derby families; the Franklin has been recognised in two historical persons, John Bussy and Stephen de Hales.[32]

[32] In a word, we would find here the same process of contamination Walter Scott described in a note to chapter xxii of *Guy Mannering*. Dandie Dinmont derives from a dozen Liddesdale yeomen Scott knew, chiefly from one James Davidson of Hindlee, breeder of the famous race of terriers he called Mustards

Unfortunately he did not, like Dante, live long enough to complete his 'structure brave'. The whole once planned along the lines suggested by the central nucleus of tales and characters, it was left to him to expand that nucleus with other stories and story-tellers; to alter some of the stories already written in order to imbue them more thoroughly with the humours of the story-tellers, to give life to secondary figures. Traces of the unfinished condition of the extant portion of the *Tales* abound. So the Shipman suddenly speaks as if he were a woman; the Second Nun calls herself 'unworthy sone of Eve', while the Man of Law announces a story in prose and actually delivers a legend in verse.

Dante in English, then, rather than an English Boccaccio. All things considered, the numerical superiority of the lines for which Chaucer is indebted to Boccaccio should not blind one to the fact of the more deeply interfused and widespread influence of Dante: an influence to which Chaucer paid due homage, mentioning the 'grete poete of Ytaille' several times in his works.

The other acknowledgement of indebtedness Chaucer makes to an Italian author concerns 'Maister Petrak', and it seems strange indeed, if we consider how slight Petrarch's influence was on his English admirer. Practically none whatever. Chaucer's acquaintance with the *Trionfi* cannot be demonstrated (all attempts so far have been, and are bound to be sterile),[33] and the insertion of a Petrarchan sonnet into *Troilus* is, in a way, a mystery. Of course, several passages in the *Filostrato* reproduce, more or less dilutedly, Petrarchan lines, in the same way as one passage imitates part of a canzone by Cino da Pistoia: so, for instance, two stanzas (v, 54–55) which Young (p. 88) says may easily be regarded as

and Peppers. See also what Proust wrote to Léon Daudet: "There is no name of imaginary character under which the author might not write sixty names of persons seen in actual life: one has posed for grimace, another for the monocle, a third for irritability, still another for the pertinent motion of the arm" (L. Guichard, *Sept Etudes sur Proust,* Cairo, 1942, p. 95).

[33] Brusendorff (p. 161, note) draws a parallel between *Clerkes Tale,* F, 995 ff., and *Trionfo del Tempo,* 127–135. I cannot see the inevitability of this parallel, the whole passage being too much of a commonplace.

a development of suggestions already present in the *Filocolo*, are, instead, an almost literal imitation of a well-known sonnet of Petrarch's (*Sennuccio, io vo' che sappi . . .*); another passage (iii, st. 84–85) derives from the still more famous *Benedetto sia 'l giorno. . . .* Was Chaucer aware of the relation between those passages in the *Filostrato* and the *Canzoniere*, and did this relation prompt him to adopt a whole sonnet as Troilus's song? Obviously he did not find the sonnet in the manuscript of the *Filostrato* he had before his eyes, because he says explicitly that Lollius writes *only* the sentence of the song.[34] One sonnet and the Latin version of the Griselda story seem hardly sufficient to justify Chaucer's homage to Petrarch and the title of 'Maister' conferred upon him, unless Chaucer actually believed Petrarch to be the author of some of Boccaccio's works.†

Chaucer's temperament—it is generally said—was much more akin to Boccaccio's than to either Dante's or Petrarch's. No wonder—I imagine Legouis saying—since Boccaccio was of French origin, like Chaucer. Still, if we consider closely enough Chaucer's indebtedness to Boccaccio, we shall not be long in perceiving how, for all the affinities existing between the two men, there are also great differences, which cause their artistic methods to be almost opposite. The relation of *Troilus* to the *Filostrato* is, not infrequently, that of a drama to a story. Boccaccio is more interested in the story itself, in its development and conclusion; for Chaucer, on the other hand, the characters overgrow the story. For Boccaccio Troilus's love for Criseyde was a simile of his own love to Fiammetta: he had undergone the same experience, he had lived the story for himself. What he did was to melt the various sources of the story into a whole, at the heat of his own love-passion. But what the Italian had *lived* from within, the English poet *saw* from without. To this difference of attitude are to be traced Chaucer's psychological superiority to Boccaccio, as well as his emotional inferiority.

[34] *Troilus*, i, lines 393–394. An error, often repeated, is to suppose that the author of the sonnet is meant by 'Lollius'. See for instance *Chaucer* by G. M. Cowling, London, 1927, p. 101.

† See also the chapter 'Petrarch in England' in the present volume.

This latter deficiency is largely compensated by the former quality; but one cannot help regretting, sometimes, the deliberate suppression, on Chaucer's part, of those fresh, direct effusions of naïve sensual love which give such a juvenile charm to Boccaccio's account:

> Or foss'io teco una notte d'inverno,
> Cento cinquanta poi stessi in inferno
>
> (*Fil.*, ii, st. 88)
>
> . . . or foss'io nelle braccia
> Dolci di lui, stretta a faccia a faccia!
>
> (*Ibid.*, st. 117)
>
> . . . anima mia,
> I' te ne prego, sì ch'io t'abbia in braccio
> Ignuda sì come il mio cor disia,
>
> (*Fil.*, iii, st. 32)

and the stanzas following this last passage, with their sensuous insistence on *in braccio* and *l' uno all' altro*, entirely vanished in Chaucer's translation (*Troilus*, iii, st. 190–191).

As C. S. Lewis has remarked,[35] *Il Filostrato* underwent first and foremost a process of *mediaevalisation* at the hands of the poet who had undertaken the task of interpreting *l'amour courtois* for the English audience: he was 'groping back, unknowingly, through the very slightly medieval work of Boccaccio, to the genuinely medieval formula of Chrestien de Troyes', that perfect fusion of narrative art, erotic doctrine, and psychology, that had been lost after Chrestien. What Chaucer intended to give was a *Filostrato* purged of all the errors Boccaccio had committed against the code of courtly love; hence, in conformity with the teaching of the love religion, *Frauendienst*, not only the traces of cynical gallantry and contempt for women which characterise the *Filostrato* disappear from the English poem, but Criseyde's conduct is defended on all points. The central theme of *Troilus* is loyalty

[35] 'What Chaucer really did to "Il Filostrato",' in *Essays and Studies by Members of the English Association*, xvii, Oxford, 1932; see also the Chaucer chapter in *The Allegory of Love*. See also my introduction to Shakespeare's *Troilus and Cressida*, Florence, 1940, pp. xvi-xxii, where what I say here is further developed.

in love; the central theme of the *Filostrato* is Troilus's sorrow for the absence of his beloved. While Criseyde has gained in subtlety in the English poem, Troilus has remained essentially the same: a proud warrior, a passionate lover, but according to all the rules of courtly love; more idealistic, therefore, than the ardent young man portrayed by Boccaccio, and more inclined to veil the torment of separation with sentimental effusions. The figure of Pandarus is profoundly altered by Chaucer: from the youth *d'alto lignaggio e molto coraggioso* he is in Boccaccio, he becomes Criseyde's uncle: an elderly man, then, but still engaged in Love's struggle, although without luck: a fascinating companion, witty, sententious, funny, 'but not, by many degrees, so broadly comic as he appears to some modern readers', for whom mediaeval sententiousness is funny by itself. Pandarus is the dominating character in *Troilus*: thanks to him the English poem is steeped in a humorous and genial atmosphere which gives it its character, just as passionate intensity is the characteristic of the Italian poem. Boccaccio's poem is dedicated to Fiammetta, and in the leave-taking (viii, st. 29–33) contains a warning to young men not to believe women too readily. Chaucer's poem is dedicated to 'moral' Gower and 'philosophical' Strode (v, st. 266), and the warning to the 'yonge fresshe folkes' is very different from Boccaccio's advice. Perhaps Boccaccio's phrase (st. 29):

> Per Dio vi prego che voi raffreniate
> I pronti passi all'appetito rio

has provided Chaucer with a starting-point for his homiletic conclusion: let young men abandon worldly vanity and turn their hearts to God, let them love Him Who died on the cross to rescue our souls, because this is true love, while the other is a passing delusion (v, st. 263–265). And Boccaccio's advice, not to abandon oneself desperately to the erotic passion ('. . . raffreniate i pronti passi all'appetito rio') becomes a complaint on 'thise wrecched worldes appetites'. Almost in order to reinforce his moral, Chaucer, in three noble stanzas (259–261) lifted from Boccaccio's *Teseida* (xx, st. 1–3, which in their turn derive from the *Somnium Scipionis*), shows us the soul of Troilus, killed by Achilles, ascending to heaven and from there despising the vanities of the world, and damning mankind's proclivity to 'blynde lust'. Thus the edifying side of Boccaccio is utilised by Chaucer to correct him who had cynically given this advice as to the choice of women:

> Ma non si vuol però scegliere in fretta,
> Che non son tutte saggie, perehé sieno
> Più attempate, e quelle vaglion meno.

[One must not, however, make a hasty choice, because not all of them are wise, although grown older, rather these latter have less value.]

And *Troilus* concludes actually with a prayer which paraphrases a famous passage of Dante's *Paradise* (xiv, 28–30): 'Quell'uno e due e tre che sempre vive . . .'

The central theme of *Troilus*, as I have said, is loyalty in love; curiously enough, the stories Chaucer borrowed from Boccaccio are all illustrations of different cases of either kept or broken loyalty. Apart from *Troilus*, the Griselda story is a *de oboedientia et fide uxoria mythologia*, as Petrarch's title runs; Chaucer's version of the *Teseida* is called *The Compleynt of feire Anelida and fals Arcite*; and the character of Dorigen (a counterpart of Tarolfo's beloved in the *Filocolo*) is revealed in a sole heartrending cry:

> Unto the gardyn, as myn housbande bad,
> My trouthe for to holde, allas! allas!

Needless to say, this moral outlook is entirely Chaucer's; in Boccaccio the problem of loyalty is, if at all, very crudely formulated.[36] Notice also that, notwithstanding his partiality

[36] Very much has been written about the difference of the condition set by 'the wife' in Boccaccio's story and in Chaucer's, but nowhere did I find stress laid on the fact that while the wife in Boccaccio merely mentions an arbitrary impossibility (a blossoming garden in midwinter), in Chaucer she really utters a sort of vow, in connexion with the return of her husband. Chaucer, similarly as in the case of Criseyde, was here anxious to justify the woman, to conciliate her binding herself to a—however impossible—condition, with her loyalty to her husband: her condition will therefore be such as to lead, if fulfilled, to the husband's safety. It is a vow. Dorigen, no less than Alcestis, is 'of love so trewe' as to be

for Criseyde, Chaucer is accused by Love, in the *Legend of Good Women*, for having discredited women's fidelity in his *Troilus*, and Queen Alceste, while defending him, engages him to sing henceforward only of such women as were faithful in love during their life; therefore the poet, in conformity with the doctrine of courtly love, writes the nine legends of Cupid's saints.

Thus much can be said about Italian literary influence on Chaucer. But Chaucer was not only a reader of books; he was also a direct observer of human life. The new spirit which breathes in his production after his first Italian journey is, doubtless, due in part to his acquaintance with Italian authors, but in part only. There is another kind of influence which cannot be easily defined and still less easily gauged: an influence which, though elusive, we find is there. Jusserand tried to specify it by conjuring up before our eyes the spectacle of Italy all alive with the dawn of the Renaissance, when Chaucer visited it. But it is hardly the sight of the paintings of Giotto and Orcagna, or the sculptures of Nicola Pisano and his school, or even the rediscovery of the ancient world, which was likely to impress the English envoy. We are too much inclined to think of those first steps of Renaissance as a pageant apt to strike the eyes of contemporaries in the same way as they strike our focussing historical outlook. We see that distant age through the magnifying glasses of posterity. Certainly, Chaucer must have felt the identity of his aims with those of the Italian forerunners of the Renaissance: he also was trying to raise the vernacular ('naked wordes in English') up to the splendour of literary language, he also was an admirer of the classics, and saw Venus 'naked fletynge in a see', her divine head crowned with a 'rose-garlond whit and red' (*House of Fame*, 133–135). But, surely, this again is literature, and what Italy had to offer to Chaucer besides literature, was actual life.

---

ready to sacrifice herself for her husband's sake. Possibly this desire to change the capricious condition into a logical one led Chaucer to alter the setting of Boccaccio's tale in the *Filocolo*: hence the scene laid on a sea-coast notoriously dangerous to sailors, hence the fiction of a Briton lay, introduced to make the story appear more authoritative.

I imagine Chaucer's experience to have been not unlike that of some Elizabethan dramatist, or, to take a more modern and clearer instance, that of Robert Browning. The intense dramatic character of Italian life does not escape a foreigner; and when I speak of dramatic character I do not necessarily imply that Italian life teems with either tragic or comic subjects. I mean that the Italians have always appeared to foreigners as wonderfully lively beings, giving outward expression to all shades of feeling, now wildly gesticulating, now summing up a whole philosophy in a rapid wink of the eye. The wonderful thing Chaucer saw in Italy was the same thing Elizabethan dramatists discovered two centuries later, the same Stendhal and Browning admired in more recent times: the wonderful thing Alfieri well expressed when he said that men 'considered as simple plants' grew in Italy 'of more vigorous mettle' than anywhere else. The spectacle of Italian everyday life no doubt sharpened still more in Chaucer the feeling for drama, both innate in him and furthered by the perusal of Jean de Meun's masterpiece, so that, coming back to his native country, the poet was able to see life round him in the light of his newly acquired experience, and to express that life in words which were 'cosin to the dede'.

BIBLIOGRAPHY

For bibliography up to 1908 see:

HAMMOND, E. P., *Chaucer: A Bibliographical Manual*, New York, 1908.

I confine myself to mentioning here the writings previous to 1908 referred to in my essay, unless already accounted for in the footnotes:

HENDRICKSON, G. L., 'Chaucer and Petrarch: two Notes on the "Clerkes Tale",' *Modern Philology*, iv (1906–97), pp. 179–192.

JUSSERAND, J. J., *Histoire littéraire du peuple anglais*, Paris, 1894 (Volume i).

KISSNER, A., *Chaucer in seinen Beziehungen zur italienischen Litteratur*, Diss. Marburg, 1867. (Excellent, still to be consulted.)

LOUNSBURY, T. R., *Studies in Chaucer*, London, 1892. (Chiefly Vol. ii, pp. 223–249.)

MOLAND, L. and D'HERICAULT, C., *Nouvelles Françoises en prose du XIVe siècle*, Paris, 1858. (The introduction.)

RAJNA, P., 'Le Origini della Novella narrata dal "Frankeleyn" nei "Canterbury Tales" del Chaucer', *Romania*, xxxii (1903), pp. 204–267. (This essay still remains the best contribution to the question of Boccaccio's influence on the *Canterbury Tales*. See also, 'L'Episodio delle Questioni d'Amore nel "Filocolo" del Boccaccio,' by the same author, *Romania*, xxxi (1902), pp. 40–47.)

RAMBEAU, A., 'Chaucer's "House of Fame" in seinem Verhältnis zu Dantes "Divina Commedia",' *Englische Studien*, iii (1880), pp. 209–268.

ROSSETTI, W. M., 'Chaucer's "Troylus and Cryseyde" compared with Boccaccio's "Filostrato",' London, 1873 (*Chaucer Society*, Ser. ii, No. 9).

SANDRAS, E. G., *Etude sur G. Chaucer considéré comme imitateur des trouvères*, Paris, 1859. (Mostly superseded.)

TEN BRINK, B., *Chaucer, Studien zur Geschichte seiner Entwicklung und zur Chronologie seiner Schriften*, Münster, 1870. *Geschichte der Englischen Litteratur*, zweite Auflage hrsg. von A. Brandl, Strassburg, 1899. (Both works fundamental.)

TYRWHITT, T., *The 'Canterbury Tales' of Chaucer*, London, 1775. (Vol. iv containing an Introductory Discourse.)

For bibliography after 1908, the following is a survey of the writings dealing with the Italian influence that appeared after that date. Incidental references are to be found also in writings not bearing directly on the subject. See also KOCH, J., 'Der gegenwärtige Stand der Chaucerforschung', *Anglia*, xlix (1925), pp. 193–243; J. E. WELLS, *A Manual of the Writings in Middle English*, New Haven-London-Oxford, 1916, pp. 866–881, and supplements; D. D. GRIFFITH, 'A Bibliography of Chaucer, 1908–1924,' *University of Washington Publications in Language and Literature*, iv, No. 1, Seattle, 1926; MARTIN, W. E., *A Chaucer Bibliography*, 1925–33, Duke University Press, 1935.

(a) GENERAL

BENNETT, H. S., *Chaucer and the Fifteenth Century*, Oxford, At the Clarendon Press, 1947.

BRUSENDORFF, A., *The Chaucer Tradition*, Copenhagen-London, 1925.

BRYAN, W. F. and DEMPSTER, G. (Editors), *Sources and Analogues of Chaucer's Canterbury Tales*, University of Chicago Press, 1941.

LÉGOUIS, E., *Geoffrey Chaucer*, Paris, 1910.

LOWES, J. L., *Geoffrey Chaucer*, Oxford University Press, 1934. (The best survey of Chaucer in relation to the culture of his time.)

SELLS, A. LYTTON, *The Italian Influence in English Poetry*, Indiana University Press, 1955.

(b) DANTE

CHAPMAN, C. O., "The Legend of Dido", "Legend of Good Women" 924–927,' *The Times Literary Supplement*, August 29, 1952, p. 565.

KELLETT, E. E., 'Chaucer as a Critic of Dante', *The London Mercury*, iv (1921), pp. 281–291. (Interesting, though the point of view it represents can hardly be accepted: Kellett interprets the *House of Fame* as a skit aimed at what he calls the 'grotesque' and 'crude' sides of the *Divina Commedia*.)

LOWES, J. L., 'Chaucer and Dante', *Modern Philology*, xiv (1916–17), pp. 129–159. (Excellent. See also two other essays by the same author, 'Chaucer and Dante's "Convivio",' *Modern Philology*, xiii (1915–16), pp. 19–33; and 'The Second Nun's Prologue, Alanus and Macrobius', *Modern Philology*, xv (1917–18), pp. 193–197).

Minor Contributions by G. L. KITTREDGE, *Chaucer Society*, Ser. ii, No. 42, p. 40 ff.; C. LOOTEN, 'Chaucer and Dante', *Revue de littérature comparée*, v (1925), pp. 545–571; the same, 'Chaucer, ses Modèles, ses Sources et sa Religion', in *Mémoires et Travaux publiés par les Professeurs des Facultés Catholiques de Lille*, 1931 (notwithstanding the promising title, an untidy and superficial work); J. S. P. TATLOCK, *Modern Language Notes*, xxix, 97, xxxv, p. 443; P. TOYNBEE, *Dante in English Literature*, London, 1909, Vol. i, pp. 1–16; *Dante Studies*, Oxford, 1921, pp. 175–176.

(c) BOCCACCIO

CUMMINGS, H. M., 'The Indebtedness of Chaucer's works to the Italian Works of Boccaccio', *University of Cincinnati Studies*, Vol. x, Part 2, 1916. (To be taken here and there *cum grano salis*. See in connexion with this essay Lowes, *Modern Philology*, xv, cited below.)

FARNHAM, W., 'England's Discovery of the "Decameron",' *PMLA*, xxxix (1924), pp. 123–139. (A good survey of the information available at that date concerning the diffusion of Boccaccio's works abroad. See also the article by the same author in *Modern Language Notes*, xxxiii (1918), p. 193.)

KIRBY, T. A., *Chaucer's Troilus, A Study in Courtly Love*, Louisiana State University Press, 1940.

LEWIS, C. S. 'What Chaucer really did to "Il Filostrato",' in *Essays and Studies by Members of the English Association*, xvii (1932).
The Allegory of Love, Oxford, 1936. (Both studies are fundamental in order to understand Chaucer's point of view.)

LOWES, J. L., 'The "Franklin's Tale", the "Teseide", and the "Filocolo",' *Modern Philology*, xv (1918–19), pp. 129–168.

LUMIANSKY, R. M., 'Aspects of the Relationship of Boccaccio's "Il Filostrato" with Benoît's "Roman de Troie" and Chaucer's "Wife of Bath's Tale",' *Italica*, xxxi, 1 (March 1954).

ROOT, R. K., 'Chaucer and the "Decameron",' *Englische Studien*, xliv (1912), pp. 1–7.
The Book of Troilus and Criseyde Edited from all the Known Manuscripts, Princeton University Press, 1926. (Excellent Introduction.)

SEVERS, J. B., *The Literary Relationships of Chaucer's Clerkes Tale*, New Haven, 1942.

TATLOCK, J. S. P., 'The Scene of the "Franklin's Tale" Visited', London, 1914 (*Chaucer Society*, Ser. ii, No. 51). (Agreeing with Rajna.)
'Boccaccio and the Plan of Chaucer's "Canterbury Tales",' *Anglia*, xxxvii (1913), pp. 69–117. (Pp. 80–108: 'striking' resemblances between the *Ameto* and the *Canterbury Tales*: for all this, the author does not consider Chaucer's knowledge of the *Ameto* by any means certain; still he does not spare us—as he himself says—a 'long and somewhat involved disquisition' on the subject.)
'The Epilog of Chaucer's "Troilus",' *Modern Philology*, xviii (1920–21), pp. 625–659.

WRIGHT, H. G., *Boccaccio in England from Chaucer to Tennyson*, University of London, The Athlone Press, 1957.

YOUNG, K., 'The Origin and Development of the Story of Troilus and Criseyde,' London, 1908 (Chaucer Society, Ser. ii, No. 40). (A standard work on the subject. See also Kittredge Anniversary Papers, Boston and London, 1913, pp. 405–417, where the same author thinks Sercambi's Novelle to have supplied Chaucer with the idea of the framework: a point of view already discussed by Rajna.)

Of minor importance: C. CHIARINI, I Racconti di Canterbury tradotti ed illustrati, Firenze, 1912–13 (Introduction and Notes); H. KORTEN, Chaucers literarische Beziehungen zu Boccaccio, die künstlerische Konzeption der 'Canterbury Tales' und das Lolliusproblem, Rostock, 1920, Akad. Preisschrift (a survey of previous opinions); V. LANGHANS, Anglia, 1, 1926, p. 8 ff. (to be read in connexion with J. L. LOWES, PMLA, xix (1904), p. 618 ff.: resemblance between B-Prol., Legend of Good Women, 11. 84–96, and Filostrato, I, st. 2–5, pointed out by Lowes, shown by Langhans to proceed from common source); L. MORSBACH, 'Chaucers Plan der "Canterbury Tales" und Boccaccio's "Decamerone",' Englische Studien, xlii (1912), pp. 43–52; the same, 'Chaucer's "Canterbury Tales" und das "Decameron",' in Nachricht von der Gesellschaft der Wissenschaften zu Göttingen, Philol.-hist. Kl. Fachgruppe 4, N. F. Bd. I, Nr. 4, Berlin, 1934; W. F. SCHIRMER, 'Boccaccio's Werke als Quelle G. Chaucers', Germanisch-romanische Monatsschrift, xii (1924), pp. 288–305 (a revision of previous opinions).

Of little value: M. BARDELLI, Qualche contributo agli studi sulle relazioni del Chaucer col Boccaccio, Firenze, 1911; M. BROWN, 'The "House of Fame" and the "Corbaccio",' Modern Language Notes, xxxii (1917), pp. 411–415 (a vain attempt to draw parallels between the two works); G. CAPONE, La Novella del Cavaliere . . . di G. Chaucer e la 'Teseide' di G. Boccaccio: assaggi di critica comparata, Sassari, 1907, 1909 and 1912 (of no value whatever); F. PRESTIFILIPPO TRIGONA, Chaucer imitatore del Boccaccio, Catania, 1923 (of no value whatever).

(d) PETRARCH

MANLY, J. M., 'Chaucer's Mission to Lombardy', Modern Language Notes, xlix (1934), pp. 209–216.

SISAM, E. K., *The Clerkes Tale*, Oxford, 1923. (Excellent Introduction.)

Of minor importance: G. L. HAMILTON, *Modern Language Notes*, xxiii (1908), pp. 169–172; A. S. Cook, *Romanic Review*, viii (1917), pp. 210–226; L. TORRETTA, 'L'atteggiumento del Chaucer verso il Petrarca e la sua interpretazione della storia di Griselda', in *Annali della Cattedra Petrarchesca*, iv (1932).

De Remediis utriusque fortunae has been compared with the Canon's Yeoman's Tale, by Kittredge, *Transactions Royal Society of Literature*, xxx, London, 1910, pp. 87–95.

(e) LOLLIUS, TROPHE, CORINNE

IMELMANN, R., 'Chaucer's "Haus der Fama",' *Englische Studien*, xlv (1912), pp. 397–431.

KITTREDGE, G. L., 'Chaucer's Lollius', *Harvard Studies in Classical Philology*, xxviii (1917), pp. 47–133. (Exhaustive essay which supplants whatever had been written before on the subject.) See also 'The Pillars of Hercules and Chaucer's Trophee' by the same author, in *Putnam Anniversary Volume*, New York, 1909, pp. 545–566.

SHANNON, E. F., *Chaucer and the Roman Poets*, Harvard University Press, 1929 (Corinne, p. 15 ff..; cf. *PMLA*, xxvii (1912), pp. 461–485).

TUPPER, F., 'Chaucer and Trophee', *Modern Language Notes*, xxxi (1916), p. 11 ff.

Of minor importance: H. BELMER, *Griefwalder Sem.-Arb.* (1919); O. F. EMERSON, 'Seith Trophee', *Modern Language Notes*, xxxi (1916), pp. 142–146; C. M. HATHAWAY, *Englische Studien*, xliv (1914), pp. 161–164 (Lollius = Raymond Lully!); F. TUPPER, 'Chaucer's Tale of Ireland', *PMLA*, xxxvi (1921), pp. 186–222 (Corinne).

(f) CHAUCER AND ITALIAN ART

BRUNNER, K., 'Chaucer's House of Fame', *Rivista di Letterature moderne*, ii, 5 (luglio-settembre 1951). (Possible suggestions in Tuscan sculpture for the statues on the pillars.)

The Politic Brain:
Machiavelli and the Elizabethans

THE popular legend of Machiavelli, the wicked politician, originated in France, as is well known, at the time of Catherine de' Medici: it represented the culmination of that anti-Italian feeling which naturally spread among French people under the rule of the Florentine sovereign. The preferments given to the Italian adventurers who crowded the French Court, the policy of the Crown in religious matters, were mainly if not solely responsible for the unprecedented amount of obloquy cast on the name of the Florentine Secretary. Upon Machiavelli's head were visited all the abuses committed by the Italian favourites, chiefly their rapacity, which rankled above all in the hearts of the French. It is only too natural that partiality to foreigners on the part of a sovereign should arouse resentment in a country. It has always been so, in all times and lands. Odium was attached to the Catalan knights in the service of the Neapolitan king, Robert of Anjou ('l'avara povertà di Catalogna'—*Paradise* viii), and to the Dutch followers of William III of Orange, no less than to the Florentine courtiers of Catherine de' Medici. The position of these latter was rendered still more odious by the religious factor. The several grounds of national and religious hatred against the Italians in France can be well studied in a curious pamphlet written in English soon after the accession of Henry IV of France, possibly by a French Huguenot. There we find that the anti-Italian feeling, in its final stage, has blossomed into a seemingly scientific theory. The title runs: A *Discovery of the great subtiltie and wonderful wisedome of the Italians, whereby they beare sway over the most part of Christendome, and cunninglie behave themselves to fetch the Quintescence out of the peoples purses: Discoursing at large the meanes, howe they prosecute and continue the same: and last of all, convenient remedies to prevent all their pollicies herein.*[1] The author draws from the first a distinction between the Septentrional and Occidental peoples and the Meridional nations: all the advantages possessed by the latter, chiefly as regards statecraft, are traced to the subtlety of the air.[2] The former, on the other hand, are described as labouring under 'a grosse humour ingendred in them, by reason of the grosnes and coldnes of the aier'. In the persons of Romulus and Numa Pompilius the writer sees prefigured two kinds of government among the Italians: Romulus founded his state on murder, Numa was a 'most subtill and ingenious inventor of a forged religion, to establish his owne government'. 'God would manifest unto us, that this nation should serve itselfe heereafter, with murthers and apparence of a counterfet religion, to laie

---

[1] London, Printed by Iohn Wolfe, 1591. Dedicated to Henry IV of France and signed at the end with the initials G.B.A.F. The author of this pamphlet shows acquaintance with the *Discorsi.* Some of his opinions seem to be conceived in opposition to Machiavelli's. Thus what he says about Romulus and Numa is antithetic to Machiavelli's chapters on those kings (*Discorsi* i, ix, xi). While Machiavelli (ch. xii) suggests transferring the Holy See to Switzerland, in order to verify its deleterious effect on the country in which it is established, the author of the pamphlet (ch. vi) would persuade the Pope 'to come into Swicerland, and into France, verie curteous and good people: to deliver themselves from the yoake of that nation which is the most corrupt in the whole world'. (See also Gentillet, *cit. infra,* p. 224.)

[2] A theory, so far as I know, held true to this day by the Italians themselves. Michelangelo says: 'Se io ho nulla di buono nell' ingegno, egli è venuto dal nascere nella *sottilità dell' aria* d'Arezzo.' And Leopardi: 'I più furbi per abito e i più ingegnosi per natura di tutti gl'italiani sono i marchegiani; il che senza dubbio ha relazione colla *sottigliezza della loro aria.*' The theory occurs already in Cicero, Hippocrates, etc. Cf. C. Iusti, *Winckelmann und seine Zeitgenossen,* Lepzig, 1923 edition, vol. iii, p. 143.

hands on others Kingdomes, and to snatch away the substance of other peoples.' The upshot of the pamphlet is that the Italians devised the domination of the pope in order to carry to Rome the 'Quintescence of the peoples purses': this money, once transported there, 'doth flie with an incredible swiftnesse'. 'It is our money they want'—so sounds the outcry of the Huguenot writer, who knew only too well how to wield the most popular of all arguments. The remedy he proposed was to 'shut up from Italians al accesse or entrance into our Countrey', following 'the good instruction that nature and the Author therof doth set before us visibly' by his 'having laid and set the Alpes most high mountaines, so firme and permanent on the one side, and the deepe Seas on the other, for bars betweene us and them, that we should not go to one another'. If only the foreign nations, for their part, had respected those natural barriers!

'A lively patterne of Italian subtiltie' is seen by the author of the pamphlet 'in the person of Katherine de Medicis, and her Florentine Counsell':

> Never were there so many died by poyson of Serpents and other venimous beasts, nor by the crueltie of Tygers, Lybbards, Crocodiles, Lynxes, Bears, and other devouring beasts, since the creation of the world, as by their tyrannous crueltie. . . . And he which would desire to know what is become of all these excessive heapes of mony levied in this kingdome: let him goe to Florence, to behold the sumptuous buildings which there have been erected by our ruine.

The charge of avarice levelled at the Florentine favourites of Catherine de' Medici, those Florentines who had come 'like poor snakes into France' and were leaving it swimming in 'wondrous wealth', became part and parcel of the Machiavellian bugbear. Gentillet, in the preface to the First Part of his famous anti-machiavellian book, wrote:

> Nous voyons à l'œil et touchons au doigt l'avarice des Italiens [Machiavellistes] qui nous mine et ruine, et qui succe toute nostre substance, et ne nous laisse rien. [3]

[3] See on p. 173 of *A Discovery* a diverting passage on *Atheistes inventeurs d'impost.*

The French origin of the Elizabethan Machiavellian is made evident by his very covetousness. Marlowe's Barabas, that 'true Machiavel', is above all a monstrous miser. His money 'was not got without my means', Machiavelli says of him in the prologue, and, in a much-quoted passage in the Second Act ('As for my selfe, I walke abroad a nights'), Barabas enumerates the stratagems which have made him rich. Nothing could be less true to the historical teaching of Machiavelli, who warned his Prince to avoid, of all things, robbing his subjects, since, he says, man forgets earlier the death of his father than the loss of his patrimony (*Principe*, xvii). He had foreseen only too well what was going to happen: men would have probably never waged such a relentless war against his name if the Florentine courtiers of Catherine de' Medici had refrained from 'fetching the quintessence' out of the purses of the French people.

After Meyer's epoch-making essay [4] it has been assumed that Gentillet's *Contre-Machiavel* was the book which caused the anti-machiavellian feeling to spread over England. Gentillet's book was published in 1576 and circulated first in the Latin translation, which went through three editions during the sixteenth century, before Simon Patericke published in 1602 his English version, which had been made in 1577, immediately after the publication of the book. Patericke's Preface has been interpreted by Meyer as giving evidence that Machiavelli was not known in England before 1577. This inference cannot be maintained, since there is evidence that Machiavelli had been known in Scotland for a long time,[*] and we find him already mentioned with a sinister connotation in the Sempill Ballads referring to Scottish political events,

---

[4] Edward Meyer, *Machiavelli and the Elizabethan Drama*, Weimar, 1897 (Litterarhistorische Forschungen, I. Heft). Clarence Valentine Boyer, *The Villain as Hero in Elizabethan Tragedy*, London, 1914, merely dilutes Meyer, without adding anything new; Wyndham Lewis, *The Lion and the Fox, the Rôle of the Hero in the Plays of Shakespeare*, London, 1927 (reprinted 1955) bases his fantastic construction on Meyer.

[*] See John Purves' introduction to *The Works of William Fowler*, Edinburgh and London, vol. III, 1940 (Scottish Text Society), chiefly pp. xcvii–xcviii.

before Gentillet's work was published in French.[5] In one of these poems, as early as 1568, we find William Maitland of Lethington, the Secretary of Mary Queen of Scots, styled 'this false Machivilian'; in another ballad, dated 1570, he is called 'a scurvie Schollar of Machiavellus lair'; in another, dated 1572, we hear of 'men of Machevillus Scuillis'; and finally, in a poem of 1583 Archbishop Adamson is called 'Matchewell'. In Buchanan's *Admonitioun* (1570) we read: 'Proud contempnars or machiavell mokkeris of all religioun and vertew'. The first of these ballads, dated 1568, is very interesting, since in it occurs for the first time in English literature the derivative form *Machiavilian*, a form which seems to presuppose an advanced stage of the Machiavelli legend.[6] As a matter of fact Secretary Lethington, who is the butt of that ballad, was popularly nicknamed the 'Mitchell Wylie' or Machiavelli of Scotland. Given the close relations between Scotland and France, we will find it very natural that the Machiavelli legend, hatched in France among the Huguenots under the rule of Catherine de' Medici, should have first found its way to Scotland and the Scottish Reformers. Moreover, Robert Sempill, to whose pen those ballads are due, was in Paris several times, and obviously was well versed in French political circumstances. Therefore, we may safely conclude that Gentillet's book was not the sole source for the English travesty of Machiavelli.[7] That book, certainly, did much towards giving wide circulation to the Machiavellian scarecrow, and fixing its abiding characteristics, but the ground on which it fell had already been prepared to receive it.[8]

[5] O. Ritter, in *Englische Studien*, xxxii, pp. 159–160, first called attention to these Ballads, without, however, drawing the consequences. The Ballads are printed in *Satirical Poems of the Time of the Reformation*, ed. by J. Cranstoun (S.T.S.), 1891–93. They bear the numbers ix, xxii, xxx, xlv.

[6] Therefore Meyer's statement (p. 27) that Robert Greene in 1583 'was the first to make in popular literature an abstract noun of the Florentine's name' is not exact.

[7] See also Irving Ribner, 'The Significance of Gentillet's "Contre-Machiavel"' in *Modern Language Quarterly*, x (1949), 153–157.

[8] E. Köppel, in *Englische Studien*, xxiv, pp. 108–118, has traced the sources of Gentillet's *Maximes*, which he read in Meyer. Much trouble would have been spared to him had he seen Gentil-

By then Machiavelli had become a sort of rallying-point for whatever was most loathsome in statecraft, and indeed in human nature at large. The political devices he had studied in past history, in order to infer from those historical premisses

---

let's text, where most of the sources are given. For B. 3, see *Discorsi* III, ii: "La nostra Religione ha glorificato più gli uomini umili e contemplativi, che gli attivi. Ha dipoi posto il sommo bene nella umiltà, abiezione, nel dispregio delle cose umane; quell' altra lo poneva nella grandezza dell' animo, nella forza del corpo, e in tutte l'altre cose atte a fare gli uomini fortissimi. . . . Questo modo di vivere adunque pare ch' abbi renduto il mondo debole, e datolo in preda agli uomini scellerati.' The source of B. 4, which Köppel could not trace, is in *Discorsi* II, v: 'E chi legge i modi tenuti da San Gregorio, e dagli altri capi della Religione Cristiana, vedrà con quanta ostinazione e' perseguitarono tutte le memorie antiche, ardendo l'opere de' Poeti e delli Istorici.' The source of Maxim C. 5 is to be found in *Discorsi* II, xix: 'E veramente simili città o provincie si vendicano contra il vincitore senza zuffa e senza sangue; perché riempiendogli de' suoi tristi costumi, gli espongono ad esser vinti da qualunque gli assalta.' Maxim C. 19 is a paraphrase of *Principe* xviii: 'Si vede per esperienzia ne' nostri tempi quelli principi avere fatto gran cose . . . che hanno saputo con l'astuzia aggirare e' cervelli delli uomini.' Maxim C. 24 is to be paralleled with *Discorsi* II, ix: 'Perché se io voglio fare guerra con un Principe, e fra noi siano fermi capitoli per un gran tempo osservati, con altra giustificazione e con altro colore assalterò io un suo amico che lui proprio.' Maxim C. 31 sums up *Discorsi* I, iv; C. 35 is drawn from *Discorsi* I, vii: 'Bisogna che i giudici siano assai, perché pochi sempre fanno a modo de' pochi.' Maxim C. 36 derives from *Discorsi* I, lv: 'Di questi nobili sono piene Napoli, Roma, la Romagna e la Lombardia: onde nasce che ivi non è mai stata alcuna vera repubblica . . . perché tali generazioni d' uomini sono al tutto nemiche d'ogni civiltà . . . In Toscana, invece, si hanno le repubbliche . . . E tutto questo segue perché non vi sono in esse signori di castella.' In this last case Gentillet condenses Machiavelli no less than in B. 8, where the French 'Moyse usurpa la Judée, comme les Goths usurperent partie de l'Empire Romain' concentrates several passages from *Discorsi* II, viii. Occasionally Gentillet's references are very vague. Such is the case of Maxims C. 13 and C. 15, which Gentillet grounds respectively on *Discorsi* I, ix and on *Discorsi* III, ii; iii. Gentillet is the source of the attack against Machiavelli's ideas contained in John Case's *Sphaera Civitatis*, Oxford, 1588; cf. D. Cameron Allen, 'An Unmentioned Elizabethan Opponent of Machiavelli' in *Italica, Quarterly Bulletin of the American Association of Teachers of Italian*, xiv, September 3, 1937.

the laws of a political science, were fathered upon him as if he had been not their expounder but their actual inventor. His original contribution to the theory of the modern state, his unprecedented method of study, could not be grasped by the contemporaries of the unfortunate Florentine. What they found in him was, as usual, what already existed, since the easiest and commonest way of reading books is to see in them what is already in ourselves. The political diseases Machiavelli had first studied scientifically were called after his name, as a physical disease is nowadays called after the doctor who has first described it: but Machiavelli was no more the inventor of Machiavellism than Graves is the inventor of Graves's disease. Machiavelli supplied a label, a *cliché*, for describing methods which had been in use since remote antiquity. One of the most popular of his maxims, on the combination of fox and lion necessary in a statesman, had been current since classical times. The character of a despotic prince had been sketched by Aristotle, St Thomas Aquinas, Savonarola, and many mediaeval and fifteenth-century writers in terms similar to those used by Machiavelli. With the difference that, whereas those writers described that character from an ethical standpoint, and therefore condemned it, Machiavelli studied it from a scientific point of view, as a system of actions and reactions operating in a moral vacuum. His shortcomings were those of all Renaissance people. The theocratic, collectivist ideals of the Middle Ages were being replaced by a conception of life based on the pre-Christian polity and the individuum. The new conception emphasised the plastic force of the individual at the expense of the surrounding atmosphere; the new hero stood out arrayed in the full glory of his strength, almost too intense to be real. The discovery of the individuum was parallel to the discovery of the nude: the draughtsmen were so engrossed in the study of the anatomy of their models that they drew the human body not as it appears to the eye but as it is known to be constituted to the scientific mind of the anatomist. Machiavelli's hero is the counterpart of the nudes painted by Signorelli or sketched by Leonardo: he is a scientific being, breathing in an element subtler than the sublunar air, no less metaphysical than the mediaeval man, but by an inverse process of exaggeration.

The mediaeval man was too much of a man in the mass; the Renaissance man, on the other hand, was isolated as a self-sufficient unit, since a reaction must go its whole length before the balance is re-established. Machiavelli's point of view was so different from that of Aristotle, St Thomas, and Savonarola that he did not suspect that his description of the Prince might have read like a monstrous travesty of the traditional description of the tyrant. No wonder, then, that that description was calculated to impress short-sighted interpreters either as a moral enormity or as an ironical *double entendre*. The scientific point of view is the great contribution of Machiavelli; once that missed, the rest was neither original nor new.

But his point of view was gaining ground among the thinkers of the Renaissance. Montaigne [9] contemplated cases in which the Prince must 'quitter sa raison à une plus universelle et puissante raison', and disregard 'son devoir ordinaire', i.e., the current moral principles; even the mediaeval-minded and morally irreproachable Sir Thomas More (who has been made a saint in our time), in a fit of anti-militarism, had caused the Utopians to adopt in war-time policies much more objectionable than those advocated by Machiavelli in *Discorsi*, III, xl ('Come usare la fraude nel maneggiare la guerra è cosa gloriosa'). And the poet whose chivalrous character, elevation of sentiment, and sense of duty and religion Professor Courthope [10] contrasts to Marlowe's exaltation of the Machiavellian principles—Edmund Spenser—did not scruple to adopt almost word for word the maxims laid down by Machiavelli in his *View of the Present State of Ireland*.[11]

The general principles of politics which are stated in Sir Philip Sidney's *Discourse to the Queenes Majesty Touching Hir Mariage with Monsieur* (1579) are principles which are almost all inherent in Machiavelli's writings, as has been shown by Dr Irving Ribner,[12] while the 'Machiavels' of the

[9] *Essais*, Livre III, ch. i, De l'Utile et de l'Honneste.

[10] *History of English Poetry*, II, xii, p. 421.

[11] See E. A. Greenlaw, 'The Influence of Machiavelli on Spenser', in *Modern Philology*, vii, pp. 187 ff.

[12] 'Machiavelli and Sidney's "Discourse to the Queenes Majesty",' in *Italica*, xxvi, 3, September 1949. At the beginning of his study Dr Ribner gives a survey of the more recent research on the influence of Machiavelli on Elizabethan literature.

Arcadia, 'rather than offer evidence that Sidney was opposed to Machiavelli's ideas, serve instead to reinforce the conclusion that Sidney and Machiavelli were in essential agreement.' [13] From the works of Sidney's friend, Fulke Greville, an impressive list has also been drawn of parallels with Machiavelli's writings.[14]

On the other hand, it cannot be said that Machiavelli's system was based solely on the corrupt political conditions of Italy. There was no such opposition as that imagined by Macaulay between foreigners, brave and resolute, faithful to their engagements, and Italians destitute of courage and sincerity. As a matter of fact, the most perfect incarnations of the Machiavellian Prince were to be found among foreign rulers. King John, Henry IV, Richard III (who is caused to say by Shakespeare: 'I can . . . set the murderous Machiavel to school'), Queen Elizabeth (who actually wrote to James VI: 'I mind to set to school your craftiest councillor'),[15] all of them English sovereigns, Louis XI of France, to cite only the most conspicuous instances, were much more cunning foxes than that desperate petty weasel Cesare Borgia, who, by the way, was no Italian either, but a Spaniard.

But in the same way as Machiavelli became a label for all sorts of political crimes, Italy was looked upon in the Renaissance as the fountain-head of all horrors and sins. Italy was no worse, in that respect, than the rest of Western Europe, but while other nations had not attracted the attention of foreign observers, Italy had appealed to them for many reasons. One of these reasons was the splendour of her civilisation, but another, no less powerful, was the exotic appeal which first was awakened in Europe, as a general phenomenon, by Italian travel. Finally, there was the religious factor, in consequence of which Rome was considered by Protestants

[13] Irving Ribner, 'Sidney's "Arcadia" and the Machiavelli Legend', in *Italica,* xxvii, 3, September 1950. See also by the same author, 'Machiavelli and Sidney: The "Arcadia" of 1590', in *Studies in Philology,* xlvii (1950), pp. 152–172.

[14] Napoleone Orsini, *Fulke Greville tra il mondo e Dio,* Milano-Messina, 1941.

[15] See W. Alison Phillips, 'The Influence of Machiavelli on the Reformation of England', in *Nineteenth Century* for December 1896, pp. 907–918.

the City of the Antichrist. All these elements combined together in creating the Elizabethan picture of a bloodthirsty, deceitful, impious, and picturesquely emotional Italy. Henceforth a tale of horror, to be popular, had to be staged in Italy,[16] just in the same way as, until quite recently, a singer had to parade a fictitious Italian name in order to attract public attention. I will quote one instance only of the *passepartout* quality possessed by the Italian frame, because it is related to our present subject, Machiavelli. In *The Duchess of Malfi*, III, v, Ferdinand writes a letter in which occurs the expression: 'Send Antonio to me; I want his head in a busines.' This phrase provokes from the Duchess the following remark:

> A politicke equivocation—
> He doth not want your councell, but your head.

We are going to see shortly how the word *politic* in this bad sense came to be an equivalent of *Machiavellian*. From all appearances, then, we are confronted with a piece of Italian Machiavellism. Mr F. L. Lucas, in his, in many respects, admirable edition of Webster, does not give any source for this remarkable equivocation, but there is a historical source. The sovereign who is actually reported to have had recourse to that sleight is Louis XI of France, who, wanting to punish the Connétable, let him be assured that he knew his faithfulness, and asked him to come, because he 'wanted such a head'. Lodovico Guicciardini, from whose *Ore di Ricreazione* I have gathered this anecdote, concludes:

> Dipoi voltatosi a un segretario pian piano disse, egli è vero che io bisogno di quel capo, ma separato dal busto, et soggiunse chi non sa simulare non sa regnare.[17]

[16] So Massinger, in *The Duke of Milan*, substitutes the Duke of Milan and his wife Marcelia for Herod and Mariamne of his source. This Italianisation was not confined to tales of horror. Massinger, again, dramatised an old English legend in his *Great Duke of Florence*. Jonson, in the first version of *Every Man in his Humour*, indulged the taste of the public and gave to the plot an Italian setting which a mere change of names showed to be only a thin veneer.

[17] Cf. Commynes, *Mémoires*, ed. Calmette, II, pp. 74–75 (Livre IV, ch. xi).

So much is it true what is written in a Caroline pamphlet, *The Atheistical Politician,* that

> if we examine the Life of *Lewis* the 11th of *France*, we shall finde he acted more ill, than Machiavill writ, or for ought we know ever thought; yet he hath wisedome inscribed on his Tomb.

But his politic equivocation had to be put in the mouth of an Italian in order to show off at its best.

But before entering into a minute study of the repercussions of the Machiavellian legend, we must observe how the great realist politician was known in his true aspect also in England. Statesmen, thinkers, philosophers, could read Machiavelli in the original, and an enterprising London printer, Wolfe, supplied the needs of this learned public by issuing the works of the Florentine with a false place of issue (Palermo or Rome instead of London) between 1584 and 1588, thus eluding censorship. But censorship forbade the publication of the translations of the *Principe* and the *Discorsi,* whose existence in the British Museum and the Bodleian was revealed by Professor Orsini,[18] so that those translations had to circulate in manuscript, whereas Gentillet's *Contre-Machiavel* was easily accessible in print and became popular thanks to the anti-Italian propaganda. Only those of Machiavelli's works which were considered harmless, the *Arte della guerra* and the *Storie,* were published in English in the course of the sixteenth century (respectively in 1562 and 1595), whereas the first printed version of the *Principe,* by Edward Dacres, appeared only in 1640.[19]

Among the most attentive readers of Machiavelli, as Professor Orsini has shown,[20] was Francis Bacon, whose apology for Machiavelli in a passage of the *Advancement of Learning* is well known: 'We are much beholden to Machiavel and

---

[18] 'Le traduzioni elisabettiane inedite di Machiavelli', in *Studii sul Rinascimento italiano in Inghilterra,* Florence, 1937. On these translations, as well as on Fowler's, see John Purves' introduction to *The Works of William Fowler,* quoted above, specially pp. cxxxix ff.

[19] Edited by W. E. C. Baynes, London, 1929.

[20] Napoleone Orsini, *Bacone e Machiavelli,* Genoa, 1936. See also Vincent Luciani, 'Bacon and Machiavelli', in *Italica,* xxiv, 1, March 1947.

others, that write what men do and not what they ought to do', because the knowledge of evil helps to defend and promote virtue. The influence of the genuine teaching of Machiavelli is evident on the *Essays or Counsels, Civil and Moral* (first edition 1597, enlarged in 1612 and 1625), which offer the quintessence of Bacon's system so far as ethics is concerned.

The logical method followed by Bacon in dealing with the moral sciences is the opposite of the one he advocated for the physical sciences: in these latter he proceeded from the particular to the universal, the idea; in the former he started from the general principles of action to end with the absolute individuality of the particular situation. Bacon saw sciences apt to catch the individuum in its purity just in those fields where until then hardly anybody had looked for a science: the fields of poetry and history. For him history is to be included under the general concept of art, as a knowledge of the particular. In order to reach this conclusion, which seems to anticipate Croce, Bacon availed himself of that immediate sense of the particular which he, in his own confession, acquired through reading Machiavelli. From Machiavelli's concrete political art he deduced, by taking a more general viewpoint, a universal economic activity, which takes place in a sphere of its own, independent from ethics, and manifests itself not only in the works of statesmen, but also in any form of practical activity, both public and private, as volition of the particular. Thus Bacon fits Machiavelli's findings to a general system of ethics, for the first time in the history of philosophy. Bacon's vigorous activism has also a Machiavellian origin: science must be at the service of action.[21]

[21] The teaching of Machiavelli elicited such an extreme doctrine of action from another Englishman, the humanist Gabriel Harvey (born *c.* 1550), that in a sense he appears as a forerunner of Nietzsche's superman. 'Il pensare non importa, ma il fare', he repeats several times in Italian: he appropriated the device of Charles V, *più oltre* (in Italian); he gave an ideal portrait of a type of superman, a paragon of activity, whom he named Angelus Furius: Angelus, i.e., a perfect intellect, Furius, i.e., impetuous in the exercise of his will. Professor Orsini, who has devoted one of his *Studii sul Rinascimento italiano in Inghilterra* (cited above) to this remarkable figure of inchoate superman, does not believe there was any important contact between Harvey and Bacon:

The applications of Machiavellism to problems and situations (specially English ones) Machiavelli had not contemplated, interest us naturally much more than the many passages (linked together by Professor Orsini) in which Bacon expounds the concrete results reached by Machiavelli in his discussion of the principles according to which nations develop and flourish. The most typical of those applications concerns practical life; in the *Faber Fortunae* (Book VIII of the *De Augmentis Scientiarum*, 1623) he makes the search after personal utility into a science, and applies its principles to the various circumstances of life in a group of essays. And here the neophyte's enthusiasm carries Bacon much beyond Machiavelli: having set himself personal utility as an ideal, the English thinker makes an absolute standard of it even in the relations which are usually considered unselfish, such as friendship and love. And he does not seem to be aware—as Professor Orsini aptly remarks—that such a complex system of cunning and precaution as the one Bacon derived from Machiavelli for private life, presupposes a radical diffidence towards mankind. This diffidence was openly declared in Machiavelli; whereas Bacon, *qua* scientist, appeared to have faith in the progress of mankind, was—in a word—an optimist. An optimist on one side, a cynic on the other: is not Bacon thus a representative man of the England of his time and of all times? You candid, simple Florentine Secretary who *aperte et indissimulanter*—these two Latin adverbs are used by Bacon in his eulogy of Machiavelli in the *De Augmentis*—were wont to speak of man's wickedness! In this manner you were handing the poisoned cup round the banquets of princes, you were guiding the hand which throttled innocent Desdemona, you were a devil incarnate!

It would, however, be unfair to stop at Bacon the expounder of the *bonum suitatis*, who is nearer to Guicciardini than to Machiavelli in his ethics of the 'particulare'. Since the whole

---

'otherwise one could have suspected an influence of the old humanist on the young philosopher, of the ideas of the *Marginalia* on those of the *Essays* and the *Faber Fortunae*. But what parallels there are are due no doubt to a common inspiration from Italian thought, particularly Machiavelli's, which both venerated' (p. 118).

is superior to the parts, the *bonum communionis* is superior to the *bonum suitatis*: Bacon sees the essence of the individual not only protected, but aggrandised in power by the State, in so far as the State gathers in itself and promulgates those ethical ideals (justice, morality, religion, etc.) that the individual is unable to bring about in their complex practical organization. In this way the ethical content of the State is stated by Bacon in a much more explicit way than by Machiavelli. The starting-point is the same: that there are two manners of fighting, one through laws, the other through violence; but whereas Machiavelli knows no better than to advise the use of violence where law is insufficient, Bacon places the objective will of the community, the *Bene Esse Civitatis*, above the opponents.

Another author who had direct access to Machiavelli's writings, and held them in great esteem, was James Harrington, whose *Commonwealth of Oceana* (published 1656) is full of references to those works.[22] Machiavelli, the 'learned diciple' of the ancients, is called 'the onely Polititian of later Ages', 'the sole retreiver of this ancient Prudence,' 'though in some places justly reproveable, yet the only Polititian, and incomparable Patron of the people'.

But Harvey, Bacon and Harrington are isolated cases; in fact at one point in *Oceana* we read that Machiavelli's books are 'neglected'. But a gross travesty of Machiavelli's political science prevailed with most, as is well illustrated by the Elizabethan use of the word *politic*. Machiavelli's use of the corresponding Italian word *politico* is instanced in these passages from the *Discorsi*:

I, lv: quelle Repubbliche, dove si è mantenuto il vivere *politico* ed incorrotto.

[22] See *James Harrington's Oceana*, Ed. with Notes by S. B. Liljegren, Lund and Heidelberg, 1924; pp. 9, 10, 12, 13, 25, 30, 32, 34, 40, 41, 42, 48, 50, 52, 53, 56, 58, 64, 87, 90, 91, 113, 114, 118, 121, 133, 135, 136, 137, 138, 139, 142, 145, 146, 169, 175, 176, 178, 179, 180, 186, 188, 189, 197, 212, 223, and notes to these pages, particularly note to p. 118 (p. 314) in which Professor Liljegren lists some anti-Machiavellian pamphlets, *Modern Policies taken from Machiavel, Borgia, and other choice Authors* (1652) ascribed to Archbishop Sancroft; *A Discourse upon Machiavell* (1656), believed to be by Francis Osborne, etc.

III, viii: Per altri modi s'ha a cercare gloria in una città corrotta, che in una che ancora viva *politicamente*.

Politico, then, in Machiavelli means 'in conformity with sound rules of statecraft'. It has a merely scientific meaning, and is opposed to *corrotto*, which is synonym to 'misgoverned'. There is no instance of the word being used in Italian in the sense of 'scheming, crafty'. The only cases quoted by dictionaries, in which the word has the connotation of 'shrewd' are not earlier than the end of the seventeenth century. In French, *politique* must have possessed the meaning of 'shrewd' in the second half of the sixteenth century, though Littré is only able to quote that use of the word in an author as late as Pascal. In Corneille's *Mort de Pompée* (1641) the evil counsellor Photin is thus referred to: 'Un si grand politique est capable de tout' (ɪɪ, iii). And, further on (ɪv, ii): 'Ces lâches politiques / Qui n'inspirent aux rois que des mœurs tyranniques.' But the word, by itself, cannot have been invested with the sinister connotation it came to possess in English, otherwise the moderate party which arose in France about 1573, and regarded political reform more urgent than the religious question, would not have been styled *politique*.

In English we find the word *policy* with the meaning of 'device' as early as 1406, in Hoccleve, where the device resorted to by Ulysses to escape the danger of the Mermaids is called a *policie* (N.E.D.). By the middle of the sixteenth century *policy* is a synonym to 'sleight, trick'. In the marginal summaries of Robynson's translation of *Utopia*, in the second edition (1556), we find: 'bellum pecunia aut *arte* declinare', translated by 'either with money or by *pollicie* to avoyde warre'; 'aliquo *stratagemate*' rendered with 'by some *pollicie*'. Another instance is supplied by Jasper Heywood's translation of Seneca's *Troas* (1559), where the Latin *dolos* (l. 569) is rendered as *pollecy*. In Studley's translation of *Agamemnon* (1566) *pollecie* corresponds to Latin *fraude* (l. 207). Other similar instances may be quoted from Newton's *Seneca*. The word is often found coupled with 'sleight', as in the following instance from *The Mirror for Magistrates* (*King Malin*, x, edition of 1587, N.E.D.): 'Secretly by *pollecy* and sleight / Hee slewe mee.' Sir William Alexander in the seventh canto ('The seventh Houre') of his long-winded poem, *Doomes-Day, or, The great Day of the Lords Judgement* (London, 1637), lists among the supporters of 'that great Arch-patron of such cunning parts' (stanzas 43, 44):

> many drawne from Southerne climes,
> Who first to tongues driv'd honestie from hearts,
> And bent to prosper car'd not by what crimes,
> The *Florentine* made famous by these Arts,
> Hath tainted numbers even of moderne times:
> Till subtilty is to such credit rais'd,
> That falshood (when call'd policy) is prais'd.
> Ah! this of zeale the sacred ardour cools,
> And doth of Atheists great abundance make, etc.

In the translation of *Utopia,* 1556, we find the famous stratagem consisting in changing the landmarks on the shore in order to destroy the navies of the enemies styled 'a *politique* device' in the marginal summary, where the Latin has *stratagema*; in the seventh tragedy of the first lot of *The Mirror for Magistrates* (*Henry Percy Earle of Northumberland*, xii, published in 1559, but written a few years before) we find *polliticke* used in the same sense of 'cunning'. In the former of the last two instances there can hardly be a sinister moral connotation, since Thomas More did not condemn the Utopian stratagem: Utopians (and More with them) held war 'a thinge very beastelye', and victory got by stratagem a thing that 'no other lyvynge creature but onely man' could achieve, 'that ys to saye, by the myghte and puysaunce of wytte'.[23] In Book II, ch. ix, it is said that the Utopians 'do marvelouslye deteste

---

[23] More's distinction is not very different from that drawn by Machiavelli (*Principe* xviii) between 'dua generazione di combattere,' of which 'quello con le leggi' is 'proprio dello uomo', 'quello con la forza' is 'proprio delle bestie'. Both More's and Machiavelli's is the typical humanistic outlook on the superiority of the mind over brutal force. The common source is Cicero, *De Officiis*, I, ix. 34: 'Nam cum sint duo genera decertandi, unum per disceptationem, alterum per vim; cumque illud proprium sit hominis, hoc beluarum, confugiendum est ad posterius, si uti non licet superiore.'

and abhorre . . . deceite, and falshed, and al maner of lyes, as next unto fraude'. Evidently those stratagems were not liable to be described so.

But with the diffusion of Machiavellism *politic* became closely associated with the disreputable principles of the Florentine Secretary. One wonders whether it was the adoption of Machiavellian statecraft, which began in England at the time of Thomas Cromwell and Henry VIII, who has been styled 'Machiavelli's Prince in action', to cast the bad connotation on the word. It is a curious question, which does not allow of a definite solution, since the evidence of extant literature must not be relied too much upon: at any rate, the date given by the N.E.D. for the first appearance of the usage of *politic* in the sense of 'scheming' seems rather too late. The instance, from Lyly's *Euphues* (1580), runs: 'For greater daunger is ther to arive in a straunge countrey where the inhabitants be *pollitique*.' To link *politic*, in the sinister sense, with Machiavelli, was customary by the end of the sixteenth century. In Lodge's *Reply to Stephen Gosson's Schoole of Abuse* (1580) we read, for instance: 'I feare me you will be *politick* wyth Machavel.' As soon as the dramatists became haunted by the character of the Machiavellian knave, they began to use the words *policy* and *politic* with an unprecedented frequency. *The Spanish Tragedy* teems with stratagems: Viluppo, Lorenzo, Ieronimo, all make use of villainous tricks. Lorenzo never gets tired of speaking of his *policy* (III, iv, 38; x, 9); he is called 'too *pollitick*' by Bellimperia (III, x, 83), and in *The first part of Ieronimo* is caused to exclaim (I, i, 123): 'O sweete, sweete *pollicie*, I hugg thee'; and to advise (II, ii, 12): 'Sly *policy* must be youre guide.' In *Soliman and Perseda* Basilisco 'held it *pollicie* to put the men children/Of that climate to the sword' (I, iii, 87–88), and Piston says (I, iv, 17): 'Oh, the *pollicie* of this age is wonderfull.'

Marlowe's Machiavellian Jew of Malta (who also uses the word *policy* a dozen times) thinks it no sin to deceive Christians, since they are all deceivers (l. 393 f.):

> I *policie*? that's their profession,
> And not simplicity, as they suggest.

In *Edward II* Lancaster says to Kent (l. 1073 f.):

> I feare me, you are sent of *pollicie*,
> To undermine us with a showe of love.

In Webster's *White Devil* the Machiavellian Flamineo says (I, ii, 341 ff.):

> We are ingag'd to mischiefe and must on.
> As Rivers to finde out the Ocean
> Flow with crooke bendings beneath forced bankes,
> Or as wee see to aspire some mountaines top,
> The way ascends not straight, but Imitates
> The suttle fouldings of a Winters snake,
> So who knowes *policy* and her true aspect,
> Shall finde her waies winding and indirect.

In that tragedy Camillo dies 'by such a *polliticke* straine,/ Men shall suppose him by's owne engine slaine' (II, i, 312–313). His fate is called 'a farre more *polliticke* fate' (II, ii, 35) than that of Isabella, who dies by kissing a poisoned picture. Marcello says to Flamineo (III, i, 60):

> For love of vertue beare an honest heart,
> And stride over every *polliticke* respect,
> Which where they most advance they most infect.

Like Ieronimo in *The Spanish Tragedy*, who had cunningly dissembled madness in order to further his revenge, Flamineo (III, ii, 318) thinks it advisable to 'appear a *polliticke* madman'; swindlers who cheat their creditors are called (IV, i, 54) '*pollitick* bankroupts'; feigned ignorance is styled (IV, ii, 82) '*politicke* ignorance'.[24] Lodovico and Gasparo whisper to dying Brachiano (v, iii, 155–156):

> You that were held the famous *Pollititian*;
> Whose art was poison. And whose conscience murder.

And, as in a litany, they draw a picturesque list of poisons, and conclude (*ibid.* 165–166):

> With other devilish potticarie stuffe
> A-melting in your *polliticke* braines.

[24] In Ford's *'Tis Pity* (IV, i) Hippolita's pretended 'reconciliation' with Soranzo on his wedding day, in order to poison him, is called a 'politic reconciliation'.

The sinister use of the words *politic, policy, politician,* may be illustrated with many other instances from Webster (none of them included in the N.E.D.); a characteristic one is found in *The Duchess of Malfi* (III, ii, 371 ff.), where Bosola says:

> A *Polititian* is the divells quilted anvell,
> He fashions all sinnes on him, and the blowes
> Are never heard.

The word *politician* is already found with a bad connotation in Nashe's *Pierce Penilesse his Supplication to the Divell* (1592): 'The Divel . . . was . . . so famous a *Polititian* in purchasing'; and in *The Unfortunate Traveller:* "Hee set his cap over his ey-browes like a *polititian,* and then folded his armes one in another, and nodded with the head, as who would say, let the French beware for they shall finde me a divell.' In Middleton's *Game at Chess* (1624), where the words *politic, policy* recur frequently, the Black Knight, i.e., the Spanish Ambassador Gondomar, is put into the bag with these words (v, iii, 201–202):

> Room for the mightiest *Machiavel-politician*
> That e'er the devil hatch'd of a nun's egg!

And W. Ralegh (*Maxims of State* in *Remains,* 1661, p. 46) has 'a cunning *Polititian,* or a Machiavilian at the least'. In most of the above instances the word *politician* is closely associated with the Devil: this very remarkable association ought to be kept in mind for what I shall say later on. A passage in John Day's *Humour out of Breath* (1607–08) conveys well the Elizabethan notion of *policy* (II, i):

> *Aspero.* How long have you bin a matchiavilian, boy?
> *Boy.* Ever since I practis'd to play the knave, my lord.
> *Asp.* Then *policy* and knavery are somewhat a kin.
> *Boy.* As neere as penury and gentry: a degree and a half
> remov'de, no more.

The word *statist* underwent a similar disparagement. In an instance of 1584 (N.E.D.) we read: 'When he plais the *statist,* wringing veri unluqqili some of Machiavels Axiomes to serve his Purpos.' In another instance of 1600 (N.E.D.) a Jesuit

who intermeddles in state affairs is called a *statist*. The association between *politic* and *Machiavellian* became so close
that actually the Italian form *politico* was used in England
with the bad connotation already illustrated (see N.E.D.
under *politico*). The discredit cast on the Florentine reflected
on all the words connected with the art of government.

The dramatists were chiefly responsible for giving currency
to the legend. A very interesting point is this: why did the
dramatists adopt so eagerly the Machiavellian type of knave?
How did Machiavelli become such an important character in
the Elizabethan drama? Here is one of the vital points in the
complex net of influences at work in the development of the
Elizabethan drama: a point which, so far as I know, has not
yet been illustrated. Among the stock characters bestowed by
Seneca upon the tragedy of the Renaissance was that of the
cruel villainous tyrant, with his ambitious schemes and unprincipled maxims of government.[25] Atreus is the most completely
portrayed among the Senecan villains. He expounds his creed in
a dialogue with his attendant.

Atreus has just disclosed his projects of cruel revenge
against his brother, and the attendant asks (*Thyestes,* ll.
204 ff.)

Satelles.	Fama te populi nihil adversa terret?
Atreus.	Maximum hoc regni bonum est, quod facta domini cogitur populus sui tam ferre quam laudare.
Sat.	Quos cogit metus laudare, eosdem reddit inimicos metus. At qui favoris gloriam veri petit, animo magis quam voce laudari volet.
Atr.	Laus vera et humili saepe contingit viro, non nisi potenti falsa. quod nolunt velint.
Sat.	Rex velit honesta: nemo non eadem volet.
Atr.	Vbicumque tantum honesta dominanti licent, precario regnatur.

[25] See also W. A. Armstrong, 'The Elizabethan Conception of
the Tyrant', in *The Review of English Studies*, xxii (July 1946),
and 'The Influence of Seneca and Machiavelli on the Elizabethan
Tyrant', *ibid.*, xxiv (January 1948).

Sat.   Vbi non est pudor
nec cura iuris sanctitas pietas fides,
instabile regnum est.

Atr.   Sanctitas pietas fides
privata bona sunt, qua iuvat reges eant.

Lycus, in *Hercules Furens*, corresponds to Machiavelli's 'principe nuovo'. He says (ll. 337 ff.):

nobiles non sunt mihi
avi nec altis inclitum titulis genus,
sed clara virtus.

Machiavelli's 'principe nuovo' relies most on his own *virtù*. Lycus goes on:

rapta sed trepida manu
sceptra obtinentur; omnis in ferro est salus:
quod civibus tenere te invitis scias,
strictus tuetur ensis.

Therefore Lycus, in order to set his power on firm foundations, decides to marry Megara, from whose noble line his newness (*novitas nostra*) shall gain richer hue (the very device adopted by Richard III). But if Megara refuses, he is determined to ruin the whole house of Hercules:

invidia factum ac sermo popularis premet?
ars prima regni est posse invidiam pati.

(ll. 352–353.)

And elsewhere (ll. 489; 511 ff.):

Quod Iovi hoc regi licet.

. . . .

Qui morte cunctos luere supplicium iubet
nescit tyrannus esse. diversa inroga:
miserum veta perire, felicem iube.

In the spurious *Octavia* Nero expounds to Seneca most of the same principles expounded by Atreus to his attendant. Among the rest, lines 456 ff. are noticeable:

Nero. Ferrum tuetur principem.
Seneca.   Melius fides.

Ner. Decet timeri Caesarem.
Sen.   At plus diligi.
Ner. Metuant necesse est—

. . . . . .

Respectus ensis faciet.

. . . . . .

tollantur hostes ense suspecti mihi.

. . . .

quicquid excelsum est cadat.

In the *Phoenissae* (*Thebais*) the tyrant's part is played by
Eteocles (ll. 654 ff.):

Regnare non vult esse qui invisus timet:
simul ista mundi conditor posuit deus,
odium atque regnum: regis hoc magni reor,
odia ipsa premere. multa dominantem vetat
amor suorum; plus in iratos licet.
qui vult amari, languida regnat manu.

. . . .

Imperia pretio quolibet constant bene.

No doubt the author of the Induction to *A Warning for Faire
Women* (1599) was right when as a first characteristic of
the Senecan drama he ranked:

How some damn'd tyrant to obtain a crown
Stabs, hangs, impoisons, smothers, cutteth throats.

It is a well-known fact that the Senecan tragedy reached
England first through the Italian imitations. The characteristic type of the Italian Senecan drama was created by G. B.
Giraldi Cinthio, and reigned supreme from 1541 to 1590. I
need not repeat here what has been exhaustively illustrated
by H. B. Charlton.[26] Almost all plots of the Italian Senecan
drama can be described as instances of the conflict between
a villain, usually a sovereign who is enabled by his position
to exert his power for his private ends, and a heroine. What
concerns us here is the type of the villain.

[26] In the Introduction to *The Poetical Works of William Alexander*, Manchester, 1921.

Now, when we come to examine closely Cinthio's characters falling under that description, we find that he developed the type of superhuman knave he found in Seneca with the help of elements derived from Machiavelli. Chiefly the character of Acharisto in *Euphimia* already possesses all the requisites of the Machiavellian bugbear of the Elizabethan stage. He is an aspiring villain who, through marrying Euphimia, daughter of the Corinthian king, has occupied the throne. He wants to enlarge his state by marrying the daughter of the king of Athens, and therefore, in order to get rid of Euphimia, accuses her of adultery: he adopts the same policy followed by the Senecan Lycus and by King Richard III. Here are some of his maxims:

> a me basta
> Ch'io sia, non men che Dio, da'miei temuto.[27]
> > (II, i)
> Il mio Dio è il mio volere, et ove questo
> Mi guida, i'voglio andare.
>
> . . . .
>
> Che dee far altro un re, che cercar sempre
> Di far maggior lo stato, di acquistarsi
> Maggior potenza? tema la ragione
> Chi pover si ritrova, a sé è ragione
> Un possente signor, sia mal, sia bene
> Ciò che di fare a lui viene in pensiero,
> Pur ch' utile vi sia, che vi sia acquisto,
> Non dee lasciar mai di condurlo al fine.
> Nessun cerca per qual modo, o qual via
> Tu sia possente, o sia fatto signore,
> Il tutto è haver, habbilo a dritto, a torto,
> Come ricco tu sei, tu sei pregiato.
> Filippo, Re di Macedonia, venne
> Col non servar mai fé, con l' usar froda,
> Col non attender mai cosa promessa,
> Signore, in pochi dì, di tutta Grecia.
>
> . . . .

[27] It is enough for me to be feared by my subjects no less than God.

Disse Lisandro, ch'ove non giungea
Il cuoio del Leon, vi si deveva
La pelle aggiunger d' una volpe. Io dico
Ch' ove giunger non puote la virtute
Cercar tu dei, che vi ti meni il vitio.
Che, quando tu acquistata hai la potenza,
Il vitio di virtù tiene sembianza.[28]
E, benché tu sia reo, tu sia malvagio,
Non manca chi ti dà lode infinite.[29]   (ii, ii)

Apart from the general Senecan tone, this passage seems to show the influence of both Machiavelli's eighteenth chapter of the *Prince* and thirteenth chapter of the Second Book of the *Discorsi*. In the former is quoted the famous passage from Plutarch's *Lysander*; in the latter we read:

Né credo si truovi mai che la forza sola basti, ma si troverà bene che la fraude sola basterà; come chiaro vedrà colui che leggerà la vita di Filippo di Macedonia.[30]

[28] Cf. Marston's *Malcontent*, v, ii: 'Mischief that prospers men do virtue call.' Ben Jonson's *Catiline*, iii, ii: 'and slip no advantage/That may secure you. Let them call it mischief;/When it is past and prospered 'twill be virtue.'

[29] 'My will is my God, and I will follow it wheresoever it leads. . . . What else should a king do, but always try to increase his state, and to acquire more power? Let him who is poor fear reason; a powerful lord has his reason in himself, whether what he intends to do is evil or good, provided there is a profit and an acquisition, he must never omit to pursue it. Nobody tries to find out in what manner or by what means thou art powerful, or hast become a lord; possession is all, have it rightly or wrongly, once thou art rich, thou art held in high esteem. Philip of Macedon, through his never keeping faith, through his using fraud, through his never fulfilling promises, became the lord of the whole of Greece in a little while. . . . Lysander said that where the hide of the lion did not reach, one had to add the skin of a fox. I say that where virtue canont reach, thou must endeavour to come to it through vice. For, once thou hast acquired power, vice has the appearance of virtue. And no matter how guilty and evil thou art, there will not be wanting people who will lavish praise on thee.'

[30] 'Nor do I believe it will ever be found that strength alone is enough, but it will be found that fraud alone suffices; as will clearly see whoever reads the life of Philip of Macedon.'

In the same drama (v, ii) one of the *consiglieri* expounds another passage from the eighteenth chapter of the *Prince*, which runs:

> Et hassi ad intendere questo, che uno principe, e massime uno principe nuovo, non può osservare tutte quelle cose per le quali li uomini sono tenuti buoni, sendo spesso necessitato, per mantenere lo stato, operare contro alla fede, contro alla carità, contro alla umanità, contro alla religione.[31]

The *consigliere* in Cinthio's drama says:

> concedianvi, che la novitade
> De gli stati fa far cose a'Signori,
> Sian boni pur, sian quanto voglian giusti,
> Che non le fanno poi, che confirmati
> Sono nel Regno, e come è da lodare
> Novo Signor, che tenga gli occhi aperti,
> E cerchi servar sé, servar lo stato,
> Dando gran pena, dando agro castigo
> A chi nascosto gli apparecchia insidie,
>
> . . . .
>
> Così indegn'è, ch'un Re si dia a far male
> A chi Signor l'ha fatto, quando alcuna
> Cagion data non gli ha di fargli offesa.[32]

The latter part reproduces a sentence in the twenty-first chapter of the *Prince*, concerning the debt of gratitude owed to the Prince by those who have achieved victory through

[31] 'And it suffices to conceive this, that a Prince, and especially a new Prince, cannot observe all those things, for which men are held good; he being often forc'd, for the maintenance of his State, to do contrary to his faith, charity, humanity, and religion" (Dacres' translation).

[32] "We grant that the newness of a state causes lords, however good or just they may be, to do things they will not do once they are confirmed in the kingdom, and as a new lord is to be praised who keeps his eyes open and exerts himself to save himself, to save his state, inflicting a heavy punishment and a bitter chastisement on those who secretly prepare snares against him . . . so it is an indignity that a king should harm those who have made him a sovereign, when they have not given him any cause to proceed against them.'

his support: 'Li uomini non sono mai sì disonesti, che con tanto esemplo di ingratitudine ti opprimessino.' [33]

In *Orbecche* the tyrant Sulmone, who holds fear to be the 'colonna dei regni', and 'n'ha sotto la fé mille traditi' (v, ii),[34] has recourse to dissimulation in order to achieve the revenge he has planned. In *Altile* (which is based on *Hecatommithi*, II, iii) the villainous Astano, who, by the way, is no king, but a simple nobleman, ruins Norrino by his treacherous simulation. His delight in making white look black is paralleled only by that of Iago, a character, we must remember, invented first by Cinthio: but we shall have to speak of Iago farther on. Astano, following the Senecan convention, discloses his mind to an attendant (I, iv):

> se fusse puro
> Questi via più che candida Colomba,
> Io lo farei parere un nero Corbo.
> Et se fusse Lamano la pietade
> Istessa, et la clemenza, io vo'che pensi
> Che col mio ingegno, più d'un Neron crudo
> (Poi ch'egli ha cominciato a darmi orecchio),
> Il farei divenire.[35]

This is the very policy adopted by Iago with Othello. Like Iago, Astano boasts the power of his words and guiles ('che potenza sia/Ne le parole mie, ne le mie insidie'): [36]

> Vuoi tu, che il finger ti succieda? fingi
> Fede, et amor, et sotto habbi il coltello
> A dar l'ultimo colpo a chi ti crede,
> Sì tosto, che l'occasion ti s'offra.[37]

[33] 'Men are never so openly dishonest as with such a notorious example of ingratitude to oppress thee.'

[34] 'column of kingdoms', 'he has betrayed a thousand who trusted his word'.

[35] 'Should this one be purer than a white dove, I would cause him to seem a black raven; and should Lamano be pity itself and clemency, I want you to believe that by my cunning I would make him more cruel than Nero, since he has begun to lend me his ear.'

[36] 'What power there is in my words, in my wiles.'

[37] 'Do you want your dissimulation to succeed? Simulate faith, and love, and underneath conceal the knife to inflict the fatal blow on him who trusts you, as soon as occasion lends itself.'

For his treacherous guiles Astano feels no more remorse than Iago, and for similar reasons:

> Né di questo debbo io biasimo havere,
> Havendomi intercetta ei la mia speme.[38]

Astano, in fact, had vainly loved Altile, much in the same way as Iago, in Cinthio's tale, had vainly loved Desdemona. Astano is represented as gnawed by envy:

> Mi sentia roder da la Invidia, come
> Ruggine rode il ferro.[39]

He promises (iv, ii) to be as solicitous of the ruin of Norrino as a mother is of the life of her own child:

> Non dubbitar, che non fu mai sì intenta
> A la salute del suo figlio madre,
> Quant'io a la costui morte sarò intento.[40]

Astano actually succeeds in showing to the king, who at first threatens him, the two lovers together, whereas Iago merely stages an appearance of offence. One of the other characters says of him:

> O perché lasci, Giove,
> Vivere in terra un huom tanto malvagio? [41]

Not only, then, do we find in Giraldi Cinthio the Senecan tyrant brought up to date on the lines supplied by the *Prince*, but also the maxims of villainous conduct, which Seneca had only put in the mouths of princes, become the property of a private person, a mere subject. Cinthio provides the link between the Senecan tyrant and the Elizabethan villain. His intentions—as Charlton says—had much in common with those of the Elizabethans, though he was devoid of all creative power and depth of human insight.

[38] 'I must not bear the blame of this, since he has cut short my hope.'

[39] 'I felt envy gnawing at my heart, as rust gnaws iron.'

[40] 'Be sure that no mother was ever so solicitous of the health of her son as I will be of his death.'

[41] 'O why dost thou, Jove, let live such an evil man on earth?'

When we have become fully aware of Cinthio's intermediate position, then a whole ingenious and seemingly plausible theory of Vernon Lee on the Italians of the Renaissance needs qualification. Vernon Lee, in a well-known essay included in *Euphorion*,[42] maintains that the Renaissance Italians 'rarely or never paint horror or death or abomination', that 'the whole tragic meaning was unknown to the light and cheerful contemporaries of Ariosto'—whereas we know that Giraldi Cinthio was the first to interpret as *horrore* the φόβος Aristotle required for tragedy, and to give to the Thyestean banquet that widespread popularity we find recorded not only in the plays themselves, but also in such descriptions of their effect on the audience as Cinthio's in his *Discorso intorno al comporre delle comedie e delle tragedie*. On the ground of her gratuitous assumption, Vernon Lee actually built a theory on the amorality of the Renaissance Italians as contrasted with the maturer ethical judgement of the contemporary English—pushing to their extreme consequences the ideas expounded in Macaulay's essay on Machiavelli:—'They did not know how wicked they were.' Suppose they did not; but, then, neither did the Englishmen of the period. Since, in the same way as the Italian Senecans placed their gruesome plots among barbarian peoples, the English dramatists chose for the favourite scene of their horrors 'the darkened Italian palace, with its wrought-iron bars preventing escape; its embroidered carpets muffling the footsteps; its hidden, suddenly yawning trap-doors; its arras-hangings concealing masked ruffians; its garlands of poisoned flowers'—as Vernon Lee very picturesquely puts it. To the Italians 'oriental themes above all presented greater opportunities for gruesome horror and spectacular luxury, and especially those depicting the Turks of their own generation, even then hammering at Italy's gates.'[43] The same exotic touch was supplied to the Italians by oriental history, to the English by Italian contemporary events: romance is more appealing when staged against an exotic background. The exotic appeal is the main reason why Italians chose to dramatise the story of some unfortunate Armenian or Persian couple

---

[42] 'The Italy of Elizabethan Dramatists'.
[43] Charlton in the Introduction mentioned above, p. lxxxix.

of lovers rather than the pathetic but too familiar story of the Duchess of Amalfi; the same exotic appeal which led English dramatists to write on the Duchess of Malfi or Bianca Cappello rather than to seek for their subjects at home, as they did in fact occasionally, in such dramas as *A Warning for Faire Women, Arden of Feversham,* and *The Yorkshire Tragedy.*

The Senecan drama was, then, the medium through which the Machiavellian principles, distorted as they had been, came to be uttered from the stage. Machiavellism, as epitomized by Gentillet, provided an up-to-date equipment of ideas to the worn-off classical tyrant; just as the essays of Montaigne supplied the dramatists with meditative passages when the Senecan aphorisms began to sound too hackneyed. But the very fact that Machiavellism was merely grafted on a pre-existent Senecan type ought to warn us to be very cautious against detecting it everywhere, as Wyndham Lewis has done in his book *The Lion and the Fox.* According to Mr. Lewis, 'the master figure of Elizabethan drama is Machiavelli . . . he was at the back of every Tudor mind.' But Seneca was at the back of every Tudor mind much more than Machiavelli, and sometimes what may be construed as Machiavellism is merely Senecan.

Senecan is, for instance, the tyrant Tancred in *Tancred and Gismund,* who is partly modelled on Giraldi Cinthio's Sulmone (in *Orbecche*); but to Simpson [44] Tancred seemed the first Machiavellian of the Elizabethan stage. Senecan is Marlowe's Tamburlaine, in whom Professor Brandl [45] imagined to discover many traits in common with Machiavelli's Prince. But the type of Tamburlaine is Seneca's Hercules: curiously enough, nobody seems to have noticed it. Tamburlaine proclaims several times to be a scourge of God, God's viceregent who executes tyrannies 'enjoin'd . . . from above,/To scourge the pride of such as Heaven abhors' (2 *Tamburlaine* ll. 3820

---

[44] *The Political Use of the Stage in Shakespeare's Time.*
[45] *Gött. Gel. Anz.* 1891, no. 18, pp. 717 ff. After Professor Brandl, the same thesis has been maintained by R. W. Battenhouse, *Marlowe's Tamburlaine, A Study in Renaissance Moral Philosophy,* Nashville, 1941, and Irving Ribner, 'Marlowe and Machiavelli', in *Comparative Literature,* vi, 4, Fall 1954.

ff.). Seneca's Hercules (in *Hercules Oetaeus*, l. 1143) had said to Jupiter: 'Ille qui pro fulmine/tuisque facibus natus in terris eram.' Tamburlaine's desperate appeals, when life forsakes him (*2 Tamburlaine*, ll. 4434 ff.), are a counterpart of Hercules' lamentations while tortured by the burning shirt:

> What daring God torments my body thus,
> And seeks to conquer mighty Tamburlaine?

His amazement is modelled on Hercules' amazement in seeing himself, a conqueror of the world, killed by a mysterious enemy (ll. 1161 ff.): 'Ego qui relicta morte . . . ego quem deorum regna senserunt tria/morior . . . sine morte vincor.' [46] Both challenge Death; Tamburlaine: 'See where my slave, the uglie monster death . . .' (*2 Tamburlaine*, l. 4459); and Hercules (ll. 1249 ff.): 'Quaecumque pestis viscere in nostro late/procede . . .' (l. 1373): 'invade, mors, non trepida . . .'; Tamburlaine's speeches are as full of hyperboles as Hercules'. Professor Brandl has thought Tamburlaine's wooing of Zenocrate a piece of Machiavellian policy, to be matched only by Richard III's proposal to Lady Anne, but Zenocrate is rather a counterpart of Iole in *Hercules Oetaeus*: she is, like her, the prisoner daughter of a king; she yields, like her, to the mighty conqueror. Tamburlaine is in so far an incarnation of Machiavelli's Prince, as he is a type of the self-confident superhuman hero, whose aspiring mind concentrates upon the attainment of a mundane end. But so is Hercules, in whom, besides, we find that craving after immortality which is also behind the vague, boundless aspirations of Tamburlaine.

The error of Professor Brandl (followed, here, by Courthope) in setting down to Machiavellism the superhuman *virtù* of Tamburlaine has been repeated by Wyndham Lewis in the case of another hero of the class of Marlowe's colossus, a hero who might be described as his issue—Chapman's Duke of Byron. At a first superficial impression, the Duke of Byron

[46] Tamburlaine compares himself to Alcides in *2 Tamburlaine*, IV, iii, (l. 3991 of the whole play): 'The headstrong Iades of Thrace, Alcides tam'd . . ./Were not subdew'd with valour more divine.' And he is compared to Alcides by Theridamas in *1 Tamburlaine*, I, ii, 159–160, and by Menaphon, *ibid.*, II, i, 10–11, *2 Tamburlaine*, v, i, 96 ff.

may indeed strike one as 'affording a spectacle of a Machiavel in the making'—as Wyndham Lewis puts it—but that first impression is dispelled as soon as we study Byron in the light of the able researches of Professor Schoell, who shows to us Chapman spell-bound by the 'moralized' image Plutarch had sketched of Alexander.[47] Machiavelli never did supply a pattern of heroism for the Elizabethan dramatists: such figures as Tamburlaine and Byron were expressions of the same spirit of *Wille zur Macht* which produced the *Prince*, but they did not derive from it directly.[48] Machiavelli only supplied characteristics of the politic villain, who, from the very beginning, was loathed at the same time as ridiculed.

It is a mistake to try to distinguish between different stages of the figure of the Machiavellian in Elizabethan drama.[49] There is no first period in which Machiavelli provides a type of heroic, unprincipled individualism, discredited in a successive stage by puritan morality. And it would be impossible to say when the Machiavellian knave, from being an object of horror, turns into an object of derision. As early as 1597 we find a caricature of the Machiavellian in the 'ugly mechanicall Captain' of Nashe's *Unfortunate Traveller*, who, persuaded by Jack Wilton that he is a 'myraculous polititian', deserts from the English to the French, but, given away by his own foolishness, is flogged back to the English, who flog him in their turn. Other Machiavellian dupes are Chapman's Gostanzo in *All Fools* (about 1604) ('these politicians . . . are our most fools'—III, i), and Beaumont and Fletcher's Lucio in *The Woman Hater* (*c.* 1606). In Ben Jonson's *Volpone*

[47] F. L. Schoell, *Études sur l'Humanisme continental en Angleterre*, Paris, 1926, p. 85.

[48] Such is also the case of Milton's Satan, in whom Professor Courthope (*History of English Poetry*, iii, pp. 415–416) has seen the embodiment of Machiavellian *virtù*. But aspiring pride had been a traditional feature of Satan, and the new touches added by Milton are rather to be traced back to Aeschylus's Prometheus than to Machiavelli's hero. Milton's Machiavellian studies form the subject of one of Professor N. Orsini's *Studii sul Rinascimento italiano in Inghilterra, op. cit.*; Professor Orsini has shown from Milton's *Commonplace Book* that Machiavelli was to the English poet chiefly a master of republican doctrine.

[49] As R. Fischer does in *Anglia-Beiblatt*, vii (May 1897–April 1898), p. 355.

(1606) the character of the Italianate Englishman Sir Politick Would-be is meant for a humorous skit on the Machiavellian fop. Like Machiavelli himself, Sir Politick loves 'to note and observe', and, though he lives free from the active torrent, he marks 'the currents and the passages of things', for his own private use, and knows 'the ebbs and flows of state'. He thinks Ulysses a poor wit,[50] and sees plots and tricks of state everywhere. His wife has come with him to Venice 'for intelligence/Of tires and fashions, and behaviour/Among the Courtezans': 'the spider and the bee suck from one flower', i.e., both are trained at the Italian school of manners. Sir Politick proves a very gullible simpleton, and is easily made a laughing-stock. Ben Jonson ridiculed again the Machiavellian statesman in the character of Bias, 'a vi-politic, or sub-secretary', in *The Magnetic Lady*. A caustic caricature of the politician is found in *Alphonsus, Emperor of Germany*, a play which, though only performed in 1636, was written, possibly by a John Poole (not, of course, by Chapman), 'not much later than the epoch-making work of Marlowe' (Parrott). The secretary Lorenzo de Cyprus, who, after having dictated to Alphonsus a grotesque epitome of the *Prince* derived from Gentillet, Phalaris-like falls a victim to his own arts, and is poisoned with his own poisons, in accordance with his rules of policy, is an evident parody of Machiavelli. As Lorenzo is a caricature of Machiavelli, so Alphonsus is modelled on the historical Cesare Borgia, whom a false report described as Machiavelli's disciple. The banquet at which Alphonsus (who, like the Borgias, is a 'viperous, bloodthirsty Spaniard') tries to poison his enemies is a repetition of Pope Alexander VI's famous feast, with the difference that Alphonsus only pretends to be poisoned himself.

In *Alphonsus*, as in most minor dramas, many influences are at work. There is a slight influence of *Richard III* (chiefly for religious hypocrisy: I, ii, 84 ff.), but the strongest influences are of Marlowe's *Jew of Malta*, and of *The Spanish Tragedy*, the two plays which gave birth to the type of the Machiavellian knave on the Elizabethan stage. Indeed the question of Machiavellian influence on Elizabethan drama

[50] Cp. *3 Henry VI*, III, ii, 189: 'I'll . . . deceive more slyly than Ulysses could.'

is complicated by the influence of those two plays, which was still more far-echoing than it is thought. Very seldom the dramatists had a first-hand aquaintance with Machiavelli's writings; most of the time the villainous traits in the characters of their dramas are borrowed from Kyd's and Marlowe's Machiavellians: at the utmost, fresh illustration was derived from Gentillet.

So, for instance, Webster's Flamineo in *The White Devil* is a Machiavellian after Kyd's Lorenzo in *The Spanish Tragedy*: in both cases, the aim of their policy is the marriage of their sister to a powerful lord, an aim which leads them to murder in each case the person to whom the sister is engaged. Webster's Romelio, in *The Devils Law-Case,* is, on the other hand, clearly influenced by Marlowe's *Jew of Malta* (see III, ii, 1 ff.).[51] Muly Mohamet in Peele's *Battle of Alcazar,* Aaron in *Titus Andronicus,* Eleazar in *Lust's Dominion,* are all progeny of Barabas.

Marlowe certainly, and Kyd very likely, had a fair knowledge of Machiavelli's doctrines. There can be little doubt in the case of Marlowe,[52] whom Greene rebuked for having imbibed the 'pestilent Machiavilian policie'. Marlowe had studied in Cambridge, where Machiavelli's writings were eagerly read: just a little time before he was entered at Corpus Christi College (1581), a Cambridge man, Gabriel Harvey, obviously influenced by Gentillet, as Meyer has shown,[53] in a Latin poem (1578) had put in Machiavelli's own mouth (*Machiavellus ipse loquitur*) a denunciation of his policy which obviously supplied the model for the prologue of *The Jew of Malta.* Later on, in London, Marlowe had further opportunity of hearing Machiavelli's principles dis-

[51] See O. Schröder, *Marlowe und Webster,* Halle, 1907, pp. 8–11.

[52] Irving Ribner, 'Marlowe and Machiavelli', cited above, sees perfectly reflected in Marlowe the peculiar ambivalence which must be considered in any discussion of Machiavelli in Elizabethan England: on the one hand we find the name of Machiavelli used as a symbol for all that is evil for Elizabethan Englishmen; on the other hand, we find Machiavelli's thought widely parallelled in Elizabethan political writings, even by those very writers who at other times make free use of the popular stereotype of Machiavellism.

[53] Meyer *cit.,* pp. 22–24.

cussed by Walter Ralegh and his circle.[54] The study of Machiavelli's doctrines formed one of the favourite subjects of Ralegh's circle. Ralegh, who has been called the forerunner, if not the founder, of British colonial power, before expounding Machiavelli's theories in his own political works, put them into practice in Ireland, where he was sent in 1580 to assist Lord Grey to subjugate the rebels.[55]

His commerce with Gabriel Harvey and Walter Ralegh may have initiated Marlowe to Machiavelli's original texts. But, so far as other dramatists are concerned, their villains are little more than further developments of the type as introduced to the stage by Kyd and Marlowe. The 'most thoroughly Machiavellian figure on the English stage' is, according to Professor Courthope, Iago,[56] but the pedigree of this character is to be found in Giraldi Cinthio rather than in Machiavelli. When we read the source of *Othello*, the seventh *novella* in the third Decade of the *Hecatommithi*, we can hardly fail to notice how much more Machiavellian Cinthio's *alfiero* is than his English counterpart, Iago. The ensign, disregarding the faith pledged to his own wife (who is described in the story as a *bella et honesta giovane*) and the friendship and obligation towards the Moor, falls violently in love with Desdemona and, when he sees that his wooing is all in vain, plots the revenge. Cinthio's ensign cannot justify his behaviour through any provocation or slight suffered at the hands of the Moor; he is the ideal knave who, finding obstacles in the way of his perverse will, seeks revenge through deceit and treachery. This type of knave has been further developed by Giraldi Cinthio in his drama *Altile*, where Astano is the exact counterpart of the ensign of the *novella* of the Moor of Venice, and,

[54] See M. C. Bradbrook, *The School of Night, A Study in the Literary Relationships of Sir Walter Raleigh*, Cambridge University Press, 1936; F. A. Yates, *A Study of Love's Labour's Lost*, Cambridge University Press, 1936.

[55] In *The Cabinet Council containing the chief Arts of Empire*, and in *The Prince or Maxims of State*, Raleigh is heavily indebted to the *Principe* and the *Discorsi*. See my essay 'Un machiavellico inglese: Sir Walter Raleigh', in *Machiavelli in Inghilterra ed altri saggi*, pp. 149–164.

[56] For Bradley (*Shakespearean Tragedy*, London, 1904, new ed. 1932), on the contrary, Iago cannot surely be taken as an instance of the popular notion of a disciple of Machiavelli.

as we have seen, anticipates in many respects Shakespeare's Iago. But Shakespeare's Iago appears to us much less of a knave if we keep in mind that he is incensed by the public report that Othello has cuckolded him. 'The ostensible plot of the play'—says Wyndham Lewis—'is really the revenge of the sex-vanity of a subordinate on his chief, the revenge taking the form of inspiring his chief with the same feelings of jealousy and wounded vanity that he has experienced himself.' On this account, Iago's story, as told by Shakespeare, finds parallels in many cases of retaliation instanced by Italian *novelle*: Iago, an accomplished Machiavellian demon in Cinthio, becomes much more human and excusable in Shakespeare. The reality of Iago's jealousy seems indeed to be doubted by some commentators. The lines (IV, i, 46–48):

> Thus credulous fools are caught:
> And many worthy and chaste dames even thus,
> All guiltless, meet reproach—

are commented upon, for instance, by H. C. Hart in *The Arden Shakespeare*, thus: 'These lines show the unreality of Iago's motives with which he formerly pretended to salve his conscience. He finds that he can ruin the happiness of innocent people. He can do it causelessly, and he is triumphant.' I would not lay so much stress on those lines, since they echo almost literally the moral of Cinthio's story:

> aviene talhora che senza colpa, fedele et amorevole donna per insidie tesele da animo malvagio, et per leggierezza di chi più crede che non bisognerebbe, da fedel marito riceve morte.[57]

A feebler replica of Iago is Iachimo, the 'false Italian' of *Cymbeline*.

An extreme development of the character of the villain is found in Webster's Bosola, who partly reminds one of Iago, but of an Iago endowed with the melancholy and the wavering conscience of Hamlet: all the acts of this 'meditative murderer

---

[57] 'It sometimes happens that, without guilt on her part, a faithful and loving woman, through a deceit engined by an evil mind, and the folly of some credulous person, is killed by a loyal husband.' This almost literal translation of Cinthio's moral could be, by the way, one of the proofs that Shakespeare knew Italian.

or philosophic ruffian'—as Swinburne calls him—are cursed, so that unwittingly he kills the very Antonio he meant to save 'above his own life'.

It has been doubted whether Shakespeare had direct access to Machiavelli's writings. Köppel [58] indeed thought he had discovered direct borrowings from Machiavelli in the portrait of King Claudius in *Hamlet*, but the parallels he quotes do not seem altogether cogent. The opinion about the awe-striking effect of the 'divinity' which 'hedges a king' was one so firmly established and widespread since remote antiquity that it cannot be traced to any particular source. 'Politic' madness such as we find in *Hamlet* had first been employed on the stage by Kyd, in the character of Ieronimo. Kyd may have derived it from *Discorsi* III, ii: 'Come egli è cosa sapientissima simulare in tempo la pazzia.' What Machiavellism is displayed in Shakespeare's historical dramas seems either to be already present in the historical sources (as in the case of *Richard III*), or to be derived from the broadcast popular legend. In *3 Henry VI* Shakespeare wrote 'And set the murderous Machiavel to school' (III, ii, 193), where *The True Tragedy* has: 'And set the aspiring Catalin to schoole.' He was merely changing a label: the facts remained the same, with a new name. In *1 Henry IV* (I, iii, 285 ff.) Worcester says:

> For, bear ourselves as even as we can,
> The king will always think him in our debt,
> And think we think ourselves unsatisfied,
> Till he hath found a time to pay us home.

This seems indeed to reproduce very closely a passage in the third chapter of the *Prince* (the chapter to which Köppel traced the similitude drawn from the hectic fever in *Hamlet*, IV, iii, 67) about the founder of a *principato nuovo*:

> non ti puoi mantenere amici quelli che vi ti hanno messo, per non li potere satisfare in quel modo che si erano presupposto.[59]

[58] See *Englische Studien*, xxiv, cited above.

[59] '. . . thou canst not keep them thy friends that have seated thee in it, for not being able to satisfie them according to their expectations' (Dacres's translation).

But the similarity is still greater in a passage in *Leycester's Commonwealth* (1584) reproducing Machiavelli's maxim:

> For that such Princes, after ward can never give sufficient satisfaction to such friends for so great a benefice received. And consequently least upon discontentment, they may chance doe as much for others against them, as they have done for them against others: the surest way is, to recompence them with such reward, as they shall never after bee able to complain of.

Indeed Machiavelli's text concludes that one cannot employ against friends *medicine forti,* 'sendo loro obligato'.[60]

Ben Jonson had a direct acquaintance with Machiavelli's writings, as appears from his *Discoveries,* from passages of the unfinished *Fall of Mortimer,* and from such occasional use of Machiavelli's terminology as in two passages of *Sejanus* (III, i; III, iii), where *fortune* and *virtue* are contrasted; [61] but, on the other hand, what in *Sejanus* might remind one of Machiavelli is, instead, almost literally borrowed from Seneca. So the dialogue about policy between Tiberius and Sejanus (II, ii) is little more than a collection of the tyrant's maxims given by Seneca in *Thyestes, Thebais,* and *Octavia.* That Meyer, who ignored the Senecan origin of those maxims, could find parallels for them in Machiavelli's writings shows once more how cautious one must be in the study of Machiavelli's influence upon the stage. Also, Tamburlaine's disciple Selimus, in the play of this name, is after the Senecan tyrant, and not after the Machiavellian Prince.

Of course, the Machiavellism of many minor characters in Elizabethan drama is unmistakable. Aspiring Guise in Marlowe's *Massacre at Paris,* Monsieur and Baligny in Chapman's

---

[60] '. . . thou canst not . . . put in practice strong remedies against them, being obliged to them.' In his essay on 'Il "Coriolano" di Shakespeare' (in *La Nuova Antologia,* no. 1863, December 1953, pp. 427–444) Professor Salvatore Rosati has shown how some of Volumnia's exhortations to her son are uniform with the Machiavellian doctrine.

[61] 'She herself [fortune], when virtue doth oppose,/Must lose her threats.' 'Men's fortune is their virtue.' A similar use of the binomial 'virtue-fortune' in Sidney's *Arcadia* was first noticed by S. L. Wolff, *The Greek Romances in Elizabethan Prose Fiction,* New York, 1912, pp. 326–327.

Revenge of Bussy d'Ambois, Piero in Marston's 2 *Antonio and Mellida*, Mendoza in *The Malcontent*,[62] Latorch in *The Bloody Brother* (by Fletcher and Jonson, (?) revised by Massinger) [63] are admittedly Machiavellian; Barnes's *Divels Charter* is a thoroughly Machiavellian play by its very argument, Pope Alexander VI's story, which Barnes derived from Guicciardini and combined with Marlowe's version of the legend of Doctor Faustus. Allusion to Machiavellian policy is very frequent in all the authors of this period, as Meyer has shown in his patient and almost exhaustive *corpus* of quotations. But most of those quotations are echoing a popular *cliché*; their import does not reach beyond a superficial passing record of a fashionable byword. On the other hand, in many authors acquainted with Machiavelli's writings, Machiavellism combined with other influences: most of the time, as I have shown, with the influence of Seneca; sometimes with that of the Greek romances, where dissimulation and stratagems were common enough: such is the case of the Machiavellian characters in Greene's novels: Pharicles, Arbasto, and Pandosto.[64]

[62] A typical passage is IV, iii, 148 ff.:

> 'They shall die both, for their deserts craves more
> Than we can recompense: their presence still
> Imbraids our fortunes with beholdingness,
> Which we abhor . . .'

[63] See, for authorship, E. H. Oliphant, *The Plays of Beaumont and Fletcher*, New Haven, 1927, pp. 457–463.

[64] See Wolff *cit.*, p. 412. For Seneca, see J. W. Cunliffe, *The Influence of Seneca on Elizabethan Tragedy*, London, 1893. (*Sejanus*, pp. 89 ff.) To the classics, rather than to Machiavelli, is also to be traced much of Corneille's 'Machiavellism'. The maxims of his villan Photin, in *La Mort de Pompée*, are borrowed from the speeches of Pothinus in Lucan, *De Bello Civ.* viii, 482 ff. But such a device as, in *Polyeucte*, Félix suspects Sévère of employing against him (v, i), of letting him reprieve Polyeucte in order to ruin him utterly in the eyes of the Emperor, is eminently Machiavellian:

> Je sais des gens de cour quelle est la politique,
> J'en connais mieux que lui la plus fine pratique.
>
> .   .   .   .
>
> De ce qu'il me demande il me ferait un crime.

We find this device noted also in *Leycester's Commonwealth*: 'the

In the cant use of the word, Machiavellism suggested chiefly two things: a treacherous way of killing, generally by poison; and atheism. A passage in Nashe's *Pierce Penilesse* [65] gives details about 'the arte of murther Machiavel hath pend' (*Summer's Last Will and Testament*, l. 1397):

O Italie, the Academie of man-slaughter, the sporting place of murther, the Apothecary-shop of poyson for all Nations: how many kind of weapons hast thou invented for malice? Suppose I love a mans wife, whose husband yet lives, and cannot enioy her for his iealous over-looking: Physicke, or rather the art of murther (as it may be used), will lend one a Medicine which shall make him away, in the nature of that disease he is most subiect to, whether in the space of a yeare, a moneth, halfe a yeare, or what tract of time you will, more or lesse.

These Machiavellian poisons, punctual like clock-work, became no less of a regular property of the Elizabethan stage than the Senecan bloody blades.[66] In *The Jew of Malta* we come across a precious powder bought at Ancona 'whose operation is to binde, infect,/And poyson deeply: yet not appeare/In forty houres after it is tane' (ll. 1373 ff.). In *Alphonsus, Emperor of Germany*, out of that powder has grown a whole box of poisons, which is given to Lorenzo de Cyprus by Julius Lentulus, 'a most renowned Neapolitan'. Other Machiavellian tricks are expounded by Lightborn in Marlowe's *Edward II* (ll. 2363 ff.):

I learnde in Naples how to poison flowers,
To strangle with a lawne thrust through the throte,
To pierce the wind-pipe with a needles point,
Or whilst one is a sleepe, to take a quill

Machiavilian sleight . . . of driving men to attempt somewhat, where they may incur danger or remaine in perpetuall suspition or disgrace'. After Polyeucte has been sacrificed by Félix, too solicitous of his own safety, Sévère addresses him thus (v, vi):

Père dénaturé, malheureux politique,
Esclave ambitieux d'une peur chimérique.

[65] Ed. McKerrow, i, p. 186.
[66] Cf. Shakespeare, *Tempest*, iii, iii, 105; *Winter's Tale*, i, ii, 321.

And blowe a little powder in his eares,
Or open his mouth, and powre quick silver downe,
But yet I have a braver way then these.

This braver way, as is shown afterwards, consists in holding
the person down on the bed with a table, and stamping on it.
Many of these picturesque devices were exploited by the most
spectacular of all Elizabethan dramatists, Webster, who set
great store on 'the rare trickes of a Machiavillian'. His Flamineo says (*White Devil*, v, iii, 194 ff.):

Those are found waightie strokes which come from th' hand,
But those are killing strokes which come from th' head.
O the rare trickes of a Machivillian!
Hee doth not come like a grosse plodding slave
And buffet you to death: no, my quaint knave—
Hee tickles you to death; makes you die laughing;
As if you had swallow'd a pound of saffron.

This passage is echoed by Middleton, in the *Game at Chess*,
where the Black Knight, the Machiavellian Gondomar, says
(i, i, 257 ff.):

And what I've done, I've done facetiously,
With pleasant subtlety and bewitching courtship,
Abus'd all my believers with delight,—
They took a comfort to be cozen'd by me:
To many a soul I've let in mortal poison,
Whose cheeks have crack'd with laughter to receive it

. . . .

They took their bane in way of recreation.

As one sees from these and dozens of similar instances, the
Elizabethans could never get over the excitement caused by
the report of 'Borgias wine', though poisoning and wholesale
murder were as rife in England as anywhere else in Renaissance Europe.

Diabolical atheism is another abiding feature of the mythi-
cal Machiavelli. The accusation dates from the first ecclesiasti-
cal campaign against the *Prince*. It will be remembered that
already Cardinal Pole had called the *Prince* a book 'Satanae
digito scriptum'. Gentillet did little else but give the finishing

touch to the dark picture the Catholic clergy had been elaborating for half a century against the anticlerical writer, whose comparison between the Pagan and the Christian religion (in *Discorsi*, II, ii) was purposely misconstrued into an atheistic argument. This accusation reflected on the popular account of Machiavelli's life. He was portrayed as a thoroughly bad and ignorant man, addicted to all vices, hating his country, banished from Florence (Gentillet), and dying in despair (Greene). They distorted his name in order to see in it an emblem of his villainy: he was called *Match a villain*, '*Machevill* that evill none can match' (Davies), *Hatch-evil*.[67] His Christian name got confused with the previously existing 'Old Nick' for the Devil.[68] Sometimes he was described as a new Simon Magus (George Whetstone, *English Myrror*, Lib. iii); he was compared with Cain, Judas, Julian the Apostate (Greene, *Groat's Worth of Wit*). But the most fruitful side of the Machiavelli myth was the representation of the Florentine as an instrument of Satan, as ridden by an incubus, as the Secretary of Hell, as the Devil himself turned moralist.[69] So much did the terms Machiavelli and Satan become interchangeable that, whereas at first the tricks attributed to Machiavelli were called devilish, later on the Devil's own tricks were styled 'Machiavellian' (Nashe, *Terrors of the Night*). By an inversion of the process which had resulted in describing Machiavelli as a devil, the Devil himself became tinged with Machiavellism. On this later development I shall have shortly a few more words to say.

Since Machiavellism had become the common denominator for sins of every description, we will not be surprised in finding not only the Senecan tyrant dressed in the new Florentine garb, but also other old stock characters of drama brought up to date with Machiavellian trimmings. In Kyd's Lorenzo and in Webster's Flamineo we have Machiavel in the role of Pandar; in Barabas, Machiavel in the role of the Miser; in Iago, Machiavel in the role of the Revengeful Cuckold; and in

[67] Meyer *cit.*, 68–69, 116–117. The Jesuit Raynaud had first given currency to the legendary account of Machiavelli's death: 'blasphemans evomuit reprobum spiritum'.

[68] Meyer *cit.*, pp. 93, 177 ff.

[69] Meyer *cit.*, pp. 20, 53 f., 80 n. 1, 97 n. 3, 103 f.

Gostanzo (*All Fools*), Machiavel as the Gullible Father of the Terentian comedy.

Machiavelli's name is found coupled with that of the other Italian scandal, Aretino, and we come across the curious hybrid form *Mach-Aretines* (in Sylvester's *Lacrymae Lacrymarum*), we hear of *Aretines Politicks* (Glapthorne) and of *veneriall Machiavelisme* (Nashe).[70] Better still, Machiavelli is associated with Ignatius Loyola, and we actually come across the monstrous combination *Ignatian Matchivell*.[71]

This latter contamination deserves to be illustrated, since it has not been noticed either by Meyer or by the others who have written on the Machiavelli legend. It may seem strange that the Jesuits, who were among the first and fiercest detractors of Machiavelli, to the point of having him burned in effigy at Ingolstadt as *Cacodaemonis auxiliator*, should have become closely connected with him in the English mind. Still, we will understand how the bringing together of the two *bêtes noires* of the Protestants became possible, if we bear in mind the character of the Society of Jesus.

The ultimate meaning of Machiavelli's doctrine had been a reassertion of terrene life and ideals against the ascetic conception of the Middle Ages, which placed the aim of human activities beyond earthly life. Against this theological outlook, Machiavelli had raised the ancient ideal of power acquired and enjoyed on earth. Against a humble and contemplative life, and the 'dispregio delle cose umane', leading men to submit themselves to their spiritual guides, Machiavelli had restored the dignity and beauty of things 'atte a fare gli uomini fortissimi' during their earthly life, and leading to the achievement of happiness on earth. To this aim he had made all the rest, even religion, subservient: he had adopted Gino Capponi's praise of those who love 'more their country than the salvation of their souls'.

Now, Jesuitism was as typical of the Renaissance as Machiavelli's political creed. Since the mediaeval ideals of humility and contemplation had been supplanted by a conception of

---

[70] Meyer *cit.*, pp. 119, 156; *Works of Nashe*, ed. McKerrow, ii, p. 153.

[71] In *Lines to the Bischopes*, attributed to Drummond of Hawthornden, ed. Kastner, ii, p. 293.

life based on will of domination and active undertaking, the
Jesuits transferred to the terrene plane the centre of the religious system, and made the glory of God coincide with the
terrestrial power of their Society. Apart from the different
denomination, their aim coincided with the aim for which
Machiavelli stood—the achievement of supremacy on earth.
Theirs was a defence of mediaeval theocracy with the very
methods which had been devised to fight against it. In the
same way as the Machiavellians conceived all manifestations
of spiritual life, first of all religion, as so many instruments of
policy, so the Jesuits adopted art, literature, in short all the
appealing side of Humanism, as instrumental to their aim of
controlling men and states. Domination was in both cases the
chief aim: everything else was degraded to the rank of tool,
to be laid aside when its function had been fulfilled. In both
cases all scruples had to be disregarded, whenever a certain
action was conducive to the aim, which in Machiavelli's case
was the glory of the country, in the case of the Jesuits the
glory of God. Political writers under Jesuit influence had in
fact so much in common with Machiavelli that, notwithstanding their apparent anti-Machiavellism, they actually reproduced Machiavelli's principles while pretending to derive
them from Tacitus.[72]

Hence, in the popular report, the doctrines of both Machiavelli and Loyola could be epitomised in the formula: 'the end
justifies (or sanctifies)the means.' One of the means of which
the Jesuits made constant use was equivocation, which was a
perfect counterpart of Machiavellian dissimulation. Equivocation became a byword in England since Henry Garnet,
superior of the Jesuits in England, used it during his trial for
complicity in the Gunpowder Plot. Therefore it was only too
natural that the two chief figures of the political and religious
world of the South should have been confused together by the
Englishmen of Queen Elizabeth's time, who had religious and

[72] See G. Toffanin, *Machiavelli e il Tacitismo*, Padova, 1921. In
this book is also to be found an interesting chapter on 'Il Valentino
e Tiberio', where it is shown how much Tiberius, as protrayed by
Tacitus, had in common with Cesare Borgia. No wonder then if
Meyer, in reading Ben Jonson's *Sejanus*, was reminded of Machiavelli.

political causes of hatred against that nation which was the secular arm of the Church—Spain. The Jesuited Politician became the butt of the English people.

An adjective frequently used in connexion with both Machiavelli and the Jesuits was *polypragmatic,* i.e., meddlesome. In the N.E.D. we find recorded: 'Polypragmaticke Papists', 'polypragmatic Machiavel', 'Iesuited Poly-pragmatiques', 'the most atheall Polypragmon Father Parsons'. From the last instance it appears that the accusation of atheism, raised against Machiavelli first of all by the Jesuits, had finally stretched also to them in the popular report. Polupragmaticus, 'Iesuita, Magus', &c., and Aequivocus, 'Iesuitae servus', are characters in Robert Burton's satirical play *Philosophaster* (1606): another character is the sophist Simon Acutus, whose nationality is Italian.

Polupragmaticus is heard teaching the other impostors of the play how to behave. Here is a passage of his dialogue with Simon:

Polu. Tuum est disputare de Infinito, Ente, Vacuo

. . . .

De Gabrielitate Gabrielis, et spiritali anima.

Sim. Vellem quod jubes si possem.

Polu. Potes fingere, et mentiri, et hoc satis.

Sim. Dabo operam.

Polu. Ne dubites; unica virtus erit impudentia

. . . .

Suum cujusque curet officium.
Ego meum, bilinguis, ambidexter, omniscius
Jactabo quidvis, prout dabitur occasio,
Callere me omnes linguas, artes, scientias,
Nescire, aut haesitare, stolidum existimo.
Sed verbo dicam Jesuitam prae me feram.

Sim. Cur Jesuitam?

Polu. Quid non audet hoc genus hominum
In regum aulas, gynaecia, quo non ruit?
Quod intentatum reliquit scelus?

Here the Jesuit is naïvely made the mouthpiece of the author, much in the way Machiavelli was caused to condemn himself

in the prologue to *The Jew of Malta*. Later on the servant
Aequivocus says of his master:

> qua non abit? huc, illuc, ubique,
> Per omnes vicos urbis noctivagus repit
> Ad horas omnes noctis, nunc virili habitu
> Nunc muliebri incedens, omnes formas induens,
> Lenae, obstetricis, interdum vero militis,
> Proteus opinor non est illo mutabilior,
> Nec vulpes mage versipelles, aut versutior.

Here the Jesuit is represented as a fox. It was not long before
the famous Machiavellian saying on the lion and the fox became applied also to him. Of such use we have a witness in
one of the thirty-two *New and Choise Characters* printed
together with Overbury's poem *The Wife:* according to Mr.
F. L. Lucas, Webster is possibly the author of these *Characters*.[73] A Jesuit, we read there among other things, 'in Rome,
and other countries that give him freedome, . . . weares a
Maske upon his heart; in England he shifts it, and puts it upon
his face. . . . To conclude, would you know him beyond
Sea? In his Seminary, hee's a Foxe; but in the Inquisition, a
Lyon Rampant.' And in a pamphlet of 1653 (*The Anabaptist
Washt and Washt, &c.,* London, Printed by William Hunt)
we see in the frontispiece a half-length figure of a Jesuit, with
an open mouth similar to the mouth of a lion's head facing
him, and above we read the words: 'Obrugiens Ore Leonino
Vulpinus Iesuita.'

Ignatius Loyola and Machiavelli are both represented as
pleading at Lucifer's Court in John Donne's *Ignatius his Conclave,* published in Latin and then in English in 1611.[74] Donne
has given to his pamphlet the form of a vision of hell. He sees
all the rooms in hell open to his sight, and, in the innermost
of them, Lucifer with a few chosen spirits. Lucifer examines
the titles of those who claim to be admitted to that secret

---

[73] *The Complete Works of John Webster,* ed. Lucas, iv, p. 42.
[74] In a print of 1605 on *The Powder Treason, Propounded by
Sathan,* &c. (Br. Mus. Cat., Political and Personal, i, n. 67) are
pictured the Mouth of Hell, the Devil holding a scroll, and
numerous evil spirits, with the words: 'Ignations Conclave'.

place, a favour granted only to people who have attempted great innovations, induced doubts and anxieties and scruples, and at length established opinions directly contrary to all established before. Ignatius Loyola, who appears in the role of Lucifer's mentor, is determined to oppose all claimants except those of his own order. After Copernicus's and Paracelsus's services have been proclaimed not sufficiently distinguished to raise them to so high a preferment in hell, Machiavelli is ushered in. Between Machiavelli and Loyola ensues a dispute which keeps enough satirical pungency to render it palatable even to modern readers. Machiavelli, seeing how Ignatius, uncalled, has thrust himself into the office of King's Attorney, and, scorning as unfit for a Florentine the patience of the two preceding German claimants, thinks at first to get some venomous darts out of his Italian arsenal to cast against the worn solder of Pampeluna, 'this *French-Spanish* mungrell', Ignatius. But, on perceiving how Lucifer approves whatever Ignatius says, he suddenly changes his purpose, and determines to direct his speech to Ignatius as to the principal person next to Lucifer, in order both to mollify him and to make Lucifer jealous and fearful lest Ignatius, 'by winning to his side politique men, exercised in civill businesses, might attempt some innovation' in his kingdom. Therefore he begins to speak thus:

Dread *Emperour*, and you, his watchfull and diligent *Genius*, father *Ignatius*, *Arch-chancellor* of this *Court*, and highest *Priest* of this highest *Synagogue* (except the Primacy of the *Romane Church* reach also unto this place) let me before I descend to my selfe, a little consider, speake, and admire your stupendious wisedome, and the gouvernment of this state. You may vouchsafe to remember (great *Emperour*) how long after the *Nazarens* death, you were forced to live a solitarie, a barren, and an Eremitical life: till at last (as it was ever your fashion to imitate heaven) out of your aboundant love, you begot this deerely beloved sonne of yours, *Ignatius*, which stands at your right hand. And from both of you proceedes a spirit, whom you have sent into the world, who triumphing both with *Mitre* and *Crowne*, governes your Militant Church there.

Machiavelli goes on praising the art of equivocation:

> For my part (ô noble paire of *Emperours*) that I may freely confesse the truth, all which I have done, wheresoever there shall be mention made of the Iesuites, can be reputed but childish; for this honor I hope will not be denied me, that I brought in an *Alphabet*, & provided certaine Elements, & was some kind of schoolmaister in preparing them a way to higher understandings.

Machiavelli has taught the Jesuits the rudiments of their art: he is therefore indignant not to be admitted straightway to the *sanctum sanctorum* of hell. If Paracelsus had some claim to the Jesuits' favour because of his having been 'conveniently practised in the butcheries and mangling of men', so much the more is Machiavelli entitled to that favour:

> For I my selfe went alwaies that way of bloud, and therefore I did ever preferre the sacrifices of the *Gentiles*, and of the *Iewes*, which were performed with effusion of bloud (whereby not only the people, but the Priests also were animated to bold enterprises) before the soft and wanton sacrifices of *Christians*.

This passage is almost a literal rendering of a passage in the notorious second chapter of the Second Book of the *Discorsi*.[75]

> But yet although the entrance into this place [goes on Machiavelli] may be decreed to none, but to Innovators, and to onely such of them as have dealt in *Christian* businesse;

[75] 'I Gentili . . . erano nelle azioni loro più feroci. Il che si può considerare da molte loro constituzioni, cominciandosi dalla magnificenza de' sacrifizii loro alla umiltà dei nostri, dove è qualche pompa più delicata (Donne: *soft*) che magnifica; ma nessuna azione feroce o gagliarda. Quivi . . . vi si aggiungeva l'azione del sacrifizio pieno di sangue e di ferocia . . . il quale aspetto sendo terribile, rendeva gli uomini simili a lui.' An echo of this point of view is to be found in Restif de la Bretonne's *Monsieur Nicolas*: in the dialogue between Pierre (i.e., the author himself) and Mirabeau, this latter says that he has caused the head of a beheaded man stuck on a pike to be brought before a relative of his, *non pas pour augmenter l'horreur des derniers moments de cet infortuné, mais pour mettre de l'énergie dans l'âme molle et vaudevillière des Parisiens par cette atrocité.*

and of them also, to those only which have had the fortune to doe much harme, I cannot see but next to the Iesuites, I must bee invited to enter, since I did not onely teach those wayes, by which, through *perfidiousnesse*, and *dissembling of Religion*, a man might possesse, and usurpe upon the liberty of free *Commonwealths*; but also did arme and furnish the people with my instructions, how when they were under this oppression, they might safeliest conspire, and remove a *tyrant*, or revenge themselves of their *Prince*, and redeem their former losses; so that from both sides, both from *Prince* and *People*, I brought an aboundant harvest, and a noble encrease to this kingdome.

By this time [says Donne] I perceived *Lucifer* to bee much moved with this Oration, and to incline much towards *Machiavel*. For he did acknowledge him to bee a kind of *Patriarke*, of those whom they call *Laymen*.

Machiavelli is, therefore, a forerunner of those *Jésuites de robe courte* who were employed in the most risky missions, first of all in killing the sovereigns who opposed the plans of the Society. Donne is here adopting a theory advanced by Cardinal Pole, and repeated by Albericus Gentilis (*De Legationibus*, Lib. III, C. ix), according to which Machiavelli, under pretence of instructing the princes, was supposed to teach the subjects how to get rid of their tyrants.

And therefore he [Lucifer] thought himselfe bound to reward *Machiavel*, which had awakened this drowsie and implicite *Laytie* to greater, and more bloody undertakings. Besides this, since *Ignatius* could not bee denied the place, whose ambitions and turbulencies *Lucifer* understood very wel, he thought *Machiavel* a fit and necessarie instrument to oppose against him; that so the skales beeing kept even by their factions, hee might governe in peace, and two poysons mingled might do no harme.[76] But hee could not hide this intention from *Ignatius*, more subtil than the *Devill*, and the verier *Lucifer* of the two: Therefore *Igna*-

[76] Gentillet C. 30–31 (Meyer *cit.*, p. 13). Cf. *Sejanus*, III, iii: 'I have heard that aconite,/Being timely taken, hath a healing might/ Against the scorpion's stroke; the proof we'll give:/That, while two poisons wrestle, we may live.'

tius rushed out, threw himselfe downe at *Lucifers* feet, and groveling on the ground adored him.

Ignatius proceeds to expose how much the 'obscure *Florentine*' has transgressed against Lucifer and the pope his image-bearer, and last of all against the Jesuit order:

Was it fit that this fellow, should dare either to deride you or (which is the greater iniury) to teach you? . . . This man, whilst he lived, attributed so much to his own wit, that hee never thought himselfe beholden to your helps, and insinuations; and was so farre from invoking you, or sacrificing to you, that he did not so much as acknowledge your kingdome, nor beleeve that there was any such thing in nature, as you. I must confesse, that hee had the same opinion of God also, and therefore deserves a place here, and a better than any of the *Pagan* or *Gentile* idolaters: for, in every idolatrie, and false worship, there is some Religion, and some perverse simplicitie, which tastes of humilitie; from all which, this man was very free, when in his heart he utterly denyed that there was any God. . . . But to proceed now to the iniuries, which this fellow hath done to the *Bishop* of *Rome*, although very much might be spoken, yet by this alone, his disposition may bee sufficiently discerned, that hee imputes to the *Pope*, vulgar and popular sinnes, farre unworthy of his greatnesse. Weake praising, is a kind of Accusing, and wee detract from a mans honour, if when wee praise him for small things, and would seeme to have said all, we conceale greater.

At this point Donne puts into the mouth of Ignatius a scurrilous attack on the sins of the popes, which covers several pages. Then Ignatius comes back to Machiavelli:

Let us more particularly consider those things, which this man, who pretends to exceed all Aunicent and Moderne *Statesmen,* boasts to have beene done by him. Though truly no man will easily beleeve, that hee hath gone farr in any thing, which did so tire at the beginning, or mid-way, that having seene the *Pope,* and knowne him, yet could never come to the knowledge of the *Divell.* . . . How idle, and how very nothings they are, which he hath shoveld together in his bookes, this makes it manifest, that some of every *Religion,* and of every profession have risen up against him and no man attempted to defend him. . . . This then is the point of which wee accuse *Machivell,* that he carried not his Mine so safely, but that the enemy perceived it still. But wee, who have received the Church to be as a ship, do freely saile in the deep sea. . . . As for that particular, wherein *Machiavel* useth especially to glory; which is, that he brought in the liberty of dissembling, and lying, it hath neither foundation nor colour: For not onely *Plato,* and other fashioners of *Commonwealths,* allowed the libertie of lying, to Magistrates & to Physicians, but we also . . . have found that doctrine [in the Fathers of the Church] . . . yet wee have departed from this doctrine of free lying . . . because we were not the first *Authors* of it. But wee have supplied this losse with another doctrine, lesse suspitious; and yet of as much use to our *Church*; which is *Mentall Reservation,* and *Mixt propositions.* The libertie therefore of lying, is neither new, nor safe as almost all *Machivells* precepts are so stale and obsolete, that our *Serarius* using I must confesse his *Iesuiticall* liberty of wilde anticipation did not doubt to call *Herod,* who lived so long before *Machivell,* a *Machiavellian.*

Loyola concludes his speech of fifty pages by saying that in all times in the Roman Church there have been friars who have far exceeded Machiavelli in his own arts. Crushed by this monumental oration, poor Machiavelli, 'often put forward, and often thrust back', at last vanishes. This truculent fight between the two Southern bugbears vies for perversity of grim humour with Richard Lovelace's account of the fight between the toad and the spider. Among the other innovators who come as claimants after Machiavelli is Pietro Aretino, but his boast of the notorious licentious pictures [77] is minimized by Ignatius's statement that the Jesuits have gone even farther, in expurgating the ancient texts not in order to destroy the obscenities, but rather in order to teach them to their disciples

[77] Illustrations, after paintings by Giulio Romano, of venereal postures. Aretino was responsible for the explanatory lines.

after having experimented 'whether *Tiberius* his *Spintria*, & *Martialis Symplegma*, and others of that kinde, were not rather *Chimeraes*, & speculations of luxuriant wits, then things certain & constant, and such as might bee reduced to an Art and methode in licentiousnes'. Donne is surprised by the rejection of Aretino, since

> hee might have beene fit, either to serve *Ignatius*, as *maister of his pleasures*, or *Lucifer* as his *Crier*: for whatsoever Lucifer durst think, this man durst speake.

At last Lucifer, wishing to get rid of Loyola, who threatens to become too powerful, suggests that he should withdraw with the rest of the Jesuits to the moon, and found a Lunatic Church there: 'without doubt after the Iesuites have been there a litle while, there will soone grow naturally a *Hell* in that world also'. Lucifer's fears were not unfounded, since two centuries later the French poet Béranger (probably deriving from a popular legend) caused the Devil to be poisoned by Loyola during a banquet; after which Loyola asked for, and obtained, his inheritance, that is the rule over Hell.[78]

Also in Middleton's political play, *A Game at Chess*, we find Machiavellism and Jesuitism, this time working in agreement, in the characters of the Black Knight, i.e., the Spanish Ambassador Gondomar, and the Black Bishop's Pawn, i.e., the Jesuit Father John Floyd.[79] The Induction to this play consists in a dialogue between Ignatius Loyola, 'the great Incendiarie of Christendome' (II, ii, 120), and Error. Among other things Ignatius says (ll. 78–79):

> I would doo anie thing to rule alone:
> Tis rare to have the world reignd in by one.

In this play, however, contrary to what we have seen in *Ignatius his Conclave*, the Machiavellian appears to be subtler than the Jesuit. The Black Knight says (I, i, 274 ff.):

> I've bragd lesse,
> But have donne more then all the Conclave on em,

[78] See A. Graf, *Il Diavolo*, 1889, pp. 453–454.
[79] *The Works of Thomas Middleton*, ed. Bullen, vii, pp. 4 and 118; and *A Game at Chess*, ed. R. C. Bald, Cambridge, 1929, pp. 1–18.

Take theire Assistant fathers in all parts,
I, or theire father Generall in to boote.

Then follows the passage about facetious poisoning already referred to. Presently the Black Knight makes an outward show
of deference towards the Black Bishop's Pawn, and says (ll.
299 ff.):

I doo this the more
T'amaze our Adversaries to behold
The reverence wee give these Guitenens,
And to beget a sound opinion
Of Holines in them and Zeale in us,
And also to envite the like Obedience
In other Pusills, by our meeke Example.

The Black Bishop's Pawn tries to commit a rape upon the
White Queen's Pawn, but when this latter accuses him to the
White Queen, the Black Knight produces a pretended alibi in
his defence. He would have the White Queen's Pawn for her
calumny to be condemned 'in a roome fild all with Aretines
pictures' to 'more then the twice twelve labours of [luxurie]'.
One sees that in the minds of the authors of the age, Machiavelli, Loyola, and Aretino were three closely associated figures.
The Black Knight is so much of a hardened politician that
when his Pawn suggests that the sad news he brings may
prick his conscience, he retorts (III, i, 124 ff.):

Mine?
Mischeife must finde a deeper Nayle and a Driver
Beyond the strength of anie Machiavill
The politick kingdomes fatten, to reach mine.

Of him says the White Duke (III, i, 221): 'Ile undertake That
Knight shall teach the devill how to lye.' His soul can 'digest
a Monster without cruditie,/A Sin as weightie as an Ele-
phant/And never wamble for 't' (IV, ii, 12 ff.). On hearing
the White Knight call dissembling a vice, he exclaims (v, iii,
164 ff.):

And call you that a Vice?—
Avoyde all prophanation, I beseech you,—

The onelie prime State-Virtue uppon earth,
The policie of Empires

. . . . . .

It is a Jewell of that pretious Value
Whose worth's not knowen but to the skillfull Lapidarie.

Throughout the play the Machiavellian is represented shelter-
ing the Jesuit and using him as a tool. Both are finally found
out and confounded.

Though a touch of ridicule had been inherent from the first
in the figure of the Elizabethan Machiavellian, since his tricks
were bound to recoil inevitably on his own head, the loath-
someness of his character was calculated to provoke chiefly
horror during the period of his greatest vogue. When the taste
for poignant tragedy died down and romantic plays swayed
the stage, the figure of the Machiavellian was doomed to lose
its more lurid colours, in order to suit the general tuning down
of passions. In an idyllic, sentimental world there was little
room for Machiavelli: the audience could no longer be
affected by his terrors, but became increasingly aware of his
ridiculousness. Ridiculousness only is left when the tamed
bugbear appears for the last time as an independent character
in dramatic literature, as Lord Machavil in Aston Cokaine's
Trappolin suppos'd a Prince (1658).[80]

Though the legend of Machiavelli had been very popular in
general, it had enjoyed the greatest vogue with the dramatists,
first of all because it had suited very well the stock character
of the villain of Senecan extraction. As a matter of fact, it is
very surprising to see how seldom popular literature of broad-
sides and satirical prints made use of it. *The Uncasing of
Machivils Instructions to his Sonne* (1613) and *Machivells
Dogge* (1617) are almost the sole instances we are able to
cite in this section, and, since the latter pamphlet is an evident imitation of the former, our list is practically exhausted
with one single item. In the whole catalogue of satirical prints

[80] M. A. Scott (*Elizabethan Translations from the Italian*,
Boston and New York, 1916, p. 214) believes the comedy to be
an adaptation of an Italian tragi-comedy in prose and verse entitled *Trappolino creduto principe*, as the Prologue explains. The
theme of the 'supposed prince' was popular in the *commedia
dell'arte* (e.g., *Arlecchino creduto principe*).

of political and personal import relating to this period in the British Museum, the only case I have come across of allusion to Machiavelli is represented by Thomas Scott's *Vox Populi*.[81] It is natural, then, that with the closing of the theatres the Machiavellian bugbear should have faded away. But the word remained in the vocabulary and was later on freely employed in the Restoration comedy as a jocular taunt: to call a subtle woman 'a Machiavel' became quite a fad, after the example of Ben Jonson (*The Case is Altered*, IV, iv).[82] As a scarecrow the Machiavellian had a short-lived revival with that belated Elizabethan, Nathaniel Lee. The Jesuit practically eclipsed the Machiavellian in the popular mind. The Politician of the times of James II was eminently a Jesuited Politician.[83]

It was Romanticism which, bringing about a taste for horrors very akin to that of the Elizabethans, restored to life the old stock characters of the tyrant, the villain, and the traitor.[84] The German Romantics were well versed in Shakespearian drama, and possibly through it they derived what Machiavellism is inherent in the characters of their fictions. Lessing was the first to revive in Germany that exotic taste for Italian

[81] *The Second Part of Vox Populi, or Gondomar appearing in the likeness of Matchiavell in a Spanish Parliament, wherein are discovered his treacherous and subtile Practises To the ruine as well of England, as the Netherlandes. Faithfully Translated out of the Spanish Coppie by a well-willer to England and Holland* (1620). To this tract, written by Thomas Scott, a Scotch Minister at Utrecht, Middleton was indebted for his *Game at Chess*.

[82] Thus for instance Thomas Andrew wrote in 1604 *The Unmasking of a feminine Machiavell* (see Meyer, *cit.*, p. 102), and Abraham Cowley, in one of his anacreontics (*The Account*) called a waiting-maid acting as a go-between, a *Matchavil*.

[83] But the figure of the legendary Machiavelli, as it had become established in the Elizabethan period, continued to reappear every now and then. Thus in *Tom Jones* (1749) we read (Book I, ch. xiii): 'One of the maxims which the devil, in a late visit upon earth, left to his disciples, is, when once you are got up, to kick the stool from under you. In plain English, when you have made your fortune by the good offices of a friend, you are advised to discard him as soon as you can.' And in ch. ii of Book VI Squire Western is represented as a perfect politician, 'though perhaps he had never read Machiavel': by 'politic' Fielding meant 'cunning', as appears from the following chapter.

[84] See for instance the character of Schedoni in Mrs Radcliffe's *Italian* (1797).

passions and horrors which Walpole's *Castle of Otranto* had shortly before revived in England. The Italian background of *Emilia Galotti* is the same traditional background of the Elizabethans. Together with the poniards and the banditti—inevitable paraphernalia—reappear the characters of the despotic prince and of the Machiavellian knave, this latter in the person of the wicked courtier Marinelli.[85] The villainous Franz Moor in Schiller's *Räuber* is admittedly a compound of Iago, Richard III, and Edmund (in *King Lear*); Präsident von Walter in *Kabale und Liebe* is Franz Moor become a prime minister of the Machiavellian type, while his secretary, Wurm, is a still fuller incarnation of the Machiavellian politician. Tieck's Andrea Cosimo, in the epistolary novel *William Lovell,* is a Machiavellian brought up to date with a study of eighteenth-century philosophers, chiefly Condillac. He is a cold, cynical dissector of souls, who takes a perverse delight in studying the rare ways in which a soul works on another. He has devised a sort of jocoserious lottery of souls for his own gratification: this gamble is his pastime.[86] This sinister figure of romantic villain was brought to perfection by Goethe in his Mephistopheles, whose name stands in our present vocabulary for many of those characteristics the Elizabethans comprehended under the description 'Machiavellian'. How much of Mephistopheles' villainy may be traced to the influence of the Machiavellian legend is difficult to say. But Machiavellism was obviously at the back of Goethe's mind in portraying that devil, as it was in sketching that miniature Mephistopheles, Clavigo's worldly-wise councillor Carlos.[87]

[85] This traditional pair continues as late as in Wilde's *Duchess of Padua.* In T. De Quincey's sensational novel, *Klosterheim* (1832), the Landgraf's confidant is Adorni, 'a subtle Italian . . . who covered a temperament of terrific violence with a mask of Venetian dissimulation and the most icy reserve' (*Collected Writings,* ed. D. Masson, xii, 49; as for De Quincey's detestation of Machiavelli see *id.,* viii, 143).

[86] See specially *William Lovell,* Book vi, Letter vii.

[87] Clavigo's story shows some similarities with the Faust-Gretchen episode; with the difference that the girl's brother here kills the faithless lover (Beaumarchais is the counterpart of Valentin). Carlos's role corresponds to Mephistopheles'. His arguments to persuade Clavigo to jilt Marie have a true Machiavellian ring. Cf. chiefly iv, i.

Shakespeare's Italy

IT has been remarked that the audience of an Elizabethan theatre must not have been very different from a modern cinema audience: they cared chiefly for the spectacular and the sensational. The influence of Senecan tragedy is responsible for the way in which the Elizabethan taste for thrillers developed, but assimilation takes place only when there exists an affinity: Seneca supplied the Elizabethan dramatists with a justification for horrors for which there was certainly a spontaneous taste. Plays like the *Yorkshire Tragedy* and *Arden of Feversham*, though posterior to the *Spanish Tragedy*, which is clearly indebted to Seneca, cannot be traced to a foreign or classical influence, but are the direct outcome of a native interest in the police-court horrors of the time. Such interest is perhaps nowhere better witnessed than in Nashe's *Unfortunate Traveller*, with its sensationalism continually over-reaching itself in the display of horrors piled upon horrors, and its iterated showman's cries: 'Prepare your eares and your teares, for neuer tyll thys thrust I ani tragecall matter vpon you.'

The English translators of Seneca's *Tenne Tragedies* were enabled to enlarge on Seneca's horrors by an inborn taste for loathsome details; but had not the foremost of the Italian imitators of Seneca, Giraldi Cinthio, already interpreted as *orrore* the φόβος Aristotle required for tragedy, had he not given to the Thyestean banquet that widespread popularity

Mephistopheles is primarily a courtier, and shows at his best at the Kaiser's court, when he advocates the famous device for restoring the finances of the state. On hearing his words about the inborn spiritual power of the gifted man—corresponding to Machiavelli's *virtù*—the Chancellor accuses him of atheism. When Faust turns conqueror, Mephistopheles turns pirate and repeats the famous maxim of Machiavellism: 'If one has might, one has right: one asks about *what*, and not about *how*.' That is, the end justifies the means. But apart from his treacherous help in killing Valentin, and from his scaring to death Philemon and Baucis, Goethe's Mephistopheles does not display a tenth of the ferocious perfidy of the Elizabethan villains. The study of the *Encyclopédistes*—who, by the way, knew their Machiavelli—has refined him thoroughly. He is the least harmful among the demons, *der Schalk*, the rogue, endowed with something of the attractive humour of Falstaff. In Mephistopheles nothing is left of the beast-like figure of the Devil, with pointed horns, flaming eyes, and protruding tusks: of the mediaeval monster only the gentle satyr's cloven foot is kept. His malign power is all concentrated in the mind, and the mind has been trained at the school of his ancient disciple become, in his turn, his master, the legendary Machiavelli.[88]

[88] Another strange offshoot of the Machiavelli legend in the nineteenth century is found in the Machiavellian interpretation of the Gioconda smile: see my *Romantic Agony*, Oxford University Press, 1951 (2nd ed.), specially p. 327: the *sourire dérobé et noir de Joconde* with which Giulia Belcredi, in E. Bourges's *Crépuscule des dieux* (1884), *masquait ses plus terribles résolutions*. Nowadays this enigmatical smile has been caricatured, by E. M. Forster in *A Room with a View* (1903) ('a Machiavellian smile'), by A. Huxley in *The Gioconda Smile* (*Mortal Coils*, 1922), by L. Durrell in *Justine* (1957) (pp. 125–26: 'For my part the famous smile has always seemed to me to be the smile of a woman who has just dined off her husband').

we find recorded not only in the very plays, but also in such descriptions of their effect on the audience as Cinthio's in his *Discorso intorno al comporre delle comedie e delle tragedie?* The effects Senecan tragedy was expected to produce in the audience were, according to Cinthio, astonishment and 'a thrill which puts the spectator beside himself' (*un certo raccapriccio che fa uscire chi l'ha veduto come di sé*). What then about Vernon Lee's theory (in her somehow charmingly antiquated essay in *Euphorion*) that the Renaissance Italians 'rarely or never paint horror or death or abomination', that 'the whole tragic meaning was unknown to the light and cheerful contemporaries of Ariosto'; do we not know now that the taste for horrors was first indulged in by the Italian Senecans? Do we not know from the Italian chronicles utilised by Stendhal how fond the crowds were of capital executions? The Italian dramatists, however, chose to dramatise the story of some unfortunate couple of Oriental lovers, rather than their own pathetic, but too familiar stories in which the English found that exotic thrill which the domestic police-court horrors lacked. The favourite background of the Elizabethan dramatists became, as we have seen,[1] 'the darkened Italian palace, with its wrought-iron bars preventing escape; its embroidered carpets muffling the footsteps; its hidden, suddenly yawning trap-doors; its arras-hangings concealing masked ruffians; its garlands of poisoned flowers.' Italy made very good copy, being considered the academy of manslaughter, the sporting place of murder, the apothecary shop of all nations.

The Elizabethan dramatist who made the most of the lurid exotic appeal of Italy is admittedly Webster. He exploits the two sides of the Italian appeal: the splendour of its princely courts, and the practice of poisoning. The taste for processions, jousts, investitures, in a word, gorgeous display of every description, was inborn in the crowds of the Renaissance: see how many shows Webster contrives to cram into his Italian plays! Webster is the supreme exponent of a school of Italianate horrors which begins with Kyd's *Spanish Tragedy* and Marlowe's *Jew of Malta*, and blossoms in such produc-

[1] See above, p. 117, in the essay on 'Machiavelli and the Elizabethans'.

tions as Massinger's *Unnatural Combat* (which is about the famous Cenci trial), Marston's *Antonio and Mellida* and *Insatiate Countess,* Tourneur's *Revenger's Tragedy* and *Atheist's Tragedy,* Middleton's *Women beware Women* and *The Changeling.*

It is a matter of no little surprise, then, when we turn to Shakespeare, to see how his Italian plays are comparatively free from the usual horrors and thrills. Horrible murders and treasons occur indeed on the Shakespearian stage but, oddly enough, not as a rule in the plays whose action takes place in Italy. Was it because Shakespeare disdained the cheap appeal of Italian criminality? Or because the broadness of his vision made him keep in the background the abject and horrible side of human nature, and stress the pure and noble one? Or because the acquaintance he had with Italian things enabled him to take a more sober view of Italian society than the current one circulated by religious or conservative fanatics and cherished by the thriller-seeking crowd?

From one among the first of his plays, *The Two Gentlemen of Verona,* to the one which is his last finished work, *The Tempest,* Shakespeare frequently brought Italian characters on the stage, and yet the majority of them is exempt from those moral monstrosities over which other dramatists used to gloat. Rather, Shakespeare's Italy is so near to that idyllic Italy which we can picture from Ariosto's and Castiglione's works that some have ventured to suggested that Shakespeare travelled there: how could he otherwise have been able to draw such a true-to-life image, when everybody round him in England was spell-bound by the myth of Italian wickedness? Every now and then, in Shakespearian criticism, we come across such statements as: 'We marvel at his intimate description of Italian life, explicable apparently only on the supposition that he was an eye-witness of the scenes he describes' (Boecker). Some have found 'a pure Paduan atmosphere' hanging about *The Taming of the Shrew* (Ch. Knight), others, that the first act of *Othello* is thoroughly Venetian in spirit. One critic observes that, as in *The Merchant of Venice* Portia is the type of the brilliant, playful, sprightly Venetian lady, so in *Othello* Desdemona personifies the gentle, loving, submissive, patient type so dear to the Italians; the

same critic (Horatio F. Brown) declares Shylock to be more
Venetian, in many respects, than Jewish. Georg Brandes
believed Shakespeáre's knowledge of Italy to have been
'closer than could have been gained from oral descriptions and
from books'. William Bliss, in his playful 'Counterblast to
Commentators', *The Real Shakespeare* (1947), actually makes
him travel round the world with Drake, and, for the second
period in which we have no record of his whereabouts (from
1586 to 1592), maintains as a paradox that he was shipwrecked on the Illyrian coast, and went to Venice, where
he met the Earl of Southampton who succoured him and remained his patron afterwards. Bliss wanted to demonstrate for
fun that anything can be plausibly argued about Shakespeare;
but there is not the slightest suggestion of leg-pulling in G.
Lambin's articles *Sur la trace d'un Shakespeare inconnu* which
appears in *Les Langues modernes* in 1951–52. For Lambin
there is no doubt that the author of the plays which go under
the name of Shakespeare visited Italy, particularly Florence
and Milan. The 'Saint Jaques le Grand' to which Helena is
supposed to betake herself on a pilgrimage in *All's Well* would
not be the well-known sanctuary in Spain but San Giacomo
d'Altopascio not far from Florence, and the palmers' hostel
'at the S. Francis here beside the port' (III, v, 37) would stand
for the oratory of San Francesco dei Vanchetoni in the neigh-
bourhood of Porta al Prato in Florence. This 'unknown Shakespeare', according to Lambin, writes passages of *All's Well*
in the style of the French pasquils about the League, with
whose workings he is shown to be intimately acquainted,[2]

[2] M Lambin displays a perverse ingenuity in trying to identify
the names of the captains given by Parolles in *All's Well*, IV,
iii, 165 ff., with historical supporters of the French League: thus
Gratii is a name which evokes so well 'les faveurs et les com-
plaisances' that it must needs be that of a minion of Henry III;
and Bentii, that is *le tordu*, bent, is surely Charles Emmanuel duke
of Savoy; the more obvious explanation, that those two names are
peculiar spellings of the Florentine family names Grazzi, Benci,
does not cross his mind. But his solving the riddle of Chitopher is
a good sample of his method: Henri, comte de Bouchage, presented himself to Henri III disguised as Jesus Christ: 'vêtu de la
"tunique" du Seigneur, celle que vont se partager les soldats:
la "chitôn" du texte grec de l'Évangile (Saint Jean xix, 23)': he
wore a chiton, so he is Chitopher. Guiltian would be a pun on

and *The Tempest* as a panegyric for Maria de' Medici. For
Maria de' Medici, M. Lambin is convinced, is Miranda, and
her father Prospero is Francis I Grand Duke of Tuscany;
Sycorax is Bianca Cappello, and Caliban, Francesco's spurious
son by her, Antonio. The key to this hidden meaning of *The
Tempest* has been supplied to Lambin by an article on the
Grand Duke he has found in the *Dictionnaire général de
biographie et d'histoire* by Ch. Dezorry and Th. Bachelet, in
which he has read about Francesco's chemical laboratory,
the *studiolo* in Palazzo Vecchio. He even goes as far as to suggest that Ariel and the famous line 'those are pearls that were
his eyes' were suggested by the figures of *amoretti* represented in that study as working at precious substances such
as coral, crystal, pearls. . . . But there is no knowing how
far Lambin is prepared to go, assisted by second-hand historical
information, which he naïvely twists to prove his assumptions.[3]

Guisian: 'le rapprochement entre "Guise" et "guilt" (crime)
[allusion to the St Bartholomew Massacre] n'est pas accidentel'. M.
Lambin's ingenuity reminds one of Raymond Roussel's *Comment
j'ai écrit certains de mes livres*.

[3] After reading Mary G. Steegmann's book on *Bianca Cappello*
(1913), 'ouvrage de vulgarisation auquel nous avons emprunté
plusieurs renseignements', Lambin draws a lurid picture of the
'morts brutales' which had 'favorisé Bianca': among them the
wife of Francesco, Joan of Habsburg, 'se rompant le col à point
voulu'. If, instead of having recourse to an 'ouvrage de vulgarisation' like Mary Steegmann's, Lambin had consulted Gaetano
Pieraccini's *La stirpe de' Medici di Cafaggiolo* (Florence, 1947,
second edition), he would have found that the Grand Duchess
died in child-birth: 'si trovò il putto fuora della matrice et il
collo della matrice stracciato' (contemporary report: the child
had broken the 'neck' of the womb). He would also have found
that, contrary to the legend which he accepts, Francesco and
Bianca were not poisoned by Francesco's brother, the cardinal
Ferdinando, but died of malarial fever. He would have found also
that Francesco, far from offering a likely model for Prospero, was
a bad prince, inclined to lechery, punctilious over petty matters
of etiquette, weak-willed and incontinent in eating and drinking:
'si è dilettato poco della virtù, non dimostra troppo bell'ingegno'
(contemporary Venetian report). Lambin seems to be aware that
The Tempest 'est avant tout une œuvre théâtrale et une magnifique
fantaisie, ne l'oublions pas. Ce n'est pas une monographie his-
torique'. But whatever part imagination plays in the actual drama,
it is nothing in comparison to the boldness of Lambin's own

There is, in fact, nothing which cannot be manipulated by Lambin into a proof: even the hackneyed Petrarchan metaphor of the *navicella* (little ship) he finds in the madrigals of Francesco (first published 1894) would have suggested to the author of *The Tempest* the episode of Prospero being abandoned in a 'rotten carcass of a boat' adrift on the sea. His is a series of arbitrary equations and far-fetched associations such as we are accustomed to find in the writings of the followers of Freud (for instance in Marie Bonaparte's study of Poe) or in Joyce. His 'discoveries' would point in the direction of M. A. Lefranc's *Découverte de Shakespeare* (Paris, 1945 and 1950): Lambin's 'unknown Shakespeare' would have utilised personal recollections of his travels in Italy and France and his contacts with people of importance in those countries: he might well be William Stanley, Sixth Earl of Derby. . . . But is this new proliferation of the old Baconian heresy in any way warranted by whatever evidence of actual acquaintance of topography of Italian cities we can safely sift from Lambin's and others' straining of the text of the plays? Madame Longworth de Chambrun, about whose hypothesis I shall have to speak further on, writes: 'What strikes us above all in Shakespeare's work, is to see how the dramatist has succeeded in giving us a true impression of Italian culture whereas, all things considered, one finds in him very little real knowledge. Shakespeare, though having a very slight acquaintance with the Italian language, gives to the spectator or the reader a very strong illusion of local colour'. On the same theme F. E. Schelling warns: 'Much nonsense has been written about Shakespeare's power of local colouring. This power he undoubtedly possesses in a high degree, but it comes from the suggestions of his sources and only the unimaginative commentator can think it needful to send him to Italy for the colouring of *The Merchant of Venice* and *Othello*, or to

---

flights. It was daring enough of Shakespeare to write about 'the cloud-capped towers, the gorgeous palaces, the solemn temples, etc.', but more daring still of M. Lambin to see there an allusion to the view of Florence which Francesco would have enjoyed from his villas.

Denmark for his *Hamlet*. Shakespeare's personages are seldom foreigners.'

Before coming to the actual question about the way in which Shakespeare may have got acquainted with Italian things, let us make a rapid survey of his Italian plays.

The scenes of *The Two Gentlemen of Verona* are Verona and Milan. The names of the chief characters are more or less Italianate, but those of the two servants, Speed and Launce, are English. Several inconsistencies have been noticed. In Act I, Scene iii, Valentine is said to attend the Emperor in his royal court; but later on we find that the court is actually a duke's court. In Act II, Scene v, which is supposed to take place in Milan, Speed is heard welcoming Launce 'to Padua'. Elsewhere we find Verona where we would expect Milan. These local inaccuracies have led critics to think that Shakespeare had written the whole of the play before he had settled where the scene was to be laid. At any rate the plot structure of *The Two Gentlemen* is modelled on that of a typical Italian *commedia dell'arte*,[4] so that Shakespeare either used as a source a thoroughly Italianate play, such as might have been the lost *Felix and Philiomena*, or he developed with devices derived from the Italian comedy the slender thread of a story such as that in Montemayor's *Diana*, which is usually given as his source.[5] The influence of the *commedia dell'arte* is already evident in Shakespeare's first comedy, *Love's Labour's Lost*, where the characters of Armado and Holofernes respectively correspond to the Spanish Captain and the Pedant of the Italian comedy. *Lazzi* and other proceedings familiar to the *commedia dell'arte* are so frequent in Shakespeare that one critic[6] has jumped to the conclusion that most of the prose of the plays must be due to the collaboration of the actors themselves.

[4] Cf. Valentina Capocci, *Genio e mestiere, Shakespeare e la commedia dell'arte,* Bari, Laterza, 1950, pp. 56 ff.

[5] O. J. Campbell, ' "Love's Labour's Lost" re-studied', and ' "The Two Gentlemen of Verona" and Italian Comedy', in *Studies in Shakespeare, Milton and Donne* by Members of the English Department of the University of Michigan, New York, 1925. See also René Pruvost, ' "The Two Gentl. of Verona", "Twelfth N." et "gl 'ingannati" ', in *Etudes Anglaises*, Jan.-Mar. 1960.

[6] Valentina Capocci, *op. cit.*, chiefly p. 113.

Does Shakespeare try to make his Italians speak like Italians? When in *The Two Gentlemen* (i, iii, 6 ff.) we hear Panthino declaring:

> other men, of slender reputation,
> Put forth their sons to seek preferment out:
> Some to the wars, to try their fortune there;
> Some to discover islands far away;

we are led by this last line to think rather of the English oversea adventurers than of the citizens of an inland town like Verona. But was Verona an inland town for Shakespeare? It is perhaps well to settle at once the curious problem of Shakespeare's Italian geography.

In *The Two Gentlemen* Valentine's father 'at the road/ expects him coming there to see him shipped' to Milan. In Act ii, Scene iii Panthino says to Launce: 'Away, ass! you'll lose the tide, if you tarry any longer', to which Launce retorts: 'Lose the tide. . . . Why, man, if the river were dry, I am able to fill it with my tears'. Verona, then, is imagined on a river with tides that ebb and flow, connected to Milan by a waterway. In *The Tempest* (i, i, 144 ff.) Prospero tells how he was put aboard a bark at the gates of Milan, with his little daughter,

> In few, they hurried us aboard a bark,
> Bore us some leagues to sea, where they prepared
> A rotten carcass of a boat, not rigg'd,
> Nor tackle, sail, nor mast. . . .
> . . . there they hoist us,
> To cry to the sea that roar'd to us. . . .

Milan, therefore, is imagined on a waterway communicating with the sea. Again, in *The Taming of the Shrew* (i, i, 42), where the scene is Padua, we hear Lucio saying: 'If, Biondello, thou wert come ashore', and later on: 'Since I have come ashore'. Gremio, a citizen of Padua, boasts (ii, i, 376) of being the owner of a large merchant vessel, an argosy. Further on (iv, ii, 81) we hear of Mantuan ships which are stayed at Venice, because of a quarrel between the two towns. Finally, we are told of a sail-maker in Bergamo, another inland town.

Sir Edward Sullivan, in an article published in *The Nineteenth Century* (August 1908) was at great pains to show that these seeming inaccuracies, far from revealing Shakespeare's ignorance of Italian geography, show an intimate acquaintance with it, since it can be proved by quotations of Italian writers of, and prior to, the seventeenth century, and with the aid of a map of Lombardy of the time, that the high road from Milan to Venice was by water, and a journey from Verona to Milan could be performed by water. G. Lambin has recently [7] added some further considerations, particularly an attempt to interpret the 'tide' as a sudden and transient flood in a torrential river, since, even supposing that Verona could be reached by the far from conspicuous tide of the Adriatic Sea, it would have been dangerous for a ship to try to descend a river against the tide.[8] The navigation of the two gentlemen and their servants is not, therefore, concludes Lambin, 'an ignorant invention of the playwright. It exactly corresponds to what was taking place in his time. A boat was the only comfortable conveyance from Verona to Milan. But one must have made use of it oneself to be so well informed.' As for the other difficulty caused by the passage of *The Tempest* in which Milan is imagined near the sea, Lambin maintains that it is a deliberate absurdity (*une absurdité voulue*), for really, according to Lambin's interpretation of that drama to which we have already referred, Milan stands for Florence, 'from which the access to the sea is of the easiest' (*l'accès à la mer est des plus aisés*), at least so it seems to M. Lambin.

Let us admit for a moment that Sir Edward Sullivan's and Lambin's demonstration of the possibility, nay, the advisability, of travelling from Verona to Milan by water is quite convincing. So far as Shakespeare is concerned, it seems wide of the mark. There are other allusions in these plays which

---

[7] *Les Langues modernes*, 1952, p. 245 ff., 'Shakespeare à Milan'.
[8] Lambin quotes a passage from *Eastward Ho!* where Sir Petronell (III, iii, 138 ff.) is warned against embarking 'against the tyde' in the Thames. However, Sir Petronell wanted to reach Blackwall, where his ship lay, with a small boat, and a storm was expected, so the warning was justified; on the other hand the Thames could be navigated by bigger ships only during the tide.

bear on the matter of local colour, but, while some of those allusions point to Italy, most of them point to England, specifically to London.

In *The Two Gentlemen* we hear of the custom of begging for 'soul-cakes' on Hallowmas (II, i, 24–25), of the pageants held at Whitsuntide (IV, iv, 163): the former allusion points to a Staffordshire custom, the latter to the Chester plays. Speed, in the same scene in which he welcomes Launce to Padua, where he ought to have said Milan, says: 'I'll to the alehouse with you presently', and Launce alludes to the custom of going 'to the ale'—a rustic festival during which ale was brewed, sold, and drunk. Now it might perhaps be shown by some painstaking antiquarian that ale was occasionally brewed in Padua even in the Renaissance (as beer is brewed to-day), but surely if Shakespeare had ever thought of Italian local colour he would have spoken of wine, and not of ale. In *The Taming of the Shrew* we hear several beginnings of English ballads sung by Italian characters, we are told of an inn in Genoa called the 'Pegasus', which was one of the popular signs of London, and of a sleeve cut like an apple-tart, which is a typical English sweet. In a similar way in *Twelfth Night* the best hotel in the Illyrian town is said to be the 'Elephant', which was the name of an inn near the Globe Theatre. In *The Merchant of Venice*, Gobbo says to Launcelot: 'Thou hast got more hair on thy chin than Dobbin my fill-horse has on his tail.' Those who maintain that *The Merchant of Venice* shows a strong Venetian local colour will not find it easy to reconcile with the town of the canals and gondolas the fact that Gobbo possesses a horse, and a horse which has such an English name as Dobbin. Perhaps an emulator of Sir Edward Sullivan and Lambin will come to tell us that horses could exist somehow in a town so peculiarly unfit for them (actual proofs are not lacking until the late sixteenth century), and that the extremely intricate system of Venetian narrow lanes allowed a horse to journey from one end of the town to the other. But the obvious explanation is that, although Shakespeare speaks of gondolas and the Rialto and the 'tranect' or *traghetto*, when he mentions the fill-horse Dobbin he is thinking of England and of his characters as English characters. And so when he speaks of alehouses and of festivals and ballads peculiar, not to Italy, but to England. Therefore the only reasonable conclusion we can draw about Shakespeare's conception of the town in which the play takes place as of a town on a river with a tide, connected with the sea, is that he was thinking of London, and using Milan and Verona as mere labels. This is after all what we should expect from a artist of Shakespeare's time, when, for instance, painters would represent the Adoration of the Magi as taking place in a familiar landscape, with figures partly dressed as Orientals, partly as contemporary Europeans. Something approaching a careful study of a historical background can be found only in Ben Jonson.

As for the characters of Shakespeare's Italian plays, none of them is so self-conscious about his supposed Italian characteristics as, for instance, Webster's Italians are in *The Devil's Law-Case*, where we come across utterances like these:

> I have not tane the way,
> Like an Italian, to cut your throat
> By practise—
>
> (II, i, 269)

and:

> Me thinks, being an Italian, I trust you
> To come somewhat too neere me—
> (*ibid.*, 325)

or such a painstaking explanation of the use of the stiletto as:

> Come forth then,
> My desperate Steeletto, that may be worne
> In a womans haire, and nere discover'd,
> And either would be taken for a Bodkin,
> Or a curling yron at most; why tis an engine,
> That's onely fit to put in execution
> Barmotho Pigs—
>
> (III, ii, 94 ff.)

words which sound like a commentary intended for the use of the English spectators.

However, the second of Shakespeare's Italian dramas,

Romeo and Juliet, displays a much stronger local colour than *The Two Gentlemen of Verona.* Romeo's love expresses itself in the metaphors of the school of Serafino Aquilano, that school of sonneteering which anticipated the *concetti* of the seventeenth century. In Romeo's speeches, much more than in Shakespeare's *Sonnets,* we find the influence of the conventional tropes of the flamboyant sonneteers. Such is for instance the passage (i, i, 137 ff.):

> Many a morning hath he there been seen,
> With tears augmenting the fresh morning's dew,
> Adding to clouds more clouds with his deep sighs.

In a sonnet attributed to Serafino, the poet boasts that his tears are able to supply Neptune with new seas, in case he were deprived of his oceans, while his sighs could compensate Aeolus for the loss of his winds. In the third Act Capulet rebukes Juliet for crying:

> How now! a conduit, girl? what, still in tears?
> Evermore showering? In one little body
> Thou counterfeit'st a bark, a sea, a wind;
> For still thy eyes, which I may call the sea,
> Do ebb and flow with tears; the bark thy body is,
> Sailing in this salt flood; the winds, thy sighs,
> Who, raging with thy tears, and they with them,
> Without a sudden calm, will overset
> Thy tempest-tossed body.
>
> (III, v, 130-138)

Here Capulet is rehearsing a very hackneyed Alexandrian *concetto,*[9] found in a Latin poem of Hercules Strozza (*Unda hic sunt Lachrimae . . .*), in an Italian sonnet attributed to Serafino, and in one of the poems (the 85th) of Watson's *Passionate Century of Love,* where it runs thus:

> Error was maine saile, each wave a Teare;
> The master, Love him selfe; deep sighes were winde, *etc.*

[9] See M. Praz, *Studies in Seventeenth-Century Imagery,* i, (1939), p. 102.

Another well-known *concetto* of the flamboyant school is
heard, improved, from Juliet's mouth (III, ii, 21 ff):

> Give me my Romeo; and, when he shall die,
> Take him and cut him out in little stars,
> And he will make the face of heaven so fine
> That all the world will be in love with night
> And pay no worship to the garish sun.

Romeo's famous passionate address in Capulet's orchard
(II, ii) consists of a string of traditional *concetti*. First: the
window is the east and Juliet the sun. Second: Juliet is like
the sun and outshines the moon. Third: her eyes are two stars;
if Juliet's eyes changed place with the stars

> The brightness of her cheek would shame those stars. . . .
> . . . her eyes in heaven
> Would through the airy region stream so bright
> That birds would sing and think it were not night. (19–22)

Fourth: Romeo wishes to be a glove upon Juliet's hand, that
he might touch her cheek. Further on Romeo wishes to be
Juliet's bird.

For each of these *concetti* parallels and analogues could be
quoted in the Petrarchan sonneteers of the flamboyant school.
And the interesting question arises whether Shakespeare deliberately aimed at portraying a passionate Italian lover on
the lines suggested by the sonneteering literature. Such an
aim seems almost to be implied in Mercutio's sneering remark:
'Now is he for the numbers that Petrarch flowed in: Laura
to his lady was but a kitchen-wench.'

In fact Shakespeare succeeds so well in imitating the language of the Italian Petrarchists that in two passages his similes coincide with those used by Romeo's counterpart, Latino,
in a tragedy by Luigi Groto, the *Adriana* (published in 1578)
which is also inspired by the story of Juliet and Romeo.
Latino, also, waiting in the garden for his beloved to appear
at the gate, says:

> . . . e par ch'io senta aprir la porta,
> La qual meglio chiamar posso oriente:
> Ecco spunta il mio sol, cinto di nubi

A mezzanotte! mira come gli astri
Dan loco al lume suo smarriti in vista.[10]

And Adriana's definition of love is similar to that of Romeo.
Romeo says:

Why then, O brawling love! O loving hate!
O any thing, of nothing first create!
O heavy lightness! serious vanity!
Mis-shapen chaos of well-seeming forms!
Feather of lead, bright smoke, cold fire, sick health!
Still-waking sleep, that is not what it is!
This love feel I, that feel no love in this.

(I, i, 182–188)

Groto's Adriana had vented a similar litany of Petrarchan
oxymora:

Fu il mio male un piacer senza allegrezza. . . .
Un ben supremo fonte d'ogni male,
Un male estremo d'ogni ben radice. . . .
Un velen grato ch'io bevvi pegli occhi. . . .
Una febbre che il gelo e il caldo mesce,
Un fèl più dolce assai che mèle o manna. . . .
Un giogo insopportabile e leggero,
Una pena felice, un dolor caro,
Una morte immortal piena di vita,
Un inferno che sembra un paradiso.[11]

The resemblance between the passages just quoted, and the
mention of the nightingale in the parting scene between the
lovers in both plays, led some critics to conclude that Shakespeare knew Groto's tragedy, though the two plays are as
different as they could be in the treatment of the story and in

---

[10] 'I seem to hear open the gate, which I may better call the
east: there my sun rises, girt with clouds at midnight! look how
the stars, dismayed, make room for its light.'

[11] 'My evil was a pleasure without mirth . . . a supreme good,
source of every evil, an extreme evil, root of every good . . . a
delightful poison I drank through my eyes . . . a fever mixing
iciness and heat, a gall far sweeter than honey or manna . . . an
unbearable and light yoke, a happy pain, a dear sorrow, an immortal death full of life, a heaven-seeming hell.'

the study of the characters. I am inclined to believe that the resemblances, which bear on commonplaces of the Petrarchan school, are due to a coincidence; and that they prove only that Shakespeare succeeded so well in depicting an Italian lover that the language he puts into his mouth may occasionally appear derived from that extremely artificial poet of the flamboyant school, Luigi Groto. If this is local colouring, and of the most effective, on the other hand when Mercutio inveighs (II, iv) against the ridiculous fashion-mongers, who use Italian fencing terms and French expressions and dresses, he is no more an Italian than the character of *The Merchant of Venice* who speaks of his horse Dobbin is 'genuinely' a Venetian; Mercutio is there a Londoner.

The local colour of *The Merchant of Venice* has been declared well-nigh astonishing. Accurate sailors' expressions are put into the mouths of Salanio and Salerio, mention is made of the 'tranect' or *traghetto* which connects Venice to the mainland, and the correct distance that Portia and Nerissa would have to travel from Belmont, i.e., Montebello, to Padua.* Portia has sunny locks, she is, therefore, the true Venetian type with red-gold hair made famous by Titian. To complete Shakespeare's Venetian canvas we have also a Prince of Morocco and his train, just as in the feasts and pageants painted by the Venetian painters there is always some turbaned Oriental or some African wearing 'the shadow'd livery of the burnish'd sun'. Against the considerable amount of accurate information (Shakespeare knows about 'the liberty of strangers' which formed one of the points of the Venetian constitution; and, in *Othello* (I, i, 183), mentions the 'special officers of night', i.e., the *signori di notte*), we may record as mere slips Gobbo's mention of his horse Dobbin, and Launcelot's objection to the conversion of the Jews: 'If we grow all to be pork-eaters, we shall not shortly have a rasher on the coals for money', which alludes to that peculiarly English dish, a fried slice of bacon. However, if Launcelot blunders apropos of food, Gobbo seems to be quite aware of the

* Belmonte is, however, already in the source, the tale in *Il Pecorone*, without a proper location, and there are several places named Montebello, so that the impression of a precise place-reference is possibly deceptive.

Venetian custom when he brings a dish of pigeons for his son's master. As for the characters themselves, one cannot say that they are more Venetian than anything else. They seem to fit the setting so well because they are lifelike in the broadest sense of the word; their type is universal, whereas the Italian characters of the picture-palace school of Elizabethan drama are generally caricatures of the seamy side of Italian life. But what about that sinister Italian knave, Iago?

As we have said,[12] Iago, an accomplished Machiavellian demon in Cinthio, would become much more human and excusable in Shakespeare if we could believe that he is actually incensed by the public report that Othello has cuckolded him: if so, Iago's story, as told by Shakespeare, would find parallels in many cases of retaliation instanced by Italian *novelle*. Needless to say, the character of Iago does not imply any acquaintance with Machiavelli's writings. What Machiavellism is displayed in Shakespeare's dramas seems either to be already present in the historical sources (as in the case of *Richard III*), or to be derived from the current popular legend.

In the last of his great plays, *The Tempest*, Shakespeare deals with a theme of Italian political intrigue. But how different his treatment is from the usual practice of the Elizabethans! Instead of the ordinary Elizabethan chain of murder, revenge, and wholesale butchery against the background of the darkened Italian palace, we seem to breathe the purified atmosphere after a sea-storm; the grace of heaven with its dews has touched the shores of the island secluded from the world, and that sweet aspersion fallen from heaven consecrates into a kind of holy mystery the human story displayed before our eyes. *The Tempest* could hardly be called a conventional study in Italian criminality; still there can be little doubt about the Italian inspiration of the play, which has been convincingly traced by Ferdinando Neri to a group of scenarios of the *commedia dell'arte*. Even the clowns, who are as a rule portrayed as Elizabethan Londoners in Shakespeare's other plays, here seem to have been borrowed from a Neapolitan farce.

[12] See above, pp. 123–124, in the essay on 'Machiavelli and the Elizabethans'.

Mr J. J. Dwyer [13] has tried to show that the poems and plays which go under the name of Shakespeare (for Mr Dwyer is a supporter of the Earl of Oxford heresy) contain many allusions to pictures which had been actually seen in Italy. But what warrant have we for identifying the source of the picture of Troy owned by Lucrece (*The Rape of Lucrece*, 1366 ff.) with Giulio Romano's paintings of that subject at Mantua, beyond the fact that we find the Gonzagas mentioned in *Hamlet*, and Giulio Romano in *The Winter's Tale*—as a sculptor, though, which would only prove that Shakespeare had a very hazy knowledge of him? If Shakespeare had actually seen those paintings during a highly hypothetical visit to Mantua with the Earl of Southampton in 1593, he would not have committed that blunder. There was, however, no need to travel to Italy to know about Titian's *Venus and Adonis*, in which Mr Dwyer has seen the starting-point of the poem on the same subject:

> Even as the sun with purple-colour'd face
> Had ta'en his last leave of the weeping morn,
> Rose-cheek'd Adonis hied him to the chase;
> Hunting he lov'd, but love he laugh'd to scorn:
>   Sick-thoughted Venus makes amain unto him,
>   And like a bold-fac'd suitor 'gins to woo him.
>
> 'Thrice fairer than myself,' thus she began,
> 'The field's chief flower, sweet above compare,
> Stain to all nymphs, more lovely than a man . . .'

In both the painting and the poem Adonis is represented as indifferent or even rebellious to the appeals of the goddess (whereas in all the ancient poets he is responsive to her love). 'One may reasonably infer that this modern interpretation of the myth had come to Shakespeare directly or indirectly from the lips of a traveller who had seen Titian's painting, or one like it; or one might even suppose he had seen it himself, though that would involve a further hypothesis,' concludes Professor Sells,[14] who has been impressed by Mr

[13] *Italian Art in the Poems and Plays of Shakespeare*, Colchester, 1946.

[14] A. Lytton Sells, *The Italian Influence in English Poetry, op. cit.*, p. 192.

Dwyer's parallel. Since *Venus and Adonis* was painted in 1554 for Philip II of Spain, it would at first seem that Shakespeare could not have had any opportunity of seeing it, and that the coincidence, if there is one, can be ascribed to the similarity of aims of the painter and the poet, who wrote in a period when the old formula *ut pictura poesis* was in full force. There is however, I find, a frequently reprinted letter of Lodovico Dolce to Alessandro Contarini, where Dolce describes the painting (which, according to Titian's habit, is called 'poesia') of Venus and Adonis made 'for the King of England' ('Fu questa poesia di Adone poco tempo addietro fatta e mandata dal buon Tiziano al re d'Inghilterra').

The letter describes the beauty of Adonis, 'grazioso ed in ogni parte sua leggiadro, con una tinta di carne amabile che il dimostra delicatissimo e di sangue reale' ('graceful and attractive in every part, with a lovely complexion which shows him very exquisite and of royal blood'). What follows is interesting in view of Venus's appeal in Shakespeare's poem ('Thrice fairer than myself, etc.'):

> E vedesi che nell'aria del viso questo unico maestro ha cercato di esprimere certa graziosa bellezza che, partecipando della femmina, non si discostasse però dal virile: vuo' dire che in donna terrebbe non so che di uomo, e in uomo di vaga donna: mistura difficile, aggradevole e sommamente (se creder dobbiamo a Plinio) prezzata da Apelle. Quanto a l'attitudine, egli si vede muovere, e il movimento è facile, gagliardo e con gentile maniera, perché sembra che egli sia in cammino per partirsi da Venere, con desiderio ardentissimo di gire alla caccia.[15]

As for the scenery: 'D'intorno v'ha splendori e riflessi di sole mirabilissimi che allumano e allegrano tutto il paese'. There

[15] 'And one sees that in the appearance of the face this unique master has tried to express a certain kind of graceful beauty which, partaking of the feminine, is not, however, unbefitting a man: I mean to say that in a woman it would show some manliness, and in a man some womanly charm: a difficult mixture, agreeable and (if we are to believe Pliny) highly prized by Apelles. As to the attitude, he is seen moving, and the motion is easy, energetic and smooth, because he seems about to part from Venus and animated by an ardent desire to go hunting.'

are several points in this letter which would yield support to Mr Dwyer's hypothesis, particularly the statement that the picture was 'fatta e mandata dal buon Tiziano al re d'Inghilterra'. This king of England was no one else but Philip II of Spain, who had married Queen Mary; actually the painting reached London in very bad condition and took some time to restore.[16] Titian's painting, then, had been seen in England; and on the other hand Dolce's letter was accessible in print: anthologies of letters by distinguished persons and noble wits were frequently published during the sixteenth century. With all that, the parallel between the painting and the poem is not such as to carry absolute conviction.

As a result of this rapid survey, the conclusion can hardly be resisted that Shakespeare not only had an acquaintance with Italian things, but that he actually knew Italian. In *Measure for Measure*, for instance, he must have taken the idea of the substitution of the bodies from Cinthio's drama *Epitia*, since that substitution does not occur in the story of the *Hecatommithi* (Deca VIII, Novella 5), of which *Epitia* is a dramatic version. Neither does it occur in Whetstone's rehandling of Cinthio's story. Since Italian books were widely read in the society in whose midst Shakespeare lived, there is nothing extraordinary in his acquaintance with Italian literature; rather, the contrary would be surprising. That this acquaintance must have been little more than superficial seems shown by the fact that Shakespeare generally has recourse to English translations and imitations; this is chiefly noticeable in the *Sonnets*, whose conventional passages recall English rather than Italian or French sources.

What seems to be more puzzling is Shakespeare's accuracy in certain local allusions. Some of them I have already discussed; and even if Lambin has overstated the case of Shakespeare's knowledge of the topography of Milan, the mention of St Gregory's Well near that town, in *The Two Gentlemen*, seems definite enough; we find moreover Bellario as a Paduan name in *The Merchant of Venice*, which in fact it is, and, in *Romeo and Juliet*, details about Juliet's funeral (found, however, already in Brooke's poem) and about the

[16] See A. Venturi, *Storia dell'arte italiana*, ix, 3, p. 158, and Cavalcaselle, *Tiziano*, vol. ii, p. 193.

evening mass in Verona. We have also noticed the inconsistencies which imperil the local colour in Shakespeare's Italian dramas, but most of them occur in the farcical scenes, where the characters are really English clowns; and the practice of the stage—in the old *commedia dell'arte* as well as in to-day's pantomimes and puppet-plays—is always to give a contemporary national character to the comic scenes, irrespective of the time and place in which the serious plot is staged. In short, even when those inconsistencies spoil the effect of Italian atmosphere, the accuracy of the occasional local allusions remains to be accounted for. How did Shakespeare get hold of these local details?

An important fact is that these allusions are confined to a very definite part of Italy: Venice, and the neighbouring towns Verona, Padua, Mantua; and Milan. Local allusions to Florence, in *All's Well*, seem only to be the fruit of Lambin's ingenuity; while Messina of *Much Ado* is clearly an imaginary town. There are two possible alternatives: either Shakespeare travelled to the North of Italy, or he got this information from intercourse with some Italian in London.

There is no evidence for the first alternative. As for the second, Shakespeare may have had frequent occasions to meet Italian merchants; the Elephant Inn, which he mentions with praise as being the one where it was 'best to lodge' in the unknown Illyrian town of *Twelfth Night*, and being, of course, nothing else but the inn called 'The Oliphant' on Bankside, was patronised by Italians.[17]

But whatever his relations may have been with those Italian tradesmen and adventurers (many of whom were Northern Italians, chiefly, as is natural, from the commercial town of Venice), it is to-day well established that Shakespeare must have come across, at least, John Florio, the apostle of Italian culture in Englnd.[18] Florio and Shakespeare moved in the same circle; they were fellow-members of Southampton's household. Florio was a teacher in both the Italian and French

[17] See G. S. Gargàno, *Scapigliatura italiana a Londra sotto Elisabetta e Giacomo I*, Florence, 1923.

[18] Madame Clara Longworth de Chambrun was the first to discuss this connexion in *Giovanni Florio, Un Apôtre de la Renaissance en Angleterre*, Paris, 1921.

languages, and it has been surmised [19] that it may have been William Cecil, Lord Burleigh, who appointed him as tutor to Southampton when he was a minor under his guardianship, possibly to report about a young man destined to be influential in the Essex camp. If Florio had this unenviable role, then it can be understood why Shakespeare would not have hesitated to ridicule him as the pedant Holofernes in *Love's Labour's Lost*. Florio supplied Ben Jonson with whatever information that dramatist shows about Venice in *Volpone*: [20] a copy of this play in the British Museum has this autograph dedication: 'To his louing Father, & worthy Freind Mr. John Florio: The ayde of his Muses. Ben: Jonson seales this testemony of Freindship, & Loue.' Florio's manuals for the study of Italian, entitled *First* and *Second Fruites*, are responsible for the Italian sentences which occur in Act I, scene ii, of *The Taming of the Shrew*, a scene, however, which is not entirely ascribed to Shakespeare.[21] The expression found in *The Taming of the Shrew*, I, i, 'Lombardy, the pleasant garden of great Italy', is similar to Florio's 'La Lombardia è il giardino del mondo' in the *Second Fruites*, and very likely Florio is ultimately responsible for the currency of the phrase 'the garden of the world' applied to England.[22] Florio's vocabulary has a prevailing Lombardo-Venetian character,[23] Venice is for him the foremost Italian town, as can be seen in the eighth chapter of the *First Fruites*; this may help us to understand why the local allusions in Shakespeare's Italian plays are limited to Venice and the neighbouring towns. Florio was a rhetorician whose taste for style sinned on the florid side; some of his sentences, studded with proverbial expressions (he also compiled a collection of proverbs) seem to anticipate Giambattista Basile's Baroque grotesqueness; nevertheless his translation of Montaigne, plethoric as it is

[19] See Frances A. Yates, *John Florio*, Cambridge University Press, 1934, p. 218.

[20] See the following essay in 'Ben Jonson's Italy'.

[21] See *The Taming of the Shrew*, ed. by J. Dover Wilson, in *The New Shakespeare*, Cambridge University Press, 1928.

[22] See letters by J. B. Leishman and others in *The Times Literary Supplement* for November 7 and 28, and December 5, 1952.

[23] See my essay on 'Ben Jonson's Italy'.

with pretended elegances, has become a classic, and a source for Elizabethan dramatists, first of all Shakespeare, who bred his Hamlet on it; his manuals of conversation and his Italian dictionary were responsible for most of the knowledge of Italian of Shakespeare's contemporaries; he was called 'the aid of his Muses' by Ben Jonson, and probably would have deserved a similar appellation from Shakespeare; he may have been a sycophant, as he certainly was a pedant, in a word, a tool for greater purposes, a help for travellers to that garden of the world, Italy, and also, strangely enough, for travellers to the eternal garden of Poesy.

Ben Jonson's Italy

'THE darkened Italian palace,' to quote again Vernon Lee's picturesque summing-up of the exotic element in Elizabethan drama, combined with the revenge motif of the Senecan tragedy to form the background of the plays of Marston, Middleton, Tourneur, Webster, and Ford—to mention only the chief dramatists in that 'choir of giants', as Adolfo de Bosis, the *fin-de-siècle* Italian poet and translator of Shelley who admired them, defined them not without some exaggeration. De Bosis's passage (which occurs in his note on his version of *The Cenci*) deserves to be quoted in full, for the dangerous generalisation it contains, reflecting the continental opinion of the Elizabethan stage in the wake of Taine: 'That choir of giants who, reaching from Marlowe down to Otway are Webster and Cyril Tourneur, Beaumont and Fletcher, Ben Jonson, Thomas Middleton, Dekker, Marston, Rowley, Chapman, Shirley, Heywood, and many others, formidable, violent, inexhaustible in horror, tenderness, and passion, wild and many-souled, the lords of life and its laws, among whom William Shakespeare is seen towering.' Leaving aside the others, Ben Jonson for one could not possibly be described by any of those titanic adjectives, least of all as 'wild' (*scomposto*), being on the contrary, as is well known, steeped in his classical models to the point of pedantry. And if Shakespeare's Italy is very different from the blood-and-thunder Italy of the Elizabethan thrillers, being rather, in many respects so close to the idyllic country which is mirrored in Castiglione's and Ariosto's works that some have gone so far as to think that he had visited it, neither can Ben Jonson's Italy be said to have been imagined according to the current pattern.

We should not make too much of the Italian names of the first version of *Every Man in his Humour* (1598; published 1601): Lorenzo di Pazzi, Prospero, Thorello, Stephano, Musco, Giulliano, Biancha: this is no more than a veneer calculated to attract the attention of the courtiers, who were Italianate in accordance with the fashion. To show how genuinely English the atmosphere of the play was, it was enough to change the names of the places and characters in the second version (about 1612; published 1616). While Lorenzo di Pazzi, Prospero, Musco and the others wandered like somnambulists through the unknown topography of an imaginary Florence (a Florence containing a 'Realto'!), they find their bearings again as Knowell, Brainworm, Cash, etc., and throb with the pulse of life at the sound of Fleet Street, Houndsditch, Whitechapel, and Artillery Garden. The Italianate comedy of humours is no more than a preliminary tuning of instruments towards that consummate orchestration of popular London *motifs* which Ben Jonson was to produce in his great *kermesse, Bartholomew Fair* (1614). And Charles Lamb, rejoicing in the Anglicisation of *Every Man in his Humour*, found that Master Kitely, Mistress Kitely, Master Knowell, etc., sounded better than 'those Cisalpines'.

Neither do we find any specifically Italian traits in the other comedy of humours, *Every Man out of his Humour* (1599), apart from a few allusive personal names (Macilente, Puntaruolo, Carlo Buffone, Deliro, Fallace, Saviolina, Sordido, Fungoso, Sogliardo), and an incident and scene derived from Castiglione's *Courtier*, as Bang has shown.[1] How, in fact, could there be anything typically exotic in a comedy in which the author, having wound up his puppets, makes them go through all the movements to which they are geared during four interminable acts, until at last he makes up his mind to associate them in a common action in the fifth? Furthermore, in order to avoid any possible misunderstanding of the characters of these puppets, each is prefixed by a brief word-portrait. Deliro who dotes on a wife who never ceases to

[1] In *Englische Studien*, xxxvi.

scold him; quixotic Puntaruolo, who never parts with his
cat and his dog; Fastidius Brisk, the fop, the hero of a comic
duel in which only the elegant clothes receive ghastly and
complicated wounds; the student Fungoso, who, in order to
ape Fastidius's smartness, squeezes money from his father
(whose name, Sordido, is transparent enough), a miser bent
over the almanacks in order to find forecasts of famine
likely to increase the value of his granaries; boorish Sogliardo,
who covets the rank of a gentleman to the point of boasting
a coat of arms no less grotesque than the one Giotto, according to Sacchetti's report, painted for a coarse artisan; malevo-
lent Macilente, who beslavers everything with his envy;
Fallace, the foolish grumbler; Saviolina, the fatuous 'witty
woman'—this gallery of grotesque abstractions set before our
eyes in order to enable the playwright to lash the follies of
his time, belongs to the tradition of humanistic satire (*The
Ship of Fools*) and would have little reason to adopt Italian
names, were it not for fashion's sake.

But a great change came about with *Volpone* (1606).
Here the Venetian local colour is rendered with such an
accuracy as to leave behind any other contemporary dramatist fond of picturesque allusion. A frequently quoted scene,
the second of the second act, reproduces in minute detail the
spectacle of a quack selling a nostrum in Saint Mark's Square:

> *Volpone.* Most noble gentlemen, and my worthy pa-
> trons! It may seem strange that I, your Scoto
> Mantuano, who was ever wont to fix my bank
> in face of the public *Piazza*, near the shelter
> of the *Portico* to the *Procuratia*, should now,
> after eight months' absence from this illustrious
> city of Venice, humbly retire myself into an
> obscure nook of the *Piazza* . . . Let me tell
> you: I am not, as your Lombard proverb said,
> cold on my feet; or content to part with my
> commodities at a cheaper rate than I accus-
> tom'd: look not for it. Nor that the calumnious
> report of that impudent detractor, and shame to
> our profession (Alessandro Buttone, I mean),
> who gave out, in public, I was condemn'd

à sforzato to the galleys, for poisoning the
Cardinal Bembo's cook, hath at all attach'd,
much less dejected me. No, no, worthy gentlemen; to tell you true, I cannot endure to
see the rabble of these ground *ciarlitani*, that
spread their cloaks on the pavement, as if they
meant to do feats of activity, and then come
in lamely, with their mouldy tales out of Boccaccio, like stale Tabarin, the fabulist: some of
them discoursing their travels, and their tedious captivity in the Turks' galleys, when,
indeed, were the truth known, they were the
Christians' galleys, where very temperately
they eate bread, and drunk water, as a wholesome penance, enjoin'd them by their confes-
sors, for base pilferies.

Sir Politic. Note but his bearing, and contempt of these.

Volpone. These turdy - facy - nasty - paty - lousy - fartical
rogues, with one poor groat's-worth of unpre-
par'd antimony, finely wrapp'd up in several
scartoccios, are able, very well, to kill their
twenty a week, and play; yet these meagre,
starv'd spirits, who have half stopp'd the or-
gans of their minds with earthy oppilations,
want not their favourers among your shrivell'd
salad-eating artisans, who are overjoy'd that they
may have their half-pe'rth of physic; though it
purge 'em into another world, 't makes no matter.

Sir Politic. Excellent! ha' you heard better language, sir?

Volpone. Well, let 'm go. And gentlemen, honourable
gentlemen, know, that for this time, our bank,
being thus remov'd from the clamours of the
canaglia, shall be the scene of pleasure and
delight; for I have nothing to sell, little or
nothing to sell. . . . I protest, I, and my six
servants, are not able to make of this precious
liquor so fast as it is fetch'd away from my
lodging by gentlemen of your city; strangers
of the terra firma; worshipful merchants; ay,
and senators too: who, ever since my arrival,

have detained me to their uses by their splen-
didous liberalities. And worthily; for, what
avails your rich man to have his magazines
stuff'd with *moscadelli,* or with the purest
grape, when his physicians prescribe him, on
pain of death, to drink nothing but water
cocted with anise-seeds? O health! health! the
blessing of the rich! the riches of the poor!
who can buy thee at too dear a rate, since
there is no enjoying this world without thee?
Be not then so sparing of your purses, honourable gentlemen, as to abridge the natural course
of life . . . For when a humid flux, or catarrh,
by the mutability of air, falls from your head
into an arm or shoulder, or any other part;
take you a ducat, or your cecchine of gold, and
apply to the place affected: see what good effect it can work. No, no, 't is this blessed
unguento, this rare extraction, that hath only
power to disperse all malignant humours, that
proceed either of hot, cold, moist, or windy
causes . . . to fortify the most indigest and
crude stomach, ay, were it of one that, through
extreme weakness, vomited blood, applying
only a warm napkin to the place, after the
unction and fricace;—for the *vertigine* in the
head, putting but a drop into your nostrils,
likewise behind the ears; a most sovereign and
approved remedy: the *mal caduco,* cramps,
convulsions, paralyses, epilepsies, tremorcordia,
retired nerves, ill vapours of the spleen, stop-
pings of the liver, the stone, the strangury,
hernia ventosa, iliaca passio; stops a dysenteria
immediately; easeth the torsion of the small
guts; and cures melancholia hypocondriaca,
being taken and applied, according to my
printed receipt. For [pointing to his bill and
his glass] this is the physician, this the medicine; this counsels, this cures; this gives the
direction, this works the effect; and, in sum, both

together may be term'd an abstract of the theoric and practic in the Æsculapian art. 'T will cost you eight crowns. And,—Zan Fritada, pray thee sing a verse extempore in honour of it. . . .

Peregrine. All this, yet, will not do; eight crowns is high.

Volpone. . . . Gentlemen, if I had but time to discourse to you the miraculous effects of this my oil, surnamed *oglio del Scoto*; with the countless catalogue of those I have cured of th'aforesaid, and many more diseases; the patents and privileges of all the princes and commonwealths of Christendom; or but the dispositions of those that appear'd on my part, before the *signiory* of the *Sanità* and most learned College of Physicians; where I was authorized, upon notice taken of the admirable virtues of my medicaments, and mine own excellency in matter of rare and unknown secrets, not only to disperse them publicly in this famous city, but in all the territories, that happily joy under the government of the most pious and magnificent states of Italy. But may some other gallant fellow say, 'O, there be divers that make profession to have as good, and as experimented receipts as yours.' Indeed, very many have assay'd, like apes, in imitation of that, which is really and essentially in me, to make of this oil; bestow'd great costs in furnaces, stills, alembics, continual fires, and preparation of the ingredients (as indeed there goes to it six hundred several simples, besides some quantity of human fat, for the conglutination, which we buy of the anatomists), but when the practitioners come to the last decoction, blow, blow, puff, puff, and all flies in *fumo*: ha, ha, ha! Poor wretches! I rather pity their folly and indiscretion, than their loss of time and money; for those may be recovered by industry: but to be a fool born, is a disease incurable. . . . And gentlemen, honourable gentlemen, I will undertake, by virtue of chymical art, out of the honourable hat that covers your head, to extract the four elements; that is to say, the fire, air, water, and earth, and return you your felt without burn or stain. For, whilst others have been at the *balloo,* I have been at my book; and am now past the craggy paths of study, and come to the flowery plains of honour and reputation. . . . You all know, honourable gentlemen, I never valu'd this *ampulla,* or vial, at less than eight crowns; but for this time, I am content to be depriv'd of it for six; six crowns is the price, and less in courtesy I know you cannot offer me; take it or leave it, howsoever, both it and I am at your service. I ask you not as the value of the thing, for then I should demand of you a thousand crowns, so the Cardinals Montalto, Fernese, the great Duke of Tuscany, my gossip, with divers other princes, have given me; but I despise money. Only to show my affection to you, honourable gentlemen, and your illustrous state here, I have neglected the messages of these princes, mine own offices, fram'd my journey hither, only to present you with the fruits of my travels.— Tune your voices once more to the touch of your instruments, and give the honourable assembly some delightful recreation.

Peregrine. What monstrous and most painful circumstance Is here, to get some three or four gazettes, Some threepence i' the whole! for that 't will come to. . . .

Volpone. Well, I am in a humour at this time to make a present of the small quantity my coffer contains; to the rich in courtesy, and to the poor for God's sake. Wherefore now mark: I ask'd you six crowns; and six crowns, at other times, you have paid me; you shall not give me six crowns, nor five, nor four, nor three, nor two, nor one; nor half a ducat; no, nor a *moccinigo.*

Sixpence it will cost you, or six hundred pound
—expect no lower price, for, by the banner of
my front, I will not bate a *bagatine*.—That I
will have, only a pledge of your loves, to carry
something from amongst you, to show I am not
contemn'd by you. Therefore, now toss your
handkerchiefs, cheerfully, cheerfully; and be
advertised, that the first heroic spirit that deigns
to grace me with a handkerchief, I will give it
a little remembrance of something besides,
shall please it better than if I had presented
it with a double pistolet.

The words of the text printed in italics are Italian words;
and they are not the usual words or vague picturesque exple-
tives one comes across in Elizabethan plays with an Italian
background. Jonson gathered facts together in a manner that
reminds one of the authors of nineteenth-century historical
plays. Like these, he is not exempt from a certain naïvety,
as when Volpone specifies the site of his bank ('in face of
the public Piazza, near the shelter of the Portico to the
Procuratia'), or when he uses the expression 'to be cold on
one's feet' (the meaning of which we shall presently see),
and glosses it with: 'As your Lombard proverb saith'. What
has happened between the comedies of humours which we
have been discussing, and *Volpone*? The poet has written
two plays on classical themes, *Poetaster* (1602) and *Sejanus
his Fall* (1603), and in his enormous respect for erudition
(typical of a person of humble origin), he has not been content with a smattering of information like Shakespeare, who, in
Ben Jonson's words, 'wanted art', but has studied the sources
accurately, and although the chief aim of *Poetaster* is a satirical allusion to the rivalries between Jonson and Marston and
Dekker, the playwright has taken pains to give us a faithful
reconstruction of the Augustan literary *milieu*, and makes
Horace and Virgil quote their own lines; and in *Sejanus* he
has had recourse to Tacitus, Dion, Juvenal, and Seneca, to
the point of giving Hazlitt the rather exaggerated impression
that the drama is an 'ancient mosaic' of 'translated bits'. We
shall have something to say later on about the deep influence

this study of imperial Rome had on Jonson's interpretation of contemporary Italy; meanwhile let us notice how, while working at these Roman plays, Jonson learned the method of historical reconstruction of a given *milieu*.

How did Jonson come by his information about Italy and Venice? What knowledge had he of the Italian language and literature? Drummond of Hawthornden, that belated sonneteer in a period in which the vogue for the sonnet had died out, could affirm in 1619, in his famous *Conversations* with Jonson, that the latter did not understand Italian, and possibly he was right, if he was judging by his own minute acquaintance with Italian writers. True, Jonson translated lines from Parabosco, but his allusions to Italian literature are rare; in the *Conversations* we find only a criticism of the *Pastor Fido*, which had appeared in English in 1591, an unfavourable opinion of John Harington's translation of Ariosto ('under all translations was the worst'), which does not necessarily imply a comparison with the original, and an attack on Petrarch whom Jonson curses for having constrained poetry in the Procrustean bed of the sonnet. Castiglione's *Courtier*, upon which Jonson drew for *Every Man out of his Humour*, could be read in Hoby's version; in *Volpone* Lady Politic, a caricature of the Italianate court-lady, says she has read 'Petrarch, Tasso, Dante, Guerrini [*sic*], Ariosto, Aretino, Cieco di Hadria,' and mentions the *Pastor Fido* (Act iii, Scene 4); we find in *Epicoene* (iv, 4) an allusion to Doni's *Moral Filosofia* which had been translated into English by Thomas North in 1570; in *The Alchemist* we read of the obscene pictures by Giulio Romano, accompanied by sonnets by Aretino—an Elizabethan commonplace recurring also in *Volpone*—and of one of Ariosto's characters, Bradamante, used as a common noun (ii, 3: 'a Bradamante, a brave piece'). And although the Italian origin of Inigo Jones's settings for Jonson's masks has been demonstrated,[2] the text of the masks is original. Bruno's

[2] Oskar Fischel, 'Inigo Jones und der Theaterstil der Renaissance', in *Vorträge der Bibliothek Warburg 1930–1931: England und die Antike*, Leipzig-Berlin, 1932. Inigo Jones had worked in Florence with Giulio Parigi; the close relations between the courts of France, England, and Tuscany especially under Charles I—Henrietta Maria was the daughter of Maria de' Medici—caused the art of the theatre to take on an international character.

Candelaio has been suggested as a possible source of *The Alchemist*, but the resemblances are vague, and on the other hand the plot is very different.[3]

In conclusion, the knowledge Jonson had of Italian literature seems neither wide nor exceptional, and it should have been exceptional indeed if he had had to derive the precise allusions and expressions used in *Volpone* from books. It has been suggested that Jonson may have gathered information from Tommaso Garzoni's *Piazza universale di tutte le professioni del mondo,* and that he found there the name of Zan Fritada and the mention of such Venetian coins as the *gazzette* and the *mocenighi;* but as Garzoni accounts only for a few allusions and words, 'some other author about Italian things with whom he was familiar' has been vaguely conjectured.[4] Briefly, we are confronted with a case similar to that offered by the mysterious references to localities in Northern Italy contained in some of Shakespeare's plays.[5] What appeared to us a probable hypothesis for Shakespeare, is a certainty in Jonson's case. A copy of *Volpone* in the British Museum has the following dedication written in the playwright's own hand:

> To his louing Father, & worthy Freind
> Mr John Florio: The ayde of his Muses
> Ben: Jonson seales this testemony
> of Freindship, & Loue.

[3] In favour of the source, C. G. Child, in the New York *Nation,* July 28, 1904; against, C. H. Herford, in the Oxford edition of Jonson's works, 1925 ff., vol. ii, p. 94 ff.

[4] P. Rebora, *L'Italia nel dramma inglese,* Milan, 1925, p. 124. Garzoni, in the *Piazza universale,* speaking of 'De' formatori di spettacoli in genere, & de' Ceretani, O Ciurmadori massime', has: 'Enough (to touch on some of their manners for making money) to say that at the corner of the piazza you see our gallant Fortunato together with Fritata making people gape for gudgeons, and entertain the company every afternoon from the twentieth to the twenty-fourth hour of the day, invent stories, devise tales, improvise dialogues, perform juggling tricks, sing extempore . . . and finally produce the begging-box and come to the point of the gazette, which their courteous and urbane chatter is intended to extract'.

[5] See above, p. 165.

Florio was about twenty years older than Jonson, but the appellative of 'father' must be understood here as a title of respect given to a master. And what help might Florio have given to Jonson if not that of acquainting him with Italian terms and customs? Miss Yates [6] sees an allusion to his *Second Fruites* in a passage of Volpone (II, 1):

Sir Politic.	What? came you forth Empty of rules for travel?
Peregrine.	Faith, I had Some common ones, from out that vulgar grammar, Which he that cri'd Italian to me, taught me.
Sir Politic.	Why, this it is that spoils all our brave bloods, Trusting our hopeful gentry unto pedants, Fellows of outside, and mere bark . . .

True, the allusion seems less than respectful, but Sir Politic is the caricature of a certain type of Englishman, so that blame in his mouth is tantamount to a praise. And as for Italian grammars, in 1606, with the exception of the jejune *Italian Schoole-Maister* by Hollyband, there were only Florio's manuals, and in fact the sixth dialogue of the *Second Fruites* concerns 'divers, necessary, profitable, civil, and proverbial precepts for a traveller.' The same act of *Volpone* (II, 1 *ad fin.*, and 2), a little before Volpone's propitiatory speech quoted above, explains how valuable a source of information teachers of languages were:

Peregrine.	Who be these, sir?
Sir Politic.	Fellows, to mount a bank. Did your instructor In the dear tongues never discourse to you Of the Italian mountebanks?
Peregrine.	Yes, sir.
Sir Politic.	Why, Here shall you see one.
Peregrine.	They are quacksalvers. Fellows that live by venting oils and drugs.
Sir Politic.	Was that the character he gave you of them?

[6] Frances A. Yates, *John Florio*, Cambridge University Press, 1934, p. 279.

Peregrine. As I remember.

Sir Politic.   Pity his ignorance.
They are the only knowing men of Europe!
Great general scholars, excellent physicians,
Most admir'd statesmen, profess'd favourites
And cabinet counsellors to the greatest princes;
The only languag'd men of all the world!

The preceding passage enables us to guess from where
Jonson derived his information for the scene of the quack in
Volpone. We shall not find the scene in the pages of the *First,*
or the *Second Fruites,*[7] nor shall we find there word for word
an Italian passage which occurs in *Cynthia's Revels,*[8] but the
Italian vocabulary of the playwright has the same quality as
that of the grammarian, i.e., a prevailing Lombardo-Venetian
flavour.[9] The Italian words used by Jonson in the scene we

[7] The *First Fruites* has been reprinted in facsimile, with notes,
by Arundell Del Re (*Memoirs of the Faculty of Literature and
Politics,* Taihoku Imperial University, Formosa, 1936, vol. iii, no. 1).

[8] Act v, Sc. 4, text in Italian: 'Signora, ho tanto obligo per lo
favore resciuto [*sic,* i.e. ricevuto, riceuto] de lei, che veramente
dessidero con tutto il core a remunerarla in parte: & sicurative
signora mea cara, che io serò sempre pronto a servirla & honorarla.
Bascio le mane de vo' signoria'.

[9] Arundell Del Re in his edition of the *First Fruites* notices the
Venetian form of the names of spices given by Florio, and conjectures that he derived what he knew on the subject from the
Venetian merchants who were the chief importers of those com-
modities. But throughout the volume of the *First Fruites* one
finds Venetian and Lombardo-Venetian forms, such as *giande* for
ghiande, ungie for *unghie, bombeligo* for *ombelico, soppiare* for
soffiare, ameda (aunt), *neza* (niece), *tegna, pizigare, malado,
miglioradi,* etc. And we notice that Jonson has *Zan Fritada,* and
not *Fritata,* as we read in Garzoni. Another fact showing that
Florio gathered his material from among merchants is the presence
of foreign words with a slight Italian veneer, as happens even
nowadays among the Italians of the United States: gallicisms like
bona cera (bonne chère), giocar di poma (cf. *jeu de paume*),
potto (pot), dangerosa (dangereuse), pilagio (pillage), inrizzato
(corresponding to *hérissé* in the phrase *castagno inrizzato*),
anglicisms like *pacuzo (packhouse), tubbaro* (the English equivalent given by Florio is *cooper,* but the word seems derived from
tub, which is the wooden vessel most commonly made or repaired by coopers: there is an obvious sound-association with
Venetian *botaro*), *pilgrimaggi (pilgrimages), scepa (Cheap,* i.e.,

have quoted are to be found in Florio's Italian-English dictionary, *A Worlde of Wordes* (1598); [10] thus, not to speak of the more common words, we find: *sforzati,* 'galley-slaves perforce'; *scartoccio,* 'a coffin of paper for spice'; *Moscadello,* 'the wine Muscadine'; *zecchino,* 'a coine of Gold currant in Venice worth about seaven shillings and six pence sterlin'; *moccenigo,* 'a kind of coine in Venice'; *gazzetta,* 'a small coine in Italie'; *bagatino,* 'a little coine in Italie'; *vertigine,* 'a sicknesse proceeding of windiness, which so troubleth some that all they see seemeth to turne round, we call it a vertigo, or giddiness, a dizzinesse or swimming in the head with a mistinesse, a dimnesse, a sparkling or glimmering of the eies, namely if one stoop or looke downward'—an uncommonly long explanation, showing Florio's special interest in this illness, which actually appears as the first in Volpone's list; *mal caduco,* 'the falling sicknesse'; *ballone,* 'great ball, footeball', recorded also among the sports in the *Second Fruites; ampolla,* 'a thin viole-glasse'; the expression *havere freddo a' piedi* explained as 'to stand or be in great neede'.[11] We find more Italian words in *Volpone: buffalo* (IV, 4) 'a buffle, or a buffe: also a blocke or logerhead'; *gazetti*

Cheapside, a street in the City of London), *Carisee* (*Carsies,* today *kersies,* a kind of cloth), *scandalezzare,* in the un-Italian sense of *to slander,* It. 'calunniare'. Once we are aware of the Lombardo-Venetian flavour of Florio's vocabulary—and Venice is for him the foremost Italian town, as we may see in chapter 8 of the *First Fruites*—we may guess why the local allusions in Shakespeare's Italian plays are limited to a well-defined part of Italy: Venice, and the neighbouring towns of Verona, Padua, Mantua; and Milan. There is, as we have already said, no local allusion in *Much Ado,* where the scene is an imaginery Messina, nor in those scenes of *All's Well* which take place in Florence.

[10] I have been able to consult only the second edition, *Queen Anna's New World of Words,* 1611.

[11] A better definition is contained in Ouden's *Dictionnaire italien et françois,* Paris, 1616, under the word *freddo: 'aver freddo ai piedi:* n'avoir point d'argent; *item*: donner sa marchandise à bon marché pour s'en aller vistement; *non aver freddo ai piedi,* ce que disent les marchands quand ils n'ont pas haste de vendre leur marchandise'. In Cherubini's *Vocabolario milanese-italiano,* Milan, 1814, vol. ii, p. 28: *'ave o ave minga i pee frec:* vale essere o non essere ricco di denaro, di beni di fortuna'.

(v, 4), 'running reports, daily newes, idle intelligences, or flim flam tales that are daily written from Italie namely from Rome and Venice'; *piscaria* (v, 7), 'a fish-street, a fish-market': together with Venetian names of institutions and localities, such as the *saffi*, the *avvogadori*, the hospital of the Incurabili, the convent of Santo Spirito, the Lazzaretto, and the Rialto. And Jonson learned of the festivities in Venice for Henry III of Valois (iii, 7). We find several Italian words and expressions also in *Cynthia's Revels*, a play written towards the end of the year 1600, which alludes to several of the so-called *giochi liberali e d'ingegno* (noble and witty games) of the Cinquecento (paradoxes, the meanings of colours, devices or *imprese*, etc.); we have already seen a phrase of the type found in conversation-manuals; another is (i, 4) on travelling (travail) which 'as the Italian saies, *vi rendi* [*sic*] *pronto all'attioni*, makes you fit for action'; also (v, 4): '*Non sapete voi parlar Itagliano?*', and names of dishes (ii, 3): *maccaroni, bovoli, fagioli* (Florio explains these words in his *World of Words; bovolo* is defined 'any round snaile, a periwinkle'—a Venetian word, which even modern visitors of Venice may remember from the name of the famous spiral staircase in the Contarini Palace near Santo Stefano), together with *caviare* (*caviaro*, 'a kinde of salt blacke meate made of roes of fishes much used in Italie'); and *babioun* (v, 4), in the sense of Italian *babbione* (Florio: 'a babuine, a gull, or sot') and *Bessogno* (in the same scene) for 'a fresh needy souldier', as Florio has it.

There can be little doubt, therefore, that Florio aided Jonson for the local colour of *Volpone*; Miss Yates suggests Florio as the author of the verses signed I.F. which, together with other tributes from several friends, are prefixed to the first edition of the play, but they are more likely due to John Fletcher; [12] the same scholar inclines also to think that Florio's influence contributed to make Jonson a partisan of the classical rules of stage 'decorum'. It is more interesting still to notice how, in between the proverbs and the scraps of conversation taught him by his Italian master, Jonson caught glimpses of the opulent and corrupt temper of sixteenth-century Venice,

[12] See the fifth volume of the Oxford *Ben Jonson*, p. 3, remarks by Percy Simpson.

and felt the sinister lure of a personage who was representative of it.

True, Ben Jonson mentions Aretino only for the obscene pictures with which his name was traditionally associated, and probably knew at least the *Marescalco* among his comedies,[13] but is it really necessary to quote passages from the *Ragionamenti* to demonstrate that the author of *Volpone*, more than any other writer of his time, has come close to the picturesque eloquence, to the art of making language ferment and seethe like the very corruption it describes, to the spell-bound contemplation of the spectacle of human turpitude, which were proper to the Scourge of Princes? That *Volpone*, in a word, is the best of Aretino's plays, the play Aretino should have written, and instead, has only inspired? But there is more to be said about the character of Volpone. Volpone, the Venetian *magnifico*, pretends to be dying in order to snatch gifts from those who hope to be his heirs, and, in league with Mosca, his parasite, makes the greedy and foolish with emblematical names, Voltore, Corbaccio, Corvino parade before him, and rejoices to see them lay bare the sores and tumours of their souls. (No doubt these pretenders would have been even more repulsive had they been linked with Volpone by family ties, but, after all, one of them goes so far as to be willing to prostitute his wife to the dying man!) The Volpone who, in between the various calls, bursts into peals of sarcastic laughter (his manner of moralizing on mankind at large), the Volpone who delights in exercising his diabolical power over men, and is more thrilled by the souls' degradation than by material gifts—what is this Volpone but the faithful image of Aretino himself, that self-portrait which Aretino was not naïve enough (as Cellini had been), or artist enough, to draw of himself? Was it through Florio's gossip that Jonson divined a new enormous and truculent way of sinning in Aretino's Venice? Indeed he saw so far into Aretino's *hubris* as to give

[13] See O. J. Campbell, *The Relation of "Epicoene" to Aretino's "Il Marescalco,"* in *PMLA*, xlvi (1931), pp. 752–762. According to Campbell, Jonson would have derived the central idea of the plot from Aretino. The publisher John Wolfe had printed in London in 1588 *Quattro Comedie del divino Pietro Aretino*, destined to circulate in Italy, where they had been put on the Index.

a foretaste of the psychic make-up of the Marquis de Sade. For it is not enough for Volpone to degrade others; he derives a subtle thrill from exposing himself to an unnecessary risk, by making Mosca his heir, and causing himself to be declared dead, in order to relish the disappointment and rage of the cheated pretenders, with the result that he sees himself betrayed by the parasite, and fallen a victim of his own snare.

Throughout Ben Jonson's work we are aware of his deep fascination with the figure of a titanic transgressor: Sejanus, Catiline, on a tragic level, Subtle the alchemist on the level of comedy. Volpone is the perfect incarnation of the type, and one cannot say in what measure the tragic elements mix with the comic to give the drama its unique temper. It is an ambiguous drama, with an ambiguous protagonist. Farce borders on tragedy, mockery is tinged with inhuman cruelty. And if, after reading Jonson's play, we look at the *mascarone* (as Gonzaga's envoy defined it in a letter) painted by Titian, we feel we are in the presence of the same audacious and malignant buffoonery. Confronted with his portrait intuitively drawn by the English playwright, Aretino might have repeated the words he actually said apropos of his likeness painted by Titian: 'Certainly it breathes, throbs with life and spirit in the very manner I do'. So we, in our turn, under Titian's figure of the man who turns his cunning and insolent face sideways, a face to which the beard fails to lend a venerable air, while the satins, velvets and brocades are amply folded round the diabolically inflated chest, feel almost tempted to write the name: Volpone.

Venice, Pietro Aretino . . . Jonson was fresh from reading the historians and satirists of imperial Rome, and contemporary Venice appeared to him like a reincarnation of the opulence and corruption of the ancient world. It has indeed been shown [14] that the central situation of the drama, of the testator who flouts the legacy-hunters, is already found in Lucian (*Dialogues of the Dead,* v-ix) and Petronius (Eumol-

[14] See the Oxford *Ben Jonson,* vol. ii, p. 49 ff., and my edition of *Volpone* for the Biblioteca Sansoniana Straniera; the principal study is J. Q. Adams, 'The Sources of Ben Jonson's "Volpone" ', in *Modern Philology,* ii (1904), pp. 289–299: see also Prof. G. D. Rea's edition of *Volpone* in *Yale Studies,* 1919.

pus's adventures in Croton), and is not typical of Jonson's times, but of the Roman world, where the figures of the *captator* was common enough. 'There is no evidence or probability,' Herford remarks 'that Jonson had discovered a Venetian Eucrates or Eumolpus'. But Aretino was a still more formidable gift-hunter than either Eucrates or Eumolpus. Venice takes on a reflected light from Rome. Volpone courts Celia with lines which recall Catullus (iii, 7: 'Come, my Celia, let us prove/While we can the sports of love . . .'), and tries to inflame her with splendours worthy of Trimalchio: [15]

> See, here, a rope of pearl; and each more orient
> Than that the brave Aegyptian queen carous'd:
> Dissolve and drink 'em. See, a carbuncle,
> May put out both the eyes of our St. Mark;
> A diamond would have bought Lollia Paulina,
> When she came in like star-light, hid•with jewels
> That were the spoils of provinces; take these
> And wear, and lose 'em; yet remains an ear-ring
> To purchase them again, and this whole state.
> A gem but worth a private patrimony
> Is nothing; we will eat such at a meal.
> The heads of parrots, tongues of nightingales,
> The brains of peacocks, and of estriches,
> Shall be our food, and, could we get the phoenix,
> Though nature lost her kind, she were our dish.

And Lady Politic, who paints her face according to the fashion of that 'curious nation', the Italians (iii, 4), and exclaims: 'This *fucus* was too coarse too . . .', reminds one of the scene of Livia's toilet in *Sejanus* (ii, 1) and of Eudemus's words: 'This same *fucus* was well laid on', with Livia's reply: 'Me thinkes, 'tis here not white'. After all, the drawing together of sixteenth-century Italy and imperial Rome was not so arbitrary. For did not the Italian Cinquecento vie with the ancient world in ostentation and refinement, did it not aim at a classicism which was at the same time colossal in the Roman way and bejewelled in the Alexandrian, massive, polished and, at

[15] The passage partly derives from Pliny's *Naturalis Historia*, ix, 117, 118, 120, 121.

the same time, variegated like rare marbles and changing like opals and amethysts? The Cinquecento of the mannerist painters and miscellaneous writers, the century of Vasari and Aretino, was divined by Jonson through Florio, in the same way he had divined the Rome of the Caesars through Tacitus, Juvenal and Petronius.

Donne's Relation to the Poetry
of His Time

THERE are few themes more harped on by sixteenth-century poets than the time-honoured one of the love-dream. Its formula, as it was broadcast throughout Europe by the Italian sonneteers, amounted to this: the poet dreams that his cruel beloved has relented and comes to solace him, but just when he is about to enjoy this godsend, sleep forsakes him. This being the bare outline, one was left an extensive choice of trimmings. You could start with a brief and elegant description of night, or with a complaint addressed to Sleep, or with a cry of joy: 'Is this the fair hair . . . ?' combined with the usual Petrarchan description of the lady; if you were at pains how to fill up the quatrains, mythology came to your rescue, with Morpheus, Endymion and Diana, Ixion, and similar pleasant purple patches; or you could quibble on the disappearance of the sun, and the rise of that other sun, the beloved, in the dead of night. . . . When, in the eighties of the sixteenth century, Thomas Watson picked up (from the Latin poems of Hercules Strozza) 'this kinde of invention . . . usuall among those that have excelled in the sweetest vaine of Poetrie', he set out with a mythological embroidery on the circumstances of his dream:

In *Thetis* lappe, while *Titan* tooke his rest,
I slumbring lay within my restless bedde,
Till *Morpheus* us'd a falsed soary iest,

Presenting her, by whom I still am ledde:
> For then I thought she came to ende my wo,
> But when I wakt (alas) t'was nothing so.

Alas, vain hope! Like Ixion's

> Embracing ayre in steed of my delight,
> I blamed *Love* as author of the guile,
> Who with a second sleepe clozd up my sight,
> And said (me thought) that I must bide a while
>> *Ixions* paines, whose armes did oft embrace
>> False darkned clouds, in steed of Iunoes grace.

But now another lady appears to the lover: she is a prosopo-poeia of Hope:

> When I had laine and slumbred thus a while,
> Rewing the dolefull doome that *Love* assign'd,
> A woman *Saint*, which bare an Angels face,
> Bad me awake and ease my troubled minde:
>> With that I wakt, forgetting what was past,
>> And sawe 'twas *Hope*, which helped thus at last.

About the same time, another minor poet, Sir Arthur Gorges, whom Spenser celebrated as Alcyon 'fit to frame an everlasting dittie' in *Colin Clout's Come Home Again,* gave this less pompous, but equally commonplace, treatment of the theme, in imitation of Desportes (*Songe,* in *Diane,* Livre II: 'Celle que j'aime tant, lasse d'estre cruelle'): [1]

> She whome I holde so deare
>> too cruell thoughe She bee
> Did in my sleepe appeare
>> this other night to me
> Sweet were the lookes shee lente
>> and with such cheare Shee spake
> As who shoulde say shee ment
>> remorce on me to take

[1] *The Poems of Sir Arthur Gorges,* ed. Helen Estabrook Sandison, Oxford, 1953, pp. 11–12.

I pressed with my payne
   sayd unto her withall
Faire one doo not disdaine
   the harte that is your thrall
And with a vapored Eye
   this onely dyd I crave
That I the death might dye
   yf grace I might nott have
Wherwith she dyd disclose
   those faire sweet Coralls twaine
And sayde receave repose
   doo thow no more Complaine
Nor from thy wastede Eyes
   drawe not such dropps of griefe
From whence thy woes dyd ryse
   from thence receave releeffe
Oh sweet Elusion straunge
   o marvell of delighte
But oh how sone did chaunge
   the pleasure off this nighte
For loe this soddayne Joye
   so strake me to the harte
As that to myn annoye
   out of this sleepe I starte
And yett dyd doubtfull stande
   tyll lyftinge upp my heade
To kisse her comelye hande
   the shape awaye was fledd
But then I did devyse
   a slumber new to fayne
And closede kept myne Eyes
   althoughe it were in vaine
Att laste awakte I sayde
   oh dreame that didst surpasse
By the I am betrayde
   as Bradamanta was
Yett that which lyked me beste
   my Mistres here shall fynde
That thoughe my Bodye reste
   I have her styll in mynde.

Of course, you will find a better treatment of the theme of the love-dream in Sidney ('Thus night while sleepe begins, with heavie wings . . .'), but, if the workmanship is superior, the spirit is much the same as in Watson's poor mythological concoction, or Sir Arthur Gorges's imitation of Desportes's *Songe*.

Let us now read side by side with these poems, which faithfully reproduce a traditional formula, Donne's *Dream:*

Deare love, for nothing lesse then thee
Would I have broke this happy dreame,
   It was a theame
For reason, much too strong for phantasie,
Therefore thou wakd'st me wisely; yet
My Dreame thou brok'st not, but continued'st it,
Thou art so truth, that thoughts of thee suffice,
To make dreames truths; and fables histories;
Enter these armes, for since thou thoughtst it best,
Not to dreame all my dreame, let's act the rest.

One has only to think that even poets like Sidney and Shakespeare paid tribute to that time-hallowed recipe of the love-dream, to realize to what extent Donne's poem meant a new departure. The poet, on his waking up, is no longer addressing a rhetorical complaint to an absent beauty. It is not the sun which awakes him, as in Sannazaro ('Quando apersi, ohimè, gli occhi, e vidi il Sole . . .'): the beloved has actually come to his room, and the brightness of her eyes rouses the poet from sleep:

As lightning, or a Tapers light,
Thine eyes, and not thy noise wak'd me;
   Yet I thought thee
(For thou lovest truth) an Angell, at first sight,
But when I saw thou sawest my heart,
And knew'st my thoughts, beyond an Angel's art,
When thou knew'st what I dreamt, when thou knew'st when
Excesse of joy would wake me, and cam'st then,
I must confesse, it could not chuse but bee
Prophane, to thinke thee any thing but thee.

The last stanza concludes with a note of hope, as in Watson,
but the tone of the two poets could hardly be more different:

Comming and staying show'd thee, thee,
But rising makes me doubt, that now,
    Thou art not thou.
That love is weake, where feare's as strong as hee;
'Tis not all spirit, pure, and brave,
If mixture it of *Feare, Shame, Honor*, have.
Perchance as torches which must ready bee,
Men light and put out, so thou deal'st with mee,
Thou cam'st to kindle, goest to come; Then I
Will dreame that hope again, but else would die.

A comparison like the one I have suggested (which could
be repeated for most of Donne's songs) brings out very well
the peculiarities of Donne's poetry: its dramatic character,[2] its
metrical originality, its crabbed and prosaic imagery. The
poem is not sung, but spoken; the poet does not sit in state
in his singing robes, with Apollo and the Muses whispering
into his ears; he has come down from the golden clouds of
abstraction, and argues with his beloved. She is not the distant
figure seen in a glimpse against the sky, hardly more human
than the sun and the evening star to which she is compared.
Such was the lady of the sonneteers, but Donne's lady is so
much of a flesh-and-blood presence that she can be invited to
'act the rest'. The poet's passionate argument does not allow for
those stately, self-contained lines whose perfection redeems
many a lifeless sonnet. There is hardly a line in Donne's poem
which makes sense by itself, or can claim the power of em-
blazoning in a musical cadence a whole state of mind. The
sense is rounded off only at the end of the stanza, or rather at
the end of the poem: the unit is not the line, as in many
sonneteers, and not even the stanza, but the entire poem
in its serpentine swerving from one excitement to another.[3]
Donne's technique stands in the same relation to the average

[2] An analysis of this poem from a dramatic point of view will
be found in Pierre Legouis's study on *Donne the Craftsman*, Paris,
1928, pp. 75–77.

[3] See on the mannerist character of Donne's poetry, Wylie
Sypher, *Four Stages of Renaissance Style*, Anchor Books, 1955,
especially p. 151.

technique of Renaissance poetry, as that of mannerist to that of Renaissance painting. His main preoccupation is with the whole effect.

Seen from this angle, Donne's songs present a marked contrast to such poetry of *concetti* as was written by Marino and by Donne himself in the *Anniversaries*. True, one finds *concetti*, even the same kind of *concetti*, both in Marino and in Donne. Marino openly confessed that the poet's aim should be to produce wonder and surprise in the reader. Donne is not so deliberate. When that surprise is brought about by him, this is due to the way his mind is working rather than to the deliberate choice of a startling simile. Marino's aim being the *concetto* for its own sake, his poems are either epigrams or fall into loose sequels of epigrams, of decorative puns. A capital instance of this kind of poetry in England is given in Crashaw's *Weeper*. But the chief thing with Donne is not the *concetti*, no matter how quaint they seem to us and how apt, in consequence, to engross our whole attention. The chief thing with him is the dialectical slant of his mind.

Of the various elements Sir Herbert Grierson distinguished [4] in the notion of 'metaphysical' poetry, the 'argumentative, subtle evolution' of the lyric strain is the thing Donne shares only with such mediaeval poets as Guido Guinizelli, Guido Cavalcanti, and Dante in his minor mood; the other metaphysical characteristic, the 'peculiar blend of passion and thought, feeling and ratiocination', of which 'learned imagery' is the consequence, is by no means such a rare thing in poetry, that traces of its may not be found in many Elizabethan writers, chiefly in the dramatists, as Miss Elizabeth Holmes has shown in a penetrating study.[5] Indeed the definition T. S. Eliot gave in his Clark Lectures: 'I take as metaphysical poetry that in which what is ordinarily apprehensible only by thought is brought within the grasp of feeling, or that in which what is ordinarily only felt is transformed into thought without ceasing to be feeling', is singularly akin to a definition Professor Martino gave [6] of Baudelaire's inspiration: 'L'idée

[4] *Metaphysical Lyrics and Poems of the Seventeenth Century*, pp. xv–xvi.

[5] *Aspects of Elizabethan Imagery*, Oxford, 1929.

[6] *Parnasse et symbolisme*, Paris, 1925, p. 100.

n'est jamais absente des *Fleurs du Mal*; il n'y a guère de
livres qui soient plus philosophiquement pensés, au sens large
du mot; mais l'idée ne cherche que bien rarement à s'abstraire;
elle arrive portée par la sensation, et encore enveloppée en
elle. C'est bien là le "frisson" dont parlait Victor Hugo.' My
bringing together of the two definitions would be welcomed,
I think, by Mr Eliot, who, in the lectures referred to above,
spoke of three metaphysical periods in European poetry: a
mediaeval period, a seventeenth-century period, and a modern
one with Jules Laforgue as its chief representative.

The quality of 'sensuous thought', prominent as it is in
Donne, is insufficient alone to describe his poetry. A passage
like the following one:

> my love
> In whom the learned Rabbis of this age
> Might find as many wondrous miracles
> As in the theorie of the world,

might be read as Donne's,[7] if we did not know that it is
Marlowe's (*2 Tamb.*, iv, 2). Or take:

> We too, that with so many thousand sighs
> Did buy each other, must poorly sell ourselves
> With the rude brevity and discharge of one.

Were it not for the last line, this passage could be sought for
in the works of Donne, instead of Shakespeare (*Troilus and
Cressida*, iv, 4).

Still nearer to Donne are the lines:

> Terms, tongs, reading, all
> That can within a man, cald learned, fall;
> Whose life is led yet like an ignorant mans:
> Are but as tooles to goutie Artizans
> That cannot use them; or like childrens arts,
> That out of habite, and by rootes of hearts,
> Construe and perce their lessons, yet discerne
> Nought of the matter, whose good words they learn:

---

[7] Cf. A *Valediction: of the booke*, 1.26 ff.:

> in this our universe
> Schooles might learne Sciences . . .

> Or, like our Chimicke Magi, that can call
> All termes of Art out, but no gold at all.

Here we seem to listen to 'a less swift and passionate Donne', as Miss Holmes calls Chapman, to whose pen the passage just quoted is due.[8] Like Donne's, Chapman's imagination is powerfully stimulated by this or that passage in the books he is reading, very often by a barren gloss, or such pieces of pedantic information as he could find in Natale Conti's mythological yarns. The poet boasts, every now and then, of the aptness and novelty of the figures and similes his own ingenuity has elicited from the sources: the thrill other poets receive from direct experience of life, he, with Donne, gets very often from either theological or ethical disquisitions, pedantic commentaries, and learned dictionaries. No doubt the 'striking affinity' Chapman has to Donne [9] is partly due to the fact that his poetry, as Mr Schoell noticed,[10] 'plonge d'aussi profondes racines dans la métaphysique du moyen-âge que celle de Donne'. But, if I may be allowed another quotation, in order to show how that affinity has been concordantly emphasised from various quarters in the last few years,

> such links are not accidental. They appear as results of a mental kinship. Donne's 'songs and sonets' were perhaps finding wide private circulation before Chapman wrote his tragedies or his *Tears of Peace*, and *An Anatomie of the World* appeared a few years earlier than Chapman's elegiac poem *Eugenia*. The two poets might well be acquainted, being both known to Ben Jonson, and both admitted to the literary circle of the Countess of Bedford. In any case Chapman must have read Donne sooner or later, but in several cases he anticipates him, for the metaphysical infection was in the air, and he was a likely subject.[11]

[8] See *The Poems of George Chapman*, ed. Phyllis Brooks Bartlett, New York, 1941, pp. 245–246 ('To yong imaginaries in knowledge').

[9] T. S. Eliot, *The Sacred Wood*, London, 1920, p. 20.

[10] F. L. Schoell, *Etudes sur l'Humanisme Continental en Angleterre*, Paris, 1926, p. 19.

[11] Holmes, *op. cit.*, p. 99.

Whether Chapman had anything to learn from Donne, is matter of speculation; but in the case of another dramatist, Webster, we have positive proofs of imitation,[12] though, of course, imitation here presupposes an analogous frame of mind. In Tourneur's *Transformed Metamorphosis* we see reflected the same chaos of a changing world which forms the background of Donne's verse.

Much of the quaintness later ages have detected in metaphysical poetry can be accounted for if we try to realise what must have been the position of those poets living between two worlds, two cultures, in an age of scientific revolution. The best illustration of this peculiar position is offered by Donne. His cultural equipment was in many ways that of a Scholastic thinker; hence the curious affinity some of his poetry shows to that of Dante's circle. With the difference that, whereas those mediaeval poets believed in the scientific and philosophical theories they accepted as the background of their verse, Donne, living in an age of scientific revolution, could not help surveying with a sceptic's eye the state of confusion presented by the changing world. On the one side he had the Holy Fathers and a curious body of mediaeval lore, on the other Copernicus and Brahe, Galileo, Kepler and Paracelsus. Though interested in thought, he was no original thinker himself. He aimed at artistic self-expression; therefore both the tentative creed of a new age, and the superannuated lore of centuries of old, merely supplied him indiscriminately with illustrations for his own poems and homilies. He was like a lawyer choosing the fittest arguments for a case in hand; not like a searcher after a universally valid truth. The scientific theories having only a value of conjectures or plausible speculations in his curious mind, do not belong to a world entirely distinct from the world of fancy, as they would in an era of settled convictions. Rather, there is a continuous interchange of suggestions from fancy to scientific thought and vice versa; and Donne is enabled to mix, in the same kaleidoscope, broken pieces of lore either old or new, and images properly belonging to the world of poetry. This state of mental osmosis, so

[12] See passages referred to in the Index to *The Complete Works of John Webster,* ed. F. L. Lucas, London, 1927.

to speak, is very likely responsible for the quality of 'sensuous thought' we detect in many Elizabethan writers.

Also of the argumentative, dramatic mood, which we find so peculiar to Donne, instances are not lacking, every now and then, among his predecessors. Miss Holmes calls our attention to a sonnet in *Astrophel and Stella* which 'plays with ideas in Donne's fashion, subtly and passionately at once'. It is the sonnet concluding with the well-known line:

> Deere, love me not, that thou may love me more.

It is not difficult to see where the taste for this and similar quibbles originated. When we read that line of Sidney, or this one of Drayton:

> You're not alone when you are still alone;

or Panfilo Sasso's:

> Tu non sei tua, ma mia, son tuo, non mio;

or Ronsard's:

> En toy je suis et tu es dedans moy,
> En moy tu vis et je vis dedans toy;
> Ains noz toutz ne font qu'un petit monde—

we are sent back to that fondness for scholastic subtleties which Petrarch retained from his predecessors. As a matter of fact a counterpart to Sidney's quibble can be found in an Italian poet of the thirteenth century, Guittone d'Arezzo:

> . . . poi che per amar m'odiate a morte
> Per disamar mi sarete amorosa.

And a rhymer of Guittone's school might well have written Donne's *Prohibition*;

> If thou love mee, take heed of loving mee;

or his *Lovers infinitenesse*:

> If yet I have not all thy love,
> Deare, I shall never have it all

> . . . .

> Or if then thou gavest mee all,
> All was but All, which thou hadst then . . .

The first of English poets to write in this dialectical style was,
I suppose, the first Petrarchist, Sir Thomas Wyatt. Do we
not see an anticipation of Donne's argumentative strain in the
following poem?

> To cause accord or to aggre
> . . . .
> That man that hath his hert away,
> If lyff lyveth there as men do say,
> That he, hertles, should last on day
> Alyve, and not to torn to clay,
>   It is impossible!
> . . . .
> Yet Love, that all things doeth subdue,
> Whose power there may no liff eschew,
> Hath wrought in me, that I may rew
> These miracles to be so true,
>   That are impossible.

If Wyatt is seen here anticipating Donne, it is because he
harks back to Petrarch:

> Talor m'assale in mezzo a'tristi pianti
>   Un dubbio, come posson queste membra
>   Dallo spirito lor viver lontane.
> Ma rispondemi Amor: Non ti rimembra
>   Che questo è privilegio degli amanti,
>   Sciolti da tutte qualitadi umane? [13]

---

[13] Sonnet 11 *in vita.*

>   Sometimes a doubt assails my deep distress:
>   How can these limbs go on living at all,
>   So far away from their soul's happiness?
>   But then Love answers me:—Don't you recall
>   That lovers have the privilege to be
>   Rid of each human trait and quality?
>   (Anna Maria Armi's translation,
>   Pantheon Books, 1946)

Yes, 'harmlesse lovers' wrought such 'miracles' already in Petrarch's time. And it would be difficult to find a better instance of metaphysical subtlety, of that subtlety which is a distinctive feature of The Extasie,[14] than Petrarch's sixty-third sonnet *in vita*:

> Quando giunge per gli occhi al cor profondo
>   L'immagin donna, ogni altra indi si parte;
>   E le virtù che l'anima comparte
>   Lascian le membra quasi immobil pondo.
> E dal primo miracolo il secondo
>   Nasce talor; che la scacciata parte,
>   Da se stessa fuggendo, arriva in parte
>   Che fa vendetta, e 'l suo esilio giocondo.
> Quinci in due volti un color morto appare:
>   Perché 'l vigor che vivi gli mostrava,
>   Da nessun lato è più là dove stava.

[14] The theory which is at the basis of Donne's *Extasie* occurs also in Giordano Bruno's *Candelaio*, I, x. Cf.: 'Our hands were firmly cemented . . . Our eye-beams twisted, and did thread/Our eyes upon one double string;/ So to entergraft our hands, as yet/Was all the means to make us one,/And pictures in our eyes to get/Was all our propagation . . ./When love, with one another so/Interinanimates two souls,/That abler soul, which thence doth flow,/Defects of loneliness controls, etc.' Bruno: 'L'esser fascinato d'amore adviene, quando con frequentissimo over, benché istantaneo, intenso sguardo, un occhio con l'altro, e reciprocamente un raggio visual con l'altro si riscontra, e lume con lume si accopula. Allora si gionge spirto a spirto; ed il lume superiore, inculcando l'inferiore, vangono a scintillar per gli occhi, correndo e penetrando al spirito interno che sta radicato al cuore; e cossì commuoveno amatorio incendio.' [Fascination by love takes place when owing to very frequent looking or to an intense, though instantaneous, look, one eye meets another, and two eye-beams reciprocally encounter, and light couples together with light. Then spirit joins with spirit; and the superior light informing the inferior one, they come to sparkle through the eyes, rushing to, and penetrating, the inner spirit which is rooted in the heart; and in this manner they kindle erotic fire.] Merritt Y. Hughes, in 'The Lineage of "The Extasie",' in *The Modern Language Review*, xxvii, January 1, 1932, has conclusively shown how Donne's poem links up with the tradition of Italian Platonism as embodied in Castiglione's *Cortegiano*, and chiefly in Benedetto Varchi's *Lezioni sopra alcune quistioni d'amore* (the question whether in honest love one feels passions).

E di questo in quel dì mi ricordava,
Ch'i' vidi duo amanti trasformare
E far qual io mi soglio in vista fare.[15]

As we survey Donne's poetry after such a distance of time, we can hardly fail to notice how much this poet who in a sense led the reaction against Petrarchism in England was himself a Petrarchist, thanks to his mediaevally trained mind. Not a Petrarchist to the extent Sidney was, who, notwithstanding his protests of independent inspiration, was rehearsing most of the hackneyed tropes of the Continental sonneteers, nay, at the very moment he claimed to be no pickpurse of another's brain, was deriving from Du Bellay's ode *Contre les Pétrarquistes*. No, Donne must have actually felt in opposition to the poetry of his day, and if he still remained a Petrarchist to some extent, this is due to the fact that, no matter how strong one's personal reaction is, one cannot avoid belonging to a definite historical climate.

One can find Donne's quality of sensuous thought in many other poets, and yet, if we restore the Donne-like passages of others to their context, we shall easily persuade ourselves that neither Marlowe, nor Shakespeare, not even Chapman, is like Donne, because, though metaphysical elements are to be found in them all, it is their frequency that gives to poetry that peculiar flavour we recognise as Donne's. Again, scholastic subtlety of thought is every now and then affected by many, but nowhere do we find it enhanced by a dramatic

[15] When through the eyes reaches the secret heart
A high image, the others dissipate,
And the virtues that are our soul's best part
Desert the members, leaving a dead weight.
And from this wonder a second sometimes
Derives its birth, and the excluded thing
Fleeing itself arrives in other climes
That revenge it and make its exile sing.
Hence in two faces comes a look of death;
Because the vigour that gave them life's breath
In neither place can stay where it had been.
And I remembered this a certain day
When I beheld two lovers' cheeks decay
And suddenly assume my usual mien.
(Anna Maria Armi's translation)

technique like that used by Donne. From this point of view, a comparison of *The First Anniversary* with *A Feaver* is very telling. *The First Anniversary*, with its central idea that the world has come to an end with the death of that young girl, Elizabeth Drury, may be considered as a mere embroidery on a theme which, in its simplest form, may be found in this sonnet by Sannazaro, also inspired by the death of a girl:

> Una nova Angioletta a' giorni nostri
> Nel viver basso apparve altera e schiva;
> E così bella poi, lucente e viva
> Tornò volando a li superni chiostri.
> Felice ciel, tu chiaro or ti dimostri
> Del lume, onde la terra è oscura e priva;
> Spirti ben nati, e voi l'alma mia diva
> Lieti vedete ogn'or con gli occhi vostri.
> Ma tu ben puoi dolerti, o cieco mondo;
> Tua gloria è spenta, il tuo valore è morto;
> Tua divina eccellenzia è gita al fondo.
> Un sol rimedio veggio al viver corto,
> Che avendo a navigar mar sì profondo,
> Uom raccolga la vela, e mora in porto.[16]

The world is worth nothing, after such a death, says Sannazaro (and God knows how many times the same thing had been said before!). 'Sicke World, yea, dead, yea putrified . . .' says Donne, bent on improving and amplifying an old *concetto*. Had Donne always written in the style of the Anniversaries, he would not rank much higher than Marino

---

[16] A new Angel appeared in our time, haughty and shy, in this lower world; then, as beautiful as she had come, bright and alive she flew back to the upper spheres.

O happy heaven, now thou showest thyself adorned with that light of which earth has been deprived; and you, blessed souls, are glad to see forever my divine beloved before your eyes.

But thou, blind world, hast reason to complain; thy glory has faded, thy valour is dead; thy supremacy has been overthrown.

I see only one remedy to our short life, that, since man has such a deep ocean to cross, he should gather the sails, and die in the harbour.

or Góngora. But when we come across the same *concetto* in
A Feaver, the impression we receive is quite different:

> But yet thou canst not die, I know;
>   To leave this world behinde, is death,
> But when thou from this world wilt goe,
>   The whole world vapors with thy breath.

The accent is here dramatic and passionate; there is none of
that splendid fustian about the 'intrinsique balm', the 'pre-
servative', and similar pseudo-scientific paraphernalia.

> Or if, when thou, the worlds soule, goest,
>   It stay, tis but thy carkasse then,
> The fairest woman, but thy ghost,
>   But corrupt wormes, the worthyest men.

I suppose when Donne wrote:

> For there's a kinde of World remaining still,
> Though shee which did inanimate and fill
> The world, be gone . . .
>   .   .   .   .
> The twilight of her memory doth stay;
> Which, from the carcasse of the old world, free,
> Creates a new world—

he meant more or less the same thing; but the dramatic live-
liness of the shorter poem makes all the difference. And the
rapid change of intonation is continued in the next stanza:

> O wrangling schooles, that search what fire
>   Shall burne this world, had none the wit
> Unto this knowledge to aspire,
>   That this her feaver might be it? [17]

---

[17] A similar use of the theory of the end of the world through
fire had been made by Tasso when he attributed to Providence the
illness which was casting a shadow on the beauty of Eleonora
d'Este. For, he argued, should that beauty appear in its full
brightness

> incenerite ed arse
> Morrian le genti . . .
>   .   .   .   .

There is in this poem a nervous elasticity which seems worlds apart from the ponderous redundancy of the *Anatomie of the World,* and was to be equalled only by another among English poets, Robert Browning. No doubt most of Donne's poems appeal to our modern taste thanks to that dramatic quality of their style.

Donne's holy sonnets come next in interest after his songs. Though they have none of the originality of the latter, they can vie with those of Michelangelo for earnestness and intensity of religious thought: indeed, they are remarkably close to them in inspiration. In both poets the 'devout fitts come and go away/Like a fantastique Ague'; faith has proved such a difficult conquest for them, that they are continually afraid of slackening in zeal. The moments of grace are so rare that Michelangelo asks God to make haste:

> Ché con più tempo il buon voler men dura.[18]

Both of them try to overcome the aridity of their hearts; they feel between their heart and God a barrier, which only God can break:

> Batter my heart, three person'd God . . .
>
> . . . .
>
> I, like an unsurpt towne, to'another due,
> Labour to'admit you, but Oh, to no end. . . .
>
> Tra 'l foco e 'l cor di ghiaccio un vel s'asconde . . .
>
> . . . .
>
> I' t'amo con la lingua e poi mi doglio,
> Ch'amor non giungie al cor . . .
>
> . . . .

> E ciò che il Fato pur minaccia, allora
> In faville converso il mondo fora.

[The nations would be burnt to ashes . . . And, what Fate still threatens, the world then would be turned into sparks (i.e., the Day of Wrath would take place).]

[18]   . . . for here
With lengthening days good thought and wishes fail.
                              (Symonds' translation)

> Squarcia 'l vel tu, Signior! Rompi quel muro
> Che con la sua durezza ne ritarda
> Il sol della tua luce. . . .[19]

Also Donne could have repeated Michelangelo's appeal to
God:

> Manca la speme, e pur cresce il desio
>
> . . . .
>
> Ammezzami la strada, ch'al ciel sale,
> Signior mio caro, e, a quel mezzo solo
> Salir, m'è di bisognio la tua 'ita.[20]

> Except thou rise and for thine owne worke fight,
> Oh I shall soone despaire. . . .

> Non mirin con iustizia i tuo' sant'occhi
> Il mio passato, e 'l gastigato orecchio
> Non tenda a quello il tuo braccio severo.
> Tuo sangue sol mie colpe lavi e tocchi
> E più abondi, quant'i' son più vecchio,
> Di pronta aita e di perdono intero.[21]

[19] Between it [my heart] and the fire a veil of ice
Deadens the fire . . .

. . . .

I love Thee with my tongue, then mourn my fill;
For love warms not my heart . . .

. . . .

Rend Thou the veil, dear Lord! Break Thou that wall
Which with its stubbornness retards the rays
Of that bright sun . . .
(Symonds' translation)

[20] Hope fades, but still desire ascends

. . . .

Shorten half-way my road to heaven from earth!
Dear Lord, I cannot even half-way rise,
Unless thou help me on this pilgrimage.
(Symonds' translation)

[21] Let not Thy holy eyes be just to see
My evil past, Thy chastened ears to hear
And stretch the arm of judgment to my crime:
Let Thy blood only lave and succour me,
Yielding more perfect pardon, better cheer,
As older still I grow with lengthening time.
(Symonds' translation)

. . . Oh! of thine onely worthy blood,
And my teares, make a heavenly Lethean flood,
And drowne in it my sinnes blacke memorie;
That thou remember them, some claime as debt,
I thinke it mercy, if thou wilt forget.

One may say that these are more or less commonplaces of religious poetry, but it is all the same remarkable that both Michelangelo and Donne strike the same notes, and only these. Idle as it perhaps would be to speculate on affinities between Donne and Michelangelo, I cannot forbear to record here another curious coincidence. Michelangelo had said in a famous sonnet:

Non ha l'ottimo artista alcun concetto
Ch'un marmo solo in sé non circoscriva
Col suo soverchio, e solo a quello arriva
La man, che ubbidisce all'intelletto.[22]

The same image occurs in *The Crosse*:

As perchance, Carvers do not faces make,
But that away, which hid them there, do take.

Donne, of course, could not have known of Michelangelo's sonnets, which were posthumously published in 1623. But in his peculiar mixture of realism and platonism, in the dramatic turn of his genius as well as in his laborious yearnings for beauty and religion, in that double character of half-baffled, half-triumphant struggle, in his power of depicting the horrors of sin and death, and the terrible effects of the wrath of God, Donne is perhaps nearer to Michelangelo than to anybody else.

[22] The best of artists hath no thought to show
Which the rough stone in its superfluous shell
Doth not include: to break the visible spell
Is all the hand that serves the brain can do.
                    (Symonds' translation)

The Flaming Heart:
Richard Crashaw and the Baroque

THERE exists in Rome, in the church of Santa Maria della Vittoria, a work of art which may be taken as an epitome of the devotional spirit of the Roman Catholic countries in the seventeenth century. Radiantly smiling, an Angel hurls a golden arrow against the heart of a woman saint languorously lying on a bed of clouds. The mixture of divine and human elements in this marble group, Bernini's Saint Teresa, may well result in that 'spirit of sense' of which Swinburne, who had borrowed the phrase from Shakespeare, was so fond of speaking. Spirit of sense as in that love song the Church had adopted as a symbol of the soul's espousals with God: the Song of Solomon, which actually in the seventeenth century was superlatively paraphrased in the *coplas* of Saint John of the Cross. Inclined as it was to the pleasures of the senses, the seventeenth century could not help using, when it came to religion, the very language of profane love, transposed and sublimated: its nearest approach to God could only be a spiritualization of sense.

While the passion of the age for rhetoric and grandiloquence expressed itself in the cult for saints conceived as victorious athletes, heroes, the strong erotic strain of seventeenth-century worshippers found an outlet in the cult of female saints and martyrs. The greatest popularity was achieved by those saints in whom the erotic element joined with the element of surprise—a metamorphosis of theatrical proportions: hence the cult of that Venus in sackcloth, Saint Mary Magdalen, who pointed out the way to Heaven to repentant sinners: the transition from profane to sacred love took place in her with that dazzling contrast in which the century recognized the essence of wit.

But Mary Magdalen was only the supreme star in a constellation of female saints which dominated the summer sky of Baroque religion: under that sky were born not only most poets in the Catholic countries, but also a few Northern ones, Vondel in Holland, and Richard Crashaw in England. Actually in the *Brieven der Heilige Maeghden, Martèlaressen* (that spiritualization of Ovid's *Heroides*), Vondel compares his band of twelve virgin and martyred saints to a Zodiac through which every year the sun of the Cross makes its round: the signs of the Zodiac being the traditional attributes of those saints, among which many are emblems of martyrdom. In another of Vondel's works, Mary Stuart is represented as a martyr of faith, falling under the blows of persecuting wrath like a ripe ear of corn: for the poet took very seriously the predestination contained in her name: *Maria Stuarta erat matura arista*. Since also Crashaw saw things from this angle, it will be opportune to become familiar with it from the outset.

An English Jesuit, arrested at the time of the Gunpowder Plot, is reported to have sworn never to have been either a seminarist or a priest, and, when found out by a confrontation with a certain Hawkesworth, to have explained that he had meant to say that he had never been a priest *of Apollo,* he had never been across the *Indian* sea, never known the said Hawkesworth *scientia scientifica,* and never seen him *in visione beatifica.* Such cases of mental reservation, common in the course of the seventeenth century, may strike us as incredible, for we find it hard to understand how serious people can have admitted a device of this kind. However, the case of mental reservation (a form of 'honest dissimulation') [1] is only

---

[1] The treatise *Della dissimulazione onesta,* by Torquato Accetto (latest reprint, edited by G. Bellonci, Florence, 1942), has been discussed in connexion with Baroque ostentation by Jean Rousset, *La Littérature de l'âge baroque en France,* Paris, 1953, p. 221 f.

a transference to the moral field of that *argutezza* (wit) which in the aesthetic field produced that typical seventeenth-century mental process, the *concetto* (conceit). Seventeenth-century men saw instances of *argutezza* in every aspect of the universe. All the phenomena of the surrounding world, all the categories of learning, supplied them with suggestions for this mental idiosyncrasy of theirs: they discovered mysterious witticisms in the aspects of the earth and the sky, heroical devices and symbols in all the creatures; animals and plants possessed a witty language for them; and full of wit was the language of God; for since man fashions God in his own image, and a cannibal imagines God as a man-eater, so a seventeenth-century man had an idea of God as a 'witty speaker, who, talking in riddles to Men and Angels, clothed his most exalted concepts with various heroical Devices, and pictorial Symbols'.[2] The seventeenth-century man saw the sky as 'a vast cerulean Shield, on which skilful Nature draws what she meditates: forming heroical Devices, and mysterious and witty Symbols of her secrets,'[3] saw the thunderbolts as 'formidable Witticisms [*Arguzie*] and Symbolical Ciphers of Nature, both dumb and at the same time vocal; having the Bolt for their body and the Thunder for their motto', saw dreams, quibbles, prodigies, oracles, monsters as so many forms of wit, or rather everything was to him a prodigy, an oracle, a monster, a quibble, and his world seems to us a dream-world, in which, thanks to a bizarre convention, everything appears to be endowed with a fictitious and absurd value. Tesauro's *Cannocchiale Aristotelico* enables us to get to the roots of the seventeenth-century frame of mind: a frame of mind which, in its striving after wit, mixed together all the aspects of the universe into one monstrous category, and knew no limits in that respect.

As everything was subservient to wit, no criterion was left to distinguish a work of art from a work of mere skill, or, worse, from the capricious product of a disordered brain; indeed mad people 'better than sane ones (believe it or not) are well conditioned to invent exhilarating metaphors and

[2] E. Tesauro, *Il Cannocchiale Aristotelico*, Venice, 1655, p. 61.
[3] Tesauro, p. 77. Cf. Plutarch, *De oraculorum defectu*, in *Moralia* 416 D.

witty symbols; Madness itself being nothing else than a Metaphor which takes one thing for another'.[4] We might perhaps say that *secentismo* is an exaggeration of that mediaevel, scholastic tendency to see the world as a figurative, mystical alphabet, a tendency which is instanced in the façades of Gothic cathedrals conceived as books displaying symbolic signs that spoke a clear, logical language to any one who had the clue to them.

Emblems, devices, anagrams, riddles, puzzles, were accounted sublime achievements of art, and the taste of the period was so engrossed with this craze for *concetti*, that a seventeenth-century man would *naturally* resort to wit in those critical circumstances of life which usually elicit simple, elementary expressions even from the most sophisticated of men: Donne, on the day when all hopes of happiness seemed to forsake him, found nothing better than a witticism: 'John Donne, Ann Donne, Undone'; and Laud, imprisoned and threatened with death, saw an ironical confirmation of the accusations of his enemies in an anagram of his name: 'William Laude—Well am a Divil'.[5]

As *arguzia* (wit), in the words of Sforza Pallavicino, was 'a marvellous observation condensed into a brief sentence', it is easy to understand why the artistic form which best suited the mind of a seventeenth-century man should be the epigram, which, by suggesting a foreshortened *tertium quid*, was the literary counterpart of a deceptive perspective of the kind of the famous Borromini colonnade in the Palazzo Spada, Rome.[6] One may say in a certain sense that the epigrammatic tendency is discernible in all the literary works of the seventeenth century; and a great impulse in that direction must no doubt have come to seventeenth-century taste from the diffusion of the *Greek Anthology* which had begun at the

[4] Tesauro, p. 97.

[5] See W. H. Hutton, *The English Church from the Accession of Charles I to the Death of Anne*, London, 1903, p. 86.

[6] See what Tesauro (p. 310) says on the metaphor: 'Metaphor packs tightly all objects into one word: and makes you see them one inside the other in an almost miraculous way. Hence your delight is the greater, because it is a more curious and pleasant thing to watch many objects from a perspective angle than if the originals themselves were to pass successively before one's eyes.'

end of the fifteenth century: [7] a diffusion which was favoured by the extreme similarity between the epigram and the sonnet, which was the prevailing poetic form at the time.[8] The *Anthology* offered an inexhaustible quarry to the sonneteers, who immediately grafted the new themes derived from the Greek epigrams onto the hackneyed ones of Petrarchan origin. The influence of the epigram on the form of the sonnet was even greater than on its contents: it accelerated and completed that process of concluding with a witty turn that was inherent in its nature. This refashioning of the sonnet on the model of the epigram was not the sole effect of the discovery of the *Greek Anthology* (the refashioning, it is worth noticing, was so deliberate that, for instance, Clément Marot called some of his sonnets 'epigrams'): another effect was the unprecedented vogue for madrigals and collections of madrigals: such seventeenth-century collections as the *Tela Cangiante,* the *Ghirlanda dell'Aurora,* the *Giardino di Rime,* the *Giardino di Fiori Toscani,* and so on, are manifestly modelled on the Garlands of Greek epigrams.

The epigrammatic tendency, which had become general in the seventeenth century, availed itself of forms like the *ottava rima* and the sonnet to sparkle like a Catherine-wheel at the end. Wonder, which was the chief aim of the seventeenth-century writers, is particularly achieved through such unexpected clashes and conflagrations of conceits as are the natural decorations of the closing lines of those metrical forms. The *ottave* of Marino's *Adone,* and even more those of the *Strage degli Innocenti,* are so many epigrams, and the madrigals and sonnets of Marino and his followers are epigrams in

[7] James Hutton, *The Greek Anthology in Italy to the year 1800,* Cornell University Press, 1935 (Cornell Studies in English, xxiii). For a further elaboration of the ideas contained in this portion of the present study, see my *Studies in Seventeenth-century Imagery,* London, 1939, ch. i, 'Emblem–Device–Epigram–Conceit'.

[8] Cf. Sebillet, *Art poétique françois,* 1548, ii, 2 (ed. Gaiffe, p. 115): 'Le Sonnet suit l'epigramme de bien pres, et de matière et de mesure; et quand tout est dit le sonnet n'est autre chose que le parfait epigramme de l'Italien, comme le dizain du François.' Already that popular form of the epigram, the *strambotto,* born in Greek Sicily, had had a passing but widespread influence on the lyric poetry of the end of the fifteenth century, particularly on Cariteo and Serafino.

the same way. The whole *Strage degli Innocenti,* if one looks
at it properly, is no other than an endless repetition of the
formula for a marvellous case we find in Martial's well-known
epigram on the child killed by a lump of ice ('Qua vicina
pluit Ripsanis porta columnis . . .'), whose closing line
('Aut ubi mors non est, si iugulatis aquae?') must have
thrilled seventeenth-century people. There is, moreover, in
Martial an exclamation that could be taken as a slogan for
the seventeenth-century craze for conceits:

O quantum est subitis casibus ingenium!

which adumbrates that wit—*ingenium*—seventeenth-century
people detected in inanimate things and events.

There was in the seventeenth century a group of Latin
poets, Jesuits as a rule, who cultivated this art of the epigram
with an ingenuity that had been well trained at the school of
casuistry, equivocation, and sacred eloquence.[9] Tesauro's
passage [10] on the *concetti predicabili* helps us to understand
the use of wit in religious subjects:

> Hence you may easily understand what are those
> *Thoughts* of Sacred Orators which are usually called
> PREACHABLE CONCEITS: received with so much favour and
> admiration by the sacred Theatre, that the word of God
> appears nowadays insipid and jejune unless it is seasoned
> with such sweets. A baffling question, this one, which, so
> far as I am aware, has escaped notice until now, and has
> never been touched upon by any writer. For from the out-
> set it is evident, that neither the wording of a Gospel pas-
> sage, nor a bare history from the Old Testament, nor the
> simple sentence of a Sacred Author, nor an article of Saint
> Thomas, are commonly liable to be called by that name of
> *Conceits,* which people find so much to their taste. Even
> less will a philosophical subtlety, or a plain and evident
> moral reason, or an example, no matter how marvellous, or
> profane erudition, howsoever curious, be called a *Preach-*

[9] The quantity of the poetical output in verse due to the Jesuits
can be gauged by glancing at the *Parnassus Societatis Iesu . . .*
Francofurti, Sumptibus Iohan. Godofredi Schonwetteri, 1654: a collection which is still far from including all the poets of the Society
who wrote Latin verse in the first half of the seventeenth century.
[10] Pp. 67–68.

able Conceit by the people. Therefore two things chiefly make up this sacred offspring of Wit: i.e., the *sacred subject* grounded on Divine Authority, and the *Witty Form*, founded on some figurative Symbol which yields a Tropological, or Allegorical, or Anagogical sense that is different from the one offered at first sight by the words of the Sacred Text literally taken. This is what we call WIT: an ingenious, unexpected, and popular Argument. Hence Theologians do not confirm their theses by such witty Conceits: but by plain and literal Arguments; on the contrary that Sacred Orator who weaves his speech with Theological Arguments, is considered a scholastic teacher rather than a popular Preacher. In order to be convinced of it, try to examine one of these ingenious products: you will find that its foundation is a *Metaphor*, a *Quibble*, a *Laconism*, or another of those Rhetorical Devices we have examined elsewhere. Therefore the PREACHABLE CONCEIT is nothing else than a *Symbolical Witticism, lightly hinted at by the Divine Mind: elegantly revealed by the mind of man: and reconfirmed through the authority of some Sacred Author*. The applause is equally divided between God for having found it, the Saint for having observed it, and the Preacher for having shown it to the world as a rare merchandise, and opportunely suited it to his purpose. The utmost praise goes to that Conceit which best fulfils the requisites of Wit: i.e., *Propriety, Novelty, Ingenious Allusion*, and *Admirable Reflexion*. Chiefly if, offering in its literal context a sense which at first is *contradictory* and difficult to explain, this sense is at last unexpectedly and ingeniously cleared as a figurative sense, either through some subtle doctrine, or rare piece of erudition, or lively similitude, or felicitous analogy with some other hard passage of the Scripture. For two obscure sentences, once put together, become luminous.

Whatever is here said about the preachable conceits can be extended to the whole class of compositions to which Richard Crashaw's first book of verse, the *Epigrammata Sacra* (1634), belongs. The words the poet addresses to his master Benjamin Laney in the preface assign to the sacred epigram an aim similar to that Tesauro recognized in the preachable conceit: 'Enimvero epigramma sacrum tuus ille vultus vel est, vel quid sit docet; *ubi nimirum amabili diluitur severum, et sanctum suavi demulcetur'*. These epigrams are usually of the same nature as those Latin inscriptions which Croce [11] reported to be carved on seventeenth-century Neapolitan monuments: they belong to the witty lapidary style (*arguta Lapidaria*) discussed by Tesauro. They are both pun and poetic image, and this ambiguity causes our modern minds to hesitate, whether to dismiss such inventions as mere play, or to receive them among the genuine products of inspired fancy. Sometimes a little touch is enough to make the scales turn one way or the other. One is reminded of the South-Seas fish of which Stevenson said:

It is a question both of time and place. A fish caught in a lagoon may be deadly; the same fish caught the same day at sea, and only a few hundred yards without the passage, will be wholesome eating: in a neighbouring isle perhaps the case will be reversed; and perhaps in a fortnight later you shall be able to eat of them indifferently from within and from without. According to the natives, these bewildering vicissitudes are ruled by the movement of the heavenly bodies. The beautiful planet Venus plays a great part in all island tales and customs; and among other functions, some of them more awful, she regulates the season of good fish. With Venus in one phase, as we had her, certain fish were poisonous in the lagoon; with Venus in another, the same fish was harmless and a valued article of diet.

If for Venus we substitute the Muse, or inspiration, the whole story of Baroque will be told without any need of further distinctions and subdivisions.[12]

Take for instance Crashaw's most famous epigram, the one on the miracle at Cana:

Unde rubor vestris, et non sua purpura lymphis?
Quae rosa mirantes tam nova mutat aquas?

[11] *Saggi sulla letteratura italiana del Seicento*, p. 424.
[12] Such as are attempted by Odette de Mourgues in *Metaphysical, Baroque and Précieux Poetry*, Oxford, 1953.

Numen (convivae) praesens agnoscite Numen:
Nympha pudica Deum vidit et *erubuit*.[13]

The conceit contained in this epigram has a rather curious
history. One finds it foreshadowed in a passage of Grotius's
Christus Patiens translated by Crashaw,[14] and more particularly in a couplet of the Jesuit Maximilianus Sandaeus placed
under the figure of a rose with an image of the Presentation of
the Virgin in the Temple in its centre: [15]

> Vin' scire unde suum rosa candida traxerit ostrum?
> Purgantem vidit Virginem et erubuit.

Later Dryden and Victor Hugo drew inspiration from the
same conceit.[16] One may say many fine things on the fourth
line of Crashaw's epigram, and see in every word of it 'a
theatre full of wonders', to use Tesauro's language. Emilio
Cecchi [17] has defined that line as 'a concentrated expression

[13] R. Crashaw, *The Poems, English, Latin and Greek*, ed. L. C.
Martin, Oxford, 1927, p. 38. Aaron Hill's free rendering runs:

> When Christ at Cana's feast by pow'r divine
> Inspired cold water with the warmth of wine:
> See! cried they, while in redd'ning tide it gush'd,
> The bashful stream hath seen its God, and blush'd.

[14] Hugonis Grotii *Poemata*, 1639, p. 399:

> Natura rerum cessit et fassa est Deum.
> Undae liquentis ebrios potus bibit
> Galilaea pubes.

Crashaw's translation runs (ed. Martin, p. 399):

> The water blush'd, and started into wine,
> Full of high sparkeling vigour: taught by mee
> A sweet inebriated extasy.

[15] Sandaeus (van der Sandt), *Maria Flos Mysticus snte* [sic]
*Orationes ad sodales in festivitatibus deiparae habitae desumpta
materia a floribus cum figuris eneis*, Maguntiae apud Godefridum
Schonwetterum, 1629, p. 24. (See note by Edward Bensly in
Notes and Queries, Series 10, x, p. 307, October 17, 1908).

[16] La nymphe de ces eaux aperçut Jésus-Christ,
Et son pudique front de rougeur se couvrit.

The same clause of the pentameter occurs in Cabilliau, *Magdalena*
(*Balduini Cabilliavi e soc. Jesu Magdalena*, Antverpiae, ex officina
Plantiniana Balthasaris Moreti, 1625), *Magdalea Silva*, lxij, 2 (p.
199): 'Monstrifero speculo vidit, et erubuit'.

[17] *Storia della letteratura inglese nel secolo XIX*, Milan, 1915,
p. 296.

of the manner in which the natural and the divine join in intimate and passionate relationship'. He adds: 'Nature's emotion particularly vibrates in the second verb: the chaste pagan nymph acknowledges the Spirit, the creator. Shut in the hard physical autonomy of the ancient world, she feels her own origin carried outside herself into a reason which contains and reveals it.' Sublime as Crashaw's idea may be, there is only a hair's breadth between it and Théophile's notorious conceit, in which successive generations have seen a typical instance of the grotesque:

> Ha! voicy le poignard qui du sang de son maistre
> S'est souillé laschement: il en rougit, le traistre!

We are reminded also of a less famous, but no less grotesque, conceit of Marino's, who apostrophised those who stoned Saint Stephen in the following terms:

> Vedete i sassi là, che de' begli ostri
> Sparsi sen van, sol per mostrarsi tinti
> Di quel rossor che manca ai volti vostri.[18]

One wonders whether Crashaw, while writing that epigram, was aware of having hit upon a much nobler invention than the one contained in his distichs on Pilate:

> ### Pontio lavanti
>
> Non satis est caedes, nisi stuprum hoc insuper addas,
>   Et tam virgineae sis violator aquae?
> Nympha quidem pura haec et *honesti filia fontis*
>   Luget, adulterio jam temerata tuo.
> Casta verecundo properat cum murmure gutta,
>   Nec satis in lacrymam se putat esse suam.
> Desine tam nitidos stuprare (ah, desine) rores:
>   Aut dic, quae miseras unda lavabit aquas.[19]

We would find it difficult to admire nowadays the amazing feats detailed in these distichs, which by far surpass whatever

[18] 'Look there at the stones, dyed in that fine purple, only to show that blush which is lacking in your faces'. No more convincing is Milton's personification of the earth who 'woos the gentle air/to hide her guilty front with innocent snow' (*On the Morning of Christ's Nativity*, 38–39).

[19] Ed. Martin, p. 57. See Crashaw's English version, *ibid.*, p. 94.

certain 'noble wits' invented apropos of a celebrated fountain mentioned by Tesauro.[20] *Attonitas hebetant docta haec miracula mentes,* declared one of them, and well may we repeat it when we think of the impression Crashaw's epigrams were calculated to produce on his contemporaries. A comparison between the Cana epigram, which achieves genuine poetry, and the other verses we have quoted, which strike us as mere documents of a passing taste, warns us not to be hasty in a wholesale condemnation of baroque wit.

Certain subjects were for Crashaw inexhaustible sources of witticism: he handled and rehandled them both in Latin and English, he took every opportunity to bring them in like ready-made purple patches. Whenever waters or tears came into question, Crashaw's wit revealed itself capable of astonishing hydraulic inventions: he makes the waters play like Versailles waterworks, and thinks to give us a quintessence of the Castalian spring in the iridescent sparkle of conceits. Let us quote another epigram, *In aquam baptismi Dominici:* [21]

Felix ô, sacros cui sic licet ire per artus!
　Felix! dum lavat hunc, ipsa lavatur aqua.
Gutta quidem sacros quaecunque per ambulat artus,
　Dum manet hic, gemma est; dunc cadit hinc, lacryma.

Word-play, ambiguities, *calembours,* are at the root of such astonishing conceits, which might as well be formulated like riddles, e.g.: Who is the man by whose body water is washed instead of washing? In fact a few years before the publication of the *Epigrammata Sacra,* a Spanish poet, Alonso de Ledesma, had composed riddles of this kind (*Iuegos de Noche Buena*).[22] In another epigram, *In natales Domini pastoribus nuniatos,*[23] not included in the 1634 volume, we read:

Pastor, an Agnus erat? Pastor, et Agnus erat.
Ipse Deus cum Pastor erit, quis non erit agnus?
Quis non pastor erit, cum Deus Agnus erit?

[20] Pp. 49, 50, 51.
[21] Ed. Martin, p. 32; Crashaw's English version, p. 85.
[22] See my *Studies in Seventeenth-century Imagery, op. cit.,* pp. 126–127.
[23] Ed. Martin, p. 355.

In another, *Ad Infantes Martyres*: [24]

> Fundite ridentes animas; effundite coelo:
> Discet ibi vestra (ô quam bene!) lingua loqui.
> Ne vos lac vestrum et maternos quaerite fontes:
> Quae vos expectat *lactea* tota *via* est.

This last epigram is very close to Marino's puns on the Innocents ('Noi della lattea via lattanti germi/d'orme sanguigne il bel candor segnammo') [25] but it is unlikely that Crashaw, who, as we shall see, was to find his favourite author in Marino, knew the *Strage degli Innocenti* (first published in 1632) in time to utilise it for his 1634 volume (Crashaw's version of the *Sospetto d'Erode* belongs almost certainly to 1637; see below); however the theme had long been among the favourite ones of Jesuit and Marinist poets.[26] On the other hand the epigram *Ad Judaeos mactatores Stephani*: [27]

> Frustra illum increpitant, frustra vaga saxa: nec illi
> Grandinis (heu saevae!) dura procella nocet.
> Ista potest tolerare; potest nescire: sed illi,
> Quae sunt in vestro pectore, saxa nocent—

recalls one of Marino's conceits (*Lira*, iii, *Nel Martirio di Santo Stefano*, sonnet: 'O cori no, ma perfidi, e maligni . . .'):

[24] Ed Martin, p. 24; Crashaw's English version, p. 88.

[25] 'We foster-children of the Milky Way marked that beautiful whiteness with blood-stained footprints'.

[26] The first idea of the *Strage degli Innocenti* can be traced back to Marino's youth. Among the other poets who drew inspiration from that subject, see specially Iacobi Bidermanni e Soc. Iesu *Herodiados Libri tres,* Sive DD. Innocentes Christomartyres ab Herode tyranno crudeliter caesi . . . Dilingae . . . Apud Uldaricum Rem, 1622 (although Bidermann's poem is modelled on the *Aeneid,* and, on this account, is very different from Marino's poem, there are many more affinities between the two poems than the identity of the subject would naturally produce; however the dates help little towards establishing priority, since the date of the publication of Marino's poem does not necessarily coincide with the date of its actual circulation); Fr. Remondi *Epigrammata,* quoted below, p. 5 (Lib. i, xii, xiii), and, among the Italian Marinists, A. Bruni, *Le Tre Grazie,* Rome, 1630, p. 422-423; etc.

[27] Ed. Martin, p. 24.

Son ben per lui crudeli e fieri ordigni
Le pietre sì, ma 'l martire dolente
Più de le vostre colpe i colpi sente
Che 'l fulminar de' rigidi macigni.[28]

In the same way another epigram, *In vulnera pendentis Domini* ('Sive oculos, sive ora vocem tua vulnera . . .' [29] is based on a conceit we find in Marino's *Alla piaga del Costato* ('Piaga dolce d'amore/già tu piaga non sei/ma bocca di quel core').[30] And the conceit derived from the theme of the Circumcision, which recurs in many epigrams of Crashaw,[31] seems suggested by Marino's sonnet on that subject (*Lira*, iii):

Questo vermiglio umor che stilla fora
    Pria ch'a forza l'esprima o chiodo, o spina,
    E per man di Simon tinge, e colora
    Del Redentor l'umanità divina,
Rassembra quasi porpora d'Aurora,
    Che 'n su la stagion fresca, e mattutina
    Suol grave pioggia annunziar talora
    Dopo 'l calar de la minuta brina.
Poiché 'l sangue purissimo, che viene
    Solo d'un sol de' santi membri suoi,
    Principio acerbo a più profonde pene,
Altro non è ch'una rugiada e noi
    Appo 'l diluvio, che l'aperte vene
    Hanno su'l duro tronco a versar poi.[32]

---

[28] 'The stones are indeed cruel and fierce weapons for him, but the aching martyr feels more the blows of your sins than the pelting of the hard rocks.'

[29] Ed. Martin, p. 41.

[30] 'Sweet wound of love, thou art not a wound, but a mouth of that heart'.

[31] Ed. Martin, pp. 38, 53, 98, 365.

[32] 'This crimson humour which is dripping before either nail or thorn forces it out, and by Simon's hand dyes and colours the Redeemer's divine humanity, is not unlike the blush of Dawn, which in the cool and early part of the day, sometimes foretells a heavy rainfall after the dropping of the light dew. Because the pure blood, which issues from only one of his holy limbs—a bitter beginning of deeper sorrows—is nothing more to us than a dew against the flood which the open veins will later pour on the hard trunk.'

Crashaw, in one of his epigrams, makes the circumcised Christ say to his Father:

> Has en primitias nostrae (Pater) accipe mortis
>
> . . . .
>
> Ira (Pater) tua de pluvia gustaverit ista:
> Olim ibit fluviis hoc latus omne suis.[33]

The epigram *In beatae Virginis verecundiam*: [34]

> In gremio, quaeris, cur sic sua lumina Virgo
> Ponat? ubi melius poneret illa, precor?
> O ubi, quam coelo, melius sua lumina ponat?
> Despicit, at coelum sic tamen illa videt—

together with the other *Deus sub utero Virginis*: [35]

> Quanta uteri, Regina, tui reverentia tecum est,
> Dum iacet hic, coelo sub breviore, Deus!

makes one think instead of a conceit already used by Donne in *The Litanie*: [36]

> Whose wombe was a strange heav'n for there
> God cloath'd himselfe, and grew.

Many inventions of the *Epigrammata Sacra* find parallels in the Latin poems of the Jesuits, and belong to that common fund of witticisms which the authors of treatises on *agudeza*, who were legion in that period,[37] strove to spread among the clergy.

---

[33] Crashaw's English version, ed. Martin, p. 98. See however Remond, p. 7: *Ad Angelum qui Christo Domino apparuit in horto Getsemani, et qui pingi solet calicem manu gestans*: '. . . Has tamen interea missas, pater, accipe guttas;/cras tibi, quod reliquum est sanguinis, ille dabit.' At a later date, in *Panteon in Pindo* by the Ascoso Accademico Gelato (C. C. Malvasia), Bologna 1691, p. 11, the same conceit recurs apropos of the Circumcision: a sign that it had become a commonplace.

[34] Ed. Martin, p. 27, Crashaw's English version, p. 89.

[35] Ed. Martin, p. 23.

[36] *Poems*, ed. Grierson, Oxford 1921, Vol. i, p. 339.

[37] Besides the Spanish theorists listed by Antonio (cf. Croce, *Saggi sulla letteratura italiana del Seicento*, Bari, 1911, p. 175), see various other works which were published on the subject during the seventeenth century by Sandaeus, e.g., his *Theologia Symbolica*,

The study Crashaw made of contemporary Latin poets [38] is witnessed also by a poem on Mary Magdalen's tears, on which he worked at different times. We had better speak of this poem at once, in order to show how those juvenile exercises (begun from school days), the epigrams, informed the subsequent developments of Crashaw's poetry with their character.

The Weeper [39] is indeed little more than a rosary of epigrams or madrigals clumsily linked together, without progression: the stanzas might be arranged in a different order (as indeed the poet arranged them in the various editions) and the poem be augmented indefinitely, or reduced (as it has been not improperly in many of the anthologies which have

---

In qua origo symbolorum, eorumque artificium, ex Sacra Scriptura potissimum eruitur, et ejusdem Symbola omnis generis explicantur: Opus Sacrae Doctrinae studiosis, et imprimis Concionatoribus, et politioris litteraturae amatoribus utile, Moguntiae, 1621. Also *Symbolica*, Ex omni antiquitate sacra, ac profana in artis formam redacta, Oratoribus, Poëtis, et Universis Philologis, ad omnem commoditatem amoenae eruditionis concinnata, 1625.

[38] Among the collections of epigrams Crashaw must have known are Bernardi Bauhusii and Balduini Cabilliavi e Soc. Iesu *Epigrammata*, Caroli Malaperti ex eadem Soc. *Poemata*, Antverpiae, ex Officina Plantiniana Balthasaris Moreti, 1624; a book which contains also seven elegies and three more compositions by Remond. This volume contains the famous line dedicated to the Virgin: 'Tot tibi sunt dotes, Virgo, quot sidera coelo', whose capacity of 1022 different combinations—the numbers of the stars known at the period—was illustrated by Erycius Puteanus in 1617: a line which was indeed 'a theatre full of wonders' (*un pien teatro di meraviglie*). Another Jesuit epigrammatist from whom Crashaw derived was Jacob Bidermann, some of whose epigrams are collected together with others by Bauhuis and Cabilliau (Lugduni, 1623). In Bidermann's *Epigrammatum Libri tres* (Dilingae, apud Melchiorem Algeyer, 1620; and other editions elsewhere) there is a composition on 'Theresa, Angeli Spectatrix'. As for other instances of the influence of Jesuits on English poets, I may add that the last two books of Quarles's *Emblems* are copied from Hugo's *Pia Desideria* of which I shall speak later: a book which saw a number of reprints and translations; and that Edward Sherburne translated (in *Salmacis, Lyrian and Sylvia*, etc., London, 1651) several Latin epigrams of the Polish Jesuit Casimir Sarbiewski, whom I mention below.

[39] Ed. Martin, p. 308 f.

included it): the unit is not the poem, but the stanza, the madrigal, the epigram, as happens in the collection of madrigals on *Maddalena ai piedi di Cristo* by Marino, which probably suggested the scheme and gave some technical hints. It is possible that the poem *The Teare* [40] which is found at the beginning of the 1646 volume, represents a first sketch of *The Weeper*: in the latter poem the stanza has a more regular construction, which seems modelled on the fifth stanza of the shorter lyric: this stanza was later on, in the 1648 edition, included in *The Weeper* [41] together with the retouched fourth stanza. The sixth and seventh stanzas of *The Teare* seem to suggest a conceit which finds a fuller expression in the fourth stanza of *The Weeper*:

The Teare

vi

Faire Drop, why quak'st thou so?
'Cause thou streight must lay thy Head
    In the Dust? ô no;
The Dust shall never bee thy Bed:
A pillow for thee will I bring,
Stuft with Down of Angels wing.

vii

Thus carryed up on high,
(For to Heaven thou must goe)
    Sweetly shalt thou lye,
And in soft slumbers bath thy woe;
Till the singing Orbes awake thee,
And one of their bright *Chorus* make thee.

[40] Ed. Martin, p. 84.

[41] That the eleventh stanza of *The Weeper* (1648, 1652) is the result of an elaboration of the fifth stanza of *The Teare* is made evident by the greater precision and perfection of the images. Against: '. . . the maiden gemme,/by the *wanton spring putt on*,/. . . blushes on the manly sunne' of *The Teare*, we find in *The Weeper*: '. . . the maiden gemme/by the *purpling Vine* put on,/. . . blushes at the *Bridegroome* Sun', in which 'purpling Vine' has evidently been suggested by 'blushes'.

The image of the drop climbing the sky [42] does not fit with that of the drop which sleeps: this latter image is laboriously drawn out of the purely incidental image of the drop which 'lays its head on the dust', i.e., falls to the ground. Although

[42] The conceit is found in the xciii sermon by Saint Peter Chrysologus (*De Conversione Magdalenae:* Migne, vol, lii, col. 463) which Baltasar Gracián, in *Agudeza y Arte de Ingenio* (first edition, 1642) gives as an illustration of *agudeza de contrariedad* (third impression, Huesca 1649, p. 10): 'En mutatur ordo rerum, pluviam terrae coelum dat semper: ecce nunc rigat terra coelum, immo super coelos et usque ad ipsum Dominum imber humanarum prosilit lachrimarum'. The rest of the passage reads in the original: 'ut juxta Psalmistam et de aquis fletuum cantetur illud: Et aquae quae super coelos sunt, laudent nomen Domini' (*Psal.* cxlviii). This latter portion has obviously suggested the lines in the 1648, 1652 versions of *The Weeper:* 'Waters above th' Heavens, what they be/We 'are taught best by thy Teares and thee'. But we can trace that conceit to *Ecclesiasticus* xxxv, 18 and 19: 'Nonne lacrymae viduae ad maxillam descendunt? . . . A maxilla enim ascendunt usque ad coelum.' These lines are quoted at p. 70 of H. Hugo's *Pia Desideria,* Antwerp 1624, a very widespread book (see M. Praz, *Studies in Seventeenth-century Imagery,* p. 131; A. Spamer, *Das kleine Andachtsbild vom XIV. bis zum XX. Jahrhundert,* Munich 1930, p. 143 ff.), the style of whose verses and quotations may have influenced Crashaw (cf. e.g., the headpiece of *The Weeper,* reproduced by Martin on p. 308, with the figures on pp. 64, 326, and with the one illustrating the passage 'Domine, ante te omne desiderium meum' in the edition of the *Pia Desideria* quoted above). The same image occurs apropos of Mary Magdalen's tears in one of Sarbiewski's epigrams, which I would not have hesitated to identify with Crashaw's source, if I had been able to establish that it was known at the time of the English poet. But this epigram does not appear in any of the contemporary editions of Sarbiewski's poems (Mathiae Casimiri Sarbievii *Lyricorum Libri IV, Epodon Liber Unus Alterque Epigrammatum,* Antverpiae, Ex Off. Plantiniana, 1632: and many other editions: see for a bibliography and information upon this Jesuit poet the reprint *Poemata omnia,* Staraviesiae, Typis et sumptibus Collegii S. J., 1892, in which the epigram in question is printed as the ccliii: as far as I can ascertain, it was never printed before 1892, but might have been circulated in MS. during the seventeenth century). Here is the epigram of the Polish poet:

Sancta Maria Magdalena flens Christum Dominum requirit

> Flebilis absentem reperit dum Magdala Sponsum,
> Inque suum Jesu pectore pectus habet:
> Bina per afflictos iverunt flumina vultus,
> Ibat et in miseram ros pretiosus humum.

the fourth stanza of *The Weeper* contains an unbearable pun, it possesses at least a logic and bizarre coherence which the very forced witticism of *The Teare* lacks altogether.

The fourth stanza of *The Weeper* in the 1646 edition appears in the following form:

> Vpwards thou dost weepe,
>   Heavens bosome drinks the gentle streame.
> Where th'milky rivers meet,
>   Thine Crawles above and is the Creame.
> *Heaven, of such faire floods as this,*
> *Heaven the Christall Ocean is.*

We may imagine a process of this kind: Crashaw developed the image of the sky-climbing tear into that of a *river of tears*; this latter would easily suggest the Milky Way, which is like a river of milk; as Mary Magdalen's tears are more precious than this milky river, they are the cream of that milk.

And as to the 'waters above the firmament' mentioned in

> Ros hic Olympiacos consueverat ire per hortos:
>   Nescio, non suetam cur modo poscat humum.
> Cum Deus in coelis, *ad coelos lacrima currit;*
>   Quando Christus humi, lacrima scandit humum.

Actually this witticism must have been obvious enough for a seventeenth-century writer. Marino (*La Galeria*, Venice, Ciotti, 1636: *Istorie*, p. 88) had already used a similar conceit apropos of Magdalen's eyes:

> Voi che già fuste a lunga schiera amante
> Ministri sol di fiamme e di faville,
> Voi voi disciolto in tepid' onde il gelo
> Bagnaste in terra (o meraviglia!) il Cielo.

('You which used to be only dispensers of flames and sparks to a long troop of lovers, having now thawed into warm waves have watered (oh wonder) Heaven on earth'.) Marino himself had come very near the conceit of 'waters above the firmament' apropos of Mary Magdalen's tears in the following passage (*op. cit.*, p. 89):

> Perdon l'acque de l'Ermo, e perdon quelle
> Appo voi, *c'hanno il fonte in Paradiso* . . .

['The waters of the Hermus (a river in Asia Minor whose sands the poets assumed to contain gold) and those which have their source in Paradise, are defeated by you'.]

Genesis (i, 7) and in the *Psalms* (cxlviii, 4), and already connected with Mary Magdalen's tears by Saint Peter Chrysologus, as we have seen, they had given origin to a scholastic question (*Summa*, i, 68) which continued to be debated: a passage of Donne (*Elegie on the Lady Marckham*, 11. 8–9) might have been in Crashaw's mind: 'Our waters then, above our firmament (teares which our Soule doth for her Sins let fall)'.[43] So much ingenuity produced at last in its final form (1648, 1652 editions) the following *concetto predicabile*:

The Weeper, iv

> Vpwards thou dost weep.
> Heaun's bosome drinks the gentle stream.
> Where th' milky rivers creep,
> Thine floats aboue; & is the cream.
> *Waters aboue th'Heauns, what they be*
> *We' are taught best by thy* TEARS & thee.

The influence of a number of contemporary Latin poets is evident in *The Weeper*. Chiefly of an epigram by the French Jesuit Remond which Crashaw must have known, since he translated a few elegies of that writer under the title *Alexias*. The epigram is entitled *De lacrymis sanctae Mariae Magdalenae, quas ad Christi pedes effudit*:[44]

> Felices nimium gemini tua lumina fontes,
>   Quaeque venit trita sedula gutta via.
> Se lacrymam esse tuam cuperet, dum vere tepenti
>   Labitur in molles humida gemma rosas.
> Si manare oculis posset Pactolus ab istis,
>   Aurifer hac iret ditior amnis aqua.
> Tam pretiosa pedes Domini nisi lamberet unda,
>   Unda, quid, ah! quererer, tam pretiosa peris?

The beginning of this epigram seems to have suggested the opening line of *The Weeper*:

> Hail, sister springs!

---

[43] Ed. Grierson, i, p. 279.

[44] Francisci Remondi Divionensis E Soc. Iesu *Epigrammata, Elegiae et Orationes* . . . Mediolani Apud Hieron. Bordonium et Petrum Martyrem Locarnum Socios, 1605, Lib. I, xxix, p. 11.

while the second distich is clearly the source of the eighth stanza:

> The deaw no more will weep
> The primrose's pale cheek to deck,
> The deaw no more will sleep
> Nuzzel'd in the lilly's neck;
> Much reather would it be thy TEAR,
> And leaue them Both to tremble here.

The fourteenth stanza in the 1646 version:

> Golden though hee bee,
> Golden *Tagus* murmurs though,
> Might hee flow from thee
> Content and quiet would he goe,
> Richer far does he esteeme
> Thy silver, then his golden streame—

seems inspired by the fourth distich of the Latin epigram, but the conceit occurs also in Cabilliau's *Magdalena*: [45]

> Si potis influere hos oculos Tagus aurifer, aurum
> Efflueret fulvi purius amne Tagi.

This Latin poem seems to have inspired part of the first stanza of *The Weeper*:

> Hail, sister springs!
> Parents of syluer-footed rills!
> Euer bubling things!
> Thawing crystall! snowy hills,
> Still spending, neuer spent! I mean
> Thy fair eyes, sweet MAGDALENE!—

since Cabilliau has (ll. 1–2):

> Magdalis ut glacies Phoebeo saucia telo
> Liquitur, et verna plus nive delacrymat.

The seventeenth stanza in the 1648 and 1652 editions:

> But can these fair Flouds be
> Freinds with the bosom fires that fill thee

[45] Liber II, *Magdalena Poenitens*, Elegia xiv, p. 59 'Magdalenae lacrymae gemmae', ll. 5–6.

Can so great flames agree
Æternall Teares should thus distill thee!
O flouds, o fires! o suns ô showres!
Mixt & made freinds by loue's sweet powres—

is comparable to one of John Owen's epigrams (*Epigrammata*, 1605, Lib. i, epigr. 74):

> *Nilo negli occhi, Etna nel cuore*
> Frigidus ardentes intravit Nilus ocellos,
>   Dum cor Ætneo carpitur Igne meum.
> Nec tantus fluvio lacrymarum extinguitur ardor,
>   Nec tanti fletus flumina siccat amor.
> Sic sibi discordes, exercent vim tamen ambo,
>   In me concordes, ignis et unda suam.

Also the distich which accompanies the headpiece in the 1652 edition seems to derive from here:

> Loe where a *Wounded Heart* with Bleeding Eyes Conspire.
> Is she a *Flaming* Fountain, or a Weeping fire!

Finally the much ridiculed conceit of the nineteenth stanza (1648, 1652 editions) (the weeping eyes following Christ like 'two faithfull fountaines;Two walking baths; two weeping motions;/Portable & compendious oceans') far from being a grotesque invention of Crashaw's—as the critics believed at one time—, before its final codification by Tesauro (see below), was used by Hugo (*Pia Desideria*, i, viii, ll. 9–12, 27–28), Cabilliau (Magdalea Silva, xlvii, p. 186 of *Magdalena*, 1625, and lxiv, wrongly numbered xliv, p. 200) [46] and in the following epigram (the eighth) by Sarbiewski which appears in all editions:

> *De D. Maria Madgalena*
> *Per vicos & plateas quaeram, quem diligit anima mea*
>   Et gemit, et miseris singultibus astra lacessit,
>   Et salso teneras irrigat amne genas.
>   Et cava per, per acuta celer, per inhospita fertur:
>   Et per aperta fugax, et per iniqua ruit.

---

[46] See these and similar pasages (by G. Markham, Southwell, Greene, Marlowe) quoted by Martin, p. 449.

Quid facit ad tantos tam prodiga lacryma cursus?
Magdalis in lacrymis navigat ipsa suis.[47]

Nor was it only from the Latin epigrammatic and elegiac poets that Crashaw gathered gems for his necklace of conceits. The image of the Angels who 'with crystall violls come/and draw' from Magdalen's eyes 'their master's Water: their own Wine' (st. vi, 1646; xii, 1648 and 1652) was probably suggested by Donne, *Twicknam Garden*, 19–20: 'Hither with christall vyals, lovers come,/and take my teares, which are loves wine'. The phrase 'crystall violls' (Donne's 'christall vyals') replaces in the 1648 and 1652 editions the prosaic 'their bottles' of the 1646 edition (st. vi). The twenty-seventh stanza of the 1648, 1652 versions (a rehandling of the fourth stanza of *The Teare*):

> So doe perfumes expire.
> So sigh tormented sweets, opprest
> With proud vnpittying fire.
> Such Teares the suffring Rose that's vext
> With vngentle flames does shed,
> Sweating in a too warm bed—

echoes lines of Marino's *Il Sudore del Sangue*:

> Suda sangue anelante,
> Vaso, che colmo di bei fiori il seno
> A quel cocente ardor, che 'n lui sfavilla,
> Liquidi odor soavemente stilla.[48]

And the conceit of the third stanza of *The Teare*: 'Each Drop leaving a place so deare,/Weeps for it selfe, is its owne Teare', had already occurred in Sidney's *Arcadia* (Lib. II, ch. xi) apropos of the water which 'seemed to weepe, that it should parte from such bodies' as those of the princesses Pamela and Philoclea.

[47] Besides those I have quoted, there are other epigrams on Magdalen in the 1892 edition of Sarbiewski: see nos. ccl, ccli, ccliv, cclv.

[48] 'He sweats reeking blood: a pot, which, its bosom filled with fine flowers, suavely distils liquid perfumes because of the burning fire with which it glows'.

The Weeper, with its reminiscences, its retouches and arabesques, is an excellent example of the manner in which Crashaw followed the practice of workers in mosaic, aiming not so much at a general effect, as at a cluster of epigrams or independent pictures. We shall see how, in apparently more homogeneous compositions also, the conceit, the image, continually tends to stand by itself, to detach itself from the context. What is lacking is a central point round which the poem should gravitate in a harmonious coordination of its parts. Now this is a trait which brings Crashaw's art not so much near to Shelley's, to which it has been compared, as to Swinburne's: we shall see how this is not the only point of contact between the two poets.

One would almost say that a rosary of epigrams such as *The Weeper* is the culmination, the final display of waterworks, of the lachrymosity which, bubbling in Petrarch's sonnets, had been steadily growing to the proportions of a river during the sixteenth century, particularly thanks to Tasso and Tansillo: [49] Mary Magdalen, contrition, and religion have little or nothing to do with the poem, and therefore it seems to us that a criticism like that of Macdonald [50] misses the point, when it blames the 'moth-like' flitting of the poet's conceits round the theme as unworthy of it and irreverent. Crashaw does neither more nor less than Marino did with his madrigals: neither religion nor love is actually at the back of such a glitter of conceits, but only indulgence in a self-congratulatory and self-complacent play of wit. For a seventeenth-century writer, according to Baltasar Gracián's words, to perceive a witticism was an eagle's task, to produce it, an angel's, 'an occupation of cherubs and an elevation of men which causes us to rise to a very exalted hierarchy'. The point was to say the most marvellous things possible on Mary Magdalen's tears, and Crashaw has collected in upwards of thirty stanzas a great part of what in such a subject seemed poetical to his contemporaries, for whom wit and poetry were synonymous. It is curious to observe how near Crashaw's poetry comes in its development and conceits to one of the

[49] See how the *motif* of tears is recurrent in Crashaw's juvenile compositions; cf. Martin, pp. 386, 390, 396.

[50] *England's Antiphon,* ch. xvii, p. 238.

themes Tesauro proposes as a model in his treatise, which was published a few years after Crashaw's death: a clear sign that certain subjects and phrases were in the air of the period.[50 bis] I feel therefore justified in quoting Tesauro's pages (534 ff.) in full, as they seem especially written to reveal the background of this poem of Crashaw's:

Now that we have spoken in detail of each kind of Urbane Enthymema [= thought, argument] I want to show you two ingenious ways of trying your wit at two very pleasant and easy Theorems . . . The other Theorem is no less pleasant and varied and profitable toward stimulating the brain and making it teem with conceits; it is this: PROPOSITUM THEMA UNUM, SINGULA PER CAUSARUM GENERA FINESQUE RHETORICOS ENTHYMEMATICE VARIARE.

This is done by playing with the said Theme, now with Adductive Reasons, now with Deductive Consequences, now with acute Reflexions. Now by exaggerating in admiration, now by taking it away. Now by Advising, now by Warning. Now by Indicting, now by Excusing. Now by eliciting Documents from it, now by expressing Affections of Love, Hatred, Pity, Indignation, Envy. By varying at the same time the formulas and manners of the Sentence. So that, the Theme being always the same, the Conceits should be different.

Let our Theme be: MAGDALENA CHRISTUM AMAT VEHEMENTER EIUSQUE PEDES LAVAT. You have to reduce this Theme to an admirable and enigmatical Reflexion, such as: MAGDALENAE OCULI AMORE ARDENT ET LACHRY-MIS MANANT. Here you see already a *complication* of two opposite Objects, which open to you a copious vein of Propositions and witty Enthymemata of every kind, *Rational, Moral,* and *Pathetic.* And since the Matter is Civil, you may reduce it to all the three kinds of the Rhetorical Causes. You have therefore to gather the Motions or cir-

[50 bis] The first appearance in English literature of those hyperbolical analogies later to be expended on 'Eyes and Tears' by Herbert, Crashaw, Vaughan and Marvell, is to be found in Robert Southwell's *Marie Magdalens Funeral Teares,* 1591; see Louis L. Martz, *The Poetry of Meditation,* New Haven, 1954, p. 201.

cumstances of these four Opposite Objects: LOVE, TEARS, FIRE, FROST: a thing which you will find very easy, if you keep the order of the two said Tables. Then by reflecting on these and those, by knitting and dividing them, you will obtain wonderful discourses of this kind . . .

Tesauro proceeds then to give a long Latin passage in which all possible combinations of those conceits are illustrated; for instance:

What is this prodigy? Water and Flame, once bitter rivals, are now reconciled like peaceful bedfellows in Magdalen's eyes. . . . You will find in them a spring and a torch, you will draw fire from the water, water from the fire. Her eyes repeat the fabulous miracle of Mount Ætna on whose top the snow is espoused to the fire. Like a new bride, Magdalen carries the wonted offerings of fire and water on the threshold. Hail, eyes, dispensers of fiery springs. Come you, sick ones, to these hot baths healthier than the Leucadian fountain, Love the bath-keeper calls you, come (*Salvete oculi largitores aestuosorum fontium. Vos ergo debiles morbidique, ad ista Vaporaria Leucadio fonte salubriora, balneator Amor accersit; venite*).[51]

After a quantity of similar inventions, Tesauro concludes:

It is your turn to continue, there is no end of it: still the Reflexion on which the discourse is founded is almost Poetical: and the jests are born solely out of the Metaphor of Proportion.

---

[51] This comparison of Mary Magdalen's eyes to thermal baths, having Love for bather, is even more shocking than Crashaw's simile, according to which the eyes were called 'two walking baths', etc. (see above p. 224). The hyperbole used by the English poet, 'portable and compendious oceans', finds an exact parallel in another passage of Tesauro (p. 432): 'If you call Love a FIRE, if you want to exaggerate, you may through a SIMPLE HYPERBOLE call him a *portable Furnace*'. Also the other hyperbole, 'a wandring mine, a voluntary mint' (st. xxi, 1648) is not uncommon in the seventeenth century. Cf. Lorenzo Morassini, *Rime,* Florence, 1641, p. 31: 'Un erario animato in costei miro' ('I see in her an animated treasury').

The irreverence with which Macdonald reproached Crashaw would have appeared incomprehensible to the poet's contemporaries, who in this respect were of the opinion of Pierfrancesco Minozzi (*Sfogamenti d'ingegno*, Venice 1641). Minozzi, while he did not approve of conceits and hyperboles in profane stories, praises and recommends them for sacred histories and the lives of the saints, since 'Saints deserve any kind of artificial amplification, and whatever you may say of them is true, and they are by themselves superior to any human adulation. Therefore in the lives of the saints even jests have the power to persuade and move, being taken seriously and not for fun. Sometimes a jest is more likely to touch because it pleases, than a simple statement having no blandishment in it.' [52]

The Weeper has an air of unbearable luxuriance like certain works of Southern baroque architecture, in which the design is obscured by stuccoed stalactites and a glitter of glassy ornaments: works which so resemble the impermanent creations of a mirage, that a breath of air seems sufficient to dispel them.

A comparison of the various versions of the poem would not suggest that it has gained by growing from twenty-two to thirty-one stanzas. The stanzas containing the more attractive similes were already present in the 1646 edition, like the one which seems miraculously to anticipate Shelley's exquisite intuition of Nature:

> Not in the Evenings Eyes
> When they red with weeping are,
> For the Sun that dyes,
> Sits sorrow with a face so faire.
> Nowhere but heere did ever meet
> Sweetnesse so sad, sadness so sweet.

Attention must be drawn to the exclusion in the following editions of three stanzas (viii, xi, xvii) which appeared

---

[52] This passage is quoted by Croce in 'I Trattatisti italiani del "Concettismo" e Baltasar Gracian', Memoria letta all'Accademia Pontaniana di Napoli nella tornata del 18 giugno 1899. *Atti,* vol. xxix, memoria n. 7, p. 18. Reprinted in *Problemi d'Estetica.*

in the 1646 version. One might perhaps congratulate the poet on having weeded out such a grotesque conceit as:

> Time as by thee he passes,
> Makes thy ever-watry eyes
> His Hower-Glasses.
> By them his steps he rectifies.
> The sands he us'd no longer please,
> For his owne sands hee'l use thy seas.[53]

But one remains perplexed at seeing the poem enriched with witticisms such as:

xix

> And now where're he [the lamb] strayes,
> Among the Galilean mountaines,
> Or more vnwellcome wayes,
> He's follow'd by two faithfull fountaines;
> Two walking baths; two weeping motions;
> Portable, & compendious oceans.

xx

> O Thou, thy lord's fair store!
> In thy so rich & rare expenses,
> Euen when he show'd most poor,
> He might prouoke the wealth of Princes.
> What Prince's wanton'st pride e're could
> Wash with Syluer, wipe with Gold.

xxi

> Who is that King, but he
> Who calls't his Crown to be call'd thine,
> That thus can boast to be
> Waited on by a wandring mine,
> A voluntary mint, that strowes
> Warm syluer shoures where're he goes!

The flow of wealthy similes (besides precious metals and gems, also balsam-sweating and amber-weeping trees are

[53] Cf. Cabilliau, *op. cit.*, p. 188, 'Magdalena in clepsydram se verti vovet.'

made to contribute) makes one suspect that the author intended to imitate the *Song of Solomon*. And it is curious to see how, while reproducing its precious and exotic atmosphere, he misses altogether the passionate spirit which pervades it: I mean the human passion whose accent is the first thing to strike a modern reader of that ancient song, and makes much more impression than the images. A passion indeed can also be detected in Crashaw's stanzas, but it is a passion of the brain, as I have said, for the play of wit for its own sake. The spirit of the *Song of Solomon* will however be found in another of Crashaw's lyrics, the hymn on the *Assumption of our Blessed Lady*. An instance of a reminiscence from the *Song of Solomon* is offered by the additional fifteenth stanza:

> O cheeks! Bedds of chast loues
> By your own showres seasonably dash'd
> Eyes! nests of milky doues
> In your own wells decently washt,
> O wit of loue! that thus could place
> Fountain & Garden in one face.

Compare the *Song of Solomon*, v, 12–13:

> His eyes are as the eyes of doves by the rivers of waters, washed with milk, and fitly set.
> His cheeks are as a bed of spices, as sweet flowers . . .

Nothing helps us more to understand the character of Crashaw's inspiration than a comparison of his translations with their originals. The most conspicuous of them both for length and importance is that of the *Sospetto d'Erode*, i.e., of the first Canto of Marino's *Strage degli Innocenti*. An authoritative manuscript copy discovered by Professor Martin [54] has next to the title the date 'November 25, 1637', probably recording the completion of the task. This was certainly not the first of Marino's works which Crashaw knew: we have seen how some of the sacred epigrams developed conceits already used in Marino's *Lira*. One of Marino's madrigals, 'Foco d'Amore diviso' (in the second part of the *Lira*) was translated by Crashaw, with the vague

[54] *Modern Language Review*, 1915, p. 378.

indication 'out of the Italian', in the brief poem 'Love now no fire hath left him'.[55] A great number of Marino's lyric poems had already been Englished by Drummond of Hawthornden.

The translation of the *Sospetto d'Erode* must have been a kind of apprenticeship for Crashaw: while transferring the contents of each *ottava* into the more capacious English stanza, Crashaw made a very deft use of the margins by embroidering clever variations on the expressions of the Neapolitan poet, which were frequently too obvious and direct. Crashaw was not a man to miss any opportunity of concentrating into one single point as many witticisms as he could manage; if the limits of human art had allowed it, nothing would have stopped him from heaping there an even greater number than the ten thousand angels who, according to the Schoolmen, could alight on the point of a single needle.

From the very outset, against the Italian of the first stanza:

E voi reggete voi l'infermo Ingegno,
Nunzi di Cristo, e testimoni invitti,
Che deste fuor de le squarciate gole
Sangue in vece di voce e di parole— [56]

the English text reads:

O be a Dore
Of language to my infant Lips, yee best
Of Confessours: whose Throates answering his swords,
Gave forth your Blood for breath, spoke soules for words.

[55] Ed. Martin, p. 190. Another madrigal 'out of the Italian' which is printed on the same page has a common source with Drummond of Hawthornden's 'Love naked' (ed. Kastner, vol. i, p. 126): this source defeated the researches of many scholars, including myself, for a long time, until I chanced on it while reading Alfredo Obertello's *Madrigali italiani in Inghilterra*, Milan, Bompiani, 1949; it is a sextet by Valerio Marcellini which was set to music by the celebrated Luca Marenzio (see my letter in *The Times Literary Supplement* for October 21, 1949, p. 681).

[56] 'And may you support my infirm talent, you announcers of Christ, and dauntless witnesses, who gave forth blood instead of voice and words from your severed throats'.

If Crashaw had limited himself to competing with the
original in wit, one might have deprecated the result. It
happens, however, that the English poet succeeds in impart-
ing poetic life to certain trite metaphors and purple patches
of Marino, thus relieving the flabbiness of the Italian poem,
a late scion of the decayed epic tradition. A neutral expression like 'in mezzo al cor del Mondo' (st. 5) acquires new
freshness in 'the worlds profound Heart pants'; a weak
personification like (st. 40):

> V'ha la Vendetta in su la soglia, e 'n mano
> Spada brandisce insanguinata ignuda [57]

breaks into vivid colour in

> There has the *purple* Vengeance a proud seat,
> Whose ever-brandisht Sword is *sheath'd in blood.*

Very frequently the image contained in the English lines is
more dramatic. Sleep who (st. 49)

>   by a gentle Tyranny,
> And sweet oppression . . .
> . . . tam'd the rebellious eye
> Of sorrow, with a soft and downy hand,
> Sealing all brests in a Lethaean band—

supplies a much more coherent and forcible image than:

> E con dolce tirannide e soave
> Sparse le tempie altrui d'acque letali,
> I tranquilli riposi e lusinghieri
> S'insignorian de' sensi e de' pensieri.[58]

Similarly (st. 51):

> Già 'l Diadema Real de la Giudea
> La progenie di Giuda avea perduto

[57] 'Vengeance sits on the threshold, brandishing in her hand a
bloody naked sword'.
[58] 'And sprinkling men's temples with Lethean waters—a mild
and sweet tyranny—tranquil and flattering repose swayed their
senses and thought'.

> E del giogo servil gli aspri rigori
> Sostenendo . . .[59]

is loosely knit in comparison with:

> And from the head of Iudahs house quite torne
> The Crowne, for which upon their necks he laid
> A sad yoake. . . .

In the place of the dull description of the blighting of the flowers by the approach of the fourth Fury (st. 48):

> Parvero i fiori intorno, e la verdura
> Sentir forza di peste, ira di Verno— [60]

we find this delicate image:

> The field's faire Eyes saw her, and saw no more,
> But shut their flowry lids for ever. Night,
> And Winter strow her way . . .

And instead of the still more indifferent stanza 54:

> Mal accorto tu dormi, e qual nocchiero,
> Che per l'Egeo, di nembi oscuri e densi
> Cinto, a l'onda superba, al vento fiero
> Obliato il timon, pigro non pensi,
> Te ne stai neghittoso . . .[61]

we seem actually to watch the rage of the elements in Crashaw's rendering:

> So sleeps a Pilot, whose poore Barke is prest
> With many a mercylesse o're mastring wave;
> For whom (as dead) the wrathfull winds contest,
> Which of them deep'st shall digge her watry Grave.

'My shining kingdoms' ('I miei regni lucenti') of stanza 27 become 'the never-fading fields of Light'; and, completing

---

[59] 'Already Judah's progeny had lost the royal diadem, and supporting the sharp severity of the servile yoke . . .'

[60] 'The flowers and vegetation all round seemed to feel the blow of the plague, or Winter's rage'.

[61] 'Incautiously you sleep, and like a pilot who in the Aegean sea encompassed by dark thick storms, lazily fails to think of the fierce wind and the swollen waves, and forgets the rudder, you remain idle'.

as usual an image left unfinished by Marino, Crashaw translates (st. 16):

> Vede aprir l'uscio a triplicato Sole
>   La reggia oriental, che si disserra [62]

with:

> He saw a threefold Sun, with rich encrease,
> Make proud the Ruby portalls of the East.

Only rarely does the English embroidering on Marino's text
result in an oddity such as:

> what wild Engines stand
> On tiptoe in their giddy Braynes?

for the plain: 'O qua' machine volge' (st. 56: 'O what
machinations does it devise'); or like that quaint 'When
'gainst the Thunders mouth we marched forth' (st. 36), which
assumes the divine thunder to be like a cannon, to signify
the assault of the rebellious angels, which is referred to
plainly in the Italian text where we find no hint of Crashaw's
conceit.

On the other hand, very frequently Crashaw succeeds
in creating a fresh and powerful poetical image for which
Marino's verse hardly offers as much as a hint. What in
Marino's seventh stanza appears to be a mere rhetorical
juxtaposition of substantives, adjectives and verbs:

> Negli occhi, ove mestizia alberga, e morte,
> Luce fiammeggia torbida, e vermiglia.
> Gli sguardi obliqui, e le pupille torte
> Sembran Comete, e lampadi le ciglia.
> E da le nari, e da le labra smorte
> Caligine, e fetor vomita, e figlia,
> Iracondi, superbi, e disperati,
> Tuoni i gemiti son, folgori i fiati— [63]

[62] 'He sees the oriental Court unbolt and throw open its gates to
a threefold Sun'.

[63] 'In the eyes, where sadness and death have their abode, flames
a troubled, crimson light. His oblique looks and crooked glances
are like comets, like meteors shine his orbs. And from his nostrils
and from his wan lips he vomits and brings forth fog and foul-
ness; angry, superb and desperate, his groans are thunder, his
breath lightning.'

expands, in Crashaw, into vistas of similitudes and echoing conceits:

> His Eyes, the sullen dens of Death and Night,
> *Startle the dull Ayre with a dismal red:*
> Such his fell glances as the fatall Light
> Of staring Comets, *that looke Kingdomes dead.*
> From his black nostrills, and blew lips, in spight
> Of Hells owne stinke, a worser stench is spread.
> > His breath Hells lightning is: and each deep grone
> > Disdaines to thinke that Heav'n Thunders alone.

Notice how the 'dismal red' of Lucifer's eyes which 'startles the dull air' surpasses in effectiveness the 'luce' which 'fiammeggia torbida e vermiglia', a phrase in which you feel that each element may be changed without serious harm: Crashaw's image is the more forcible as it describes the effect of the thing on the surrounding world. Thus comets appear more terrible through the vision of kingdoms whose destruction they portend; whereas 'sembran comete' is little more than a stale metaphor. The succession of images in the version of the tenth stanza is thicker and more coherent than in the original:

> Misero, e come il tuo splendor primiero
> Perdesti, o già di luce Angel più bello?
> Eterno avrai dal punitor severo
> A l'ingiusto fallir giusto flagello.
> De' fregi tuoi vagheggiatore altero,
> De l'altrui seggio usurpator rubello,
> Trasformato e caduto in Flegetonte,
> Orgoglioso Narciso, empio Fetonte.[64]

> Disdainefull wretch! how hath one bold sinne cost
> Thee all the Beauties of thy once bright Eyes?
> How hath one blacke Eclipse cancell'd, and crost
> The glories that did guild thee in thy Rise?

[64] 'Wretched one, and how didst thou lose thy pristine splendour, O one-time fairest Angel of light! Thou shalt receive from the severe punisher a just pain for thy unjust crime. Thou proud idolater of thy own adornments, thou rebellious usurper of another's seat, transformed and fallen into Phlegethon, vain Narcissus, impious Phaëton'.

>   Proud Morning of a perverse Day! how lost
>   Art thou unto thy selfe, thou too selfe-wise
>   *Narcissus*? Foolish *Phaeton*? who for all
>   Thy high-aym'd hopes, gaind'st but a flaming fall.

The beginning of stanza 15 seems actually to shine with the
light of paradise:

>   Hee saw how in that blest Day-bearing Night,
>   The Heav'n-rebuked shades made hast away;
>   How bright a Dawne of Angels with new Light
>   Amaz'd the midnight world, and made a Day
>   Of which the Morning knew not . . .

whereas Marino's text offers only a piling-up of adjectives:

>   Vede de la felice e santa notte
>   Le tacit'ombre, e i tenebrosi orrori
>   Da le voci del Ciel percosse, e rotte,
>   E vinte da gli angelici splendori.[65]

Finally, we miss in Marino's seventeenth stanza:

>   Vede dal Ciel con peregrino raggio
>   Spiccarsi ancor miracolosa stella,
>   Che verso Bettelem dritto il viaggio
>   Segnando va folgoreggiante, e bella;
>   E quasi precursor divin Messaggio,
>   Fidata scorta, e luminosa ancella,
>   Tragge di là da gli odorati Eoi
>   L'inclito stuol de' tre presaghi Eroi— [66]

the prodigious conflagration of images of the English counterpart:

>   He saw Heav'n blossome with a new-borne light,
>   On which, as on a glorious stranger gaz'd
>   The Golden eyes of Night: whose Beame made bright

---

[65] 'He sees the silent shadows and darksome horrors of the
happy and blessed night smitten and broken by Heaven's voices,
and dispelled by the angelic splendours'.

[66] 'He sees also a miraculous star move through Heaven with
a wandering beam, and mark the straight way to Bethlehem in a
fine flashing trail; like a forerunning divine messenger, a trusty
guide, and luminous handmaid, it draws the illustrious band of
the three wise heroes from beyond the perfumed East'.

> The way to *Beth'lem,* and as boldly blaz'd,
> (Nor askt leave of the Sun) by Day as Night.
> By whom (as Heav'ns illustrious Hand-maid) rais'd
>   Three Kings (or what is more) three Wise men went
>   Westward to find the worlds true *Orient.*

The image of the first three lines may have been suggested by an excessive valuation of the word *peregrino* (peregrine), which in Marino means 'wandering'. The epigrammatic close contains a conceit of the same kind as a famous one used by Dante apropos of Saint Francis (*Paradise,* xi, 53–54): a conceit which was a favourite with Crashaw.

What I have been saying does not presume to exhaust the remarks which can be made apropos of this admirable version of the *Sospetto d'Erode,* parts of which Milton must have remembered while describing the appearance of his Lucifer.[67]

Among the other Italian poems translated by Crashaw, a delightful little song by Ansaldo Cebà [68] is rendered in a masterly way. Crashaw is less happy in his variations on religious hymns and psalms: the difference from the originals is too great to admit of minute comparisons. Crashaw takes even more liberties than his contemporaries were used to doing in such cases: he sets in motion a complicated machinery of similes which falls short of the powerful simplicity of the sacred compositions. If not even Dante succeeded in imitating the vivid immediacy of the Latin originals in his paraphrases of prayers, what can we expect from poets of a lesser rank like Crashaw and Marino? What are the variations of these two poets on the *Stabat Mater* in comparison with that crude and sublime hymn? Their fireworks pale against that broad daylight: [68 bis]

---

[67] See M. Praz, *The Romantic Agony,* ch. ii, 'The Metamorphoses of Satan', p. 53 ff.

[68] Ed. Martin, p. 188. *Rime* di Ansaldo Ceba, In Aversa, Appresso Martino Nutio, 1596, p. 25. ('Dispiegate guance amate . . .'). This song appears with a different text (touched up with religious unction) in the 1611 edition of the *Rime,* Rome, Zannetti.

[68 bis] However Louis L. Martz in his excellent study on *The Poetry of Meditation* (*op. cit.,* p. 115 ff.) says of Crashaw's 'descant': 'Throughout the poem, with a vividness never approached in the

Her eyes bleed TEARES, his wounds weep BLOOD.
O costly intercourse
Of deaths, & worse,
Diuided loues. While son & mother
Discourse alternate wounds to one another.

. . . .

Shall I, sett there
So deep a share
(Dear wounds) & onely now
In sorrows draw no Diuidend with you?

Against the plain passage:

Fac me plagis vulnerari,
Fac me cruce inebriari,
In cruore Filii—

the following divagation appears wordy and even grotesque:

O let me suck the wine
So long of this chast vine
Till drunk of the dear wounds, I be
A lost Thing to the world, as it to me.

And yet, considered for itself, Crashaw's lyric effusion has
flashes of undeniable beauty, and could hardly be termed
a cold exercise; it would be unfair to condemn it by comparing it with a text with which, after all, it has only the
theme in common; to do so would be to act like those re-
storers of Roman churches who, in order to bring them back
to their mediaeval simplicity, did not scruple to demolish
seventeenth-century ornaments, which, though of a different
character, had a beauty of their own. We must bear this
in mind while examining the paraphrases of *Vexilla Regis
prodeunt, O Gloriosa Domina, Lauda Sion Salvatorem, Dies*

---

hymn, the mind is' focused intensely through the eyes of the
Mother. . . . From this dramatic intensity of vision follows a passionate directness of colloquy, implicit, but unmatched, anywhere
in the simple pleas of the hymn. . . . Crashaw has left the hymn
far behind, and appears to be developing his variations according
to the kind of procedure suggested in Luis de la Puente's *Medita-
tions upon the Mysteries of our Holie Faith* (St. Omer, 1619)'.

irae and *The Office of the Holy Cross*: in place of the straightforward energy of the Latin text we find a winding circumlocution, which, though it has occasionally a cloying sweetness, and is clearly much less noble, does not lack a certain grace. Defects and merits are well illustrated by the versions of the twenty-third and hundred-and-thirtyseventh psalms.

Psalm xxiii proceeds through a quick succession of acts: it has a skeleton-like quality, so apparent are the vertebrae of the verbs, unimpeded by an adipose tissue of adjectives:

> The Lord is my shepherd: I shall not want.
>
> He maketh me to lie down in green pastures: he leadeth me beside the still waters.
>
> He restoreth my soul: he leadeth me in the paths of righteousness for his name's sake, etc.

George Herbert had translated this psalm in a hymn of plain and popular character:

> The God of love my Shepherd is,
>   And he that doth me feed:
> While he is mine, and I am His,
>   What can I want or need?
>
> He leads me to the tender grass,
>   Where I both feed and rest;
> Then to the streams that gently pass:
>   In both I have the best.
>
> Or if I stray, He doth convert,
>   And bring my mind in frame:
> And all this not for my desert,
>   But for his holy name.

Let us read now Crashaw's paraphrase of those first three sentences: [69]

> Happy me! ô happy sheepe!
> Whom my God vouchsafes to keepe
> Even my God, even he it is,

[69] Ed. Martin, p. 102.

That points me to these wayes of blisse;
On whose pastures cheerefull spring
All the yeare doth sit and sing,
And rejoycing smiles to see
Their greene backs were his liverie:
Pleasure sings my soule to rest,
Plenty weares me at her breast,
Whose sweet temper teaches me
Nor wanton, nor in want to be.
At my feet the blubb'ring Mountaine
Weeping, melts into a Fountaine,
Whose soft silver-sweating streames
Make high Noone forget his beames:
When my waiward breath is flying,
Hee calls home my soule from dying,
Strokes and tames my rabid Griefe,
And does woe me into life:
When my simple weaknesse strayes,
(Tangled in forbidden wayes)
Hee (my Shepheard) is my Guide,
Hee's before me, on my side,
And behind me, he beguiles
Craft in all her knotty wiles:
Hee expounds the giddy wonder
Of my weary steps, and under
Spreads a Path cleare as the Day,
Where no churlish rub saies nay
To my joy-conducted Feet,
Whil'st they Gladly goe to meet
Grace and peace, to meet new laies
Tun'd to my great Shepheards praise; etc.

The cheerfulness of this song offers a sharp contrast to
the severe and almost sententious character of the psalm, and
also, in part, of Herbert's version. There is nothing, in these
two compositions, recalling the fantastic personifications
which people Crashaw's lyric like the allegorical figures in
a pageant. Nature, in this lyric, is instinct with human feelings: the mountain weeps, the streams sweat silver, and so
on. Bold, ornate images spring up in quick succession: the

green backs of the pastures wearing the Lord's livery, the giddy wonder of the weary steps. The psalm is a recitative, Herbert's hymn a plain song, but Crashaw's lyric is an allegretto, a fugue, and gives the same impression of mirth as Milton's *Allegro*.

This musical spirit pervades also the version of Psalm cxxxvii, which, with the variety of its verse, presents a pattern of very lively motion and seems almost to anticipate the virtuosity of Dryden's *Alexander's Feast*. Here again a curious comparison might be made with Campion's version, conceived according to the same traditional character of hymn-writing illustrated in Herbert's version quoted above.

'We hanged our harps upon the willows in the midst thereof', says the Psalm. 'Our silent Harps we pensive hung', runs Campion's version. But Crashaw has: 'Our Harpes . . . nodding on the willows slept'. And here is his rendering of the passage:

> If I forget thee, O Jerusalem, let my right hand forget her cunning.
>
> If I do not remember thee, let my tongue cleave to the roof of my mouth; if I prefer not Jerusalem above my chief joy.

> Ah thee *Jerusalem!* ah sooner may
>   This hand forget the mastery
>   Of musicks dainty touch, then I
>   The Musicke of thy memory.

> Which when I lose, ô may at once my Tongue
>   Lose this same busie speaking art
> Vnpearcht, her vocall Arteries unstrung,
>   No more acquainted with my Heart,
>   On my dry pallats roofe to rest
>   A wither'd Leafe, an idle Guest.

> No, no, thy good, Sion, alone must crowne
>   The head of all my hope-nurst joyes.[70]

[70] Ed. Martin, p. 105.

The weak point of Crashaw's style is manifest in the manner in which he renders that terrible close: 'Happy shall he be, that taketh and dasheth thy little ones against the stones', whose bareness Campion strives to imitate in:

> Blest shall they be thy babes that take
> And 'gainst the stones dash out their braines.

Crashaw paraphrases thus:

> Laugh, till thy childrens bleeding bones
> Weepe pretious Teares upon the stones—

which through its impropriety and circumlocution shows how incapable the poet was of feeling the power of the original.[71] One might make further interesting remarks on these paraphrases: see for instance how he trims them with puns and alliterations such as:

> Not *wanton,* nor in *want* to be (Psalm xxiii)
> When *Harpes* and *Hearts* were drown'd in teares (Psalm cxxxvii).

This tendency, common in the seventeenth century, and brought to its climax by Marino, can be illustrated with plenty of instances in Crashaw:

[71] The study of the paraphrase of the Office of the Cross is also of great interest. I limit myself to quoting the original text and Crashaw's version of the hymn *Ad primam de Cruce* (ed. Martin, p. 267):

> Hora prima ductus est Iesus ad Pylatum.
> Falsis testimoniis multum accusatum.
> In collo percutiunt manibus ligatum.
> Vultum dei conspuunt lumen coeli gratum.

> The early Prime blushes to say
> She could not rise so soon, as they
> Call'd Pilat vp; to try if He
> Could lend them any cruelty.
>   Their hands with lashes arm'd, their toungs with lyes,
> And loathsom spittle, blott those beauteous eyes,
> The blissfull springs of ioy; from whose all-clearing Ray
> The fair starrs fill their wakefull fires the sun himselfe drinks
>   Day.

Non *parere* sed *perire* ceu *parata* [72]

> (Martin, p. 224)

Lo the faint *Lamb,* with weary *limb*
Beares that huge tree

> (Martin, p. 270)

the *close closet* of aeternity

> (Martin, p. 388)

each *Leafe* you meet
Is her *Lifes* wing

> (Martin, p. 397)

The Greek text of Moschus' *Runaway Love* which, literally translated, reads 'being a little torch he sets the Sun itself on fire', is rendered by Crashaw: [73]

> His Torch Imperious though but small
> Makes the Sunne (of flames the sire)
> Worse than Sun-burnt in his fire.

As for alliterations, one should quote in their entirety the translations of Remond's elegies and the *Description of a religiuous house* taken from Barclay's *Argenis,* in which every line is tuned to an alliteration, such as:

> Whole *d*ayes & suns *d*euour'd with endlesse *d*ining
> *M*ix the *m*ad sons of *m*en in *m*utuall blood [74]

Other mannerisms in Crashaw's style can be clearly seen in his versions of Psalms where they are emphasised by the contrast with the originals. Thus the mixed metaphor resulting in an impropriety: that phrase of his version of Psalm xxiii, 'silver-sweating streames', illustrates a tendency which is exhibited flagrantly in:

> This shall from henceforth be the masculine theme
> Pulpits and pennes shall sweat in— [75]

---

[72] A similar word-play occurs in the modern Jesuit poet G. M. Hopkins. See instances of it in the essay 'T. S. Eliot and Dante' in the present volume, p. 371.
[73] Ed. Martin, p. 160.
[74] Ed. Martin, p. 338.
[75] Ed. Martin, p. 139.

reminding one of the first line of a famous sonnet of Achillini's: 'Sudate, o fochi, a preparar metalli'.[76] Finally, it is significant that the only passage of Psalm xxiii Crashaw translates literally is 'thou anointest my head with oil; my cup runneth over', whose opulent oriental images it was impossible to enrich:

> How my head in ointment swims!
> How my cup orelooks her Brims!

A study of Crashaw's versions shows how incapable he is of a concise style, of rendering severe and manly feelings in a few strokes; how, on the contrary, he makes capital out of whatever lends itself to florid divagations and to description of tender and delicate emotions. Grace is not denied to him, but Strength is beyond his reach. His happiest moments come when he can abandon himself to fantastic visions which do not obey any other law but the natural one which postulates a relaxation after a period of intense stress.

Therefore the most typical of his versions is that of a Latin composition introduced by the Jesuit Famianus Strada into his *Prolusiones Academicae* (Lugduni, 1617, Lib. II, Prol. vi) by way of imitation of Claudian's style. The popularity of this Latin poem, if we consider where it appeared, seems to us little short of miraculous: and perhaps it can be explained if we think how widespread Jesuit literature was during the seventeenth century. We have already seen, indeed, Crashaw deriving inspiration from Jesuit elegiac and epigrammatic poets whose works saw several reprints at the time and are now completely forgotten. If we bear in mind that Strada's composition was also imitated in England by Ford (*The Lover's Melancholy*, Act I, sc. i), Ambrose Philips, Browne (*Britannia's Pastorals*, Book II, song iv, 463 ff.), and others, without taking allusions into account; [77] in Italy by Marino

[76] 'Sweat on, ye fires, to get metals ready'.
[77] See Martin, pp. 439–440, and Saintsbury, *Minor Caroline Poets*, i, 408: Benlowes, 'Theophila's Love-Sacrifice':

> Sic amet, omnis Amans, sic immoriatur Amanti:
> Ut lyra Lusciniae Vitaque Morsque fuit.

> Lovers so love, as for the lov'd to die,
> As Strada's lute was life and destiny.

(*Adone*, vii, st. 32 ff.); in France by Sautel; [78] in Spain by Don García Coronel in the commentary to a passage in Góngora which referred to it; [79] in Holland by the poetess Tesselschade Visscher in *Wilde Zangster* (very likely through Marino); we will not be far from the truth in seeing in the diffusion of this theme a witness to the popularity of that Jesuit literature which today is almost forgotten. Perhaps Crashaw came to know Strada's poem through Ford, who is the only playwright he mentions in his works; or vice versa. [80]

For a while the English poet follows more or less Strada's text, though endeavouring to insert conceits as in:

in whose gentle aires
Hee lost the Dayes heat, and his owne hot cares—

which elaborates

sonanti
Lenibat plectro curas, aestumque levabat;

or else condensing the elements offered by his model into fine images: thus 'a cleare unwrinckled song' is more forcible than 'nulloque plicatile flexu/carmen init'. But after having translated line 40: 'et infuscat ceu Martia classica pulset',

---

[78] *Lusus poetici allegorici sive Elegiae oblectandis animis et moribus informandis accomodatae*, Auctore P. Petro Justo Sautel, S.J., Parisiis, Typis Josephi Barbou, 1754. Elegia Decima: *Philomela in certamine moriens*. The bravura of certain lines by Sautel vies with Crashaw's:

Nunc vocem infuscat, jaciens nunc fusile carmen
Productis longum tractibus arva replet.

. . . .

Nunc revolubilium torquet glomeramina vocum

. . . .

Et strepit et tinnit, pipatque lipitque pipitque.

The contest is alluded to also by Etienne Binet, in *Essai des merveilles de nature et des plus nobles artifices, pièce très nécessaire à tous ceux qui font profession d'éloquence*, par René François, prédicateur du Roi, Paris 1639 (2nd ed.). See on the contest, Della Giovanna in 'Atene e Roma', 1904–05.

[79] Góngora, *Obras comentadas por Don García Coronel*. Segunda parte del tomo segundo, Madrid, 1648, p. 259.

[80] See the epigram 'Upon Ford's Tragedies', ed. Martin, p. 181.

Crashaw soars on his own account into a giddy spiral of images which find no counterpart in the Latin text:

> as when the Trumpets call
> Hot Mars to th'Harvest of Deaths field. . . .

Lines 54–104 and 112–126 of *Musicks Duell* may be said to create in verse an effect similar to that of many a famous baroque building, and to illustrate the fundamental baroque tendency to avoid a closed composition, to develop single parts irrespective of the ensemble, to emphasise the picturesque and spectacular to the detriment of design and balance. Crashaw lets himself be waylaid by all the attractive images which ogle him at every turning, ventures into dangerous ascents which lead nowhere, gets lost in intricate mazes of conceits, and thus achieves a dazzling effect which may remind us of the impressionist technique.

This quality of 'dazzling intricacy and affluence in refinement' is, oddly enough, a characteristic of Swinburne, the poet who thus characterised Crashaw.[81] The inspiration of both is of Dionysian character, lets itself be overwhelmed by a world of images without ever succeeding in controlling it; and, incapable of fixing a limit, might continue endlessly in its giddy ascent, were it not that the very impulsion slackens by a natural law. The fancy of both poets finds an apt definition in what Swift says in his *Tale of a Tub*: 'Fancy, flying up to the imagination of what is highest and best, becomes overshot, and spent, and weary, and suddenly falls, like a dead bird of paradise, to the ground': and we should note that both poets, by a strange coincidence, were likened to birds of paradise. If we compare certain passages of *Tristram of Lyonesse* with *Musicks Duell*, we shall be astonished at the similarity of technique: while occasionally Swinburne's alliteration and word-play have a seventeenth-century flavour, Crashaw's random shots hit sometimes such bold similes, even for his century, that one would think them the fruit of a modern brain: e.g., Apollo's music making 'Heavens selfe

[81] Whereas this description is apposite, the comparison the same writer makes between Crashaw and Théophile in his essay on this latter (posthumously published by Gosse, London, 1915) is ill-chosen and inconclusive. Perhaps Swinburne was misled in this case by his anti-religious bias.

looke higher' (l. 118). Such effects of transposition of terms, which Marino usually brings about mechanically, through devices like those recommended by Tesauro [82] in order to widen the field of metaphors (such as 'una piuma canora, un canto alato' [83]—*Adone*, vii, 37), which Mallarmé and Valéry achieve through a refinement of the same process, seem to come naturally to the heated imagination of Crashaw and Swinburne: these poets lose themselves in a shapeless and universal mode of being in which sensations become merged and confused. This is what Crashaw says of the name of Jesus: [84]

> Fair, flowry Name; in none but Thee
> And Thy Nectareall Fragrancy,
>   Hourly there meetes
> An vniuersall SYNOD of All sweets
>
> . . . .
>
> SWEET NAME, in Thy each Syllable
> A Thousand Blest ARABIAS dwell;
> A Thousand Hills of Frankincense;
> Mountains of myrrh, & Beds of spices,
> And ten Thousand PARADISES . . .

A passage of the *Hymn of the Nativity* [85] (in the 1646 edition of *Steps to the Temple*) which has puzzled the interpreters, supplies a good illustration of the Dionysian 'impressionism' of our poet. The Virgin lulls the Divine Child to sleep:

> Shee sings thy Teares asleepe, and dips
>   Her Kisses in thy weeping Eye,
> Shee spreads the red leaves of thy Lips,
>   That in their Buds yet blushing lye.

[82] Tesauro, *op. cit.*, p. 120.

[83] 'a singing feather, a winged song'.

[84] ed. Martin, p. 244. Crashaw's lines develop a hint from the *Song of Solomon*, i, 2: 'Oleum effusum nomen tuum'. Cf. Ludovici Cellottii (Louis Cellot) Soc. Iesu *Opera Poetica*, Parisiis, Apud Sebastianum Cramoisy, 1630: 'De Sanctissimo Iesu Nomine.' See an analysis of Crashaw's poem in the light of Mauburnus's *Scala Meditatoria*, in L. L. Martz's *The Poetry of Meditation, op. cit.*, p. 331 ff.

[85] Ed. Martin, p. 108.

> Shee 'gainst those Mother-Diamonds tryes
> The points of her young Eagles Eyes.

Similes and conceits form in these few lines a monstrous cluster: the viewpoint shifts with such speed that what we see is a throbbing and dazzling chaos instead of a definite pattern.[86] A sudden darting of animal and vegetable beings, a succession of quick mysterious acts, is all we perceive in that dim process in which tears are likened to infants lulled to sleep, kisses are seen diving into tears as into a pool, lips are like blushing buds, the eyes of the Virgin are like diamonds (mother-diamonds in their relation to the Son's eyes), and, it is understood, they shine like the sun, and as the sight of the sun is tolerated only by eagles, the eyes of the Child are like a young eagle's, and she tries their points, i.e., their glances, against those unscratchable diamonds.[87]

Another illustration of Crashaw's dizzy imagination is supplied by the Latin poem *Bulla,* first published at the end of Heinsius's *Crepundia Siliana* (Cambridge, 1646.) Written in a humanistic Latin, far from unusual in that period (see for instance some of Murtola's *Neniae,* Macerata, 1618), it deals with a theme which was then familiar, the soap bubble, to which it was customary for moralists to compare human life (Erasmus, *Adagia,* II, iii, 48: 'Homo bulla').[88] Knowing

---

[86] However, the point of view of the seventeenth century may be put in Tesauro's words apropos of another author: 'You see with what speed and through how many degrees in a single moment your thought has to sweep in order to reach his conceit: and what an amount of perspicacity and quickness of wit is necessary both for him who makes the metaphor and for him who seizes it'. (p. 279)

[87] Cf. Thomas Randolph, *A Maske for Lydia:*
> Close up those eyes, or we shall finde
> Too great a lustre strike us blinde!
> Or if a Ray, so good
> Ought to be seene, let it but then appeare
>   When Eagles doe produce their brood,
> To try their young ones there.

[88] See for instance the figure in *Quadriga Aeternitatis,* Monaci, ap. Raph. Sadelerum, 1619: a child with a bubble-pipe leans against a skull; above are the words: 'Homo bulla', and underneath: 'Bulla quid est fragilis, vernans Flos, Fumus in aura?/Est nihil, an vita est his potiore loco.'

next to nothing of the humanist literature of which *Bulla* is a product, modern readers may find the poem akin to certain of Shelley's lyrics, such as *The Cloud* or the fifth stanza of *To Jane: The Recollection*.[89] Of the former of these poems we are reminded while reading:

> Sum venti ingenium breve
> Flos sum, scilicet, aëris,
> Sidus scilicet aequoris;
> Naturae jocus aureus,
> Naturae vaga fabula,
> Naturae breve somnium, etc.

were it not that this string of elegant comparisons belongs to a kind of rhetorical artifice not uncommon in the seventeenth century.[90] In the course of this astonishing lyric Crashaw places before our eyes a kaleidoscope of

> Sweet views which in our world above
> Can never well be seen,[91]

minature landscapes, faery spectacles of diminutive revolutions, rendered with an exquisite verbal craftsmanship which often results in highly poetical images like that

> . . . grex velleris aurei
> Grex pellucidus aetheris;
> Qui noctis nigra pascua
> Puris morsibus atterit—

that 'flock of the golden fleece, the bright flock of ether, which with pure bites browses the black pastures of the Night'. Even more extraordinary for his period, the awareness the poet seems to possess of the spiritual reality of his world: 'Cur vixit? adhuc tu nempe legebas'. In *Bulla* Crashaw aims at an effect which would seem attainable only by a painter, just as in *Musicks Duell* he strives to produce in the reader's mind a state which only pure sounds seem capable of provoking. This virtuosity of his is no mere playing, because his fancy imparts

[89] Ed. Martin, p. 216 ff.
[90] We find remarkable analogies with Crashaw's style in *Partheneia sacra*. See my *Studies in Seventeenth-Century Imagery*, vol. i, pp. 150–157.
[19] Shelley, *To Jane: The Recollection*.

an exceptional incandescence to the verbal medium. In these bold attempts at surpassing the limits and possibilities of his own art, Crashaw, better than any of the poets who were his contemporaries, achieves a result which may be said to have been the common aspiration of baroque art: that inextricable complexity of presentation, that one universal Art in which all the arts should blend and become an indistinguishable whole. *Bulla* and *Musicks Duell* are masterpieces of an age which had a painter's view of architecture, and tried to obtain plastic and musical effects from poetry, that age that created as the supreme fruit of its experiments the opera, where the word, music, and painting concur in bringing about a *tertium quid* which transcends its components.

The poetics at the back of Crashaw's lyrical poetry can be better determined through the words of Pope, a critic professing opposite principles, who in poetry most valued design, a logical pattern, and a well-defined elaboration of parts, a critic who was an eminent representative of that classicism which arose as a reaction to the spirit of impassioned fantasy, asymmetric and limitless rambling, and impressionism, which were proper to baroque art. In his letter of December 17, 1710 to Henry Cromwell, Pope wrote: 'All that regards design, form, fable (which is the soul of poetry), all that concerns exactness, or consent of parts (which is the body) will probably be wanting; only pretty conceptions, fine metaphors, glittering expressions, and something of a neat cast of verse (which are properly the dress, gems, and loose ornaments of poetry), may be found in these verses'. And chiefly: 'And (to express myself like a Painter) their [i.e., of poets like Crashaw] colouring entertains the sight, but the Lines and Life of the Picture are not to be inspected too narrowly'. Pope considered frivolous certain traits of Crashaw's art which have instead a deeper root.

Crashaw's idea of poetry partakes more of the spirit of baroque art than Marino's superficial definition:

> E' del poeta il fin la meraviglia,
> Chi non sa far stupir vada alla striglia,[92]

[92] 'The poet's end is to strike with wonder; whoever fails to astonish deserves the whip'.

which accounts only for the crude and showy side of *secentismo*: verbal artifices, alliterations, word-play, and witticisms are included in that definition, but nothing is said about that marvellous energy of soaring imagination which produced so many masterpieces in the visual arts. In fact an Italian poet, hampered by tradition (to be an Italian poet meant being a 'Tuscan' poet), being himself a refiner of the far-fetched compliments of the Petrarchan school, rather than a revolutionary, could be baroque only half-heartedly. The yoke of tradition weighed less heavily on the painters, and if a new spirit was hardly apparent in those who were incapable of ridding themselves of old conventions, there were many, chiefly in the South, who, feeling the ties of academic tradition but weakly, let themselves go in orgies of colour. If baroque art in Italy, then, did not assert itself vigorously so far as poetry was concerned, and, though shining here and there with outstanding beauty, failed to reach supreme expression in painting, and achieved perfection only in architecture, outside Italy, instead, in countries where the Renaissance had come only at a second remove, and minds were not saturated with the classical tradition, baroque art was to enjoy its main triumphs.

It would be unfair to call Crashaw a Marinist just because he was trained to turn surprising *concetti* [93] in Marino's school: Crashaw's poetry, in its more peculiar aspects, is the

---

[93] Besides the parallels we have already examined, many more might be listed. In the hymn *In the holy Nativity* (ed. Martin, p. 248) whose structure, like an amoebaean song, perhaps derived from Sannazaro's *De Partu Virginis* (Lib. II, 170 ff., specially 197–232), lends itself to an epigrammatic treatment, one finds variations on a conceit used by Marino in his sonnet 'Nella Notte di Natale': 'Felice notte, ond' a noi nasce il giorno/di cui mai più sereno altro non fue,/che fra gli orrori e sotto l'ombre tue/copri quel Sol, ch' a l'altro Sol fa scorno . . .' ['O happy night, out of whom the serenest day of all is born to us, thou, who coverest with thy horrors and shadows that Sun, who puts the other sun to scorn'] (cf. a similar conceit in Shakespeare's *Romeo and Juliet*; see 'Shakespeare's Italy', above.) In the three couplets *On our crucified Lord, naked and bloody* (ed. Martin, p. 100) the Crucifix appears clothed with the purple of his own blood, according to an image used by Marino in the *Sudore del Sangue* which can be traced to Saint Bonaventure's *Lignum Vitae*.

literary counterpart, though a minor one, to Rubens's apotheoses, Murillo's languors and El Greco's ecstasies.

Marino's distich conveying his narrow idea of poetry is a poor match for the lines in which Crashaw speaks of poetical inspiration (in *To the Morning, Satisfaction for Sleepe*); [94]

> . . . nimble rapture starts to Heaven and brings
> *Enthusiasticke* flames, such as can give
> Marrow to my plumpe *Genius,* make it live
> Drest in the glorious madnesse of a Muse,
> Whose feet can walke the milky way, and chuse
> Her starry Throne; whose holy heats can warme
> The Grave, and hold up an exalted arme
> To lift me from my lazy Vrne, to climbe
> Vpon the stooped shoulders of old Time;
> And trace Eternity . . .

Such an inspiration can be defined, to use other words of the poet,[95] 'a sweet inebriated extasy': an ecstasy which breaks forth into dithyrambs, into hymns of many-hued splendour, now nimble, soaring up in dizzy spirals, now solemn, wrapped in the silken folds of azure singing robes, veiled by clouds of incense. 'Love is eloquence' says Crashaw,[96] and though he believes in that dumb eloquence which manifests itself through glances and tears (the kind of eloquence the painters of the period used to signify ecstasies):

> Eyes are vocall, Teares have Tongues,
> And there be words not made with lungs;
> Sententious showers, ô let them fall,
> Their cadence is Rhetoricall— [97]

though he believed in this dumb eloquence and daily practised it in the vigils at Little Gidding and the adorations at Little St. Mary and in the chapel of Peterhouse, his faith belongs to the kind which finds an outlet in expressions now

[94] Ed. Martin, p. 183.
[95] Ed. Martin, p. 399.
[96] Ed. Martin, p. 136.
[97] Ed. Martin, p. 167.

torn and eager with longing, now instinct with melting sweetness. It is a faith completely diverse from that of the Protestants; completely steeped in contemplation and an exulting
amazement before the divine wonders, it ignores the tone of
homily and the pedestrian sermon. It is the faith of a Southern
Latin cast, of a soul which is *naturaliter* Roman Catholic. One
of Crashaw's English critics, Eric Shepherd,[98] has properly
drawn attention to the exclamatory, ecstatic tone of the titles
of Crashaw's later poems, and has tried to explain this
'hymning quality' by the fact that the poet was a convert,
astonished by the glory and magnitude of his discovery: however, the state of 'sweet inebriated extasy' is previous to the
conversion, is inborn, and may be discerned even in his secular
poem, *Wishes to his (supposed) Mistresse.*

'Fac me cruce inebriari/et cruore Filii', said the sequence
of the *Stabat Mater*. 'Sanguis Christi, inebria me', repeated
Saint Ignatius. 'Let my soul swell/with thee, strong wine of
love', exclaims Crashaw. Metaphors drawn from blood, wine,
fire, recur in him with an insistence which seems extraordinary
even in a Catholic, accustomed to meditate on the eucharistic
mystery: an insistence he has in common with Swinburne, the
poet whose inspiration is curiously somehow akin to his own.
Such metaphors are like mottoes and emblems of the fiery
imagination of such poets; though in one case they refer to
profane and in the other to sacred objects: to the blood of
love's martyrdom, the wine of the intoxication of the sense,
the fire of Dionysian frenzy in the singer of Anactoria; the
blood of religious martyrdom, the wine of the celestial harvest,
the fire of the ecstatic fervour, in the singer of Saint Teresa.

Crashaw's pages are decked with red, purple, and flame—
colour, like a church decked for the feasts of the Most Precious
Blood and the commemoration of the martyrs. Had such
pages been paintings, those ruddy hues would have distinguished them like Rubens' compositions. Crashaw vies with
this painter in sumptuousness and triumphal pomp: both
sound the most high-pitched notes of the Heroic Catholicism
born out of the Council of Trent. The poet, paraphrasing one

[98] *The Religious Poems of Richard Crashaw*, with an introductory
Study by R. A. Eric Shepherd, London, 1914, p. 9 ff.

of Remond's elegies, writes of the martyrs Cecilia and Valerian: [99]

> Both mixt at last their blood in one rich bed
> Of rosy MARTYRDOME, twice Married.
> O burn our hymen bright in such high Flame.

Of the Cross: [100]

> Large throne of loue! Royally spred
> With purple of too Rich a red.

This Rubensian opulence stands out in the hymn *To the Name above every Name, the Name of Jesus*,[101] as perhaps in no other poem of the *Carmen Deo Nostro*. As in other cases, Crashaw's hymn is an exquisite string of variations on a Latin text: the text having been supplied this time (I have not seen it noticed by Martin nor by Martz) by *Jubilus de nomine Jesu*, attributed to Saint Bernard.[102] But see what riot of imagery Crashaw has conjured up from the plain Latin verse!

> Iesu dulcis memoria,
> Dans uera cordi gaudia;
> Sed super mel et omnia
> Eius dulcis praesentia.
>
> Nil canitur suauius,
> Nil auditur iucundius,
> Nil cogitatur dulcius
> Quam Iesu dei filius.
>
> Iesus spes paenitentibus,
> Quam pius es petentibus
> Quam bonus te quaerentibus,
> Sed quid inuenientibus?

[99] Ed. Martin, p. 337. Remond (Elegia ii) has: 'Sanguis utrumque iterum foecunda in morte maritat:/Ornat utrique manum palma, corona caput./ Noster Hymen tali caleat face'.

[100] Ed Martin, p. 278.

[101] Ed. Martin, p. 239 ff.

[102] See André Wilmart, O. S. B., *Le 'Jubilus' dit de Saint Bernard* (Etude avec textes), Rome, 1944, Edizioni di 'Storia e Letteratura'.

Iesu, dulcedo cordium,
Fons uiuus, lumen mentium,
Excedens omne gaudium
Et omne desiderium.

. . . .

Mane nobiscum, domine,
Et nos illustra lumine
Pulsa mentis caligine,
Mundum replens dulcedine.

Amor Iesu dulcissimus
Et uere suauissimus,
Plus millies gratissimus
Quam dicere sufficimus.

. . . .

Iesu, decus angelicum,
In aure dulce canticum,
In ore mel mirificum,
In corde nectar caelicum.

. . . .

Iesu, sole serenior
Et balsamo suauior,
Omni dulcore dulcior,
Caeteris amabilior.

Cuius gustus sic afficit,
Cuius odor sic reficit,
In quo mea mens deficit,
Solus amanti sufficit.

These and suchlike accents find a multiple echo in Crashaw's hymn: [103]

Lo, where Aloft it comes! It comes, Among
The conduct of Adoring SPIRITS, that throng
Like diligent Bees, And swarm about it.
    O they are wise;
And know what SWEETES are suck't from out it.
    It is the Hiue,

[103] The first portion of Crashaw's hymn enlarges upon the theme of st. xiv: 'Cum digne loqui nequeam,/De te tamen ne sileam:/Amor facit ut audeam,/Cum de te solum gaudeam.'

By which they thriue,
Where all their Hoard of Hony lyes.
Lo where it comes, vpon The snowy DOVE's
Soft Back; And brings a Bosom big with Loues.
WELCOME to our dark world, Thou
  Womb of Day!
Vnfold thy fair Conceptions; And display
The Birth of our Bright Ioyes.
  O thou compacted
Body of Blessings: spirit of Soules extracted!
O dissipate thy spicy Powres
(Clowd of condensed sweets) & break vpon vs
  In balmy showrs;
O fill our senses, And take from vs
All force of so Prophane a Fallacy
To think ought sweet but that which smells of Thee.
Fair, flowry Name; In none but Thee
And Thy Nectareall Fragrancy,
  Hourly there meetes
An vniuersall SYNOD of All sweets;
By whom it is defined Thus
  That no Perfume
  For euer shall presume
To passe for Odoriferous,
But such alone whose sacred Pedigree
Can proue it Self some kin (sweet name) to Thee.
SWEET NAME, in Thy each Syllable
A Thousand Blest ARABIAS dwell;
A Thousand Hills of Frankincense;
Mountains of myrrh, & Beds of spices,
And ten Thousand PARADISES
The soul that tasts thee takes from thence.
How many vnknown WORLDS there are
Of Comforts, which Thou hast in keeping!
How many Thousand Mercyes there
In Pitty's soft lap ly a sleeping!
Happy he who has the art
  To awake them,
  And to take them
Home, & lodge them in his HEART.

The heroic note is not so frequent in Crashaw as a strain of feminine tenderness by which some of his poems seem to be related to Murillo's delicate and mellow sacred paintings. The exceeding *morbidezza* of these lyrics, the lavish use of such adjectives as 'sweet', 'dear', the refined grace of the similes and the diluted fluency of the verse, seem to proceed from that world where tender saints with motherly fondness stretch out their soft arms towards the rosy radiant Child in rooms filled by mysteriously opalescent shadows: that world which is lit by the mild lunar gleam of the glory of the *Purísima,* among wreaths of festive cherubs. We find gestures similar to those of Murillo's Saint Anthony in the adoring shepherds of the hymn *In the holy Nativity,* who weave exquisite madrigals round the crib where the divine Baby lies in a halo; and there is a close kinship between one of Murillo's Immaculate Virgins and the Virgin of the Assumption in the hymn dedicated to her, breathing the erotic exaltation of the *Song of Solomon:* [104]

> . . . Purer & brighter
> Then the chast starres, whose choise lamps come to
> light her
> While through the crystall orbes, clearer than they
> She climbes; and makes a farre more milkey way.
> . . . .
> Heaun calls her, & she must away.
> Heaun will not, & she cannot stay.
> GOE then, goe GLORIOUS
>   On the golden wings
> Of the bright youth of heaun, that sings
> Vnder so sweet a Burthen
> . . . .
> LIVE, rosy princesse, LIVE. And may the bright
> Crown of a most incomparable light
> Embrace thy radiant browes. O may the best
> Of euerlasting ioyes bath thy white brest.
> LIVE, our chast loue, the holy mirth
> Of heaun; the humble pride of earth.
> Liue, crown of woemen; Queen of men.

[104] Ed. Martin, p. 304.

Liue mistresse of our song. And when
Our weak desires haue done their best,
Sweet Angels come, and sing the rest.

Much of this fervent suavity is found in the famous *Hymn
to Saint Teresa*,[105] but in the songs dedicated to the Spanish
saint who had such a deep influence on the religious life of
the poet, there are much higher notes than those of gorgeous
festivity and melting sweetness. Accents of mystical eloquence
had already come from Crashaw's lips in the ode 'praefixed
to a little Prayer-book given to a young Gentlewoman' [106]

. . . that sacred store
Of hidden sweets & holy ioyes
WORDS which are not heard with EARES

[105] E. I. Watkin, *The English Way*, London, 1934, has compared passages of Crashaw's hymn to the Latin hymn sung in the
vespers of the feast of the saint: 'Terris Teresa barbaris/Christum
datura aut sanguinem'; cf. ll. 55–56: 'So shall she leave amongst
them sown/Her Lord's Blood; or at lest her own'; 'Sed te manet
suavior/Mors, poena poscit dulcior,/Divini amoris cuspide/In
vulnus icta concides./O caritatis victima . . .'; cf. l. 65 ff.: 'Sweet,
not so fast! . . . T' embrace a milder Martyrdom . . . Thov art
love's victime . . . His is the Dart must make the Death . . .'
Fénelon was to say in a later age (*Panégyrique de Sainte Thérèse*):
'La grande sainte ne savait pas encore que ce ne seraient pas les
tortures qui la feraient souffrir, mais l'amour'. Another passage:
'Scarse has she Blood enough . . .'' recalls a passage of St Ambrose's panegyric of St Agnes (*De Virginibus* Liber I, cap. 2:
Migne, vol. xvi, col. 190) which Gracián in *Agudeza y Arte de
Ingenio* quotes as an instance of *agudeza de improporción y
disonancia* (p. 23 of the 1649 Huesca edition): Saint Ambrose
'contrapuso con grande artificio la pequeñez de su [i.e., St. Agnes's]
cuerpo a la grandeza de su espíritu' in these words: 'Fuitne in illo
corpusculo vulneri locus? Et quae non habuit quo ferrum reciperet,
habuit quo ferrum vinceret . . . Nondum idonea poenae, et jam
matura victoriae: certare difficilis, facilis coronari'. The passage
omitted by Gracián: 'mori adhuc nescia, sed parata' is recalled by
Crashaw's 'What death with love should have to doe . . .', while
the lines: 'Love knowes no nonage, nor the Mind./'Tis Love, not
Yeares or Limbs that can/Make the Martyr . . .' find a counterpart in a passage from an epistle of St Ambrose on St Agnes
(Migne, vol. xvii, col. 737): 'Fides enim non in annis, sed in
sensibus geritur; et Deus omnipotens mentes magis comprobat
quam aetates'.
[106] Ed. Martin, p. 329–330.

(Those tumultuous shops of noise)
Effectuall wispers, whose still voice
The soul it selfe more feeles than heares;
Amorous languishments; luminous trances;
SIGHTS which are not seen with eyes;
Spirituall & soul-piercing glances
Whose pure & subtil lightning flyes
Home to the heart, & setts the house on fire
And melts it down in sweet desire
    Yet does not stay
To ask the windows leaue to passe that way;
Delicious DEATHS; soft exalations
Of soul; dear & diuine annihilations;
    A thousand vnknown rites
Of ioyes & rarefy'd delights;
A hundred thousand goods, glories, & graces,
    And many a mystick thing
    Which the diuine embraces
Of the deare spouse of spirits with them will bring
    For which it is no shame
That dull mortality must not know a name.

Ecstasy is here more described than lived through; but already in the *Hymn to Saint Teresa,* mere enumeration, though sumptuous, gives way to a magnificent presentation of the beatific vision: [107]

So soon as thou shalt first appear,
The MOON of maiden starrs, thy white
MISTRESSE, attended by such bright
Soules as thy shining self, shall come
And in her first rankes make thee room;
Where 'mongst her snowy family
Immortall wellcomes wait for thee.
    O what delight, when reueal'd LIFE shall stand
And teach thy lipps heau'n with his hand;
On which thou now maist to thy wishes
Heap vp thy consecrated kisses.
What ioyes shall seize thy soul, when she

[107] Ed. Martin, p. 320.

Bending her blessed eyes on thee
(Those second Smiles of Heau'n) shall dart
Her mild rayes through thy melting heart!

. . . .

Thou shalt look round about, & see
Thousands of crown'd Soules throng to be
Themselues thy crown.

There is still something detached and of a descriptive nature in this composition: the poet does not yet possess the adequate lyric heat for the mystical experience. Very likely Crashaw never reached that state of ardent rapture which fired Jacopone da Todi with divine madness,[108] but he came nevertheless very close to it. Through his intense yearning he touched the fringe of bliss in that brief lyrical flight, with its close series of invocations which the poet (inverting the *mulier formosa* process of composition criticised by Horace) tried to combine with an exercise of that Marinesque wit with which at an earlier date he had protracted through no less than eighty-five lines a conceit on Saint Teresa and the darting Seraphim. The first portion of the poem concluded with an idea which the Petrarchan sixteenth century had fully exploited: [109]

. . . in loue's feilde was neuer found
A nobler weapon than a wovnd.
Loue's passiues are his actiu'st part.
The wounded is the wounding heart—

and, rather generically, he admonished the wise souls to be 'the love-slain witnesses' of the Saint's life. Witnesses, but not partakers in a common ardour. However, in the ill-welded

[108] 'Amore, amore che sì m'hai ferito,/altro che amore non posso gridare . . . Per te voglio pasmare,—amor ch'io teco sia,/amor per cortesia,—famme morir d'amore' [Love, love who has so wounded me, I cannot shout anything but love . . . For thee will I waste away,—love, let me be with thee, love, I beg of thee, make me die of love.']

[109] See for instance in Cesare Rinaldi's verse: 'Che 'n restar vinto è vera gloria', and in Boscán's *Obras:* 'por más que esté perdido, siempre será vencedor/quien de vos queda vencido,' etc.

fragment which stands by itself in its own halo of flame, without intimate connexion with what precedes, the intonation becomes very personal and deeply felt and soars dizzily into an impassioned invocation, so that the rather rhetorical summons of the close of the preceding passage becomes a direct, fervid experience: the poet wants to tear himself from his own life, and his yearning for ecstasy is so powerful and desperate that he almost seems to have reached it: [110]

> O thou vndanted daughter of desires!
> By all thy dowr of LIGHTS & FIRES;
> By all the eagle in thee, all the doue;
> By all the liues & deaths of loue;
> By the larg draughts of intellectuall day,
> And by thy thirsts of loue more large than they;
> By all the brim-fill'd Bowles of feirce desire
> By thy last Morning's draught of liquid fire;
> By the full kingdome of that finall kisse
> That seiz'd thy parting Soul, & seal'd thee his;
> By all the heau'ns thou hast in him
> (Fair sister of the SERAPHIM!)
> By all of HIM we haue in THEE;
> Leaue nothing of my SELF in me.
> Let me so read thy life, that I
> Vnto all life of mine may dy.

In the whole course of seventeenth-century literature there is no higher expression of that spiritualisation of sense which is condensed here in a portentous, dizzy soaring of red-hot images. We may find a counterpart in El Greco's paintings, where, among shreds of ghost-like clouds, convulsed phantoms of saints lift tearful faces lit by a light that never was seen in this world. The voluptuous raptures of Lanfranco's and Bernini's ecstatic saints, Saint Margaret surprised by the Celestial Spouse, Saint Teresa pierced by the angelic archer, the Blessed Ludovica Albertoni in the throes of expiring, the paradisial languour of so many saints, martyrs and blessed women whose effigies people Italian and Spanish churches and art galleries, these images whose character leaves us in

[110] Ed. Martin, p. 326–327.

suspense as to whether it should be termed holy or profane, become suddenly clear, as if we were given a commentary on them in the light of these few lines of a great 'minor' English poet, which transcend them and seem to contain *in nuce* the quintessence of the whole seventeenth century.

Petrarch in England

DANTE seems to have offered a different aspect to each one of the periods in which he has been appreciated, and although his fame in England suffered a long eclipse almost from the death of Chaucer to the beginning of the modern era, there is hardly an ancient foreign author more popular than he is among poets writing in English today. If we consider the chief exponents of the Dante tradition in England, Chaucer, Byron, Shelley, Rossetti, T. S. Eliot, we can hardly find anything in common among them, not even the cult of Dante, since each of them saw a different Dante.

The cult of Petrarch, on the other hand, offers a striking contrast. His personality seems to have become fixed in the mind of his readers from the very beginning. He is the creator of a poetic language as permanent as the classical orders of architecture: interpretation of his work can vary only within very narrow limits. One must either accept him as he is, or reject him: there is no possibility of presenting him from a different angle. Chaucer's Dante, Shelley's Dante, Eliot's Dante, seem hardly the same poet; this many-sidedness of Dante is, of course, the reason for his appeal to distant ages. Petrarch, on the contrary, appealed to the English Renaissance with an intensity unparalleled by any other foreign poet, perhaps; he set a vogue in Europe which established a new literary *genre*, the Petrarchan sonnet, and created a widespread school with conventions almost as fixed as those of

Byzantine painting. For a couple of centuries the Petrarchan manner created a kind of *lingua franca* for love-lyrics throughout Europe. Then the convention died out, never to be revived again, just as has happened with Byzantine painting (except in Russian industrial art).

But before proceeding to the study of the Petrarchan convention and its crystallising effect on literature (not unlike, as I have just said, that of an iconographical tradition in painting), let us consider the isolated case of Chaucer's imitation.

As we have seen,[1] the next Italian author after Dante to whom Chaucer confesses his indebtedness is 'Maister Petrak', and this seems strange indeed if we consider how slight Petrarch's influence was on his English admirer. Petrarch's Latin version of the Griselda story, the source of the *Clerk's Tale*, seems hardly sufficient to justify Chaucer's homage to Petrarch and the title of 'Maister' conferred upon him, unless Chaucer actually believed Petrarch to be the author of some of Boccaccio's works he was imitating. Then there is one of the sonnets of the *Canzoniere* of which Chaucer gives a translation in the First Book of his *Troilus*:

> If no love is, O God! what fele I so?
> And if love is, what thing and which is he?
> If love be good, from whennes comth my woe?
> If it be wikke, a wonder thynketh me.

The translation takes three stanzas, and concludes a long list of rhetorical questions thus:

> Allas! what is this wonder maladie?
> For hete of cold, for cold of hete I dye.

Two things strike us at once. The first, that Chaucer entirely disregarded the sonnet form and confined himself to borrowing the ideas. The second, that these ideas appear to us, nowadays, far from deserving translation into a foreign language. Why did Chaucer not attempt to imitate the sonnet form? Why did that spirit of experiment, which caused him

[1] See the essay on 'Chaucer and the Great Italian Writers of the Trecento', in this volume, p. 78.

to fit into English prosody most of the French lyric metres, fail to be stirred by the Italian sonnet?

The probable answer is that the sonnet form did not impress him sufficiently because it came to him in an isolated instance. As for the contents of the sonnet, and their appeal to Chaucer's mind, they conformed too well to the rhetorical *exempla* of the poetics followed by Chaucer to escape his attention. Here we come across a fundamental difference between to-day's taste and the taste of the age of Chaucer, and not only of that age, but also of the age which saw the full blossoming of the sonneteering literature, the Elizabethan age. As a matter of fact, when England discovered Petrarch in the twenties of the sixteenth century, what sonnets did the translators choose for their experiments? Are those sonnets the same we moderns would choose? The sonnets which seem to have chiefly appealed to Sir Thomas Wyatt and the Earl of Surrey, the two courtiers who are responsible for the introduction of the sonnet into England, are those which abound in artificial antitheses, oxymora, briefly those witticisms we usually associate with euphuism. This was the novelty, so far as contents go, which struck the two poets, whose other compositions still breathe a mediaeval spirit. The mannerisms of the two early English sonneteers are explained when we learn that foreign attention to the Italian sonnet was drawn not so much to Petrarch himself as to those among the Italian Petrarchists who can be said to have anticipated the extravagant conceits of the metaphysical school, those sonneteers whose work falls in the last quarter of the fifteenth century, and who were immensely popular in Italy at the time of the short-lived conquest of Charles VIII of France. Cariteo, Tebaldeo, Serafino Aquilano, Panfilo Sasso, Baldassarre Olimpo da Sassoferrato, these are the names of the poets who represent what may well be called 'the flamboyant period' of the sonnet. At this point it seems necessary to say something about the history of the sonnet.

The sonnet—as seems safely established today—was invented by the Sicilian poet Giacomo da Lentino, who flourished in the first half of the thirteenth century. There has been much speculation about the structure of this Italian poem. Briefly, it is based on a musical principle. The first part, of eight hendecasyllabic lines rhyming alternately—in which the form of the popular Sicilian metre, the *strambotto,* is easily recognisable—is arranged according to a scheme consisting of an even number of constituents; in the second part (two tercets) there is an odd number. The cause of this double arrangement is to be sought in the fact that the poem was set to music and the tune changed in the second part.

From the very beginning the sonnet showed a tendency to gravitate towards the second part. Its very musical structure postulated this: the second part represented the conclusion, a conclusion which was a culmination. Hence the tendency to build the first part of the poem as a sort of preparation for the idea which displayed its full import in the tercets. In this way the sonnet became the equivalent of the epigram of the ancients: so much so that, when the Greek Anthology and Anacreon were rediscovered in the sixteenth century, the poets, who were well aware of the similarity of the two forms, transfused into their sonnets the whole world of the Greek epigrammatists. By its very structure, then, the sonnet asked for a *concetto,* a witty invention, at the end; in the same manner in which the two premises of a syllogism are summed up in the conclusion. The emphasis of the discourse was bound to bear on that part which was originally accompanied by the closing bars of the air.

To this same reason is to be traced the tendency of the sonnet to be concluded by a couplet. But in Italy, though the disposition of the rhymes in the tercets admits of a final couplet, this is by far the rarest form of arrangement. And it is easy to see why: the couplet with its single rhyme is based on an even number, and the recurrence of such an even number in the second part of the sonnet is apt to destroy the balance of the whole composition, which is to be even in the first portion, odd in the second. Therefore, whenever the principle of concluding the sonnet by a couplet, or *rima baciata,* as it is called in Italian, prevailed, the couplet was added to the sonnet after the second tercet. Thus there originated a sonnet-form which enjoyed a certain vogue during the fourteenth century, the *sonetto caudato,* with a tail.

Now both in France and in England the form of the sonnet was thoroughly misunderstood. In France the sonnet became crystallised in the form given to it by Clément Marot: it consists of three four-line stanzas (quatrains) of which the third is separated from the other two by a couplet. Occasionally this couplet comes at the end. In Thomas Wyatt the two tercets are reduced to a quatrain plus a couplet. In order to explain this latter form it is not necessary to advance a theory according to which Wyatt, while in Italy, heard declaimed, or saw in mansucript, some among Benedetto Varchi's sonnets which conform to that pattern, or came across that form in the collection of early Italian poets called *Giuntina di rime antiche* which was published just in that year 1527 when Wyatt happened to be in Italy.[2] The tendency to end the sonnet with a couplet suggested itself naturally enough to anyone who overlooked the musical principle (i.e., an even part contrasted with an odd one) on which the sonnet was based. In the form it eventually took in French and English poetry, the Italian sonnet is hardly recognisable; and any metrical similarity ceases to exist in degenerated forms like Thomas Watson's would-be sonnet, which consists of three four-line stanzas each of them followed by a couplet: a provincial development of the French *sonnet marotique*. This, in brief, is the history of the sonnet in so far as its metrical structure is concerned. Let us now consider how the tendency to gravitate towards the second part influenced the contents of the poem.

I have called the end of the fifteenth century the 'flamboyant period' of the sonnet. To be more accurate, I should perhaps have called it 'the second flamboyant period', since in that very thirteenth century which saw the birth of the sonnet, the Tuscan poet Guittone d'Arezzo and his school fitted to the sonnet all the far-fetched inventions of the Provençal poets, many of which coincide with the *concetti* of the Roman erotic poets (and, therefore, of the Greek epigrammatists) on the one hand, and of the metaphysical school of the seventeenth century on the other. The school of Guittone, on the

[2] See W. L. Bullock, 'The Genesis of the English Sonnet Form', in *PMLA*, xxxviii (1923).

lines of the *trobar clus* of the Provençals, developed the artificial possibilities of the sonnet to their extreme limits. With Guido Guinizelli, Guido Cavalcanti, and chiefly Dante, the reaction against that artificiality took place under the banner of 'the sweet new style' (*il dolce stil nuovo*). The reaction was well over when Petrarch wrote his *Canzoniere*; rather, with him, the wind began to blow again in the earlier direction. Petrarch was too great a poet ever to make of the sonnet a simple matter of wit; but many of his sonnets show again a tendency to adopt the artificialities of the Provençal poets, and to end with a *concetto*. At any rate Petrarch represented a supreme stage of development; and, as in all supreme stages, one can detect in him the seed of the flamboyant aftermath which blossomed by the end of the fifteenth century and in the first quarter of the sixteenth. Petrarch is an end, not a beginning, and his *Canzoniere* is an epitome of the love theory and the modes of courtship invented by the Provençal poets and the poets of the *dolce stil nuovo*. So far as psychological subtlety is concerned, Petrarch was ahead of his times, so it was impossible for his imitators to invent anything new in this direction. Ingenuity could be successfully displayed only in the trimming of details, in the new presentation of old situations. The success of such a poor poet as the celebrated Serafino Aquilano, at the beginning of the sixteenth century, is only due to his knack for fantastic inventions. Each one of his sonnets aims at surprising the reader like a jack-in-the-box. His poems were really epigrams, and those among them which enjoyed most popularity were his *strambotti*, or eight-line stanzas the last two lines of which formed a couplet. Serafino's poems were reprinted several times and gave currency to a number of metaphors and similes which after then were sure to be found in every new book of verse. It would be possible to write a repertory of the main *motifs* employed by the sonneteers; such a repertory has been attempted for the Elizabethan sonnet sequences by Lisle Cecil John (Columbia University Press, 1938), who, however, has not tried to trace foreign sources and analogues, considering Miss Scott's *Les Sonnets élisabéthains* satisfactory enough in this respect. Serafino and his North Italian fellow-poet, Tebaldeo, mapped out the whole *Royaume de Tendre*. The Provençal conception of the woman as an angelic being, and the Neoplatonic theory of love, supplied the background but the foreground was entirely occupied with the little Cupid of the ancients, and his tricks. Why was Cupid painted blind, naked, winged, a boy with a bow? This *motif* of the Greek Anthology is one of the mainstays of Serafino's inspiration; the aspect and the arrows of Cupid supply him with an inexhaustible mine of puns. Another source of conceits is the state of the lover; his being deprived of his heart, which, of course, is for ever imprisoned in the bosom of his beloved one; his wonderful condition of being hot and cold at the same time; the floods of tears issuing from his eyes, the whirlwinds of sighs breaking out of the furnace of his breast: all the metaphors which Petrarch handled with a light hand were taken *au pied de la lettre* by Serafino and Tebaldeo, and dealt with as if they represented something real and of everyday occurrence. Real life was lost sight of, in the artificial atmosphere of the courts. In those hothouses such flowers could blossom which exposure to fresh air would have killed.

The excesses of this second flamboyant school, as is natural, provoked a new reaction, and this reaction against the degenerated form of Petrarchism was led by Cardinal Bembo, who, however, did not preach a return to nature, as the exponents of the *dolce stil nuovo* had done, but simply a return to Petrarch, that is to Petrarch the poet, not to the occasional mannerist. In the thirties of the sixteenth century the whole of Italy had become converted to *Bembismo*. *Concetti* were avoided, and the *canzonieri* came out strongly tinged with the Platonic theories expounded in such works as the dialogues of Leone Ebreo and Bembo himself, and the treatises on love with which the Cinquecento abounded. The poems in the manner of Serafino and Tebaldeo are bad, but amusing, those of the school of Bembo are dull, and their only merit consists in the high standard of metrical skill and flawless style achieved by even minor writers of verse. Those sonnets have a pleasing sound—and that is all: *vox et praeterea nihil*.

But the *concetti*, after a banishment of twenty years or so, came to a rally. The second flamboyant period, whose chief representative was Serafino, had originated in South Italy with Cariteo, a Catalan knight in the service of the Aragonese king of Naples. And now it was in South Italy again that the standard of *concettismo* was raised for the third time, by three Neapolitan poets, Angelo di Costanzo, Berardino Rota, and Luigi Tansillo. And this time the vogue was to enjoy a long spell, since from the time of the poets just mentioned, who became famous in the sixties, to the advent of G. B. Marino at the end of the century, there is no break caused by a new reaction: and with Marino *concettismo* became firmly established for a whole century. By the end of the sixteenth century the epigrammatic edge or *concetto* of a poem was so much the principal thing, that the sonnet saw its supremacy threatened by a rival as dangerous as the *strambotto* had been at the beginning of the century—the madrigal.

These, in brief, are the successive developments of the sonnet during the sixteenth century. They were echoed abroad, first of all in France, where imitation began under the influence of the school of Serafino. The French Serafino was the Lyonese poet Maurice Scève, whose *dizains* (ten-line stanzas) stand to the successive French poets in the same relation in which Serafino's *strambotti* stand to the Italians. With Ronsard and Du Bellay the influence of Bembo penetrates into France; with Philippe Desportes the third flamboyant wave is in full swing.

Now a peculiar fact about England is that the sonneteering literature, started by Wyatt and Surrey under the influence of the school of Serafino, was continued only at the end of the century by poets who were primarily under the influence of the French school, which was dominated by what I have called the third flamboyant period. So that the reaction of Bembo was felt only in a very indirect and feeble way; and the English sonneteers were in the first instance always imitating flamboyant models. The first English output of sonnets is almost contemporary with the work of Serafino's French disciple, Maurice Scève; Wyatt's and Surrey's sonneteering falls in the thirties, and Scève's *Délie* was published in 1544. So far English poets drew from the original source, Italy, and were independent from the French. But Watson and

Sidney, the two fathers of the Elizabethan sonnet, wrote in the eighties, when the main work of the French Pléiade had been done, and the names of Ronsard, Du Bellay, Desportes, had become no less celebrated than those of the Italian sonneteers. Though Thomas Watson follows both Italian and French models, his *Passionate Century of Love* is distinctly the work of a provincial follower of Ronsard.

Sidney's *Astrophel and Stella* offers a curious instance of the belatedness of the English sonneteering literature. On the one side Sidney echoes the anti-Petrarchist strain which had inspired Du Bellay's ode *Contre les Pétrarquistes*. But Du Bellay's ode was published in 1553, when Bembo's reaction against the extravaganzas of Serafino's school had reached France. And Sidney wrote in the eighties, when the reaction was well over, and Du Bellay, as well as Ronsard, had changed again after the latest Italian fashion. So that Sir Philip Sidney, while professing to listen only to the voice of his heart, and to despise the Petrarchan crowd, actually writes in the extravagant style of the most artificial among the Petrarchists. He offers a queer contrast, as if he were half dressed for a dinner-party, half for a cricket match. Let us listen to Sidney's anti-Petrarchist outbursts:

XV

You that do dictionary's method bring
Into your rhymes running in rattling rows;
You that poor Petrarch's long deceasèd woes,
With newborn sighs and denizened wit do sing,
You take wrong ways! Those far-fet helps be such
As do bewray a want of inward touch;
And sure at length stolen goods do come to light. . . .

XXVIII

You that with allegory's curious frame
Of others' children changelings use to make . . .
. . . I, in pure simplicity,
Breathe out the flames which burn within my heart,
Love only reading unto me this art.

LXXIV

I never drank of Aganippe's well,
Nor never did in shade of Tempe sit:
. . . .
Poor Layman, I! for sacred rites unfit
. . . .
I am no pickpurse of another's wit. . . .

I

I sought fit words to paint the blackest face of woe,
Studying inventions fine, her wits to entertain,
Oft turning others' leaves, to see if thence would flow
Some fresh and fruitful showers upon my sunburnt brain.
But words came halting forth . . .
Fool, said my Muse to me, look in thy heart and write.

In these lines Sidney seems to repeat the cry of all the rebels
against an established fashion of artificiality. Indeed his mani-
festo sounds not unlike that of the *dolce stil nuovo* which
has been embodied in a famous passage of Dante:

> I' mi son un, che quando
> Amor mi spira, noto, ed a quel modo
> Ch'e'ditta dentro, vo significando.

> [I am one who hearkens when
> Love prompteth, and I put thought into word
> After the mode which he dictates within.]

But Sidney, as I was saying, while claiming to be no pickpurse of another's wit, is actually deriving from Du Bellay's
ode *Contre les Pétrarquistes*. Du Bellay says there:

> J'ay oublié l'art de Petrarquizer,
> Je veulx d'Amour franchement deviser,
> Sans vous flatter, et sans me déguizer:
>   Ceulx qui font tant de plaintes,
> N'ont pas le quart d'une vraye amitié.

[I have forgotten the art of Petrarchising; I want to discourse of Love with simplicity, without flattering you, without disguise; those who make so many lamentations, have not the quarter part of a true affection.]

The last two lines find a counterpart in Sidney's Sonnet LIV:

Because I breathe not love to every one
. . . .
Nor give each speeche a full point of a groan
. . . .
'What he!' say they to me, 'now I dare swear
He cannot love' . . .
Dumb swans, not chattering pies, do lovers prove.
They love indeed who quake to say they love.

And when Sidney in Sonnet XXVIII says:

I beg no subject to use eloquence,
Nor in hid ways to guide Philosophy,
Look at my hand for no such quintessence—

one recognises at once Du Bellay's passage:

Quelque autre encor' la terre dédaignant
Va du tiers ciel les secrets enseignant,
Et de l'amour, où il se va baignant,
    Tire une quintessence.

[Somebody else, scorning the earth, is teaching the secrets of the third heaven, and squeezes a quintessence out of the love in which he is bathing.]

Du Bellay goes on :

Nos bons Ayeulx, qui cest art demenoient,
Pour en parler, Petrarque n'apprenoient,
Ains franchement leur Dame entretenoient
    Sans fard ou couverture.

[Our good ancestors, who took pains about this art, did not study Petrarch in order to talk of it, but entertained their Ladies with simplicity, without disguise or flattery.]

This is manifestly echoed in Sidney's first sonnet I have already quoted: 'I sought fit words . . . her wits to entertain'.

Notwithstanding his protests of simplicity and genuine inspiration, we find Sidney rehearsing most of the hackneyed tropes of the flamboyant sonneteers of the Continent. He also, with Petrarch, compares his beloved to a palace whose front is of alabaster, whose roof is of gold; he also addresses his bed, invokes Sleep, and envies his lady's lapdog, as every sonneteer was expected to do; he also implores conquering Stella to spare him, since 'noble conquerors do wracks avoid', or urges her to kill him at once, since 'a kind of grace it is, to slay with speed' ('Un modo di pietade uccider tosto' was Petrarch's expression echoed numberless times by his imitators); he too entreats his lady not to love him, since the result of her loving him is the wish to see him give up his loving her: 'Deere, love me not, that you may love me more'. In this last case the quibble is of the type affected by Guittone d'Arezzo, who said:

> Poi che per amar m'odiate a morte,
> Per disamar mi sarete amorosa.

[Since my loving you makes you hate me in deadly fashion, my ceasing to love you will make you fall in love.]

Sidney, too, boasts victory because his beloved has twice said no to him; since two negatives make an affirmative, according to the rules of grammar. He does not disdain the tritest puns on Cupid, like the one which represents Cupid burning his wings in the fire of the lover's heart, or that other one which gives the lady's eyebrows to Cupid for bows; or the commonest of all, which shows Love darting arrows from the eyes of the beloved. Finally, what could be more in the manner of Serafino than Sonnet xxix, in which Stella, like some weak lord, is supposed to surrender to Love—a mighty neighbouring king—all her externals (her lips, eyes, etc.), in order to keep free the chief city, her heart. What could be more decadent than Sonnet c:

> O tears! no tears but rain from beauty's skies
> Making those lilies and those roses grow

> . . . .

> O honeyed sighs! which from that breast do rise,
> Whose pants do make unspilling cream to flow
>
> . . . .
>
> O plaints! conserved in such sugared phrase,
> That eloquence itself envies your praise. . . .

Indeed 'Sydnaean showers/Of sweet discourse', as Richard Crashaw said, with whom, evidently, this sonnet and CII must have been favourites. This is the kind of style Shakespeare put into the mouth of his Romeo when he wanted to depict a passionate southern lover. For each one of Romeo's *concetti* parallels and analogues could be quoted in the Petrarchan sonneteers of the flamboyant school; and that Shakespeare deliberately aimed at portraying a lover on the lines suggested by the sonneteering literature seems to be almost implied in Mercutio's sneering remark: 'Now is he for the numbers that Petrarch flowed in: Laura to his lady was but a kitchen-wench'.[3]

Despite all we have been saying, Sidney is no servile imitator, and his sonnets, though unmistakably written under the influence of the flamboyant Continental style, well entitle him to the epithet of 'English Petrarch'. Sidney's psychological subtlety is no second-hand acquisition, and his genuine passionate oubursts soar infinitely above the ludicrous 'passions' of a Thomas Watson. The praise which was bestowed on the pedantic author of the *Hekatompathia* could have been bestowed on Sidney with much more truth:

> The stars, which did at Petrarch's birthday raigne
> Were fixt againe at thy nativity. . . .

Yet, in the character of his affection, Sidney comes much nearer to Ronsard than to Petrarch. Michael Drayton also, while he repeats Sidney's very protests of being no pickpurse of another's wit, and in his *Remedy for Love* satirises the Petrarchan stage properties, imitates all the same the Continental, chiefly the French, sonneteers, and rehearses their commonplaces. The chief merit of poets like Drayton and Constable consists in their having paved the way for Shake-

[3] See the chapter on 'Shakespeare's Italy' above, p. 158.

speare. They made a first provisional appropriation of foreign models; they naturalised their themes; and it is through their medium that Shakespeare derived whatever he has in common with the other sonneteers.

The position of Edmund Spenser is not very different from that of the direct imitators. His world is the same which is familiar to us in the conventional Petrarchists of the flamboyant school. From the very beginning:

> Happy ye leaves when as those lilly hands,
> Which hold my life in their dead doing might,
> Shall handle you . . .

The first bars of Spenser's music reveal at once a familiar sound. It is Tebaldeo's:

> Beata carta ne la man raccolta
> Che del mio triste cor tien la radice . . .
> [O happy leaves collected within that hand which holds the root of my heart . . .]

To Tebaldeo Spenser owes a *concetto* suggested by the mirror: why does his lady not leave her mirror aside and look into the poet's heart, which reflects an idealised image of her?; from Tebaldeo he derives the sonnet about that love which is a pleasing pain, and from Tebaldeo's fellow-poet, Serafino, he has learned how to quibble on the contrast between ice and fire. Other commonplaces dear to Serafino's school are sedulously borrowed by Spenser. This is one of the most widely circulated: the drops wear the stone, the wheel bites the hardest steel, but the poet's tears are unable to soften the hard heart of the beloved. Even when derived from Bembo's and Tasso's poems, in which a loftier strain prevails than mere *concettismo*, Spenser chooses for imitation those which contain some euphuistic trait:

> Fayre is my love, when her fayre golden heares
> With the loose wynd ye waving chance do marke:
> Fayre when the rose in her red cheekes appeares
> . . . .
> But fayrest she, when so she doth display
> The gate with pearles and rubyes richly dight . . .

This is from Tasso, as well as the simile, occurring in another sonnet, between the lover's heart and a bird flying to the hand which offers food. And from a sonnet of Bembo:

> Bella guerriera mia, perché sì spesso
> V'armate incontra me?

he has derived his 'sweet warriour, when shall I have peace with you', and the other 'Tell me when shall these wearie woes have end'.

Gabriel Harvey, in his defence of Spenser against the charge of subservience to the habit of *pétrarquiser,* pointed out that 'Petrarch's invention is love itself; Petrarch's elocution pure beauty itself'. True, but the Petrarch one finds in Spenser's *Amoretti* is the Petrarch seen in the distorted mirror held forth by his flamboyant imitators. He is not so much Petrarch as Serafino. The only case of direct imitation from Petrarch seems to be that of the sonnets on the eyes of the beloved (vii, viii, ix) which echo many expressions in Petrarch's three famous sister songs, *le tre canzoni sorelle,* on Laura's eyes. But you need only compare the several passages to realise the enormous difference between Petrarch and Spenser. Petrarch is by far the more modern poet of the two. Spenser may use the very same images, but the psychological subtlety of the Italian poet is absent. He borrows scattered images and a general outline, he misses the fine rhythm of Petrarch's thought. This is a far more important difference between Petrarch and his English imitators than the rather external ones listed by Dr John in his study of the Elizabethan sonnet sequences, namely differences relating to the scope and length of the collections of poems. To find something similar to the *Canzoniere* in intensity and seriousness we must turn to Shakespeare. The peculiar fact about Shakespeare's sonnets lies in the two or three threads recurring from beginning to end, threads which we can follow up to a certain point, though the head of the skein is lost for us. Nothing like this unity of inspiration do we experience while reading other Elizabethan sonnet sequences. And yet, it is just Shakespeare's sonnets that disintegrators have chosen as the field of their not uniformly amusing experiments. While the disintegrators imagine fantastic theories of collaboration, they seem to forget some important aspects of Shakespeare's sonnets. First of all that, apart from the last two poems of the collection, the theme of which is ultimately to be traced to the Greek Anthology, none of these sonnets can be shown to derive directly from a Continental source. This fact is almost unique in Elizabethan literature. Secondly, that whatever parallels in single expressions may be alleged, the really important ones are with sonnets of English authors, Sidney, Constable, Drayton. This tallies very well with what we know of Shakespeare's culture from his works of sure attribution. Continental themes reach him always filtered through a native medium. Of conventional *motifs* there is a comparatively small proportion in Shakespeare's sonnets. The theme of immortality secured by poetry, the theme of the apparition of the beloved in the poet's dream, the theme of absence, the contrast between the eye and the heart, a catalogue of things which cause annoyance (a Provençal *enueg*), the *motif* of jealousy towards an object touched by the beloved, these almost exhaust the list of commonplaces for which many parallels can be found, and still none that might be termed a direct source. So that when Shakespeare says:

> So is it not with me as with that Muse
> Stirr'd by a painted beauty to his verse,
> Who heaven itself for ornament doth use
> And every fair with his fair doth rehearse,
> Making a couplement of proud compare
> With sun and moon, with earth and sea's rich gems—

we may confidently say that of all the utterances of nonconformity with the Petrarchan tradition poets ever made, this is the only genuine one. Several times in his plays he satirises the conventional description of beauty, as when in *Twelfth Night* Olivia, while reproached by Cesario for leaving no copy of her 'nonpareil of beauty' to the world, promises to bequeath each feature in her will: '*Item*, two lips, indifferent red; *Item*, two grey eyes with lids to them; *Item*, one neck, one chin, and so forth' (Act I, scene 5, ll. 266–268). And the

Dark Lady of the *Sonnets* is deliberately described in an anti-
Petrarchan strain, for instance in the famous Sonnet CXXX:

> My mistress' eyes are nothing like the sun;
> Coral is far more red than her lips' red;
> If snow be white, why then her breasts are dun,
> If hairs be wires, black wires grow on her head.
> I have seen roses damask'd, red and white,
> But no such roses see I in her cheeks;
> And in some perfumes there is more delight
> Than in the breath that from my mistress reeks.
> I love to hear her speak, yet well I know
> That music hath a far more pleasing sound:
> I grant I never saw a goddess go,
> My mistress, when she walks, treads on the ground:
>   And yet, by heaven, I think my love as rare
>   As any she belied with false compare.

Dr John's words deserve to be repeated in this connexion: 'The
Dark Lady presents a strange appearance indeed among the
galaxy of Elizabethan sonnet beauties. She merits one distinction, however, that of freeing at least one cycle from the
meaningless phraseology employed by most of the poets of
the day.'

There is only one other English poet among Shakespeare's
contemporaries who showed so much, and even more, freedom
from the Petrarchan convention: John Donne. One has only
to think that even poets like Sidney and Shakespeare paid
tribute to the time-hallowed recipe of the love-dream, to
realise to what extent Donne's *Dream* meant a new departure.[4]
However, as we survey Donne's poetry after such a distance
of time, we can hardly fail to notice how much this poet, who
in a sense led the reaction against Petrarchism in England,
was himself a Petrarchist, thanks to his mediaevally trained
mind. If, notwithstanding his opposition to the poetry of his
day, he still remained a Petrarchan to some extent, this is due
to the fact that, no matter how strong one's personal reaction
is, one cannot avoid belonging to a definite historical climate.
Nothing, for instance, would seem more peculiar to Donne

[4] See above, p. 189.

than his argumentative, dramatic mood. Still, when in his *Lovers infinitenesse* he plays with ideas in a subtle and passionate way:

> If I have not all thy love,
> Deare, I shall never have it all
>
> . . . .
>
> Or if then thou gavest mee all,
> All was but All, which thou hadst then—

are we not reminded of Guittone's lines I have quoted before, and of Sidney's 'Deere, love me not, that thou may love me more', and of Drayton's 'You're not alone when you are still alone'? And it would be difficult to find a better instance of metaphysical subtlety, of that subtlety which is a distinctive feaure of *The Extasie*, than Petrarch's sixty-third sonnet *in vita*.[5] It is chiefly in the first quatrain of this sonnet that we find the elements of *The Extasie*: we find there the beloved image penetrating to the heart through the eyes ('And pictures in our eyes to get/Was all our propagation'), and chiefly the motionless, statue-like appearance of the lovers. And we find, most of all, the same argumentative development of the idea, and the paradoxical assumption of miracles wrought by lovers.

When the vogue for sonnet sequences was over, Petrarch's popularity decayed in England; William Drummond of Hawthornden's translations and imitations, published in 1616 and 1627, betray an outdated taste; the same can be said about the belated group of Italianate poets who gathered round Thomas Stanley, the pupil of the son of Tasso's translator, Edward Fairfax. Foreign travel contributed to deepen Stanley's acquaintance with fashionable authors in Italy, France and Spain, so that when, towards the close of the Civil War, he settled down in the Middle Temple and engaged in literary work, he became the soul of a small cenacle of minor poets, to whom he communicated his taste and preferences; Petrarch is only one out of the many poets they translated, mostly Marino and his followers in Italy and abroad.

[5] For this and other parallels, see 'Donne's Relation to the Poetry of His Time', in this volume.

Milton's apprenticeship was first to the Greek and Latin poets, chiefly Ovid; but as soon as, acting on his father's advice, he had learned French and Italian, he found more congenial sources of inspiration in Dante and Petrarch. The results of Milton's new allegiance are indicated in the *Sonnet to a Nightingale* and more directly in the early sonnets, English and Italian, whose date can be assigned with a fair certainty to 1630. Dr John Smart has shown that in 1629 Milton purchased a copy of the 1565 edition of the sonnets of Giovanni della Casa; and it was on Della Casa's sonnet form that Milton modelled his own, which marked a new start in the history of the English sonnet. As I have said, the sonnet form adopted by the Elizabethans differed from the Italian average model, chiefly for the use of the final couplet. Now when, after a period during which the sonnet had suffered almost complete neglect in England, Milton revived it, he did not follow the Elizabethans, but went directly to the fountain-head, the Italians, for the form of the poem, thus setting the example to later poets. The sonnet form adopted by Milton was not only generally Italian, but specifically coincided with that of Giovanni della Casa. Della Casa first consistently adopted the practice of treating the sonnet as a whole, drawing quatrains and tercets closer together by disregarding the pauses suggested by the division of the metre, whereas in the regular Petrarchan form the pauses required by the sense occur with almost perfect regularity at the ends of lines. Della Casa, in a word, practised what the French romantics were to call *enjambement*. Della Casa's type of sonnet is manifestly the model of Milton's sonnets to Cromwell, Vane and Lawrence, on the Massacre in Piedmont, on his blindness, and on the death of his wife. The sonnets Milton wrote in Italian are addressed to Milton's friend, Carlo Diodati, and sing the praise of an Italian lady, Emilia, whom presumably he had met in the circle of the Diodati family in London; they show a wide acquaintance with the stock-in-trade of Petrarchan commonplaces of the school of Bembo, but every now and then, by a clumsy turn of phrase or the bizarre use of adjectives, betray a foreign hand; however, some of Milton's Italian lines achieve such a high standard that the modern Italian poet Carducci said that they would not seem out of place in Dante or Petrarch. Petrarch's lines are here and there echoed in the Italian sonnets, as Dr Smart and Professor Federico Olivero have pointed out; for instance 'Quando tu vaga parli, o lieta canti' recalls 'E come dolce parla e dolce ride', 'ma sotto nuova idea Pellegrina bellezza' reminds one of Petrarch's famous sonnet: 'In qual parte del ciel, in quale idea/Era l'essempio, onde Natura tolse/Quel bel viso leggiadro' ('In what part of heaven, in what idea,/Was the example from which Nature wrought/That charming lovely face . . .'); 'Poiché fuggir me stesso in dubbio sono' of the last sonnet is another Petrarchan tag: 'Né pur il mio secreto e 'l mio riposo/Fuggo, ma più me stesso e 'l mio pensero'. Verbal parallels are to be found also with minor and now forgotten sonneteers; for instance the first line of the first Italian sonnet: 'Donna leggiadra, il cui bel nome onora', is modelled on a line by Gandolfo Porrino: 'Alma mia luce, il cui bel nome onora'.

As for the English sonnets, Milton, at the end of the sonnet on the Massacre in Piedmont, echoed a sonnet of Petrarch's he also quotes in his prose treatise *Of Reformation in England:*

> Fontana di dolore, albergo d'ira,
> Scola d'errori, e tempio d'eresia,
> Già Roma, or Babilonia falsa e ria,
> Per cui tanto si piagne e si sospira.

[Fountain of sorrow, dwelling of revolts, The school of errors, place of heresy, Once Rome, now Babylon wicked and false, For which the world suffers in infamy.]

With the waning of the Italianate tradition in English literature, Petrarch ceased to play an important role in England, at least among the major authors. Joseph Warton, in his *Essay on the Genius and Writings of Pope* (1756) had no liking for the 'metaphysical' Petrarch, asserting that, compared with him, 'Metastasio is a much better lyric poet'. His remarks supply a curious document of changing taste:

> The stanza of Petrarch . . . displeases the ear by its uniformity, and by the number of identical cadences. And indeed, to speak the truth, there appears to be little valuable in Petrarch except the purity of his diction. His sentiments,

even of love, are metaphysical and far fetched; neither is there much variety in his subjects, or fancy in his method of treating them.

Gray, however, by a quotation from Petrarch at the end of his *Elegy* (which opens with a quotation from Dante) heralded a minor wave of popularity. Susannah Dobson's *Life of Petrarch* (1775), though merely a condensation of the Abbé de Sade's *Mémoires pour la vie de François Pétrarque*, again called English attention, after a hundred and fifty years of neglect, to the poet of love whom William Drummond of Hawthornden had proclaimed about 1615 'the best and most exquisite poet of this subject, by consent of the whole senate of poets'. During the eighteenth century Petrarch's name had become a byword for an unmanly attitude in matters of love, that of the scorned and yet clinging lover. With the spreading of the new romantic sensibility, which found in Goethe's *Werther* a supreme expression, it became possible for Englishmen once more to weep for love and die of sorrow. Mrs Dobson's *Life of Petrarch* made him a hero of pre-Romantic sensibility and cleared him of the charge of an invented 'metaphysical' passion by demonstrating, in Sade's footsteps, the real existence of Laura. Just at that time (about 1770) Petrarch was translated again by John Langhorne, Sir William Jones, the anonymous author of *Odes translated from the Italian of Petrarch* (1777), John Nott (*Petrarch Translated*, 1808), Thomas Le Mesurier, Alexander Fraser Tytler, the Earl of Charlemont, Lady Dacre and others. The growing popularity of Petrarch in the last quarter of the eighteenth century caused the Italian sonnet to appear an ideal form for the expression of sorrow, disappointment and despair, in brief, of the then fashionable melancholy mood. Out of a host of sonneteers of this period, there emerge only Mrs. Charlotte Smith and William Lisle Bowles. Bowles' *Fourteen Sonnets, Written Chiefly on Picturesque Spots during a Tour* (1789) show him wandering, like Petrarch, 'solo e pensoso' (alone and pensive):

> Languid, and sad, and slow, from day to day
> I journey on, yet pensive turn to view . . .
> The streams, and vales, and hills, and steal away.

In the following sonnet from Mrs Smith's *Elegiac Sonnets* (1784) we perceive a distinct echo of Petrarch and a faint anticipation of Keats (the fifth stanza of the *Ode to a Nightingale*):

Again the wood and long-withdrawing vale
    In many a tint of tender green are drest,
Where the young leaves, unfolding, scarce conceal,
    Beneath their early shade, the half-form'd nest
Of finch or wood-lark; and the primrose pale,
    And lavish cowslip, wildly scatter'd round,
Give their sweet spirits to the sighing gale.
    Ah! season of delight!—could aught be found
        To soothe awhile the tortur'd bosom's pain,
Of Sorrow's rankling shaft to cure the wound,
        And bring life's first delusions once again,
'Twere surely met in thee:—thy prospects fair,
Thy notes of harmony, thy balmy air,
Have 'power to cure all sadness but despair'.

While for these minor poets Petrarch was the ideal character of a melancholy lover, to Gibbon he appeared chiefly as a patriotic poet. His letters, orations, and love of ancient republican freedom were, in Gibbon's opinion, the real titles which caused the Romans to revive for him the rite of coronation in the Capitol. This was, however, an aspect of Petrarch which remained always secondary in the minds of the English who became aware of it. Ugo Foscolo's *Essay on Petrarch*, which appeared originally in London and in English in 1821 for private circulation (and again, for sale, in 1823), and contained in an appendix Lady Dacre's translations, contrasted Dante, the poet of action, of the indomitable will, to Petrarch, the poet whose chief trait was a delicate suffering. To Shelley, as I have already said, Petrarch supplied little beyond the title for his Dantesque *Triumph of Life*. Though Dr John, in the introduction to his *Elizabethan Sonnet Sequences*, has written that 'a Petrarchan sequence in its entirety is often dismissed today as a genre dead and "nayled in his cheste" along with Petrarch himself', and though Pound, in *How to Read* (1931), dismissed Petrarch as a flabby imitator, it is actually from America that the most successful complete translation of the poet, by Anna Maria Armi, an American of Italian origin, has come (in 1946) to show that the fame of the singer of Laura, though by much inferior to that of Dante, is still well alive.[6]

[6] Mention ought to be made also of a faithful enough verse translation of *Some Sonnets and Songs of the Divine Poet M. Francesco Petrarca made in Laura's Lifetime* by William J. Ibbett, Shaftesbury, 1926 (edition limited to 105 copies).

Ariosto in England

THE history of Petrarch's fortune in the sonneteering literature
of the Elizabethan period finds a close parallel in what was
happening in lyric poetry in France; in fact, as we have seen,
France was in many cases the medium through which Italian
poetical conventions passed on to England. There is no such
parallel for Dante, whose reputation in England follows a
different course from its course in France; and there is no such
parallel for Ariosto. In France Ariosto's poetry began to be
widely appreciated and imitated about 1550 among lyric
poets: the *Olive* of Du Bellay (published in 1549), the *Odes*
and *Amours* of Ronsard (1550 and 1552), and the *Méline*
and *Francine* of Baïf (1552 and 1555) are all indebted to
the *Orlando Furioso* for stray passages; but Ariosto's epos as
a whole did not inspire any similar undertaking. Although
French writers speak of Ariosto only as an epic poet, and
affect to ignore his minor compositions, they know and imitate these too, chiefly the sixth sonnet: 'La rete fu di queste
fila d'oro', a string of pleasant *concetti*; the twenty-second
sonnet, 'Madonna, sete bella, e bella tanto', a whimsical description of the poet's lady; and the sixth elegy, 'O più che
il giorno a me lucida e chiara', a spicy narration of a love-
adventure: Du Bellay and Magny imitate also Ariosto's
satires. Joseph Vianey and after him Alice Cameron [1] have

[1] *The Influence of Ariosto's Epic and Lyric Poetry on Ronsard
and his Group,* The Johns Hopkins Press, 1930.

shown that it was the ardent, voluptuous character of Ariosto's verses that chiefly attraced the members of the Pléiade; Ariosto's erotic passages are singled out for imitation: such as the descriptions of the beautiful enchantress Alcina (*Orlando Furioso*, vii, 10–16) and of the Princess Olimpia, bound naked to a rock as a sacrifice to the Orc (xi, 65–71), the latter passage finding a counterpart in some of Tintoretto's paintings and witnessing therefore to a peculiar taste of the period. Also the five lamentations of Bradamante, inspired by the absence of her lover, Ruggiero (xxx, 82, 83, xxxii, 18–25 and 37–43, xxxiii, 62–64, xlv, 32–39), the letter of Bradamante to Ruggiero (xliv, 61–66), and the tragic story of the death of Isabella's lover, Prince Zerbino of Scotland (xxiv, 77–87), were very popular. Ariosto's becoming a favourite with French lyric poets is explained through the close intellectual, commercial, and diplomatic ties which bound France with Ferrara, where Ariosto had his home: in 1528, Renée of France, the sister of Francis I, was married to Ercole d'Este, eldest son of the Duke of Ferrara; Renée surrounded herself with a group of cultivated French people, intensely interested, as she was herself, in art, music and literature; at the same time Ercole's brother Francesco was residing at the French court, another brother, Ippolito, became archbishop of Lyons in 1539, and was known as a patron of art and literature. These intellectual exchanges must have helped considerably to establish the reputation of Ferrara's greatest poet in France.

There was no such link between Italy and England, so that Ariosto's name became known together with those of the other Italian writers, not all of them first-rate, who were in demand in a *milieu* saturated with Italian influence as the English cultured classes were at the period. How many references are there to Ariosto, how many times are his verses imitated in England? More than thirty-five years ago Anna Benedetti collected a number of those references and imitations in a book copiously informed, though indifferent from a scholarly point of view, *L' 'Orlando Furioso' nella vita intellettuale del popolo inglese*. But an author's fortune is not so much measured by a tabulation of quotations, as by the impulse his work gives to original creation, or else by the place he occupies in popular imagination as a legendary figure.

This latter was the case of Machiavelli, and in a lesser degree of Aretino, thanks to his licentious sonnets. Ariosto, on the other hand, while taking a place alongside other quoted and imitated Italian authors for his satires and comedies, and being, on this account, one out of many, provided with his *Orlando Furioso* the second great contribution Italy made to the establishment of an original literary tradition in England: the first contribution had taken place, as we have seen, in Chaucer's time, when this English poet changed allegiance from the weak French followers of the *Roman de la Rose* to the powerful triad of Italian authors, Dante, Petrarch and Boccaccio, and for the first time caused English literature to rank in the forefront of the literary output of Western Europe. I have used the phrase 'an original literary tradition', although *Troilus and Criseyde* may be on the whole described as a *rifacimento* of Boccaccio's *Filostrato*, and Spenser's *Faerie Queene* may seem to be a moralised medley of Ariosto's *Orlando Furioso* and Tasso's *Gerusalemme liberata:* but the idea of originality prevailing in the Renaissance was different from the one which has taken shape after the advent of romanticism; and a writer or painter was then considered not less great if he conformed to a set of literary or iconographical conventions, just as, for that matter, did Ariosto himself by resorting to all those sources which Pio Rajna detailed in a famous study.

But before coming to Spenser, let us reply to a question: Was Ariosto's popularity in England due to the same reasons for which the poet is appreciated nowadays? Was it due to those qualities of aerial and magical fantasy, which make us feel that opening his book is like entering a forest astir with winds that bend the trees and take dim shapes of flying horsemen and ladies as elusive as changeful leaves, or simulate sounds of clinking armour and distant trumpets? Had they an ear for the rhythm of Ariosto's verse? If this can be said to be so up to a point in the case of Spenser, as we shall see, we must also admit that Ariosto at the outset was for the English only a story-teller, so that we may safely assume that the first English followers of Ariosto failed to see the wood for the trees. They saw first of all *The Historie of Ariodanto and Ieneura, daughter to the King of Scottes:* this story, whose appeal must have been partly due to the local association (Scotland), partly to the subject, which was the redress of the wrong done to an innocent lady (a subject always apt to stir English feeling), was translated into rugged English verse by Peter Beverley and printed by Thomas East about 1566.[2] This is the first English version, or rather paraphrase, of a portion of the *Orlando Furioso,* and the poet (if you like to call him so) responsible for it, while he fell short of Chaucer's adroitness in his borrowings from Boccaccio, did not fall behind him in his passing over in silence the name of the foreign poet from whom he derived, since neither the dedication of his 'rude Booke' to Peter Reade nor the epistle to the reader does as much as mention Ariosto by name. And perhaps Beverley was wise in doing so, because palming off as Ariosto's the ill-conceived embroideries with which the English poem abounds chiefly in the first part, would have been a lie and an insult. The poem, written in the same metre which at about the same time was used in the English versions of Seneca's plays, is even less faithful than these to the spirit of the original. This passage about the pastimes at the Scottish court is enough to give an idea:

> The courtiers rise that use disportes, as pleaseth best their will,
> Some Hauks reclayme, some Coursers ride and some do daunce their fill,
> Some joye in reading Histories and some in Musikes art,
> Thus time is spent in comly sportes, as pleaseth best their hart.

In this rude disguise *Orlando Furioso* entered into English literature, or, let us rather say, into that vast class of works which form the greatest portion of what in the manuals of literary history goes by the name of literature, and ought rather to be called semi-literary or paraliterary production.

[2] Reprinted by Charles T. Prouty in *The Sources of Much Ado About Nothing, A Critical Study,* together with the text of Peter Beverley's *Ariodanto and Ieneura,* Yale University Press, 1951.

While the French were attracted by the voluptuous passages in the *Orlando*, the English were struck by a moral tale of an innocent lady slandered and persecuted: are we wrong in seeing in the type of choice a clue to the character of the two nations?

And what was it that appealed to the first English translator of the whole of *Orlando Furioso*, John Harington? Was it rhythm, the harmonious ebb and tide of the resounding poem? Not at all, but again a tale. Because the report goes that his celebrated version of the *Orlando Furioso* was undertaken as a penance Queen Elizabeth inflicted on Harington, who was her godson, for having divulged his translation of the licentious story of Giocondo (Canto xxviii) among the Queen's maids of honour: he was not to be permitted to come to court again unless he translated the remaining forty-five cantos. So Harington withdrew to his Kelston estate near Bath, and there we may imagine him sitting by the fire, winter after winter, sighing for the distant court, bent on rendering into English the epic poem born under the Italian sun. The translation was published in 1591, when Ariosto's poem was already well-known to English courtiers and literary people; the story of Ariodante and Ginevra had already been translated twice and had supplied the subject for a play, and Angelica was currently alluded to as a type of scornful beauty. Possibly Harington's translation stimulated Robert Greene to write his romantic comedy *Orlando Furioso*, which, however, does not follow its source. Toward the end of the sixteenth century, thanks to the popularity of Ariosto's poem, there entered into the English vocabulary the words *paladin, rodomont, rodomontade* (and *rodomontado*), *hippogriff*. A Scotsman, John Stewart of Baldynneis, had dedicated to James VI a curious version of the story of Orlando and Angelica, isolated from the rest of the poem.

Harington used the edition of 1584, printed by Porro, with notes by Fornari. The Italian commentaries, particularly those by Fornari (*Sposizione sopra l'Orlando Furioso*, Florence, 1549) and by Toscanella (*Bellezze del Furioso*, Venice, 1574) which tended to interpret Ariosto's poem in the light of the well-known mediaeval theory, according to which the fables of the poets adumbrate moral and philosophical truths, found great favour with the Elizabethans, who were fond of allegories and moralities. In the preface of his version, Harington discusses the method of allegorial interpretation, with its traditional four branches: literal, moral, allegorical, and anagogical senses.

The allegorical method prevails in the greatest of Ariosto's imitators, Edmund Spenser. The problem of the sources of the *Faerie Queene* is not so simple as it may appear at first, neither can it be reduced to a tabulation of parallel passages like the one produced by Anna Benedetti. No doubt the list of Spenser's borrowings from Ariosto and Tasso is impressive; and it can be safely assumed that without the *ottava* of Ariosto the Spenserian stanza would not have been born, though this latter possesses an individuality of its own thanks to the final Alexandrine which gives it a dreamy reverberating cadence. And Spenser was the first in England to use the Italian word *canto* for each single division of a long poem. But for all the precise correspondence of parallel passages, for all the evident derivations of characters and episodes, the resemblance between Spenser and Ariosto remains a superficial one. Rather than the list of the sources, consider the atmosphere of the two poems; read the first canto of the *Orlando Furioso*, and then the first canto of the *Faerie Queene*. The materials of the kaleidoscope are the same, but the hands that turn it have a different twirl, so that the pieces of coloured glass, the beads, the bits of elastic and the small cylinders, combine in a different way and accordingly give a different vision of the world. The stress of Ariosto's canto is on love, and the poem opens with a great blind-man's-buff of knights who pursue, horses that break in, more knights who complain near a river, and the whole is dominated by two apparitions, the one fluttering in the measure of a fugue, an irresistible *allegro con brio*, Angelica fleeing through dark terrifying forests, and the other a static apparition, an emblem caressed with a slow elegiac motion, the rose which is the image of a virgin, and, indeed, of whatever blossoms, lives, and decays. *Carpe diem* is the motto of the rose, *carpe diem* seems the meaning of that fugue which foreshadows what a later poet, Andrew Marvell, has condensed into two famous lines:

> But at my back I always hear
> Time's winged chariot hurrying near.

Carpe diem, says the courtly and pleasure-seeking society of Ariosto's time, in the faces of the human roses painted by Raphael and Titian, Isabellas, Leonoras, Beatrices, caught in a moment of grace and withered to-morrow, in the faces of the gentlemen and the warriors who clasp the hilt of a sword or hold a scented glove or a flower in those hands which to-morrow will be only bundles of tired bones and muscles, and then nothing but graceless and insentient dust. It was a society of young tyrants and women of pleasure which had come to blossom in the little Italian states, had brought about a splendid and ephemeral restoration of the feudal world when it had nearly faded out, and consequently had revived the taste for poems of chivalry and painted devices, those devices sported by the invading French armies which just then were ringing the knell of that very world of loves, leisures and conspicuous waste. Ariosto created that feudal world anew, and dissolved it at the same time, Paolo Giovio wrote his *Dialogues on military and amorous devices* (*Dialoghi delle imprese militari e amorose*): and there were tournaments, cavalcades, triumphs, all kinds of shows; the favour, grace, and beauty of a moment, the emblem of the rose. The *Orlando Furioso* brought back to Northern Europe those chivalric subjects which had originated there, but brought them back under the ensign of omnipotent Love, who disarms and maddens the heroes, and under the ensign of the rose, which lasts only a short season. It was the time-hallowed Mediterranean sex-centered point of view which triumphed in the *Orlando.* How did the Protestant North understand and welcome it?

Let us now call to our minds the first canto of the *Faerie Queene.* Spenser too, like Ariosto, will sing 'of Knights and Ladies gentle deeds', and declare: 'Fierce warres and faithful loves shall moralize my song', and invoke, next, Mars, Venus, and Cupid. But that Red Cross Knight sent to a great adventure by the Faerie Queene, to fight 'a Dragon horrible and stearne', does he not remind us of Beowulf? And the Virgin Una 'upon a lowly Asse more white than snow,/Yet she much whiter', leading 'by her, in a line, a milkewhite lambe', does she not look as if she came out of a mystery-play? They lose their way, like Ariosto's heroes, but their surroundings have more the nature of adumbrations and symbols than of real things:

'Ah Ladie,' (sayd he) 'shame were to revoke
The forward footing for an hidden shade:
Vertue gives her selfe light through darknesse for to wade.'

The Red Cross Knight penetrates into the den of the monster, who is half woman and half serpent, not unlike one of Bronzino's allegorical figures; and no doubt this monster who has a thousand young ones 'sucking upon her poisnous dugs', is the same monster who terrifies Rinaldo in the forty-second canto of Ariosto, with a difference, though, because Spenser warns us from the outset about the allegorical import of the monster, and puts us on our guard: 'God helpe the man so wrapt in Errours endlesse traine!', and actually causes the monster to have a fit of allegorical sickness: 'Her vomit full of bookes and papers was'. Further on, when night falls, the Knight and his companions come across 'an aged Sire, in long blacke weedes yclad,/His feete all bare, his beard all hoarie gray': this hermit is the pernicious Archimago, who offers them hospitality and sends a messenger to Morpheus' house to ask him to delude the Knight with a false dream, and in the meantime makes a false image of Una who will appear to the Knight like 'a loose Leman to vile service bound', instead of the chaste virgin he knew. Ariosto had described the house of Sleep in his fourteenth canto, and before him there had been descriptions by Ovid, Statius, and Chaucer, who, in his turn, had imitated both Ovid and Ovid's imitator, the French poet Machaut in his *Dit de la Fonteinne Amoureuse*. Spenser borrows from Ariosto, but comes closer to Ovid and Chaucer. A *motif* which occurs in these latter, but not in Ariosto, is that of the little waterfall inducing sleep: a *motif* of which Spenser gives a very musical treatment that was bound to appeal to Tennyson for his 'Lotos-eaters'. It is to passages of

this kind that Spenser owes his reputation as a 'poets' poet'.
A comparison with Ariosto's description results in a contrast
between the neat, Mantegna-like world of the Italian poet,
and the vague, musical dreamland of the English. Here is
Ariosto's House of Sleep:

> Giace in Arabia una velletta amena,
> lontana da cittadi e da villaggi,
> ch'all'ombra di duo monti è tutta piena
> d'antiqui abeti e di robusti faggi.
> Il sole indarno il chiaro dì vi mena;
> che non vi può mai penetrar coi raggi,
> sì gli è la via da folti rami tronca:
> e quivi entra sotterra una spelonca.

> Sotto la negra selva una capace
> e spaziosa grotta entra nel sasso,
> di cui la fronte l'edera seguace
> tutta aggirando va con storto passo.
> In questo albergo il grave Sonno giace;
> l'Ozio da un canto corpulento e grasso,
> da l'altro la Pigrizia in terra siede,
> che non può andare, e mal reggersi in piede.

> Lo smemorato Oblio sta su la porta:
> non lascia entrar, né riconosce alcuno;
> non ascolta imbasciata, né riporta;
> e parimenti tien cacciato ognuno.
> Il Silenzio va intorno, e fa la scorta:
> ha le scarpe di feltro, e 'l mantel bruno;
> et a quanti n'incontra, di lontano,
> che non debban venir, cenna con mano.

A literal translation will bring out the sober outline of Ariosto's
picture better than any of the existing verse translations:

There lies in Arabia a pleasant dell, far away from towns
and villages, which in the shadow of two mountains is thick
with old firs and sturdy beech trees. In vain the sun leads
there the bright daylight; its beams cannot penetrate inside,

to such an extent is their path obstructed by the entangled branches; there sinks a cavern underground.

Under the black forest a wide and roomy grotto hollows the rock, whose front is entirely crept over by the climbing ivy with its twisted path. Heavy Sleep lies in this abode: at one side Idleness corpulent and fat, at the other side Sloth is sitting on the ground, who cannot walk, and is hardly able to stand.

Forgetful Oblivion stands by the gate: she does not allow anybody in, nor does she recognise anybody; she does not listen to messages, nor relate them; and drives everybody away. Silence goes about and keeps watch: he has felt shoes, and a dark cloak; and from afar motions away whomsoever he meets.

This is no doubt an allegorical description, but it has a plastic character, such as we see, for instance, in Mantegna's *Virtue fighting Vice*, a picture which once hung in the closet of Isabella d'Este. Here, as a contrast, is Spenser's rather musical than plastic description:

He, making speedy way through spersèd ayre,
And through the world of waters wide and deepe,
To Morpheus house doth hastily repaire.
Amid the bowels of the earth full steepe,
And low, where dawning day doth never peepe,
His dwelling is; there Tethys his wet bed
Doth ever wash, and Cynthia still doth steepe
In silver deaw his ever-drouping hed,
Whiles sad Night over him her mantle black doth spred.

Whoe double gates he findeth lockèd fast,
The one faire fram'd of burnisht Yvory,
The other all with silver overcast;
And wakeful dogges before them farre doe lye,
Watching to banish Care their enimy,
Who oft is wont to trouble gentle Sleepe.
By them the Sprite doth passe in quietly,
And unto Morpheus comes, whom drownèd deepe
In drowsie fit he findes: of nothing he takes keepe.

And more to lulle him in his slumber soft,
A trickling streame from high rock tumbling downe,
And ever-drizling raine upon the loft,
Mixt with a murmuring winde, much like the sowne
Of swarming Bees, did cast him in a swowne.
No other noyse, nor peoples troublous cryes,
As still are wont t'annoy the walled towne,
Might there be heard; but careless Quiet lyes
Wrapt in eternall silence farre from enimyes.

Notwithstanding the evident borrowing from Ovid (*Metamorphoses,* xi):

            Saxo tamen exit ab imo
Rivus aquae Lethes, per quem cum murmure labens
Invitat somnos crepitantibus unda lapillis—

a passage which Spenser has combined with another from Chaucer's *Book of the Duchess,* notwithstanding this classical borrowing, Spenser's description is already steeped in an almost romantic atmosphere, with its deliberate insistence on the shadows and chiefly on the soft sleep-enticing murmurings: the atmosphere of Morpheus' house is dim, mysterious, very different from the Mantegna-like cavern of Ariosto. There are closer imitations of the *Orlando Furioso* in *The Faerie Queene,* but what has happened in the passage we have just read can be found happening to a greater or lesser extent everywhere in the poem. The same or similar adventures take place, the same battles, or nearly the same, are fought; but those of Ariosto are on the earth, and those of Spenser in the sky, among rainbow clouds, in mid-air, so to speak; or, to use another image, you see the lively, human combats which had taken place under Ariosto's broad daylight reflected with uncertain magical contours in the misty opalescent water of a northern pond in the midst of a forest. And what has happened to the rhythm, Ariosto's whirling motion whose play resulted in a sense of universal harmony? The air has become thicker; one could repeat for Spenser what a great modern Italian essayist, Emilio Cecchi, has written in some enlightening pages on King's College Chapel, Cambridge: [3]

[3] 'Cambridge', in *Pesci rossi,* trans. by F. Guercio, 'An Italian in Cambridge', in *The London Mercury,* xvii, 99, January 1928.

But more mysterious in quality and at the same time closer does this atmosphere become in the chapel of King's College. A green polar light from the nave windows brings to mind images of light in a submarine forest. In the dry and precise clarity of our climate, our columns and arches bear the weight of buildings with a logical economy of resources and with a sincere expression of human labour and resistance. In this denser atmosphere, things seem lighter, the effort of supporting them not so great, and thus their freedom of order and arrangement increases. The column, which with us is an element of strength and duty, becomes here one of elegance and phantasy. With us it is a serene slave of stone. In the chapel of King's College it is a lively vegetation: it imitates the lanceolation of leaves, it mounts and multiplies itself in veins and stalks. Our ceilings are static theorems, resolved into naked lines of energy and beauty. Here the static theorem becomes a motive for the creation of a heraldic vaulting or a flowery canopy. But this free play of the imagination, this romantic dreaming in stone, does not occur except in a less vivid reality, where some things have lost weight merely because others, which establish their relations of gravity, are more solid and heavy. There is a greater freedom in a poorer interplay of elements. Our architecture is the relation of stone and air. In the chapel of King's College, I am rather led to feel the weaker, less dynamic relation of plant and water. And there is less scrupulous care for style and beauty in this laxer relationship. The statues on our noble buildings are almost always noble; but on these noble constructions the statues are almost invariably grotesque. Henry the Eighth, on the precious door of Trinity College, stands unsteadily on his legs, with his golden crown awry as though he were a fairy king. The rampant beasts on the mural coats-of-arms have smooth, tapering bodies like those of the chilly, hairless monsters that glide among the algae. This luxuriant monotony, this leaden magnificence, is indeed the North.

'Luxuriant monotony', 'leaden magnificance': could one not repeat these very words apropos of the heraldic, allegorical fantasies of *The Faerie Queene*? Spenser not only utilises the allegorical elements already present in Ariosto, but allegorises also figures and episodes which had no allegorical meaning in the *Orlando Furioso*. Ruggiero's and Astolfo's adventures in the Italian poem symbolised the path of temperance; but Spenser's Guyon is no such dynamic character as Ruggiero; from the very beginning he is the stiff, stylised, heraldic personification of Continence, of which he bears the name almost embroidered in the border of his cloak, like a figure in a Renaissance pageant. There is no allegorical hint he finds in the Italian commentators that Spenser fails to develop. According to Fornari, Atlante represents lust, Bradamante, sacred or spiritual love; the jars full of fire which keep Atlante's castle standing are the flames and sighs of love. . . . We find this very fire at the door of the enchanter Busirane in *The Faerie Queene:* there it symbolises the flames of lust, which do not touch pure Britomart, a personification of Chastity triumphing over physical passion. According to Toscanella, another of Ariosto's commentators, Angelica's flight symbolised the dangers to which beauty is exposed when wandering by herself; according to Fornari, another commentator, it meant that flight was the only means of safety against lustful passion. Spenser's treatment of Angelica is typical of his complex imagination. Angelica, in *The Faerie Queene,* branches off into three different figures, all of them with a symbolical import. As Florimel, she is the type of chaste beauty fleeing from her assaulters. But Ariosto's Angelica was also a coquette and a vamp. This side of her is utilised by Spenser in the false Florimel, or Snowy Florimel, who is chaste only in the outward appearance, and ends by yielding to Braggadocchio, the faked knight, just as Angelica yielded to Medoro, a base soldier. But Angelica was also a proud beauty who despised men, and later was moved by wounded Medoro: and here we have Spenser's Belphoebe, a proud queen, who dresses Timias' wounds; but, instead of a repetition of the Angelica-Medoro episode, it is Timias who falls in love with his nurse, sees his love rejected, and grows mad like Orlando.

There is not only a moral allegory in *The Faerie Queene*; there is also a political one, according to which Gloriana, whom Arthur seeks in vain and sees only in his dreams (a

repetition of the Angelica-Medoro episode), is Queen Elizabeth: Arthur is probably the Earl of Leicester. But one side
of Elizabeth, who for political reasons flirted with various
European princes, deluding them with hopes of marriage, is
reflected in Snowy Florimel, and Braggadocchio is possibly
the Duke of Alençon, and Spenser's Ferraù is Don John of
Austria. It should not be imagined that these are fantasies of
modern critics. Spenser's age was fond of recondite allusions,
devices and mottoes, mysterious for the multitude but transparent for the few; chivalry had been reduced to a masqued
tournament, courtly love was a game in cipher; an Alexandrian
and at the same time mediaeval aura suffused an age fond of
allegories, emblems and stories with a key.

Allegory, which is something superadded in the *Orlando
Furioso*, permeates Spenser's poem; Spenser's novelty, from
this point of view, consisted in presenting the romantic epic
in an allegorical garb: thus Spenser, compared with Ariosto,
marks a return to the Middle Ages, just as Chaucer did in
respect of Boccaccio, when in *Troilus and Criseyde* he meant
to give a *Filostrato* purged of all the errors Boccaccio had
committed against the code of courtly love, whose formula
had been fixed by Chrestien de Troyes. And in his return to
the Middle Ages Spenser has tastes and proceedings in common with the Italian mannerist painters (just as he had in
common with them his taste for emblems, devices, pageants).
Only, when all this has been said, we must add that this also
represents in Spenser only a surface, conspicuous and fascinating as it is. There is underneath, as has been pointed by C. S.
Lewis,[4] a deep concern about the basic antitheses of the
world, about light and darkness, life and death, a religious
conception of a struggle of principles, such as we find in
Calderón's *autos sacramentales* and in Shelley. And the humility, the honesty, with which the poet faces these supreme
antinomies, his Platonism, which, for all its Florentine origins,
remains profoundly Protestant and austere, are aspects that
link Spenser with such differently tempered writers as the
authors of *Piers Plowman* and of the *Pilgrim's Progress*, Lang-

[4] *The Allegory of Love*, Oxford University Press, 1938.

land and Bunyan, aspects which give to his work a distinctly English flavour, just as distinctly English as his melodious indefiniteness, his ornate and impalpable setting of fairyland.

There is, however, in English literature another work which has more affinity with *Orlando Furioso* than *The Faerie Queene:* I mean a spiritual affinity, because the evidence for a material derivation is very slight indeed in this case. That work is one of Shakespeare's plays, not, however, the one whose source can be traced to the Ariodante-Ginevra episode, *Much Ado about Nothing.* No one of the commentators has mentioned the name of Ariosto apropos of *Midsummer Night's Dream.* The mainspring of this drama is, as in the *Orlando,* love, capricious and despotic love, which changes allegiance, maddens the heroes and the heroines, making them dote on a base object. Angelica becomes fond of the soldier Medoro, Titania of Bottom with an ass's head. Both are cases of punished arrogance. Oberon, in order to humiliate Titania, asks Puck, the symbol of the whims of love, to fetch him a certain magic flower whose juice, pressed on the eyes of Titania while she is asleep, will cause her to fall in love with the being she first sees when she wakes. Titania, after the love-juice has been placed on her eyelids, wakes to find Bottom, whom Puck has disfigured with an ass's head. Titania at once falls in love and dallies with Bottom. In the nineteenth canto of the *Orlando Furioso,* Angelica

> in tanto fasto, in tanto orgoglio crebbe,
> ch'esser parea di tutto 'l mondo schiva.
> Se ne va sola, e non si degnerebbe
> compagno aver qual più famoso viva;

[grew into such haughtiness and pride, that she seemed to avoid each and all. She goes by herself, and would not deign to have the most celebrated person for a companion.]

Angelica is indignant at the thought of having had Orlando as a lover; she feels she has lowered herself while making eyes at Rinaldo:

> Tant'arroganzia avendo Amor sentita,
> più lungamente comportar non volse:

> dove giacea Medor si pose al varco,
> e l'aspettò, posto lo strale all'arco.

[Love, having noticed such an arrogance, decided not to tolerate it any longer: he lay in wait where Medoro was lying on the ground, and fitted an arrow to his bow.]

Angelica sees Medoro wounded, feels an unusual pity and tenderness for him, and proceeds to prepare a juice of salutary herbs to heal his wounds; she recollects having seen a certain herb on a pleasant slope, whether dittany or panacea, possessing a virtue to stanch blood, and goes to seek it. Is it a coincidence, or is there actually some relationship, against the background of a similar situation, between the juice of the flower Oberon has shown once to Puck, and now asks him to fetch, and the juice of the herb Angelica is seeking? Once Medoro's wound has healed, Angelica becomes madly fond of him: her love-wound grows wider and sharper, the more Medoro's actual wound gets narrower and sounder: 'la sua piaga più s'apre e più incrudisce, quanto più l'altra si ristringe e salda.' Here too we find a proud woman in the arms of a menial.

There are further illustrations of Love's tyrannical capriciousness in *A Midsummer Night's Dream*. Hermia, ordered by her father to marry Demetrius, refuses, because she loves Lysander, while Demetrius is loved by her friend Helena, whom he has abandoned for Hermia. Under the law of Athens, Theseus, the duke, gives Hermia four days in which to obey her father; failing this, she has to suffer death, or take vows of chastity. Among the words Theseus addresses to Hermia in order to persuade her to marry there is a comparison with the rose:

> But earthlier happy is the rose distilled,
> Than that which, withering on the virgin thorn,
> Grows, lives, and dies in single blessedness.

The simile, which finds a parallel in Erasmus's *Colloquia* (in the dialogue between the suitor and the maid): 'Ego rosam existimo feliciorem, quae marcescit in hominis manu, delectans interim et oculos et nares, quam quae senescit in fruitice', seems to contradict the famous stanzas of Ariosto on the rose:

> Ma non sì tosto dal materno stelo
> rimossa viene, e dal suo ceppo verde . . .

[But not so soon from the green stock where she grew, the rose is plucked, and from the branch removed, as lost is all favour, grace and beauty that flowed from heaven and earth.]

'The virgin thorn' in Shakespeare's passage recalls 'la nativa spina' (the native thorn) in Ariosto's verse:

> La verginella è simile alla rosa
> ch'in bel giardin, su la nativa spina
> mentre sola e sicura si riposa . . .

[The virgin is like the rose which in a beautiful garden, while alone and safely she rests on her native thorn . . .]

Let us go back now to the plot of *A Midsummer Night's Dream*. Hermia and Lysander agree to leave Athens secretly in order to be married where the Athenian law cannot pursue them, and to meet in a wood a few miles from the city. Hermia tells Helena of the project, and Helena tells Demetrius. Demetrius pursues Hermia to the wood, and Helena Demetrius, so that all four are that night in the wood. Hazlitt said about this play: 'The reading of this play is like wandering in a grove by moonlight.' This sentence would equally well describe our impression in reading the *Orlando Furioso*, as we have seen in our brief survey of its first canto. Lovers pursuing each other in a wood, a blind-man's-buff breathing gallantry and mischievous frolicsomeness. That love of which Lysander talks to Hermia, is it not the very same intense and ephemeral love which was familiar to Ariosto, and to the society of Ariosto's time, love whose motto was *Carpe diem*?

> momentary as a sound,
> Swift as a shadow, short as any dream;
> Brief as the lightning in the collied night,
> That, in a spleen, unfolds both heaven and earth,

And ere a man hath power to say, 'Behold!'
The jaws of darkness do devour it up:
So quick bright things come to confusion.

Overhearing Demetrius in the wood upbraiding Helena for
following him, and desirous to reconcile them, Oberon orders
Puck to place some of the love-juice on Demetrius's eyes, but
so that Helena shall be near him when he does it. Puck, mis-
taking Lysander for Demetrius, applies the love-charm to
him, and it so happens that Helena is the first person whom
Lysander sees: Lysander, accordingly, at once makes love to
her, so that now Helena is wooed by two. The ladies quarrel,
and the men go off to fight for Helena. Later, Puck is ordered
by Oberon to throw a thick fog about the lovers; they are
brought all together, unknown to one another, and fall asleep.
While they sleep, Puck applies to their eyes a herb which
dissolves the spell, so that when they awake they return to
their former loves. Croce has already remarked that these
changing vicissitudes of love and dislike recall 'the strange
complications which took place in Italian chivalric romances
thanks to the two famous neighbouring fountains, one of
which filled the heart with amorous desire and the other
turned the original ardour into iciness'. Ariosto speaks of them
in the forty-second canto:

> Signor, queste eran quelle gelide acque,
> quelle che spengon l'amoroso caldo,
> di cui bevendo, ad Angelica nacque
> l'odio ch'ebbe di poi sempre a Rinaldo.
> E s'ella un tempo a lui prima dispiacque,
> e se ne l'odio il ritrovò sì saldo,
> non derivò, Signor, la causa altronde,
> se non d'aver beuto di queste onde.

[My lord, these were those icy waters which quench the
heat of love: drinking of these, Angelica conceived the
hatred she henceforth bore to Rinaldo. And if she at one
time was hateful to him, and found him so stubborn in his
dislike, the cause of it, my lord, is only that he had drunk
of these waves.]

Rinaldo drinks again at the magic well, and a single draught is enough to quench his thrist and his love in his ardent breast:

> e cacciò, a un sorso del freddo liquore,
> dal petto ardente e la sete e l'amore.

The date assigned to *A Midsummer Night's Dream* is 1593–94, when Harington's version of the *Orlando Furioso* had been in print for a couple of years. It is possible that Shakespeare had read it, and derived inspiration from it for the most fantastic of his plays; but even without speaking of an actual source, one cannot help noticing a deeper affinity than with any other work of the period in English literature. Ariosto's world was, in its very essence, alien to Spenser, but Shakespeare, the same Shakespeare who in his Italian plays represented the Italians like men, and not like the frantic puppets who formed the stock-in-trade of the Elizabethan blood and thunder tragedies, Shakespeare could seize the spirit of Ariosto's poem.

The rest of our rapid survey of Ariosto's fortune in England is rather matter for chronicle than for history. As I have said at the beginning, one could compile a volume of Ariosto allusions in English literature, from John Webster's *The Devil's Law-Case* (1623) in which one of the characters is called Ariosto, down to the end of the eighteenth century when William Beckford, as one would expect from the fanciful author of *Vathek*, confessed in his letters to a partiality for the *Orlando Furioso*. Among the most popular lines were those at the beginning of the thirty-first canto:

> Che dolce più, che più giocondo stato
> saria di quel d'un amoroso core?

which George Gascoigne as early as in 1561 had paraphrased thus:

> What state to man so sweete and pleasant weare,
> As to be tyed in linkes of worthy love?

Perhaps the earliest English madrigal, set to music by William Byrd, was 'La verginella è simile alla rosa', 'The

fayre yong virgin is like the rose untainted', the passage of
Ariosto's poem which was the most widely known. The
advice and assistance of Giuseppe Baretti, who in the *Italian
Library* vindicated in 1757 the beauties of Ariosto against
the strictures of French criticism which found the poet's inventions absurd, were enlisted by William Huggins. This
affluent gentleman had been working for twenty years at a
translation of Ariosto into *ottava rima*: a few of the cantos
were translated by Temple Henry Croker. Huggins' enthusiasm went so far as to raise to Ariosto in his park 'an hexagonal
temple', over whose 'Gothic Arches', typical of pre-Romantic
taste, he inscribed the following stanza:

> Per me se'n va l'incerto Viandante:
> Qui non s'alberga un orribil Gigante,
> Né della Fata Alcina il bel Sembiante;
> Castello non son io del Mago Atlante;
> Ma benché rozzo un Cumulo, son posto
> Pegno d'Amor verso il Divino Ariosto.

These lines are poor enough, and Huggins' English version of
the *Orlando* was not much superior in quality: Baretti tried
his best to improve it, and after forty days of hard toil was
rewarded with a fifty guinea watch, besides a sum of money
and the use of a house and garden adjoining Huggins' park.
The Gothic shrine and the no less Gothic translation, which
appeared in 1755, were not the only pledges of Huggins' love
for Ariosto: he defended the poet against the attacks of
Thomas Warton, who in his *Observations on the Faerie
Queene of Spenser* (1754) had vied with Rapin and Voltaire
in reviling Ariosto. Unfortunately Huggins' arguments were
not more conclusive than his exclamatory appreciations in the
Notes, such as: 'Most elegant comparison! Most delicate
stanza!', or, 'What a sweetly finished landscape!'. In 1779–80
an Irish clergyman, Henry Boyd, translated or rather paraphrased the *Orlando* into Spenserian stanzas, compressing
what he called pleonastic sentiment in order to 'add to its
poetical effect . . .', and freely altering or entirely omitting
the licentious passages. Another version appeared in 1783,
due to John Hoole, who had already translated Tasso: Hoole

had the merit of restoring the two Italian poets to some popularity among English readers, though his translation is rather dull, and his critical taste very uncertain (needless to say, he, too, pruned the sensual passages throughout the poem). Finally in 1825 William Stewart Rose published the best English version of the *Orlando Furioso*, in *ottava rima*, which Ugo Foscolo praised in these terms: 'Rose has left us one of the best models in the treatment of the English stanza in his version of Ariosto.' In 1771 a magnificent edition of the Italian text, illustrated by renowned artists was published in Birmingham by Baskerville.

It was through Hoole's version that Walter Scott and Robert Southey first became acquainted with the *Orlando*. Southey derived from his reading hints for his diligent and nowadays nearly forgotten poems, of which he had such a high opinion as not to hesitate to say of *Thalaba* that he did not know of any other poem which could claim a place between it and the *Orlando*, adding: 'Perhaps, were I to speak out, I should not dread a trial with Ariosto'. And who reads now Leigh Hunt's paraphrases of the Cloridano and Medoro episode and of the idyl between Medoro and Angelica? Or his other renderings of Ariosto included in *Stories from the Italian Poets* (1846)? I do not know how many English people read Ariosto in our time: in theory one would think that of the masterpieces of Italian literature the *Orlando Furioso* should be their favourite, because Ariosto's humorous lack of logic is not without affinity with the nonsense of *Alice in Wonderland*. Still, whereas, thanks to T. S. Eliot, the name and work of Dante are familiar to English literary people of today, chiefly to the poets, I remember having come across only one lover of Ariosto, the late professor of University College, London, Edmund Gardner, who dedicated to Ariosto his chief work. But, except in the case of John Donne, whose fortune has begun with Grierson's edition in 1912, has the enthusiasm of a professor ever made the fortune of a poet?

Tasso in England

IT IS NO wonder that, eager as she was for all Italian novelties, Elizabethan England should soon have learnt to admire Tasso. The Queen herself had committed to memory many stanzas of the *Gerusalemme liberata*,[1] and considered the Duke of Ferrara, 'for having his praise sung by such a poet', as lucky as Achilles 'for having had the great Homer'. In 1584 the Latin version of the *Gerusalemme* in the 'very pleasing and polished'[2] lines of the jurist Scipio Gentili was published in London, and dedicated to Queen Elizabeth.[3] An early inter-

---

[1] Giacomo Castelvetro's letter to Lodovico Tassoni dated 'London, June 22, 1584, old style'. I derive this, as well as other, information from Alberto Castelli's *La Gerusalemme liberata nella Inghilterra di Spenser*, Milan, 1936. I have been unable to see: H. M. Priest, *Tasso in English Literature, 1575–1675*, Northwestern University, Summaries of Dissertations, i, 1933. See also: H. H. Blanchard, 'Imitations from Tasso in the "Faerie Queene"', in *Studies in Philology*, xxii (1925), pp. 198–221; C. B. Beall, 'A Tasso Imitation in Spenser', *Modern Language Quarterly*, iii (1942), pp. 559–560.

[2] Tasso's words: 'leggiadrissimi e politissimi'; see C. Guasti, *Le Lettere di T. Tasso*, Florence, Le Monnier, 1853, n. 785, with the date 'Mantua, March 29, 1587'.

[3] *Torquati Tassi Solymeidos Liber Primus*, 1584, and *Scipii Gentilis Solymeidos Libri Duo priores*, 1584. In July 1594 the Admiral's Men performed the second part of a play *Godfrey of Bulloigne*; the first part might have been the play *Jerusalem* acted by Strange's Men on March 22 and April 25, 1592; see E. K. Chambers, *The Elizabethan Stage*, Oxford, At the Clarendon Press, 1923, vol. ii, p. 143, and iii, p. 340–341.

est in England for the biographical vicissitudes of the poet is
evidenced by the fact that a drama with the title *Tasso's
Melancholy* enjoyed some popularity between 1590 and
1595, to judge by the number of performances.[4] It has been
conjectured that *Aminta* may have been the pastoral play
performed by Italian actors in Reading in July 1574, in the
description of which mention is made of such paraphernalia
as staves, hooks and lambskins for shepherds, arrows for
nymphs, a scythe for Saturn, and 'horstayles for the wylde
mannes garment': *Aminta* had been produced at Ferrara the
year before.[5] It is only, however, through Spenser's imitations in *The Faerie Queene* that Tasso really penetrated into
English literature, with an accent which was to be found
typical of him also in the following centuries, the accent of
voluptuous enchantment and elegiac peace, a languorous
and suave perfection calculated to satisfy that very taste which
later found a paragon of beauty in the paintings of Guido
Reni.[6]

There are several analogous situations and more or less
free renderings of passages taken over by Spenser from the
Gerusalemme; but in Book II, Canto xii of the *Faerie Queen*
Armida's enchanted garden is reborn English, and the idea
contained in the lines:

> E quel che'l bello e 'l caro accresce a l'opre,
> L'arte, che tutto fa, nulla si scopre.

> Stimi (sì misto il culto è co'l negletto)
> Sol naturali e gli ornamenti e i siti.

[4] In the second edition of his *Essais* (1582) Montaigne says he
has seen at Ferrara, in the full horror of his pitiful madness,
Torquato Tasso; see L. F. Benedetto, 'Il Montaigne a Sant'Anna',
in *Uomini e tempi*, Naples, 1953. In 1588 there had appeared an
English version of the dialogue *Il Padre di famiglia* due to Thomas
Kyd: *The Householders Philosophie*: Tasso appears there as a
fugitive, persecuted by fortune and mighty men ('The wrath of
Fortune and of mightie men I shun . . .'; 'You are peradventure
one of those of whom the crye is come into our Country, who
uppon some common fault are fallen into mis-fortunes, whereof
you are . . . worthy to be pardoned.')

[5] Saturn's scythe, however, does not appear to be required for
Tasso's play.

[6] Stendhal found a likeness between Tasso and Guido Reni.

Di natura arte par, che per diletto
L'imitatrice sua scherzando imiti—

thus rendered by Spenser:

And, that which all fair works doth most aggrace,
The art which all that wrought appeared in no place.

One would have thought (so cunningly the rude
And scorned parts were mingled with the fine)
That Nature had for wantonness ensued
Art, and that Art at Nature did repine;
So striving each th'other to undermine,
Each did the other's work more beautify—

this idea of Nature playing at imitating her own imitatress,
Art, was to be re-echoed in the following ages, and to reappear in Oscar Wilde's paradox (in *The Decay of Lying*), that
life imitates art more than art imitates life; that a great artist
invents a type, and life tries to copy it, and reproduce it in
a popular formula. In Tasso's garden everything seems to
proceed like clock-work: the scene takes on a musical symmetry, the birds sing like the automata of Heron of Alexan-
dria, or like the birds of Haydn's *Toy Symphony*:

Vezzosi augelli infra le verdi fronde
Temprano a prova lascivette note,
Mormora l'aura, e fa le foglie e l'onde
Garrir, che variamente ella percote.
Quando taccion gli augelli alto risponde;
Quando cantan gli augei, più lieve scote;
Sia caso od arte, or accompagna ed ora
Alterna i versi lor la music'òra.

The joyous birds, shrouded in cheerful shade,
Their notes unto the voice attempred sweet;
Th'angelical soft trembling voices made
To th'instruments divine respondence meet;
The silver sounding instruments did meet
With the base murmur of the water's fall;
The water's fall with difference discrete,
Now soft, now loud, unto the wind did call;
The gentle warbling wind low answerèd to all.

Thus Le Nôtre's gardens took shape in Tasso's sublime rhetoric, while the famous stanzas on the rose, which develop a suggestion from Ariosto (*Orlando Furioso,* i, 42), present a theme which, introduced into English by Spenser, was destined to echo in the Choric Song of Tennyson's 'Lotus-Eaters':

> Deh mira, egli cantò, spuntar la rosa
> Dal verde suo modesta e verginella,
> Che mezzo aperta ancora, e mezzo ascosa,
> Quanto si mostra men, tanto è più bella.
> Ecco poi nudo il sen già baldanzosa
> Dispiega: ecco poi langue, e non par quella,
> Quella non par, che desïata inanti
> Fu da mille donzelle e mille amanti.
>
> Così trapassa al trapassar d'un giorno
> De la vita mortale il fiore e il verde. . . .

> The whiles someone did chant this lovely lay:
> Ah! see, whoso fair thing doest fain to see,
> In springing flower the image of the day.
> Ah! see the Virgin Rose, how sweetly she
> Doth first peep forth with bashful modesty,
> That fairer seems the less ye see her may.
> Lo! see soon after how more bold and free
> Her bared bosom she doth broad display;
> Lo! see soon after how she fades and falls away.
>
> So passeth, in the passing of a day,
> Of mortal life the leaf, the bud, the flower.

Tennyson's lines follow the same idea:

> Lo! in the middle of the wood
> The folded leaf is woo'd from out the bud
> With winds upon the branch, and there
> Grows green and broad, and takes no care,
> Sun-steep'd at noon, and in the moon
> Nightly dew-fed; and turning yellow
> Falls, and floats adown the air.

Lo! sweeten'd with the summer light,
The full-juiced apple, waxing over-mellow,
Drops in a silent autumn night.
All its allotted length of days
The flower ripens in its place,
Ripens and fades, and falls, and hath no toil,
Fast-rooted in the fruitful soil.[7]

Tasso in these stanzas of the *Gerusalemme* invented a scene
and a cadence [8] which came to be recognised as one of his
typical moods. Another *motif*, that of innocent pastoral life
contrasted with the lies of court life—one of the main themes
of *As You Like It*—penetrated into English literature through
the episode of Erminia among the shepherds (Canto vii):

Tempo già fu, quando più l'uom vaneggia
Ne l'età prima, ch'ebbi altro desio,
E disdegnai di pasturar la greggia,
E fuggii dal paese a me natio:
E vissi in Menfi un tempo, e ne la reggia
Fra i ministri del re fui posto anch'io,
E, ben che fossi guardian de gli orti,
Vidi e conobbi pur l'inique corti.

Pur lusingato da speranza ardita
Soffrii lunga stagion ciò che più spiace;
Ma poi ch'insieme con l'età fiorita
Mancò la speme e la baldanza audace
Piansi i riposi di quest'umil vita
E sospirai la mia perduta pace;
E dissi: O corte, addio. Così, a gli amici
Boschi tornando, ho tratto i dì felici.

---

[7] The theme is, in a way, a hackneyed one; cf. P. Matthieu
quoted by J. Rousset, *La Littérature de l'âge baroque en France*,
Paris, 1953, p. 273: 'Le fruit sur l'arbre prend sa fleur et puis se
noue,/Se nourrit, se meurit, et se pourrit enfin,/L'homme naist, vit
et meurt, violà sur quelle roue/Le temps conduit son corps au
pouvoir du destin.'

[8] Mark the repetition: 'e non par quella,/Quella non par', and
see the repetitions in Tennyson's 'Lotos-Eaters', e.g., st. vii: 'Only
to hear and see . . . Only to hear were sweet . . .'.

The time was once, in my first prime of years,
When pride of youth forth pricked my desire,
That I disdain'd amongst mine equall peares
To follow sheepe and shepheards bare attire:
For further fortune then I would inquire;
And, leaving home, to roiall court I sought,
Where I did sell my selfe for yearely hire,
And in the Princes gardin daily wrought:
There I beheld such vainenesse as I never thought.

With sight whereof soon cloyd, and long deluded
With idle hopes which there doe entertaine,
After I had ten yeares my selfe excluded
From native home, and spent my youth in vaine,
I gan my follies to my selfe to plaine,
And this sweet peace, whose lacke did then appeare:
Tho, backe returning to my sheepe againe,
I from thenceforth have learn'd to love more deare
This lovely quiet life which I inherite here.

> (*Fairie Queen*, Book VI, c. ix, 24–25)

Compare the Duke's words at the beginning of Act II of *As You Like It*:

Now, my co-mates, and brothers in exile,
Hath not old custom made this life more sweet
Than that of painted pomp? Are not these woods
More free from peril than the envious court?

. . . .

And this our life exempt from public haunt
Finds tongues in trees, books in the running brooks,
Sermons in stones, and good in everything.

In this brief survey of the influence of Tasso on English literature, I shall not linger on passages translated or imitated by Spenser, Daniel (who derived from *Aminta* his praise of the Golden Age), Drayton, Giles Fletcher and so many others; [9] but rather emphasise those themes and forms

[9] For lyric poems imitated by Spenser, see the introduction and notes to the translation of *Amoretti* and *Epithalamion* by Anna Maria Crinò, Florence, 1954. For the other poems, see Castelli's volume, *op. cit.*

of Tasso which led to important developments in English literature that deserve particular attention. We have just seen some of these themes inspired by either a sensuous or an elegiac strain.[10] A different kind of *motif* is that of the Infernal Council which Tasso introduced into the fourth canto of the *Gerusalemme* chiefly from Claudian's *De raptu Proserpinae* and Vida's *Christias*. This *motif* was further developed by Marino in the *Strage degli Innocenti* by casting over Satan a trace of the 'original splendour' (Satan's eyes in Marino harbour sadness and death, instead of terror and death, as in Tasso), and reappeared in the first book of *Paradise Lost*, where the figure of Satan is invested with the glamour of the dauntless rebel which belonged to Aeschylus' Prometheus and Dante's Capaneo.[11] Also Phineas Fletcher in his description of the Infernal Council in *The Purple Island* had Tasso's episode in his mind.

The *Gerusalemme liberata* became accessible in an English translation at an early date; and it was Fairfax's translation, rather than the Italian original, which made William Browne acquainted with the episode of Olindo and Sofronia which he imitated in that of Coelia and Philocel in his *Britannia's Pastorals*. There were two Elizabethan versions, a partial one (limited to the first five cantos) with the title *Godfrey of Bulloigne* (1594) by R. C., identified with the local historian and topographer Richard Carew (1555–1620), a translation

[10] The sensuous theme of Armida's garden (the nymphs of Canto xv) is found also in Camoens' *Lusiads* (ix, x ff.): the nymphs to whom is entrusted the task of luring and entertaining Vasco da Gama's companions are closely akin to those who tempt the two warriors who go to free Rinaldo in Canto xvi of the *Gerusalemme*.

[11] See M. Praz, *The Romantic Agony*, ch. ii, 'The Metamorphoses of Satan', and Olin H. Moore, 'The Infernal Council', in *Modern Philology*, vol. xvi, pp. 169–193, and xix, pp. 47–64. The Infernal Council first appears in the *Descensus Christi ad Inferos* which forms the second part of Nicodemus's Gospel (third century): it was one of the themes treated in the mystery plays of the Middle Ages. The first canto of the *Strage degli Innocenti*, containing the Infernal Council, had been translated by Richard Crashaw, and Milton knew both the Italian original and the translation. Milton derived also from the Latin poem *Georgius* by Baptista Mantuanus; see Edward S. Le Comte, 'Milton's Infernal Council and Mantuan', in *PMLA* for September 1954.

which was never very widely circulated and on the merits of which opinions have differed, although it has the merit of faithfulness; [12] and the famous version by Edward Fairfax, *Godfrey of Bulloigne, or The Recoverie of Jerusalem* (1600), which, contrary to the opinion of David Hume, who praised its 'exactness, which for that age' was 'surprising', is very free; Fairfax, for instance, does not scruple to add many mythological ornaments, contravening the precepts of Tasso, who would have liked to exclude mythology altogether from a Christian epos: in this and other features the English translator follows Spenser rather than Tasso.[13] Not unlike the English translators of Seneca,[14] or Crashaw in his rendering of Marino's *Strage degli Innocenti*, Fairfax frequently develops Tasso's descriptions and crowds them with details, thanks to the shortness of English words which enables him to gain space within the compass of a stanza, and while occasionally his amplifications exaggerate the colour of the text, as when the 'terror and death' of Lucifer's eyes becomes 'feare, death, terror and amazement', and the demons are caused to gnaw the 'chiome d'angui attorte' 'that on their shoulders hing', and their tails not only lash like whips ('si ripiega e snoda'), as in Tasso, but

> Some their forked tailes stretch forth on hie,
> And teare the twinkling stars from trembling skie—

while occasionally we come across exaggerations of this type, in other cases, as with Crashaw, the elaboration of the image is a source of new beauties, as in the passage in which Sofronia goes to King Aladdin:

> And forth she went, a shop for merchandise
> Full of rich stuffe, but none for sale exposed,
> A vaile obscur'd the sunshine of her eyes,
> The rose within her selfe her sweetnes closed,

[12] This version has been studied by R. E. N. Dodge and W. L. Bullock in *PMLA*, xliv (1929), pp. 681–695, and xlv (1930), pp. 330–335.

[13] For these translations, see Castelli, *op. cit.*, ch. iv, pp. 66–112. See also Charles G. Bell, 'Fairfax's Tasso', in *Comparative Literature*, vi, 1 (Winter 1954).

[14] See M. Praz, *Il Dramma elisabettiano*, Rome, 1946, p. 22 ff.

whereas the corresponding Italian text (ii, 18) has no image whatsoever:

> La vergine tra 'l vulgo uscì soletta;
> Non coprì sue bellezze, e non l'espose;
> Raccolse gli occhi, andò nel vel ristretta,
> Con ischive maniere, e generose.

Fairfax's version, in which the lines tend to combine into couplets, reducing Tasso's enjambments, while accentuating the antitheses and parallelisms of the original, had a certain influence on the evolution of the heroic couplet towards the form which was to triumph with Pope. The translator introduces antithesis and symmetry of members also into passages of the original where those rhetorical figures were either slightly hinted at, or latent. For instance:

> O più bel di maniere e di sembianti,
> O più eccelso ed intrepido di core—
> > (*Gerusalemme liberata*, i, 45)

becomes:

> With majesty his noble countenance shone,
> High were his thoughts, his heart was bold in fight.

Feelings become more explicit and schematic, the rhetoric of phrases is emphasised, an epigramamtic effect is the constant aim, single lines are apt to stand by themselves instead of blending with their neighbours, and the caesura gives a sharper turn to sententiousness. Here again the monosyllabic character of the English language is a determinant factor, allowing as it does a precise scansion, a staccato rhythm instead of the legato one we find in Tasso's flowing hendecasyllabics. Edmund Waller, whose smooth and balanced couplets deserved him the title of forerunner of Pope, declared he had refined his art after the model of Fairfax's stanzas.[15]

[15] Dryden reports in the preface to his *Fables* Waller's statement 'that he derived the harmony of his numbers from *Godfrey of Bulloigne*'. On Fairfax's importance in the history of English prosody, see Ruth C. Wallerstein, 'The Development of the Rhetoric and Metre of the Heroic Couplet, especially in 1625–1645', in *PMLA*, L (1935), pp. 166–209.

Edward Fairfax's son, William, contributed to the spread of interest in Italian poetry in England; he particularly influenced Thomas Stanley (1625–78) and his circle of minor poets, who translated and imitated the Italians, Tasso among others.[16] But Tasso's example was chiefly followed by the last of the so-called metaphysical poets, Abraham Cowley, who introduced the Pindaric ode and the heroic poem into England after Tasso's model. He fails, however, to acknowledge his debt; for he writes:

As for the Pindarick Odes . . . I am in great doubt whether they will be understood by most Readers. . . . They either are, or at least were meant to be, of that kind of Style which Dion. Halicarnasseus calls, *megalophuès kaì hedù metà deinótetos*, and which he attributes to Alcaeus: The Digressions are many, and sudden, and sometimes long, according to the Fashion of all Lyriques, and of Pindar above all Men living. The Figures are unusual and bold, even to Temerity, and such as I durst not have to do withal in any other kind of Poetry.

Thus the English reader was led to believe that Cowley had taken the idea from the Greeks, whereas the vogue for Pindaric poetry had already lasted for some time in Italy and France. Among the first Italians to write in a Pindaric style we find Tasso, who on the other hand had formulated the principles of the Christian epos after the *Poetica* of Gerolamo Vida, the author of *Christias*.

When Cowley, about 1638 in Cambridge, began to write his heroic poem on David's vicissitudes, the *Davideis,* the religious epos of the kind inaugurated by Tasso was enjoying popularity in Italy, where Marino's *Strage degli Innocenti* had been published posthumously in 1632, and in France, with the Biblical poems of Saint-Amant and Godeau. Cowley, in the passage of his Preface to the 1656 *Poems* relating to *Davideis*, professes to imitate Homer and Virgil 'whom we should do ill to forsake to imitate others', but in fact repeats

[16] See M. Praz, 'Stanley, Sherburne and Ayres as Translators and Imitators of Italian, Spanish and French Poets', in *Ricerche anglo-italiane*, Rome, 1944.

Tasso's arguments [17] that the subject should be taken from
history, against the idea that lying is essential to good poetry,
and against the use of mythological fables, which were good
enough for a time when there was no other religion, 'and
therefore that was better than none at all', but not for us,
who deride their folly. (Tasso had said: 'in the ancient poets
these things must be read with a different criterion, and
almost with another taste, not only for their being then accepted by the common people, but for being approved by
that religion, no matter what it was'.) Doctor Johnson, quoting in his *Life of Cowley* Rymer's opinion about the superiority of the *Davideis* to the *Gerusalemme*, wondered why the
two poets should be compared at all, such was the difference
of their manners. But the debt of the English poet to the
Italian one can easily be proved through minute comparisons,
beginning with the very first lines of the *Davideis*, the Propo-
sition and the Invocation, in which latter, however, Cowley,
following the fashion, has substituted Mary Magdalen for
the sacred Muse. A good instance of Cowley's method is
offered by his description of the archangel Gabriel taking a
human shape in order to appear to David (ii, 792 ff.):

When Gabriel (no blest spirit more kind or fair)
Bodies and cloaths himself with thicken'd Air,
All like a comely Youth in Life's fresh Bloom,
Rare Workmanship, and wrought by heav'nly Loom!
He took for Skin a Cloud most soft and bright,
That e'er the mid-day Sun pierc'd through with Light:
Upon his Cheeks a lively Blush he spread,
Wash'd from the Morning Beauties deepest Red.

[17] *Discorsi del poema eroico*, Libro II. Cowley's very declara-
tion of strict adherence to classical models repeats Tasso's (see
further, p. 324: 'Niuna cosa si dee considerare senza l'esempio
de' principi della poesia greca e latina; però che il ricercar nuove
strade porta seco maggior riprensione che lode'. Also William
Davenant, in his preface to the heroic poem *Gondibert* (*Discourse
upon Gondibert*, 1650) made use of Tasso's *Discorsi del poema
eroico*, which had been translated into French by Jean Baudoin
in 1638.

An harmless flaming Meteor shone for Hair,
And fell adown his Shoulders with loose Care.
He cuts out a silk Mantle from the Skies,
Where the most sprightly Azure pleas'd the Eyes.
This he with starry Vapours spangles all,
Took in their Prime e'er they grow ripe, and fall.
Of a new Rainbow e'er it fret or fade,
The choicest Piece took out, a Scarf is made.
Small streaming Clouds he does for Wings display,
Not virtuous Lovers Sighs more soft than they.
Those he gilds o'er with the Sun's richest Rays,
Caught gliding o'er pure Streams on which he plays.

Cowley merely embroiders on the comparatively short passage he has found in Tasso about Gabriel's materialisation (*Gerusalemme,* i, 13–14):

La sua forma invisibil d'aria cinse
Ed al senso mortal la sottopose:
Umane membra, aspetto uman si finse;
Ma di celeste maestà il compose:
Tra giovene e fanciullo età confine
Prese, ed ornò di raggi il biondo crine.

Ali bianche vestì, c'han d'or le cime . . .[18]

Johnson remarks: 'This is a just specimen of Cowley's imagery: What might in general expressions be great and forcible, he weakens and makes riciculous by branching it into small parts.' This very passage would have confirmed Johnson's criticism, had he taken the trouble to go back to Tasso and examine Cowley's source. In Cowley's note to this passage of the *Davideis* we find no mention of Tasso, but Saint Thomas and Virgil are duly cited, as if Cowley had derived his idea from a combination of them both.

[18] 'He surrounded his invisible shape with air, and subjected it to mortal sense; he fashioned for himself human limbs and a human appearance, but filled it with celestial majesty; he assumed an age hovering between boyhood and adolescence, and trimmed his golden hair with sunbeams. He donned white wings tipped with gold . . .'

We have seen how Tasso utilised the Infernal Council as an element of the marvellous in the epic poem. Cowley, following in his footsteps, has also an Infernal Council in his First Book, modelled on Tasso's and enriched with suggestions from Crashaw's version of the Infernal Council in Marino's *Strage degli Innocenti,* thus forerunning Milton who, in dealing with the same subject, derived, as we have said, from Tasso, Marino, and also (for Lucifer's complaint) from the *Davideis.* Cowley's Lucifer says:

Oh my ill changed condition! Oh my Fate . . .

And Milton's Satan (*Paradise Lost,* i, 48 ff.):

If thou beest he—but Oh how fallen! how changed
From him, etc.

Doctor Johnson humorously called attention to the fact that Cowley's Lucifer 'to give efficacy to his words, concludes by lashing *his breast with his long tail'.* Here, however, Cowley only applied to the arch-devil a habit common to Tasso's demons (iv, 4):

E lor s'aggira dietro immensa coda
Che quasi sferza si ripiega e snoda.[19]

The rest of this stanza of the *Gerusalemme,* describing the gathering of the infernal deities, was imitated by Cowley in Book II (768 ff), where some of the devils also 'stamp their cloven Paws' (Tasso: 'Stampano alcuni il suol di ferine orme'), others 'tear the gaping snakes from their black-knotted Hair' ('E 'n fronte umana han chiome d'angui attorte', showing the probable influence of Fairfax's version).[20]

The precepts about writing a heroic poem which Tasso usually laid aside when he came to write under inspiration—so that, while preaching a strict classicism, he was in fact

[19] 'And immense tails curl at their backs, which bend and lash like whips'.

[20] The verb *to tear* appears in the same stanza in which Fairfax speaks of 'snakes that on their shoulders hing'.

transforming it by the mellow and tender colours of his own palette—were followed by Milton methodically. It would be difficult to illustrate Tasso's precepts, as expounded in his *Discorsi dell'arte poetica* and *Discorsi del poema eroico*, from his own practice:

La composizione . . . avrà del magnifico, se saranno lunghi i periodi, e lunghi i membri de' quali il periodo è composto. . . . Il trasportare alcuna volta i verbi contro l'uso comune, benché di rado, porta nobiltà a l'orazione.[21]

La lunghezza de' membri e de' periodi, o delle clausole che vogliam dirle, fanno il parlar grande e magnifico non solo nella prosa, ma nel verso ancora.[22]

I versi spezzati, i quali entrano l'uno nell'altro . . . fanno il parlar magnifico e sublime.[23]

L'antipallage similmente, che si può dire mutazione de' casi, può accrescer la magnificenza del parlare.[24]

E 'l cominciar il verso da casi obliqui suole esser cagione del medesimo effetto nel parlare, il quale si può chiamar obliquo, o distorto, come in que' versi: 'Del cibo, onde 'l signor mio sempre abbonda, Lacrime e doglia, il cor lasso nudrisco.'[25]

Si può annoverar con queste il pervertimento dell'ordine, quando si dice innanzi quel che dovrebbe esser detto dopo;

[21] 'The composition will have a magnificent character, if the sentences and the members of which a sentence is composed are long. . . . Occasionally transferring the verbs against the common use, although seldom, lends nobility to the oration' (*Prose diverse*, ed. C. Guasti, Florence, 1875, vol. i, p. 54).

[22] 'The length of the members and sentences, or clauses as we may call them, makes the speech grand and magnificent not only in prose, but also in verse' (*ibid.*, p. 217).

[23] 'The breaking of the lines, so that they pass into each other . . . makes for magnificence and sublimity' (*ibid.*, p. 219).

[24] 'Similarly *anthypallage*, that is the substitution of one case for another, may increase the magnificence of the speech' (*ibid.*, p. 222).

[25] 'Beginning a line with oblique cases usually produces the same effect in the speech, which may therefore be called oblique or tortuous, as in those lines: "Of that food of which my lord has always plenty, tears and woe, I feed my wearied heart"' (*ibid.*, p. 223).

perché al magnifico dicitore non si conviene una esquisita diligenza.[26]

E la trasposizione delle parole, perch'ella s'allontana da l'uso comune . . . E 'l perturbar l'ordine naturale, posponendo quelle che doveriano esser anteposte . . . E l'*hyperbaton*, che si può dir distrazione, o interponimento.[27]

[Il poeta eroico] elegga fra le cose belle le bellissime; fra le grandi, le grandissime; fra le meravigliose, le meravigliosissime; ed alle meravigliosissime ancora cerchi di accrescere novità e grandezza.[28]

All these stylistic devices were appropriated by Milton, and the very fact that he abandoned his early plan of writing a tragedy, and wrote an epic poem instead, may be due to the influence of Tasso's arguments, for whom, of all poetic forms, heroic poems held first place:

Non posso già negare che la tragedia in minor tempo non conduca la sua favola a fine, e che quel piacere non sia più ristretto; ma avviene del diletto, il quale è nella tragedia e nella commedia, come della virtù de' corpi piccioli e de' grandi; perché niuno è ch'eleggesse d'esser picciolo, quantunque la virtù sia più unita, e più dispersa

[26] 'One may cite alongside of these the reversal of the order, when one says before what should be said after; because a fastidious precision does not suit a magnificent speaker' (*ibid.*, p. 232). Cf. p. 55: 'Per non incorrere nel vizio del gonfio, schivi il magnifico dicitore certe minute diligenze . . .' ('In order to avoid the defect of turgescence the magnificent speaker ought to dispense with a minute accuracy').

[27] 'And the transposition of words, because it departs from the common usage . . . And the alteration of the natural order, postponing words which should be placed in front . . . And the *hyperbaton*, which may be called a pulling apart or interposition of words or clauses' (*ibid.*, p. 233).

[28] 'Let the heroic poet choose the finest among fine things, the greatest among the great ones, the most marvellous among the marvellous ones; and let him study to increase the novelty and greatness of the most marvellous things' (*ibid.*, p. 125). The same principle is upheld by Tasso in his dialogue *Il Conte, o vero De l'imprese*: the body of a device has to be noble; see M. Praz, *Studies in Seventeenth-century Imagery*, i, London, The Warburg Institute, 1939, p. 61.

quella de' grandi: ma a l'incontro, è maggior virtù quella
d'un corpo grande; così anco è maggiore il piacere del-
l'epopeia, anzi è vero piacere; là dove quello della tragedia
è mescolato co'l pianto e la lagrime, e pieno tutto d'amari-
tudine. . . . Ma non voglio già concedere che la tragedia
meglio conseguisca il fine; anzi si move a quello per
obliqua e distorta strada: ma l'epopeia per diritta: perciò
che essendo duo modi del giovar con l'esempio, l'uno
d'incitarci a le buone operazioni mostrandoci il premio
dell'eccellentissima virtù e del valor quasi divino, l'altro
di spaventarci da le ree con la pena; il primo è proprio
dell'epopeia, l'altro della tragedia.[29]

Lo stile eroico . . . non è lontano da la gravità del
tragico, né da la vaghezza del lirico; ma avanza l'uno e
l'altro nello splendore d'una meravigliosa maestà.[30]

The very defects T. S. Eliot[31] finds in Milton, that his
'images do not give the sense of particularity', such as
Shakespeare's give, and that the complication of his syntax
is 'dictated by a demand of verbal music', can be traced to

[29] 'I cannot deny that tragedy employs less time in bringing its
tale to an end, and that there is in this case a condensation of
pleasure; but the delight pertaining to tragedy and comedy can be
compared with the virtue of small bodies as contrasted with big
ones; for there is no one who would choose to be small, although
virtue is more compact in this case, whereas it is scattered in big
bodies: however, the virtue of a big body is greater; so the pleasure
of epic poetry is greater, nay, it is the true pleasure; whereas that
of tragedy is mingled with tears, and thoroughly full of bitter-
ness. . . . I will not grant that tragedy better achieves its end;
rather it moves toward it through an oblique and tortuous path;
but epic poetry follows a straight one: for, there being two
ways of assisting with example, the one by stirring us to good
deeds by showing us the reward of excellent virtue and almost
divine valour, the other by deterring us from evil deeds by showing us the punishment; the former is proper to epic poetry, the
latter to tragedy' (ibid., p. 272-273).
[30] 'Heroic style . . . is neither far from the gravity of the
tragic style, nor from the pleasantness of the lyric; but surpasses
both with the splendour of a marvellous majesty' (ibid., p. 213)
[31] 'Note on the Verse of John Milton', in Essays and Studies by
Members of the English Association, vol. xxi, Oxford, At the Clarendon Press, 1935.

Tasso. In comparing Homer with Virgil, one may doubt whose virtues are greater:

> perché l'uno mette più le cose innanzi a gli occhi e le particolareggia, come disse il Castelvetro; l'altro, cioè Virgilio, sta più su l'universale: e, come pare al Castelvetro, per difetto d'arte; ma, come io stimo, per dir le cose più magnificamente, o più gravemente: perché il discriverle minutissimamente non porta seco né l'una né l'altra virtù.[32]
>
> Nel poema eroico si richiede principalmente la musica, la qual conservi il decoro de' costumi, e la maestà, come faceva la dorica . . .[33]

Tasso, in theory at least, advocates a close imitation of the classics:

> Niuna cosa si dee considerare senza l'esempio de' principi della poesia greca e latina; però che il ricercar nuove strade porta seco maggior riprensione che lode.[34]
>
> Lodiamo quelle orazioni e que' poemi i quali sono esattissimi ed insieme magnificentissimi, e somigliano le statue di Fidia, ch'erano fatte con politissima arte, ed aveano insieme dell'esquisito e del grande.[35]

The ideal beauty of a Greek statue seems to have haunted both painters and poets in that late phase of humanism. It hovered before the eyes of Annibale Carracci and Tasso, who, however, were inoculated against the spell by the

---

[32] *Prose diverse*, vol. i, p. 262: 'because the former puts things under our eyes in all their details, as Castelvetro said; the latter, that is Virgil, keeps more to the universal, owing to lack of art, Castelvetro thinks, but rather, it seems to me, in order to say things with more magnificence and gravity: because by describing them minutely one misses both virtues.'

[33] 'The chief need of a heroic poem is music, which should ensure ethical decorum and majesty, as the Dorian mode did' (*ibid.*, p. 267).

[34] 'In everything one must follow the example of the chief Greek and Latin poets; for the quest of new roads entails more blame than praise' (*ibid.*, p. 162).

[35] 'We praise those orations and poems which are at the same time very exact and magnificent, and resemble Phidias' statues, which were made with a very polished art, and were both exquisite and great.'

centuries of classicism they carried in their blood. But Poussin and Milton,[36] once they had espoused the ideal of classical beauty, were bewitched by it, like the young man who, according to the legend, put his ring on the finger of the marble statue of Venus.

Magnificence and gravity were the constant rules for Milton; he achieved them not only in his epic poem, with its sentences 'variously drawn out from one verse into another' (cf. Tasso: 'i versi spezzati, i quali entrano l'uno nell'altro . . . fanno il parlar magnifico e sublime'), but also in his sonnets, modelled, as J. S. Smart has shown, on those of Giovanni della Casa. Now on Casa's sonnet *Questa vita mortal* Tasso had remarked in his youth: [37]

Le parole di questo sonetto sono in modo congiunte, che non v'è quasi verso che non passi l'uno nell'altro; il qual rompimento de' versi, come da tutti gli maestri è insegnato, apporta grandissima gravità: e la ragione è che 'l rompimento de' versi ritiene il corso dell'orazione, ed è cagione di tardità, e la tardità è propria della gravità: però s'attribuisce a i magnanimi, che son gravissimi, la tardità così de' moti come delle parole.[38]

I was saying that it is by no means easy to illustrate Tasso's precepts from his own compositions, whereas Milton's epic verse is much closer to Tasso's idea of 'magnificence' and 'music'. One may find that the length of the clauses and the rhythm of the hendecasyllabic in that late poem, the *Sette*

[36] I repeat here what I wrote in an essay on 'Milton and Poussin' included in *Seventeenth-Century Studies presented to Sir Herbert Grierson*, Oxford, At the Clarendon Press, 1938. See the rest of that essay for the references to Poussin and Carracci.

[37] 'Lezione sopra un sonetto di Monsignor della Casa', in *Prose diverse*, vol. ii, p. 125. This lecture given at the Accademia of Ferrara was included from the earliest editions in the second part of the *Rime e prose del Tasso*. It was reprinted with Casa's works.

[38] "The words of this sonnet are joined in such a way that there is hardly any line that does not pass into another; which breaking of the lines, as it is taught by all the masters, greatly contributes to gravity: and the reason is that the breaking of the lines slackens the course of the oration, and causes tardiness, and tardiness is proper to gravity: therefore tardiness both of motions and words is ascribed to magnanimous men, who are very grave'.

Giornate del Mondo Creato, give it, occasionally, a neoclassical ring which seems to anticipate Foscolo. It is not at all clear, as F. T. Prince would have it,[39] that the *Gerusalemme liberata* and the *Sette Giornate del Mondo Creato* show, if we consider them in relation to the *Discorsi,* what Tasso proposed to do, or that the new method of writing blank verse had never been used so deliberately and consistently in Italian as by Tasso in the *Mondo Creato.* The passages Dr Prince quotes from this poem (from the *Primo Giorno,* 19 ff. and *Settimo Giorno,* 383 ff.) do not come so close to Tasso's ideal as *Paradise Lost* does on every page.[40] There is, however, a passage in the *Torrismondo* that comes nearer than any other in Tasso to Milton's epic verse: it occurs towards the end of the second Act, when Torrismondo orders festivities for the arrival of King Germondo; as this passage has never been considered in relation to the technique of *Paradise Lost,* I give it in full:

> Ora a voi, cavalieri, a voi mi volgo,
> Giovani arditi. Altri sublime ed alto
> Drizzi un castel di fredda neve e salda,
> E 'l coroni di mura intorno intorno:
> Faccian le sue difese, e faccian quattro
> Ne' quattro lati suoi torri superbe;

[39] *The Italian Element in Milton's Verse,* Oxford, At the Clarendon Press, 1954.

[40] Milton met in Naples in 1639 the pompous G. B. Manso, Marquis of Villa, who had been Tasso's last patron; the *Mondo Creato* had been begun in 1592 at the instigation of Donna Vittoria Loffredo, Manso's mother (Solerti, *Vita di T. Tasso,* 1895, vol. i., p. 716). On the style of Tasso's final phase, see the critical edition of the *Mondo Creato,* ed. by Giorgio Petrocchi, Florence, 1951, p. xxvi ff. Whereas in the young Tasso there was a marked distinction between the three styles (*magnifico, mediocre, umile*), 'the language of his last compositions is the result of the amalgamation of the three styles'. It is therefore not surprising that Milton, who kept to Tasso's precepts on the 'magnificent' style, should offer a better illustration of those precepts than the late *Mondo Creato,* whose style represented a compromise. With the passage on the Phoenix in the *Mondo Creato* (*Quinto Giorno,* 1287–1591) a passage from Milton's *Epitaphium Damonis* has been compared by Rudolf Gottfried, 'Milton, Lactantius, Claudian, and Tasso', in *Studies in Philology,* 1933, pp. 497–503.

E di candida mole insegna negra,
Dispiegandosi a l'aure, a 'l ciel s'innalzi;
E vi sia chi 'l difenda e chi l'assalga.
Altri ne'l corso, altri mostrar ne'l salto
Il valor si prepari, altri lanciando
Le palle di gravoso e duro marmo:
Altri di ferro, il qual sospinge e caccia
La polve e 'l foco, il magistero e l'arte.
Altri si veggia in saettar maestro
Ne la meta sublime; e in alto segno
D'una girevol asta in cima affisso,
Quasi volante augel, balestri e scocchi
Rintuzzate quadrella, insin ch'a terra
Caggia disciolto. Altri in veloce schermo
Percuota o schivi e 'n su l'avversa fronte
Faccia piaga il colpir: vergogna il cenno
De le palpebre a chi riceve il colpo.
Altri di grave piombo armi la destra,
E d'aspro e duro cuoio l'intorni e cinga
Perché gema il nemico a 'l duro pondo.
Altri sovra le funi i passi estenda
E sospeso ne 'l ciel si volga e libri.
Altri di rota in guisa in aria spinto
Si giri attorno; altri di cerchio in cerchio
Passi guizzando e sembri in acqua il pesce;
Altri fra spade acute ignudo scherzi;
Altri in forma di rota o di grande arco
Conduca e riconduca un lieto ballo,
D'antichi eroi cantando i fatti eccelsi:
A la voce de'l re, ch'indrizza e regge
Co'l suon la danza, i timpani sonanti
E con lieti sonori altri metalli
Sotto il destro ginocchio avvinte squille
Confondan l'alte voci e 'l chiaro canto.
Ed altri salti armato a 'l suon di tromba
O di piva canora or presto or tardi,
Facendo risonar ne'l vario salto
Le spade insieme e sfavillar percosse.
Altri, dove in gran freddo il foco accenso
De gli abeti riluce e stride e scoppia,

Con lungo giro intorno a lui si volga;
Sì che l'estremo caggia in viva fiamma
Rotta quella catena, e poi risorto
Da' compagni s'innalzi in alto seggio.
Altri là dove il gel s'indura e stringe
Condurrà i suoi destrier quasi volanti.
Ed altri a prova su 'l nevoso ghiaccio
Spinga or domite fere, e già selvagge,
C'hanno sì lunghe e sì ramose corna
E vincer ponno a'l corso i venti e l'aura.
Ed altri armato di lorica e d'elmo
Percuoterassi urtando il petto e il dorso,
Di trapassar cercando il duro usbergo
E penetrare il ferro e romper l'aste.
Ed io (ch'è già vicino il re Germondo
A la sede real) gli movo in contra
Con mille e mille cavalieri adorni,
Vestiti a 'l mio color purpureo e bianco,
Che già fra tutti gli altri a prova ho scelti.
L'altre diverse mie lucenti squadre
A cavallo ed a piè frattanto accolga
Il mio buon duce intorno a l'alta reggia,
E i destrier di metallo, onde rimbomba
La fiamma ne l'uscir d'ardente bocca
Con negro fumo, e' miei veloci carri;
E lungo spazio di campagna ingombri
Sotto vittoriosa e grande insegna.[41]

[41] 'Now to you, knights, to you I turn, bold youths. Let some
of cold and firm snow raise a castle sublime and high, and crown
it with walls all round; let them strengthen it with buttresses, and
four proud towers at its four corners; and let a black ensign rise
to the sky from such a white pile and flutter in the wind; and some
defend it, and some attack it. Let others prepare to show their
valiance in the race, others in jumping, others in hurling balls of
heavy and hard marble: let others show the skill and art of iron,
which pushes and expells powder and fire. Let another be proclaimed master of shooting at a lofty target: let him aim and
discharge rebounding arrows at a high mark fixed on the top of a
revolving pole like a flying bird, until it falls loose to the ground.
Let others hit or parry in a quick fencing, and their blows inflict a
wound on the opponent's forehead: shame to him who should
blink on being hit. Let others arm their right hands with a heavy

The sustained heroic rhythm of these lines, in which Tasso describes the military games with details supplied by Olaus Magnus [42] seems actually to be the model of the metre of *Paradise Lost*:

Nigh on the Plain in many cells prepar'd,
That underneath had veins of liquid fire
Sluc'd from the Lake, a second multitude
With wondrous Art founded the massie Ore,

---

lead wrapped round with hard and rough leather, so that the adversary shall groan under the hard weight. Let another venture his steps on a tight rope and balance himself suspended in mid air; another be sent spinning on high like a wheel; another pass through hoop after hoop with a fish-like glide; another naked play amid sharp swords; others lead to and fro a merry dance in the form of a wheel or a great bow, while singing the mighty deeds of ancient heroes: at the king's command, whose sound directs and controls the dance, ringing timbrels and bells tied behind the right knee together with other cheerful resounding metals will drown the piercing voices and the clear song. Let others armed leap, now slow, now quick, at the sound of a shrill trumpet or bagpipe, causing the swords to clash and clang and sparkle during the various leaps. Let others, where in the frost a fir-wood fire is blazing and crackling and sizzling, move round it in a long dance in a ring, until the last one, once the chain is broken, falls into the blazing fire, and, standing up again, is hoisted by his fellows to a high seat. Others where the ice is hard and compact will lead their nearly flying horses, others will push along the snowy ice the once wild, now tame, beasts with long and branched horns which race the fastest winds. Others wearing a breastplate and a helmet will joust striking the breast and back and try to pierce the hard cuirass and bore the iron and break the spears. As for me, since King Germond is approaching the royal seat, I ride to encounter him with many thousands of adorned knights whom I have chosen from among the rest wearing my crimson and white livery. My other various glittering squadrons on horseback or on foot will be gathered in the meantime by my good commander-in-chief round the lofty royal palace, together with my metal steeds, out of whose burning mouths the flame thunders issuing forth with black smoke, and my speedy chariots; and a great tract of land will disappear under my great victorious banner.'

[42] *Historia de Gentibus Septentrionalibus*, xv, ch. 23 and 24–30. See E. Gigas, 'En nordisk Tragedie af en italiensk Klassiker', in *Nordisk Tidskrift for filologi*, N.S., vol. vii, pp. 187–206, quoted by G. Carducci in his essay on the *Torrismondo* (*Opere minori in versi di T. Tasso*, Bologna, 1895, vol. iii). Cf. also Virgil, *Aen.*, vi, 642 ff.

Severing each kinde, and scum'd the Bullion dross:
A third as soon had form'd within the ground
A various mould, and from the boyling cells
By strange conveyance fill'd each hollow nook,
As in an Organ from one blast of wind
To many a row of Pipes the sound-board breaths.
Anon out of the earth a Fabrick huge
Rose like an Exhalation, with the sound
Of Dulcet Symphonies and voices sweet,
Built like a Temple, where Pilasters round
Were set, and Doric pillars overlaid
With Golden Architrave; nor did they want
Cornice or Freeze, with bossy Sculptures grav'n,
The Roof was fretted Gold.

(i, 700–717)

As when to warn proud Cities warr appears
Wag'd in the troubl'd Skie, and Armies rush
To Battel in the Clouds, before each Van
Prick forth th'Aerie Knights, and couch their spears
Till thickest Legions close; with feats of Arms
From either end of Heav'n the welkin burns.
Others with vast Typhœan rage more fell
Rend up both Rocks and Hills, and ride the Air
In whirlwind; Hell scarce holds the wild uproar.

(ii, 533–541)

These in their dark Nativitie the Deep
Shall yeild us, pregnant with infernal flame,
Which into hollow Engins long and round
Thick-rammd, at th'other bore with touch of fire
Dilated and infuriate shall send forth
From far with thundring noise among our foes
Such implements of mischief as shall dash
To pieces, and orewhelm whatever stands
Adverse, that they shall fear we have disarmd
The Thunderer of his only dreaded bolt.

(vi, 482–491)

Tasso's influence on Milton was not limited to the technique of heroic verse. One has heard much about the Spenserian character of *Comus*, but nobody seems to have been aware that Tasso's *Aminta* [43] is his real model. Comus's arguments to persuade the Lady to forsake her virginity are a development of those Dafne uses with Silvia at the beginning of Tasso's pastoral drama; Comus himself acts the part of Tasso's Satyr. *Comus* is a spiritualised *Aminta*; the Satyr binds Silvia naked to a tree and tries to violate her, but Comus's fetters are the invisible work of a spell. Thus sensuality has been carried away from the senses. Tasso's pastoral, with its tender atmosphere, its passions, and its despair gushing out so easily, so melodiously, its discreetly introduced mythological background (only Love's Prologue has a distinct Hellenistic ring), has been transformed almost beyond recognition into a morality in antique garb.

In his Introduction ('Of Heroique Plays') to *The Conquest of Granada* (published 1670) Dryden quotes the opening lines of Ariosto's *Orlando Furioso* ('Le donne, i cavalier, etc.') and adds that 'an Heroick Play ought to be an imitation, in little, of an Heroick Poem'; Tasso, however, more than Ariosto, supplied him with a model for his heroes, as Professor Roswell Gray Ham has rightly observed [44] Apropos of Dryden's claim that Rinaldo and Achilles had been his models for Almanzor:

> The Rinaldo of Tasso was more surely the prototype of Almanzor than the Achilles of Homer, or, less certainly, the Artéban of La Calprenède. Though Dryden professed to admire the Grecian demigod beyond the ruffled French hero, it was nevertheless the chop-logic of the latter and the unparalleled magnanimity of the noble Rinaldo that together composed the *mélange* which was Almanzor.

And, more generally:

> The heroic lovers of Dryden had cast away discretion, and, in their striving to achieve in tragedy the effects of Rinaldo in epic poetry, had merely risen to the realm of the baroque.

[43] The *Aminta* had been translated into English in 1628 by Henry Reynolds: *Tasso's Aminta Englisht*, London, printed by Aug: Mathewes for William Lee. Another version, by John Dancer, appeared in 1660.

[44] *Otway and Lee, Biography from a Baroque Age*, Yale University Press, 1931, pp. 34, 39–40.

It seems indeed needless to trace the impression of Tassesque atmosphere to single scenes of Dryden's (as for instance the Enchanted Wood in *King Arthur*), so closely does his sensibility seem, at times, to be related, to that of the author of the *Gerusalemme*. No more apposite emblem could be imagined of the kind of heroic infatuation which reached its climax in England with Dryden, and in the South with Metastasio's operas, than the figure of Tasso's woman-warrior, soft-breasted beneath her glittering armour.[45] *Amore alma è del mondo,* Tasso had sung in a famous sonnet; and in order to let them be vanquished by love Dryden conjured up the stately allegories of the French stage, Virtue, Honour, Renown, like so many symbols of Ripa's *Iconologia,* and disposed them in various attitudes of dismay, fear, and surrender, at the feet of the triumphant Monarch of the soul. There occurs in Dryden also the theme, destined to become a typical one with the romantics, of the *Liebestod,*[46] which is so clearly announced in the episode of Olindo and Sofronia:

> Ed oh mia morte avventurosa a pieno!
> Oh fortunati miei dolci martiri!
> S'impetrerò che giunto seno a seno
> L'anima mia ne la tua bocca spiri:
> E venendo tu meco a un tempo meno
> Con me fuor mandi gli ultimi sospiri.[47]

In *Don Sebastian* Almeyda says:

> How can we better dye than close embrac'd,
> Sucking each others Souls while we expire?

The precept that 'an Heroick Play ought to be an imitation, in little, of an Heroick Poem' had as a consequence not only

[45] See the fine essay on *Clorinda* by F. Chiappelli in *Studi tassiani,* n. 4, 1954.

[46] See M. Praz, *The Romantic Agony, op. cit.,* p. 33 ff. Rousseau, who adored Tasso (see "J. J. Rousseau e Torquato Tasso", in *Uomini e tempi* by L. F. Benedetto, *op. cit.*) was moved to tears when he read the Olindo-Sofronia episode with his 'pauvre voix cassée et tremblotante'.

[47] 'And ah! my death, fortunate to the full! Ah, happy my sweet martyrdom! If I obtain that, joined with thee breast to breast, I may exhale my soul into thy mouth: and thou, fainting at the same time, mayst breathe out thy last sighs together with me.'

that 'Love and Valour ought to be the subject of it', but also that the rules given by Tasso for the heroic poem could be applied to a heroic play, and as Tasso had said: 'Let the heroic poet choose the finest among fine things, the greatest among the great ones, the most marvellous among the marvellous ones; and let him study to increase the novelty and greatness of the most marvellous things', so Dryden ascribed to his characters hyperbolical feelings, showed them absurdly striving to outdo each other in generosity, interpolated long splendid similes after the model of Homer into dramatic passages, splendid images suited to the noble style, and introduced also (in *Don Sebastian*) a deliberate 'roughness of the numbers and cadences', 'a more noble daring in the Figures, and more suitable to the loftiness of the Subject' (it will be remembered that Tasso recommended also that the order of the speech be altered, 'because a fastidious precision does not suit a magnificent speaker').

Notwithstanding his great debt to Tasso, and his early opinion of him as 'the most excellent of modern poets, and whom I reverence next to Virgil',[48] Dryden would not have been Dryden if he had remained constant in this opinion: though *Paradise Lost* had already appeared in 1671 when Dryden expressed his admiration of Tasso in his preface to the *Mock Astrologer*, he had not yet fallen under Milton's influence. In 1677 he grouped Milton with Homer, Virgil, and Tasso.[49] In 1693 in his *Discourse concerning the Original and Progress of Satire*, which introduced his versions of Persius and Juvenal, he found occasion to censure Tasso:

> Tasso, whose design was regular, and who observed the rules of unity in time and place more closely than Virgil, yet was not so happy in his action: he confesses himself to have been too lyrical, that is, to have written beneath the dignity of heroic verse, in his episodes of Sophronia, Erminia, and Armida. His story is not so pleasing as Ariosto's: he is too flatulent sometimes, and sometimes too dry: many times unequal, and almost always forced; and, besides, is full of conceits, points of epigram, and witti-

---

[48] *Essays*, ed. W. P. Ker, i, p. 145.
[49] *Ibid.*, p. 182.

cisms: all which are not only below the dignity of heroic verse, but contrary to its nature: Virgil and Homer have not one of them. . . . But to return to Tasso: he borrows from the invention of Boiardo, and in his alteration of his poem, which is infinitely for the worse, imitates Homer so very servilely, that (for example) he gives the king of Jerusalem fifty sons, only because Homer had bestowed the like number on King Priam; he kills the youngest in the same manner, and has provided his hero with a Patroclus, under another name, only to bring him back to the wars, when his friend was killed.

These strictures did not prevent Dryden from continuing to draw on Tasso; his last great work, the *Fables,* shows the influence of the Italian poet in the more heroic stories. At one time Dryden had planned an epic poem on King Arthur; had he written it, he would hardly have avoided the influence of the *Gerusalemme.*

The merits of the various epic poets continued to be frequently compared; John Sheffield, Duke of Buckingham, in his *Essay upon Poetry* (1682), preferred Spenser to Tasso; Pope preferred Tasso to Ariosto, and in his *Observations on the Iliad* named him more often than any other poet, except Virgil and Milton, for his imitations of Homer; he showed a detailed knowledge of episodes, characters, and lines, which he quoted in Italian; he found, however, that the story of Tancred's love for Clorinda was 'ill-placed and evidently too long for the rest', and that the episode of Erminia pointing out the chief Christian warriors to the King from the walls of Jerusalem was copied 'too closely and minutely' from Homer; [50] and he confessed to his early friend and mentor, Walsh, that were he to write a pastoral play he would imitate the *Aminta,* 'not only in the simplicity of his [Tasso's] thoughts, but in that of the fable too'. He praised the *Aminta* because its plot lacked complexity and there was nothing in it 'but happens by mere chance'.

After the middle of the seventeenth century the interest in Italian literature declined considerably in England. Addison,

[50] See A. Warren, *Alexander Pope as Critic and Humanist,* Princeton University Press, 1929, pp. 204–205.

in *The Spectator* (No. 5, March 6, 1711) remarked that 'the finest Writers among the Modern Italians express themselves in such a florid Form of Words, and such tedious Circumlocutions, as are used by none but Pedants in our own Country': this apropos of the Preface to the opera *Rinaldo,* in which sparrows were made to fly about the stage in order to give verisimilitude to the scene of the enchanted garden [51] (the song of the birds was produced however by musical instruments placed behind the scenes), and the audience was entertained with plenty of thunder and lightning, illuminations and fireworks under the strict watch of firemen; 'and as for the Poet himself, from whom the Dreams of this Opera are taken, I must entirely agree with Monsieur Boileau, that one verse in Virgil is worth all the *Clincant* or Tinsel of Tasso'. Although Boileau's adverse opinion had a following in England, whatever interest there was for Italian poetry in this period of disfavour was almost solely due to Tasso. In the first part of the eighteenth century the singer and poetess Mrs Elizabeth Rowe gave short versions of some of the spookiest and most sensuous passages of the *Gerusalemme;* other poets translated from one to three cantos apiece. At the same time new or revised translations of the pastorals of Tasso and Guarini kept Englishmen from altogether forgetting that Italy had a theatre.[52] Fairfax's version, which appeared in 1749 in a new edition, inspired a stanza of William Collins's *Ode on the Popular Superstitions in the Highlands,* and an *Epistle to the Editor of Fairfax his Translation of Tasso's Jerusalem,* which was never printed and is considered lost. In the *Ode* Collins recalls his impressions on reading the episode of Tancredi in the enchanted wood:

> How have I trembled, when, at TANCRED's stroke,
>   Its gushing blood the gaping cypress pour'd;
> When each live plant with mortal accents spoke,
>   And the wild blast up-heav'd the vanish'd sword!

[51] Steele remarks in No. 14 of *The Spectator* that 'instead of perching on the Trees and performing their Parts, these young Actors either get into the Galleries or put out the Candles'.

[52] Roderick Marshall, *Italy in English Literature, 1755–1815,* Columbia University Press, 1934, p. 14.

How have I sat, when pip'd the pensive wind,
  To hear his harp, by British FAIRFAX strung.
Prevailing poet, whose undoubting mind
  Believ'd the magic wonders which he sung!
Hence, at each sound, imagination glows;
  Hence his warm lay with softest sweetness flows:
Melting it flows, pure, num'rous, strong and clear,
And fills th'impassion'd heart, and wins th'harmonious ear.[53]

Giuseppe Baretti tried to react against Tasso's monopoly by making the English understand that Italy had in Dante a far greater poet, and that Ariosto's reputation had been too long overshadowed by that of Tasso. Baretti held *Aminta* in no small esteem, but, among Italian tragedies, he called the attention of the English to the *Torrismondo*, which actually, so far as dramatic power is concerned, had little to teach to Shakespeare's fellow-countrymen, crystallised as it is in its empty classical pattern, thanks to which a princess is inevitably accompanied by a nurse and a king by a no less inevitable counsellor; and where the protagonist, at one point, is supposed to deliver a monologue of fourteen solid pages: [54] a drama which is both puerile and decrepit, unable to stand comparison with any minor Elizabethan play whatsoever.

William Huggins, who in 1755 had published a translation of Ariosto, derived from Baretti his preference for this poet over Tasso, whom he showed in the act of tearing out the leaves of Ariosto's *Orlando Furioso* with his teeth in an emulous poetic rage. In his *Essay on the Genius and Writings of Pope* (1756) Joseph Warton admired Tasso for having shown 'how fine an epic poem the Italian language, notwithstanding

---

[53] There appeared in *The Student* for 1751 (No. 8, vol. ii, pp. 313–315) a satirical *Ode to Horror, in the Allegorical, Descriptive, Alliterative, Epithetical, Fantastical, Hyperbolical and Diabolical Style of our Modern Ode Wrights and Monody Mongers*, in which Tasso is thus alluded to:

    O thou that erst on fancy's wing
    Didst terror-trembling Tasso bring
    To groves, where kept damn'd furies dire
    Their blazing battlements of fire.

[54] Exactly 375 lines in a scene of 592 from an act of 907, as Carducci remarked in his essay on *Torrismondo, op. cit.*, p. lxvii.

the popular imputation of effeminacy, was capable of supporting'. In 1758 Abraham Portal dramatised the episode of
Olindo and Sophronia, which he never submitted to the
theatre managers, being certain they would damn it, 'as a
strain of Piety runs through many of the Scenes . . .' The
chief changes which Portal made were to give King Aladine
a kind old counsellor, Orcano, who turns out to be Olindo's
father, and to inflame Aladine with a lustful desire for
Sophronia's beauties. This play, in the author's intention,
should have afforded 'a rational and agreeable Entertainment
in the Closet, where vicious Fashion does not tyrannize, and
where Men need not blush to appear pleased with *natural
Sentiment*, and touched with *just Distress* . . .' In 1761 there
appeared in Dublin a translation by an Irishman, Philip
Doyne, *The Delivery of Jerusalem*, in blank verse of a
Miltonic type, not free from errors; for instance the passage
in Canto xvi, st. 24:

> Ma bel sovra ogni fregio il cinto mostra,
> Che né pur nuda ha di lasciar costume,[55]

is thus misunderstood:

> the zone
> That bound her graceful waist, and which, unloos'd
> Naked the lovely wanton was.

Doyne had his version prefaced by Henry Layng's *Life of
Tasso* (taken from *Several Pieces in Prose and Verse*, 1748)
and by an essay of his own on the *Gerusalemme*: he maintained that Tasso excelled both Homer and Virgil, and often
Milton himself, because his subject was nobler than those
of the pagan poets, supplying him with 'an endless stock of
sublime ideas, and excellent sentiments, productive of every
kind of virtue'. Besides, Tasso had an 'enchanting way of interesting us for his heroes', which made us love them better than
the vengeful Achilles or the unscrupulously 'pious' Aeneas.
In the third place, the *Gerusalemme* worked more success-

---

[55] 'But, finer than all other ornaments, she shows the zone,
which she is wont never to quit, even naked'.

fully toward a climax than the *Aeneid* or *Paradise Lost*. The only thing Doyne found unsatisfactory in Tasso was his fondness for witchcraft. Layng, in his *Life of Tasso*, accepted the legend spread by G. B. Manso as early as 1621, and expatiated on Tasso's misfortunes, making him into the type of unpractical poet lost in a hard-hearted world: the figure which Goethe in his drama (1807) and Byron in *The Lament of Tasso* (1817) were to make immortal.

In 1762 there appeared a 'dialogue of the dead' in which Tasso and Milton compared their own lives and works in minute detail: *Il Tasso, A Dialogue: the Speakers John Milton, Torquato Tasso, in Which New Light Is Thrown on Their Poetical and Moral Characters:* both poets agreed, in Milton's words ,that 'we possess unrivalled the summits of the modern Parnassus.' The same year saw the publication of Richard Hurd's *Letters on Chivalry and Romance*, in which the charm of the 'Gothic romances' received due recognition: the supernatural element in them, according to Hurd, had made the fancies of our great modern poets 'more sublime, more terrible, and more alarming than those of the classic fablers'. 'What are Virgil's myrtles dropping blood to Tasso's enchanted forest?' The heart tells us that 'these Lyes of Gothic invention' are one of their greatest charms. Hurd's praise of Tasso could not have served more opportunely to introduce a new complete version of the *Gerusalemme* due to John Hoole, which appeared in 1763. Hoole adapted Ariosto and Tasso to the taste of his times, by translating the stanza in well-trimmed and symmetrical heroic couplets on the model of *The Rape of the Lock*. This version, even more than the original, would have deserved Gibbon's praise (in *The Decline and Fall of the Roman Empire*, 1788, ch. lxx) stressing 'the regular beauties of Tasso'. Here is stanza 23 of Canto xvi as rendered by Hoole:

> Poi che intrecciò le chiome, e che ripresse
> Con ordin vago i lor lascivi errori,
> Torse in anella i crin minuti, e in esse,
> Quasi smalto su l'òr, consparse i fiori;
> E nel bel sen le peregrine rose
> Giunse a i nativi gigli, e 'l vel compose.

Now in a braid she bound her flowing hair:
Now smooth'd the roving locks with decent care.
Part, with her hand, in shining curls she roll'd,
And deck'd with azure flowers the waving gold.
Her veil compos'd with roses sweet she dress'd
The native lilies of her fragrant breast.

This version met with the approval of Doctor Johnson, who recommended the book to the Queen in a dedicatory epistle which Boswell thought a masterpiece of elegance: this letter stressed Tasso's peculiar claim to the Queen's favour, 'as follower and panegyrist of the House of Este, which has one common ancestor with the House of Hanover', and lamented that Tasso had not lived in a happier time 'when he might among the descendants of that illustrious family have found a more liberal and potent patronage'.[56]

It was in Hoole's translation that young Scott and Robert Southey first read Tasso and Ariosto. The *Gerusalemme* and the *Orlando* opened out a whole new world to Southey: 'It was for the sake of their stories that I perused and reperused these poems with ever new delight; and by bringing them thus within my reach in boyhood, the translator rendered me a service which, when I look back upon my intellectual life, I cannot estimate too highly.'[57] In 1792 Hoole produced a version of the *Rinaldo*. In his 'Life of Tasso' prefixed to the translation, Hoole repeated the story of Tasso's love for Leonora d'Este, who returned it, and of his imprisonment by the hard-hearted Duke of Ferrara; he introduced into this biographical essay some translations of Tasso's lyric verse, the first to appear since the times of Thomas Stanley.

In 1763 the Italian text of the *Gerusalemme* was printed in Glasgow; in 1780 Baretti promised to edit a London edition, a project which was never carried out; but Agostino Isola published a Cambridge edition, with literary and historical notes. More editions appeared in London in 1796 (edited by Nardini and Polidori), and in 1806 (edited by Zotti). The *Aminta* was published in Leeds in 1796. In 1803

[56] Boswell, *Life of Dr. Johnson*, beginning of 1763.
[57] *Poetical Works*, i, pp. vii–viii; cf. Jack Simmons, *Southey*, London, 1945, p. 17.

Lorenzo da Ponte advertised a London edition of the *Rinaldo*, of which no copies are known. In 1770 the *Aminta* appeared in a translation by Percival Stockdale, with a preface in which he defended Tasso from Boileau's and Addison's strictures (Tasso's *clinquant*) and proclaimed him a greater poet than Virgil. We notice a similar strain in the author (either Edward Taylor or William Richardson, a professor at Glasgow University) of *Cursory Remarks on Tragedy* (1774), who found 'more instances of the beauty of sentiment and simplicity in the works of Tasso than in any other poet (the ancients excepted)', quoted the description of Satan in order 'to prove that the Italian language has energy and powers equal to the boldest and most sublime images', and doted on Tasso's 'wonderful distinction of characters'. The same author praised the 'genuine and sublime poetry' of the choruses of the *Torrismondo* and its moving plot, and the touching naïveté of the *Aminta*, though admitting that some of the sentiments of this play may be 'too refined for common pastoral'. Stockdale had said of those sentiments that, if not altogether 'characteristick of rural life' as it is, they were fitting for what we may imagine of the golden age, and that whoever cannot take pleasure in Tasso's idealised view of the 'innoxious life' is 'lost to a sense of peace, innocence and virtue'. In his *Essay on Epic Poetry* in verse (1782) William Hayley celebrated Tasso and defended him against Boileau:

> The Muse of Sion, not implor'd in vain,
> Guides to the impassion'd soul his heavenly strain.
> Blush, Boileau, blush, and for that pride atone
> Which slander'd Genius far above thy own;
> And thou, great injur'd Bard, thy station claim
> Amid the Demi-gods of Epic name. . . .

A defence against Boileau's attacks is one of the recurrent themes of these years; we come across it also in *A Poetical Tour* (1787) by William Parsons, who belonged to that circle of English writers residing in Florence known as the Della Cruscans.

It was inevitable that the hopeless love affair of Tasso

and Leonora should be likened to that of Héloïse and Abélard which enjoyed such popularity during the eighteenth century; thus in the fourth edition of Thomas Warwick's *Abelard to Eloisa* (about 1787) we find an imaginary epistle, 'Leonora to Tasso', suggested by Henry Layng's *Life of Tasso*, and, from the point of view of the form, by Pope's *Eloisa to Abelard*; like Pope's heroine, Leonora, unable to help Tasso to escape from prison, is left to wander at twilight over the scenes they have loved: Tasso is already presented in a romantic light, as an idealistic poet lost in a conventional, hard, self-seeking, and deceitful world.

Hoole's *Jerusalem Delivered* was reprinted in 1797, 1802, 1807, and 1810. In Sir Brooke Boothby's *Sorrows, Sacred to Penelope* (1796) we find a blank-verse translation of Clorinda's death; in Francis Lathom's play, *Orlando and Seraphina; or, the Funeral Pile*, performed and published at Norwich about 1799, the story of Olindo and Sofronia was clumsily rehandled. While in Portal's drama the kind counsellor Orcano turned out to be Olindo's father, in Lathom's Ismeno, the cruel counsellor and sole persecutor of the lovers, turns out to be the father of Seraphina, i.e. Sofronia! He is stabbed to death by Clorinda when she comes to the rescue of the doomed lovers, Clorinda who is violently in love with Orlando, i.e., Olindo.

A more reliable life of Tasso than Layng's was issued in two handsome quarto volumes in Edinburgh in 1810 by John Black, who consulted Crescimbeni, Tiraboschi, and Serassi's *Vita di Torquato Tasso* (1785): he discredited the legend of Tasso's love for Leonora and presented the poet's incarceration as a device of the thoughtful Duke's in order to save Tasso, rather too much given to wine and walking in the rain, from pneumonia. It must have been fashionable by the end of the eighteenth century to quote Tasso's lines, for Mrs Radcliffe puts them into the mouth of Ellena in *The Italian* as well as other heoines of her tales, and Sydney Owenson (later Lady Morgan) makes her lovers quote them in *The Novice of Saint Dominick* (1815). In 1815 William Hazlitt, in a famous review of Sismondi's book *De la littérature du midi de l'Europe*, published in *The Edinburgh Re-*

view (June), preferred Ariosto to Tasso, though admitting parts of Tasso to be 'exquisitely beautiful':

> the incidents in Ariosto are more lively, the characters more real, the language purer, the colouring more natural . . . Tasso was the more accomplished writer, Ariosto the greater genius. . . . The perusal of the one leaves a very high relish behind it; there is a vapidness in the other, which palls at the time, and goes off sooner afterwards. Tasso indeed sets before us a dessert of melons, mingled with roses:—but it is not the first time of its being served up. . . .

The favourite passage of Hazlitt was the stanza (xv, 20) 'Giace l'alta Cartago; a pena i segni/De l'alte sue ruine il lido serba': reflecting Tasso in a virile mood, whereas Keats (we should hardly have expected it to be otherwise with the poet of *Endymion*) seems to have stuck to the scenes in the enchanted garden, for in his *Ode to Apollo* he gives this portrait of Tasso next to those of Homer, Virgil, Milton, Shakespeare and Spenser:

> Next thy Tasso's ardent numbers
>   Float along the pleased air,
> Calling youth from idle slumbers,
>   Rousing them from Pleasure's lair:—
> Then o'er the strings his fingers gently move,
> And melt the soul to pity and to love.[58]

But the English romantic poet whose name first comes to mind when we speak of Tasso is Byron who, in *The Lament of Tasso*, crystallised the legend of his unhappy life and transmitted it to one who drew inspiration from it for works of a higher artistic value than was Byron's rather mannered and rhetorical monologue, I mean Eugène Delacroix. In 1817 Byron went to Rome, passing through Ferrara rather than Mantua, for, he said: 'I would rather see the cell where they caged Tasso than the birthplace of that harmonious plagiary

[58] In Keats's letters we find (September 21 or 22, 1818) a quotation of 'Gather the rose', probably from st. 15 of Canto xvi of the *Gerusalemme*.

and miserable flatterer'—Virgil—'whose cursed hexameters were drilled into me at Harrow'. In Florence, where he stayed a single day, Byron wrote *The Lament of Tasso* and sent it straightaway to John Murray: it was published in July 1817. The poem is preceded by an Advertisement in which we read that 'the cell where Tasso was confined in the hospital of St. Anna attracts a more fixed attention than the residence or the monument of Ariosto—at least it had this effect on me'. As always in Byron, Tasso is but one of the masks of his own personality: the same was to be true for Dante in *The Prophecy of Dante*. The poet who says:

> I stoop not to despair;
> For I have battled with mine agony,
> And made me wings wherewith to overfly
> The narrow circus of my dungeon wall—

is evidently Byron rather than Tasso.

This poem offers a remarkable literary interest, being the model of Browning's and Swinburne's lyrical monologues. An apostrophe like that of the ninth stanza:

> Go! tell thy brother, that my heart, untamed
> By grief, years, weariness,—and it may be
> A trait of that he would impute to me—
> From long infection of a den like this,
> Where the mind rots congenial with the abyss,—
> Adores thee still; and add—that when the towers
> And battlements which guard his joyous hours
> Of banquet, dance, and revel, are forgot,
> Or left untended in a dull repose,—
> This, this, shall be a consecrated spot!
> But *Thou*—when all that Birth and Beauty throws
> Of magic round thee is extinct—shalt have
> One half the laurel which o'ershades my grave—

is manifestly echoed in Swinburne's *Anactoria*:

> Yea, thou shalt be forgotten like spilt wine,
> Except these kisses of my lips on thine
> Brand them with immortality; but me—

> Men shall not see bright fire nor hear the sea,
> Nor mix their hearts with music . . . .
>
>   . . . .
>
> But in the light and laughter, in the moan
> And music . . .
> Memories shall mix and metaphors of me.

Both Tasso and Sappho recede into the background, after having offered to the romantic poet a pretext to assert his pervasive personality. This personality, in the case of Byron, so impressed Goethe that, comparing him with Tasso, he found Byron superior to this latter 'for spirit, breadth of vision and creative power. . . . Byron is the burning bush which consumes to ashes the holy cedar of Lebanon. One may poison the whole *Jerusalem Delivered* with a single line from *Don Juan.*'

The very year of Byron's death, 1824, saw the publication of another version of the *Gerusalemme,* in Spenserian stanzas, by Jeremiah Holme Wiffen, a Quaker, son of a small ironmonger. Wiffen was librarian to the Duke of Bedford and author of poetical compositions (*Aeonian Hours* and *Julia Aspinula*) which he quotes after his name on the title-page of the translation: a specimen of this (the Fourth Book) had already been brought out in London by the publisher John Warren in 1821. This translation, not devoid of merit, and certainly superior to Hoole's, which Foscolo called 'wretched' ('sciagurata'), had the honour of a long review from the poet of the *Grazie,* who must have known Wiffen through his friend Lord John Russell, the sixth son of the Duke of Bedford. This long essay by Foscolo, translated by Thomas Roscoe, appeared in the *Westminster Review* for October 1826, on the occasion of the second edition of Wiffen's version printed in that year; it is published, in the Italian original, in the tenth volume of the National Edition of Foscolo's Works (Florence, 1953). Foscolo, though finding in Wiffen many defects, admits that he possesses a heart and an imagination which place him much above the 'frozen' ('temprato di gelo') Hoole. A specimen of Foscolo's minute analysis (Wiffen had at least this merit of having given rise to it) will be enough. 'Le mamme acerbe e crude' of young Armida (iv, 31) become in English:

> Ripe as the grape just mellowing into wine
> Her bosom swells to sight.

Foscolo's remarks, which are only summed up by Roscoe, read in the English version:

> However, we do not mean to cast upon Mr. Wiffen the slightest reproach because he has not sacrificed to his author whatever compact he may have entered into with his own religious feelings. But in such cases he ought to content himself with a mere translation, without attempting either to add or suppress any idea. 'Ripe' is just the contrary of 'acerbe e crude'; it would scarcely be applied to the bosom of the Medicean Venus, whilst it is to be admired in the noble statue recently brought to light in Greece and which probably represented the Venus Mother among the ancients. But in the gallery of the Duke of Bedford, three virgin bosoms with 'mamme acerbe e crude', in the group of the Graces by Canova, might have inspired an exact and beautiful interpretation of the text of Tasso.

Foscolo was alluding here to the Three Graces by Canova, a group in the gallery of the Duke of Bedford of whom, as we have said, Wiffen was librarian: that marble group which in 1822 had been reproduced in a sumptuous folio containing, among other things, 'fragments of a Greek hymn to the Graces', i.e., actually Foscolo's *Grazie*.[59]

Wiffen's version was reprinted during the Victorian period, but the story of Tasso's reputation in England during the Victorian period is uneventful. A dialogue like the following one in *Daniel Deronda* (1876) (ch. v) is typical: 'I dote on Tasso,' says Gwendolen. Then Tasso's relations with Leonora are discussed. 'I know nothing of Tasso except the *Gerusalemme liberata*, which we read and learned by heart at

[59] *Outline Engravings and Descriptions of the Woburn Abbey Marbles*, 1822, containing 'Fragments of a Greek Hymn to the Graces', and 'Dissertation on an Ancient Hymn to the Graces' by Ugo Foscolo.

school.' To which Mrs Arrowpoint replies: 'Ah, his life is more interesting than his poetry. I have considered the early part of his life as a sort of romance. When one thinks of his father Bernardo, and so on, there is so much that must be true.'

I do not think many read the *Gerusalemme* in England nowadays; certainly the poem is not read and learned by heart in the schools. In the works of modern English authors, particularly poets, it is not uncommon to come across quotations from Dante, but we have grown so accustomed to the absence of our other great poets, that one feels no little surprise in finding Tasso as the chief topic in a BBC transmission published in *The Listener* for January 24, 1952. In *Millom Delivered* Norman Nicholson, one of the best known among the young English poets, says that after having contemplated from the opposite bank of the River Duddon, on the very border of the Lake District which Wordsworth celebrated, the Millom Ironworks standing like a battleship with all her funnels smoking and a great wash of steam about her bows, he had come home and had to stay in bed for a few days with a chill, and as he lay there, reading the *Gerusalemme*, Tasso's poem, Millom and Jerusalem got all muddled together in his mind; and Millom began to take on the look of Jerusalem as Tasso describes it in the stanzas beginning 'Gierusalem sovra duo colli è posta' (iii, 55–56), and the dry, sandy, barren desert of the old mines seemed well described by 'la terra intorno nuda d'erba', so that the poet, inspired, began to write some verses on Millom Ironworks in Tasso's own stanza. There are three stanzas of it (the final couplet of the last one was never written), and they may be quoted as the only modern English attempt at reproducing Tasso's *ottava* (whereas poems in Dante's *terza rima* are to be found in the verse of Eliot, Auden, and Allen Tate):

> This ridge commands the estuary. Here,
> Among the cow-licked green, the limestone walls,
> I gaze across grey, gulping sands to where
> The city watches from her window-sills.
> Her tilted roofs are high with sunlight; her
> Foundations are upon the holy hills:

Her feet are firm as rivets in the rock;
Her arms enclose the slagback and the dock.

The desert lies around her; wry and dry,
Long twisted dunes of rubble, screes of ore,
Shelvings of ash, ponds where reflected blue
Turns sour as bile and rots the willows bare;
A blowing grind of grit that scours the sky
And stuffs the snuffy rat-holes, mouth and ear—
And scabs of haematite on walk and wood
Where men's veins drain into the land's own blood.

Viscous and salt the sea; bitter and black,
The boil of scum dries among welts of mud;
The half-choked mussels huddle to the rock;
Plantain and sallow thrift and gutterweed
Creep like a cuticle down crack and creek
And the flat limbs of silt are stripped and dead.

'But why, you may ask,' says the poet, 'why try to imitate
Tasso at all when I was standing beside the river so closely
associated with Wordsworth? Why, when I have got the
"Duddon Sonnets", when I have got "The Prelude" and
"Resolution and Independence"—why quote the Italian epic?
It is because on Midsummer Eve I wanted an epic. I saw the
landscape as a heroic landscape; I wanted not "Resolution
and Independence" but "Attack and Triumph": *così vince
Goffredo*.' I will not repeat here Nicholson's contention that
modern man is closer to the epic mood of strife and conquest
than to Wordsworth's contemplation of the natural landscape;
but I cannot refrain from noticing how even Tasso, the softest
and most musical of poets, may appear, to the eyes of a poet
of our Age of Anxiety, in the unusual garb of the singer of a
waste land. Never before in the course of centuries, so far as
I know, had Tasso appeared in that light: another proof, if
any be needed, that in our time the point of view of the
artists has really undergone a revolution.

T. S. Eliot and Dante

It is curious to look at Eliot's relation to Dante from an Italian point of view, for, while there is an established tradition of Dante worship to which all, both Italians and foreigners, more or less conform—a tradition that affords little variety of manifestations,—T. S. Eliot's tribute could not easily be disposed of in a supplement to Paget Toynbee's monumental collection of references and allusions.[1] Eliot's relation to Dante is too intimate for that, and the fact of this intimacy, and the way in which it was brought about, have in them something entirely novel and, as I have hinted in what I hope may not seem a light-hearted beginning— curious.

Mr Matthiessen, in his penetrating study of Eliot,[2] has established a connection between him and the line of Dante scholarship at Harvard (from Longfellow through Charles Eliot Norton, Santayana and Charles Grandgent); and since Eliot himself in the Preface to his *Dante* acknowledges his debt to Grandgent's *Dante* and to Santayana's essay in

[1] *Britain's Tribute to Dante in Literature and Art: a Chronological Record of 540 Years*, London, 1921.

[2] *The Achievement of T. S. Eliot*, Oxford University Press, 1935, Enlarged edition, 1947. On the Boston milieu at the end of the nineteenth century—the milieu in which Eliot was educated—see Van Wyck Brooks, *New England, Indian Summer, 1865–1915*, New York, 1940, pp. 409 ff., 435, 442, 515 ff.: 'Eliot's mind was a mirror of Boston Alexandrianism.'

Three Philosophical Poets, there is no reason to minimise the part played by traditional scholarship in the formation of Eliot's estimate of Dante. However, it is not through the quiet ways of the school-room and the library that Eliot learnt to admire Dante. As in other fields (the metaphysical poets, the Elizabethan dramatists), he may owe much to scholars for broadening his knowledge, but his discoveries have been made thanks to non-academic critics, to free lances of culture. Arthur Symons revealed to him Laforgue; Ezra Pound, through his book on *The Spirit of Romance* (1910), and still more through his table-talk, made him aware of the greatness of Dante, gave him that shock of surprise that no recognised authority on the poet could have communicated. Before he knew *The Spirit of Romance* and had opportunities of intercourse with Pound in London, Eliot had read a smattering of the early Italian poets, especially the two Guidos and Cino, but it was Pound who sharpened his interest in these writers, who made them alive to him.[3]

No matter how much serious scholars may laugh at Pound's amateurishness and inaccuracy (and whoever has seen his pretentious and futile edition of Cavalcanti published in Genoa in 1932 is likely to underrate Pound's merits), he had the power of bringing to life the Provençal and early Italian poets, of seeing them 'as contemporary with himself'. 'Any scholar'—says Eliot in his *Introduction* to the *Poems* of Ezra Pound—'can see Arnaut Daniel or Guido Cavalcanti as literary figures; only Pound can see them as living beings.' Pound could give to his Dante that flavour of experience for which one would vainly seek in the pages of orthodox scholars. Not the least reason why Eliot's relation to Dante is out of the beaten track of Dante worship lies, no doubt, in the manner in which he discovered him through Pound. The deep resonance throughout Eliot's work of the 'superb verses of Arnaut Daniel in his Provençal tongue': [4]

> Ara vos prec, per aquella valor
> que vos guida al som de l'escalina,

[3] Private letter.

[4] *Dante,* p. 40. Ezra Pound draws attention to these lines on p. 16 of *The Spirit of Romance:* 'Arnaut speaks not in Italian, but in his own tongue; an honour paid to no one else in the *Commedia.*'

sovenha vos a temps de ma dolor!
Poi s'ascose nel foco che li affina—

bears witness to that origin, points to a strong appeal to the 'auditory imagination' of Eliot,[5] an appeal infinitely deeper than the bare meaning of the passage would have made. One may doubt whether, without the stimulus of the actual delivery of those lines on the part of such a *gourmet* of pure sounds as Pound, Eliot's imagination would ever have crystallised round them. For, I think, one may trace to Pound that aspect of Eliot which consists in investing a quotation in a foreign language with a significance infinitely more potent than its verbal import, a significance which in Eliot achieves an emblematical pregnancy.

Traces of initiation by Pound are to be seen not only in this peculiar attitude to the musical spell of the verse, but also in the critical ideas Eliot has ex*pound*ed (this was not an intentional pun!) on Dante in his early essay, in *The Sacred Wood* (1920), in his lecture on *Shakespeare and the Stoicism of Seneca* (1927), and in his *Dante* (1929).

The aim of this last work, 'to persuade the reader first of the importance of Dante as a master—I may even say, *the* master—for a poet writing to-day in any language', coincides with the climax of *The Spirit of Romance*, whose Chapter vi, ushered by the solemn 'Advenit Magister' at the end of Chapter v, deals with *Il Maestro*. At the outset Pound declares: 'This book is not a philological work . . . I am interested in poetry,' and proceeds with an onslaught on the stupidity of philologists. Nothing could be more alien to Eliot than such a slapdash manner; his way of approach is more modest and subtle, but his essay is shown, in conclusion, to possess the same characteristics as Pound's book: 'If my task had been to produce another brief "introduction to

---

[5] The last line appears in *The Waste Land* among the 'fragments . . . shored against [the poet's] ruin' (line 427); *Ara Vos Prec* is the title of the 1919 book of verse; the words 'Sovegna vos' appear in *Ash-Wednesday*; the third section of this poem was at first published separately under the title *Som de l'Escalina*; etc. See Matthiessen, p. 101, and the whole of Chapter iv for the 'auditory imagination.'

the study of Dante" I should have been incompetent to perform it. But in a series of essays of "Poets on Poets" the undertaking, as I understand it, is quite a different one. . . . I am not a Dante scholar, etc.' Pound makes dramatically a solemn oath to speak only out of first-hand acquaintance of the texts, more plainly he declares that 'throughout the book all critical statements are based on a direct study of the texts themselves and not upon commentaries', and apropos of early Italian poems (p. 98): 'After a few hours with the originals, criticism becomes a vain thing.' Eliot's advice is to the same effect, though couched in a more guarded manner (p. 68): 'Read in this way it [the *Vita Nuova*] can be more useful than a dozen commentaries [on the *Comedy*]. The effect of many books about Dante is to give the impression that it is more necessary to read about him than to read what he has written, etc.' In either case, then, the author emphasises the fact that he is a poet, that his chief concern is with the texts themselves, that commentaries are apt to obscure one's appreciation, that the way of approach of the philologist is not his own (Pound goes a step further, and shows the utmost contempt for academic critics).[6]

Pound's idea of poetry (p. 5) as of 'a sort of inspired mathematics, which gives us equations, not for abstract figures, triangles, spheres, and the like, but equations for the human emotions', may be said to be the starting-point of Eliot's theory of the 'objective correlative': [7] 'The only way of expressing emotion in the form of art is by finding an "objective correlative"; in other words, a set of objects, a situation, a chain of events which shall be the formula of that *particular* emotion; such that when the external facts, which must terminate in sensory experience, are given, the emotion is immediately evoked.' Pound's statements are not so clearcut as Eliot's, but I think that by reading in the light of the definition of poetry quoted above, the following passages, we have the chief elements of Eliot's theory of the 'objec-

[6] Whom, needless to say, he quotes inaccurately; for instance the author of the *Grundriss* is Gröber, not Grüber.

[7] 'Hamlet and his Problems', in *The Sacred Wood*, p. 92.

tive correlative',[8] as well as of his interpretation of Dante's vision:

> The cult of Provence had been a cult of the emotions; and with it there had been some, hardly conscious, study of emotional psychology. In Tuscany the cult is a cult of the harmonies of the mind. If one is in sympathy with this form of *objective imagination* [9] and this quality of vision, there is no poetry which has such enduring, such, if I may say so, indestructible charm (p. 103).

Apropos of Guinizelli's sonnet *Vedut'ho la lucente stella diana,* Pound writes: (p. 92)

> Here the preciseness of the description denotes, I think, a clarity of imaginative vision. In more sophisticated poetry an epithet would suffice, the picture would be suggested. The dawn would be 'rosy-fingered' or 'in russet clad'. The Tuscan poetry is, however, of a time when the seeing of visions was considered respectable, and the poet takes delight in definite portrayal of his vision. The use of epithet is an advance on this method only when it suggests a vision not less clear, and its danger is obvious. In Milton or Swinburne, for example, it is too often merely a high-sounding word, and not a swift symbol of vanished beauty.

In general, on Tuscan poetry (p. 104):

> Faults this poetry may have . . . this virtue it ever has, it is not rhetorical, it aims to be what it is, and never pretends to be something which it is not.

And on the *Vita Nuova* in particular (p. 114):

> Any-one who has in any degree the faculty of vision will know that the so-called personifications are real and not artificial. Dante's precision both in the *Vita Nuova* and in the *Commedia* comes from the attempt to reproduce exactly the thing which has been clearly seen. The 'Lord of terrible

---

[8] The term 'objective correlative' is first found used by Washington Allston in *Lectures on Art,* 1850. See R. W. Stallman, *The Critic's Notebook,* University of Minnesota Press, 1950, p. 116.

[9] The italics are mine.

aspect' is no abstraction, no figure of speech. There are some who can not or will not understand these things.

This passage must be read in connexion with what Pound says of allegory (p. 85):

> With the Romaunt of the Rose we come to a third thing . . . we get the allegory, a sort of extension of the fable. . . . In the romances he [the mediaeval author] has told of actions and speech and has generalized about the emotions. In the allegory he learns to separate himself, not yet from complete moods, but from simple qualities and passions, and to visualize them.

These are, then, the points made by Pound in *The Spirit of Romance*: allegory is a means for the poet to separate himself from the emotions, to visualise them; this kind of vision is not a pretence; there is nothing rhetorical about it; in the Middle Ages the seeing of visions was considered respectable; the attempt of the poet to reproduce exactly the thing he has *actually* seen makes for clarity.

If now we read what Eliot says on the same subject in his *Dante* we will easily perceive the affinities:

> . . . the simplicity of Dante has another detailed reason. . . . What is important for my purpose is the fact that the allegorical method was a definite method not confined to Italy; and the fact, apparently paradoxical, that the allegorical method makes for simplicity and intelligibility. We incline to think of allegory as a tiresome cross-word puzzle. We incline to associate it with dull poems (at best, *The Romance of the Rose*), and in a great poem to ignore it as irrelevant. What we ignore is, in a case like Dante's, its particular effect towards lucidity of style. . . . We have to consider the type of mind which by nature and *practice* tended to express itself in allegory; and for a competent poet, allegory means *clear visual images*. . . . Allegory is only one poetic method, but it is a method which has very great advantages. Dante's is a *visual* imagination. . . . It is visual in the sense that he lived in an age in which men still saw visions. . . . We have nothing but dreams, and we have forgotten that seeing visions . . .

was once a more significant, interesting, and disciplined kind of dreaming. . . . All I ask of the reader, at this point, is to clear his mind, if he can, of every prejudice against allegory, and to admit at least that it was not a device to enable the uninspired to write verses, but really a mental habit, which when raised to the point of genius can make a great poet as well as a great mystic or saint. And it is the allegory which makes it possible for the reader who is not even a good Italian scholar to enjoy Dante. Speech varies, but our eyes are all the same. . . . Dante's attempt is to make us see what he saw.

This passage (*Dante,* pp. 22–23) is closer to *The Spirit of Romance* than the passage on allegory in the short essay in *The Sacred Wood,* but the conclusion is the same. In the short essay Eliot justifies the usefulness of allegory in a poem of so vast an ambit as the *Commedia,* but he calls it an artificial and mechanical framework, where intelligence is not necessary: 'the emotional structure within the scaffold is what must be understood, the structure made possible by the scaffold. This structure is an ordered scale of human emotion. . . . Dante's is the most comprehensive, and the most *ordered* presentation of emotions that has ever been made'.

Of Dante's use of elaborate imagery such as that of the figure of the eagle composed by the spirits of the just in the *Paradise* (xviii and following cantos), Eliot says (p. 54): 'Such figures are not merely antiquated rhetorical devices, but serious and practical means of making the spiritual visible'.

Another passage of Pound's (p. 117) illustrated for the *Commedia* the point of view which is in everything but in name Eliot's theory of the 'objective correlative':

There is little doubt that Dante conceived the real Hell, Purgatory, and Paradise as states, and not places. Richard St Victor had, somewhile before, voiced this belief, and it is, moreover, a part of the esoteric and mystic dogma. *For the purposes of art* and popular religion it is more convenient to deal with such matters *objectively*; this also was most natural in an age wherein it was the poetic convention to personify abstractions, thoughts, and the spirits of the eyes and senses, and indeed nearly everything that could be regarded as an object, an essence, or a quality. It is therefore expedient in reading the *Commedia* to regard Dante's descriptions of the actions and conditions of the shades as descriptions of men's mental states in life, in which they are, after death, compelled to continue: that is to say, *men's inner selves stand visibly before the eyes of Dante's intellect*.[10]

We shall see how Eliot as a poet has tried to revive this practice chiefly in *Ash-Wednesday*: to find clear images, or rather symbols, appealing to the senses, apt to evoke the emotions of which they are the 'objective correlative'.

It may be noted incidentally that Pound's definition of the nature of an image in such a way as to stress the union of sense and thought, the presence of the idea *in* the image ('An "Image" is that which presents an intellectual and emotional complex in an instant of time') [11]—a definition intimately connected with Pound's knowledge of Dante's practice—was capable of establishing at once a link between the poetry of Dante and his circle and that of the English metaphysical poets of the seventeenth century of whom Eliot was to write [12] that they felt 'their thought as immediately as the odour of a rose. A thought to Donne was an experience, it modified his sensibility'.[13]

[10] The italics in this passage are mine.

[11] Pound's essay reprinted in *Pavannes and Divisions*, 1918. See Matthiessen, pp. 60 and 72.

[12] Essay on 'The Metaphysical Poets', in *Homage to John Dryden*, 1924, reprinted in *Selected Essays*. This essay was originally a review of Grierson's *Metaphysical Lyrics and Poems of the Seventeenth Century*, Oxford, 1921. Grierson wrote (p. xiii) of metaphysical poetry of the highest sort that its themes are 'the boldest conceptions, the profoundest intuitions, the subtlest and most complex classifications and "discourse of reason", if into these too the poet can "carry sensation", make of them passionate experiences communicable in vivid and moving imagery'.

[13] In the eighth of his Clark Lectures (not published) Eliot defined metaphysical poetry as 'that in which what is ordinarily apprehensible only by thought is brought within the grasp of feeling, or that in which what is ordinarily only felt is transformed into thought without ceasing to be feeling.' In the seventh lecture Eliot stressed the difference between Dante and Donne, which I had tried to define myself in *Secentismo e marinismo in Inghilterra*, Florence, 1925, p. 107.

In the brief comparisons of Dante with Milton and Shakespeare, Eliot is also sharing Pound's viewpoint. His slighting allusion to Milton's Satan as 'the curly-haired Byronic hero of Milton' (p. 33) agrees with Pound's '*Paradise Lost* is conventional melodrama, and later critics have decided that the devil is intended for the hero, which interpretation leaves the whole without significance' (p. 165).[14] As for Shakespeare, Pound says: 'Shakespear alone of the English poets endures sustained comparison with the Florentine. Here are we with the masters; of neither can we say, "He is the greater"; of each we must say, "He is unexcelled." . . . Dante would seem to have the greater imaginative "vision" . . . Shakespear would seem to have greater power in depicting various humanity, and to be more observant of its foibles.' Eliot (pp. 17 and 51) says substantially the same thing: 'What I have in mind is that Dante is, in a sense to be defined (for the word means little by itself), the most *universal* of poets in the modern languages. That does not mean that he is "the greatest", or that he is the most comprehensive—there is greater variety and detail in Shakespeare . . . Dante and Shakespeare divide the modern world between them; there is no third. . . . Shakespeare gives the greatest *width* of human passion; Dante the greatest altitude and greatest depth.'

The short essay on Dante concludes with these words:

> Dante, more than any other poet, has succeeded in dealing with his philosophy, not as a theory (in the modern and not the Greek sense of that word) or as his own comment or reflection, but in terms of something *perceived*. When most of our modern poets confine themselves to what they had perceived, they produce for us, usually, only odds and ends of still life and stage properties; but that does not imply so much that the method of Dante is obsolete, as that our vision is perhaps comparatively restricted.

We have accounted for the origin of the first portion of this statement. As for the latter part, one must bear in mind

[14] Cf. 'Dante', in *The Sacred Wood*: 'About none of Dante's characters is there that ambiguity which affects Milton's Lucifer.'

what Santayana, to whom Eliot confesses himself indebted, had written: [15]

Our poets are things of shreds and patches; they give us episodes and studies, a sketch of this curiosity, a glimpse of that romance; they have no total vision, no grasp of the whole reality, and consequently no capacity for a sane and steady idealization. This age of material elaboration has no sense for perfection. Its fancy is retrospective, whimsical, and flickering; its ideals, when it has any, are negative and partial; its moral strength is a blind and miscellaneous vehemence. Its poetry, in a word, is a poetry of barbarism.

With these poets Santayana contrasts Dante, whom he characterises with words that Eliot may have remembered:

Dante gives a successful example of the *highest species* of poetry. His poetry covers the whole field from which poetry may be fetched, and to which poetry may be applied, from the inmost recesses of the heart to the uttermost bounds of nature and of destiny. If to give imaginative value to something is the minimum task of a poet, to give value to all things, and to the system which things compose, is evidently his greatest task.

In another passage, this one in the book on Dante, Eliot is taking to task the modern mind (pp. 62–63):

It appears likely, to anyone who reads the *Vita Nuova* without prejudice, that it is a mixture of biography and allegory; but a mixture according to a recipe not available to the modern mind. When I say the 'modern mind', I mean the minds of those who have read or could have read such a document as Rousseau's *Confessions*. The modern mind can understand the 'confession', that is, the literal account of oneself, varying only in degree of sincerity and self-understanding, and it can understand 'allegory' in the abstract. Nowadays 'confessions', of an insignificant sort, pour from the press; everyone *met son cœur à nu,* or pretends to; 'personalities' succeed one another in interest. It is difficult to conceive of an age (of many ages) when

[15] *Interpretations of Poetry and Religion,* and *Three Philosophical Poets.*

human beings cared somewhat about the salvation of the
'soul', but not about each other as 'personalities'. Now
Dante, I believe, had experiences which seemed to him of
some importance; not of importance because they had
happened to him and because he, Dante Alighieri, was
an important person who kept press-cutting bureaux busy;
but important in themselves; and therefore they seemed
to him to have some philosophical and impersonal value.

It is interesting, in view of the development which this
theory of 'impersonality' had received in the essay on *Tradition and the Individual Talent*,[16] to trace it back to the reading of Professor Grandgent's *Dante* (New York, 1916), a
book to which Eliot gives the first place in the list of works
that have influenced him. Says Professor Grandgent (pp. 289–
290):

In no respect, perhaps, do medieval writings differ more
patently from modern than in their dignified impersonality.
Contrast this attitude for a moment with our present-day
effusiveness, our pitiful eagerness to disclose to anyone who
will listen, each petty detail of our bodily and spiritual
existence. Think of the flood of trivial self-revelation that
pours from the lips of the catchpenny scribbler or the
sublimated chorus-girl.[17] And some people must care to
read these confidences, else they would not be printed:
that is the strangest part of it. Such display would once
have seemed almost indecent as walking naked in the
street. If the exhibition of the ego was foreign to medieval
taste, the observation of self was scarcely less so. Intro-

[16] 'The progress of an artist is a continual self-sacrifice, a continual extinction of personality. . . . The point of view which I
am struggling to attack is perhaps related to the metaphysical
theory of the substantial unity of the soul: for my meaning is, that
the poet has, not a 'personality' to express, but a particular medium
which is only a medium and not a personality, in which impressions and experiences combine in peculiar and unexpected ways.
Impressions and experiences which are important for the man
may take no place in the poetry, and those which become important in the poetry may play quite a negligible part in the man,
the personality'.
[17] Compare with Eliot's passage quoted above: 'Nowadays "confessions," of an insignificant sort, *pour* from the press, etc.'

spection was confined, in the main, to religious experience, where it is legitimate and necessary.

We have thus seen how some of the most characteristic utterances of Eliot as a critic—his theory of the 'objective correlative', the other of the 'impersonality of the poet'—arose in connexion with his study of Dante. The ideas he finds in Santayana and Grandgent witness to that moral idealism and that dread of vulgarity which are typical of the Puritan mind; [18] the ideas he develops under the stimulus of Pound, *il miglior fabbro*,[19] concern rather the technique of poetry, the finding out of a pattern of clear visual images capable of evoking immediately the underlying emotion. Pound quoted also (p. 150) Arthur Symons on Cary's translation: 'To translate Dante is an impossible thing, for to do it would demand, as the *first* requirement, a *concise* and *luminous* style equal to Wordsworth at his *best*.' (The italics are Pound's.)

The blend of these various elements gives to Eliot's interpretation of Dante that peculiar character which is likely to strike an Italian as unfamiliar and curious—as I said at the beginning. Possibly Symons' words have led Eliot to perceive a similarity between the language of Dante and that of Dryden and Pope. The whole first paragraph of his chapter on the *Purgatory* and the *Paradise* deserves to be quoted:

> For the science or art of writing verse, one has learned from the *Inferno* that the greatest poetry can be written with the greatest economy of words, and with the greatest austerity in the use of metaphor, simile, verbal beauty, and elegance. When I affirm that more can be learned about how to write poetry from Dante than from any English poet, I do not at all mean that Dante is thereby greater than Shakespeare or, indeed, any other English poet. I

[18] See Matthiessen, pp. 7–8 (1947 ed., pp. 9–10).

[19] *The Waste Land* is dedicated to Pound, *il miglior fabbro,* according to the description of Arnaut Daniel in Dante (*Purgatory,* xxvi, 117), which Pound had adopted as the title of the second chapter of *The Spirit of Romance.* As for the title of *The Waste Land,* Professor Renato Poggioli, in a private conversation, suggested a possible reminiscence of *Inferno,* xiv, 94, where Crete is called 'un paese guasto'.

put my meaning into other words by saying that Dante can do less *harm* to anyone trying to learn to write verse, than can Shakespeare. Most great English poets are *inimitable* in a way in which Dante was not. If you try to imitate Shakespeare you will certainly produce a series of stilted, forced, and violent distortions of language. The language of each great English poet is his own language; the language of Dante is the perfection of a common language. In a sense, it is more pedestrian than that of Dryden or Pope. If you follow Dante without talent, you will at worst be pedestrian and flat; if you follow Shakespeare or Pope without talent, you will make an utter fool of yourself.

It will perhaps surprise Eliot if an Italian qualifies his statement in so far as his own literature is concerned. Whenever Italians have tried to imitate Dante, they have produced sometimes flat and pedestrian verse, but more frequently have written precisely in that stilted and forced style which Eliot thinks proper to the worst imitators of Shakespeare: witness the two following passages—chosen at random out of many equally to the point—one by Vincenzo Monti, the other by Gabriele D'Annunzio:

> D'italo nome troverai qui tali
>   che dell'uman sapere archimandriti
>   al tuo pronto intelletto imprennâr l'ali.
> (*In Morte di Lorenzo Mascheroni*, i, 82 ff.)

> Ei nella solitudine si gode
>   sentendo sé come inesausto fonte.
>   Dedica l'opre al Tempo; e ciò non ode.
>   (*La Tregua*, in *Laudi*, Libro III)

Italians who read Shakespeare, on the other hand, frequently find his language direct and possessing the very accent of life. In either case it could be easily shown that the illusion is caused by the ignorance in which one naturally is of the conventions of a foreign language. What matters for us here is not to ascertain to what extent Dante's style can be considered *simple* (in fact, Dante fits his language to the theme so that examples of all kinds of style can be found in him), but to know that to T. S. Eliot that style *seems* simple, that 'in twenty years he has written about a dozen lines in that style successfully; and compared to the dullest passage of the *Divine Comedy*, they are "as straw".'

When Chaucer wanted to imitate Dante, he wrote thus:

> O noble, O worthy Petro, glorie of Spayne,
> Whom Fortune heeld so hye in magestee,
> Wel oghten men thy pitous deeth complayne!

and Shelley:

> As in that trance of wondrous thought I lay,
> This was the tenour of my waking dream:—
> Methought I sate beside a public way . . .

Such passages sound Dantesque enough to an Italian ear, no less Dantesque than the passages of Monti and D'Annunzio quoted above. They are conceived in what literary historians call the Dantesque manner. This Dante, needless to say, has nothing to do with the inspirer of the dozen lines or so of which T. S. Eliot is proud.

Eliot's indebtedness to Dante ranges from the quotation and the adaptation of single lines or passages to the deeper influence in concrete presentation and symbolism. Actual quotations bear out well Eliot's appreciation of Dante as the poet who achieves the perfection of a common language, who teaches 'that a straightforward philosophical statement can be great poetry'. All the following passages have in common a quality of plain statement which is not couched in a very different form than it would be in prose:

> Or puoi la quantitate
> comprender de l'amor ch'a te mi scalda,
> quand'io dismento nostra vanitate,
> trattando l'ombe come cosa salda.
> (*Purgatory*, xxi, 133–136; motto to *Prufrock*)[20]

[20] I quote from the 'Testo critico della Società Dantesca Italiana'. These lines are given wrongly in the editions of Eliot's *Poems*, thus:

> la quantitate
> Puote veder del amor che a te mi scalda, etc.

Inaccuracies have also slipped into the next quotation; *torno* should be *tornò*.

S'i'credesse che mia risposta fosse
a persona che mai tornasse al mondo,
questa fiamma staria sanza più scosse;
ma però che già mai di questo fondo
non tornò vivo alcun, s'i'odo il vero,
sanza tema d'infamia ti rispondo.

(*Inferno*, xxvii, 61–66; motto to *The Love
Song of J. Alfred Prufrock*)

E 'n la sua volontade è nostra pace.

(*Paradise*, iii, 85)

La forma universal di questo nodo
credo ch'i' vidi, perché più di largo,
dicendo questo, mi sento ch'i' godo.

(*Paradise*, xxxiii, 91–93)

These last two quotations are favourites with Eliot; of the
whole passage from which the last quotation is taken, he
says (p. 54): 'Nowhere in poetry has experience so remote
from ordinary experience been expressed so concretely, by a
masterly use of that imagery of *light* which is the form of certain types of mystical experience.' [21]

From such passages one can infer that the influence of
Dante could lie for Eliot only in the strengthening of that
tendency to use a language not different from the ordinary,
and at the same time capable of philosophical turns, that he
had found in his early model, Laforgue.

After what Eliot says apropos of the *Commedia*, that 'genuine poetry can communicate before it is understood' (p. 16),
after what he says elsewhere on the 'auditory imagination',[22]
one would expect to find in his poems traces of the rhythm
of Dante. However, direct imitation of the *terzina dantesca*,
such as poets like Chaucer and Shelley attempted, with little
success, is not a thing which would have appealed to a poet
as subtle as Eliot.[23] Moreover, the *terzina* is apt to have a
somewhat stilted and forced sound; when Eliot says that
Dante communicated to him a poetic emotion before he

[21] Cf. Matthiessen, p. 153 (1947 ed., p. 152), for an attempt
of Eliot's to produce a similar effect in *The Rock*.
[22] See Matthiessen, Ch. iv.
[23] See, however, the passage of *Little Gidding* discussed in
the last portion of the present essay, which has been added.

properly understood the text, the appeal to his auditory imagination must have been more an appeal of words than of rhythm in its flow: 'The style of Dante has a peculiar lucidity—a *poetic* as distinguished from an *intellectual* lucidity. The thought may be obscure, but the word is lucid, or rather translucent' (p. 18).

Here again we shall get a clearer idea of the impression Dante's poetry must have made on Eliot's auditory imagination, if we refer to what Ezra Pound felt about *la dolce lingua toscana* (p. 103):

> The best poetry of this time appeals by its truth, by its subtlety, and by its refined exactness. Noffo Bonaguida thus expresses himself and the peculiar introspective tendency of his time:
>
>> Ispirito d'Amor con intelletto
>> Dentro dallo meo cor sempre dimora,
>> Che mi mantiene in gran gioia e 'n diletto
>> E senza lui non viveria un'ora.

In his chapter on *Il Maestro*, Pound remarks (p. 148):

> There are beautiful images in the *Paradiso*, but the chief marvel is not the ornament. Such lines as Canto v, 7–12:
>
>> Io veggio ben sì come già risplende
>>   nello intelletto tuo l'eterna luce,
>>   che, vista sola, sempre amore accende;
>> e s'altra cosa vostro amor seduce,
>>   non è se non di quella alcun vestigio
>>   mal conosciuto, che quivi traluce— [24]

lose too much in a prose translation, illuminated though they be in essence. . . . Though it be true that no man who has not passed through, or nearly approached, that spiritual experience known as illumination—I use the word in a technical sense—can appreciate the *Paradiso* to the full, yet there is sheer poetic magic in a line like (Canto vii, 130)—

>> Gli angeli, frate, e il paese sincero

which no lover of the highest art can fail to feel.

[24] This is the text given by Pound; the 'Testo critico' is somewhat different.

Other passages are quoted by Pound in Italian, as their beauty of sound cannot be rendered in any other language; they are passages of philosophical import (e.g., *Paradise*, vii, 136–144), rich in Latin polysyllables, or plain lines, whose charm would strike only a refined ear, like the line quoted above from *Paradise*, vii, or:

> In queste stelle, che intorno a lor vanno

(from the same Canto, 138) which possibly conveys to Pound more than to an average Italian ear, for he says that 'with the suave blending of the elided vowels, [it] has in its sound alone more of the serene peace from that unsullied country than can be conveyed in any words save those flowing from the lips of a supreme genius.'

In a similar way, Eliot's feeling for syllable and rhythm in Dante is more for the common qualities of the *dolce lingua toscana* than for the actual metrical skill of the poet.

In Eliot's imitations of Dantesque lines, true, we detect an echo of Dante's unmistakable *endecasillabo*:

> A crowd flowed over London Bridge, so many,
> *I had not thought death had undone so many.*
> > (*The Waste Land*, 62–63)
> sì lunga tratta
> di gente, ch'io non averei creduto
> *che morte tanta n'avesse disfatta.*
> > (*Inferno*, iii, 55–57)
> Highbury bore me. Richmond and Kew
> Undid me.
> > (*The Waste Land*, 293–294)
> Siena mi fe', disfecemi Maremma.
> > (*Purgatory*, v, 133)
> Issues from the hand of God, the simple soul
> > (*Animula*)
> *Esce di mano a lui che la vagheggia*
> . . . .
> l'anima semplicetta che sa nulla
> > (*Purgatory*, xvi, 85–88)

But such passages need not detain us for long: one can find similar deft insertions in dozens of other poets. The shock of surprise they give us adds no doubt to the effect of the poem,[25] but it is not from them that we can learn what Dante's influence has meant for Eliot.

That influence is closely connected with Eliot's interpretation of Dante's allegory along the lines suggested by Ezra Pound—as we have seen above. Clear visual images, a concise and luminous language: these are the two qualities of Dante Eliot has in mind. The former are the 'objective correlative' of the emotions they intend to suggest, the latter appeals to the auditory imagination: there is an element of extreme precision and an element of vagueness in both; for the mind of the reader is stirred by the symbolical import of the precise images, whereas—in contrast with the apparent terseness of the vocabulary—'the feeling for syllable and rhythm penetrates far below the conscious levels of thought and feeling, invigorates every word; sinks to the most primitive and forgotten, returns to the origin and brings something back, seeks the beginning and the end.' [26]

How much a Dantesque influence of this kind differs from a traditional imitation can be seen by reading side by side Eliot's *La Figlia Che Piange* and Rossetti's *Blessed Damozel:*

Stand on the highest pavement of the stair—
Lean on a garden urn—
Weave, weave the sunlight in your hair—
Clasp your flowers to you with a pained surprise . . .

The blessèd Damozel leaned out
　　From the gold bar of Heaven;

　　·　·　·　·　·　·　·　·

She had three lilies in her hand,
　　And the stars in her hair were seven.

Rosetti's images are directly derived from the *stil nuovo*, but are almost degraded to stage properties; they suggest only an archaic ornamentation, while their original spirit has vanished. The poet speaks in disguise. It is interesting to read what

[25] See Matthiessen, p. 20 (1947 ed., p. 22) for an analysis of these insertions.
[26] Essay on Arnold.

Eliot says of Rossetti's poem (*Dante,* p. 48): 'First by my rapture and next by my revolt, [it] held up my appreciation of Beatrice by many years'. When Eliot wrote his *Blessed Damozel, La Figlia Che Piange,* the pattern of the Pre-Raphaelite poem may have haunted the dim corners of his memory, but the clear visual images which rose in his mind had nothing of the stiff fastidiousness of Rossetti; the picture conjured up is taken from our everyday experience, not from the exquisite conventions of a *fondo oro*; but how much more suggestive of light is Eliot's image than Rossetti's! 'Weave, weave the sunlight in your hair'—'And the stars in her hair were seven': we have only to read these two lines one after the other to become fully aware of the difference of the two methods.[27]

In *Ash-Wednesday,* however, Eliot's method seems to come strangely near to Rossetti's. The beginning of the second section of that poem appears difficult to distinguish from the Pre-Raphaelite manner:

> Lady, three white leopards sat under a juniper-tree
> In the cool of the day, having fed to satiety
> On my legs my heart my liver and that which had been
>   contained
> In the hollow round of my skull. And God said
> Shall these bones live? shall these
> Bones live?

[27] That *The Blessed Damozel* was actually at the back of Eliot's mind while writing *La Figlia Che Piange* may be seen also from the curious recurring of the Rossettian pattern in the last stanza:

> She turned away, but with the autumn weather
> Compelled my imagination many days,
> Many days and many hours:
> Her hair over her arms and her arms full of flowers. . . .

Compare:

> . . . to them she left, her day
> Had counted as ten years.
> (To one, it is ten years of years.)
> . . . Yet now, and in this place,
> Surely she leaned o'er me—her hair
>   Fell all about my face. . . .
> Nothing: the autumn fall of leaves . . .

We seem instantly to breathe the atmosphere of the *Vita Nuova*, with its quaint allegorical devices (the famous dream in the Third Chapter, Love feeding the Lady with the poet's heart), and its mixture of the sensuous and the ethereal. Besides, the poem begins with that significant address, 'Donna' (Lady), which had quite a special connotation in Dante's circle. It is only in the following lines that we find again Eliot the admirer of the plain philosophical statements of Dante, with their lucid polysyllables: [28]

> And that which had been contained
> In the bones (which were already dry) said chirping:
> Because of the goodness of this Lady
> And because of her loveliness, and because
> She honours the Virgin in meditation,
> We shine with brightness.

Evidently the Lady of the poet is a sister of Dante's *donne benedette*. When we read further:

> The Lady is withdrawn
> In a white gown, to contemplation, in a white gown—

and, in the fifth section:

> Will the veiled sister pray
> . . . .
> Will the veiled sister between the slender
> Yew trees pray . . .

our recollection becomes more precise. Have we not met this Lady in those last cantos of the *Purgatory* of which Ezra Pound exalted the magnificence? The connexion of those cantos with the *Vita Nuova* is stressed by Eliot (*Dante*, p. 48): 'We cannot understand fully Canto xxx of the *Purgatorio* until we know the *Vita Nuova*'; and he proceeds immediately to quote:

> sovra candido vel cinta d'uliva
> donna m'apparve
> (*Purgatory*, xxx, 31–32)

[28] For other instances of this style see *Burnt Norton*, in *Poems*, 1936.

All commentators explain that white is the hue of faith. Eliot
continues in *Ash-Wednesday:*

> Let the whiteness of bones atone to forgetfulness.
> There is no life in them. As I am forgotten
> And would be forgotten, so I would forget
> Thus devoted, concentrated in purpose.

Eliot's poem seems to be written in the same key as Canto
xxx of the *Purgatory:* 'In the dialogue that follows we see the
passionate conflict of the old feelings with the new; the effort
and triumph of a new renunciation, greater than renunciation at the grave, because a renunciation of feelings that
persist beyond the grave. In a way, these cantos are those
of the greatest *personal* intensity in the whole poem. . . . it
is in these last cantos of the *Purgatorio,* rather than in the
Paradiso, that Beatrice appears most clearly.' If we assume
that Eliot found in those cantos the inspiration of *Ash-
Wednesday,* the symbolism of this poem seems to become
suddenly transparent. The three white leopards belong to
the same animal symbolism as the eagle, the fox, and the
dragon in *Purgatory,* xxxii, and, of course, the three beasts in
Inferno, i. And we seem to discover an uncanny correspondence between the bones 'scattered and shining' (ii), and the
'membra in terra sparte' (*Purgatory,* xxxi, 50–51), between
the fountain (iv) and the 'fontana' (xxviii, 124),[29] between
the 'jewelled unicorns' which 'draw by the gilded hearse' and
the triumphal chariot of Dante's vision (xxix, 106 ff.), between the wings which 'are no longer wings to fly' (i), and
'non ti dovea gravar le penne in giuso' (xxxi, 58); and no
doubt between the beginning of the fourth section of Eliot's
poem and the apparition of Matelda:

> Who *walked* between *the violet and the violet*
> Who walked between
> The *various* ranks of *varied green* . . .

[29] 'But the fountain sprang up'. 'L'acqua che vedi . . . esce di
fontana salda e certa.'

una donna soletta che *si gia*
cantando e scegliendo *fior da fiore*

. . . .

la gran *variazion* de' freschi *mai*
(*Purgatory*, xxviii, 40–41, 36)

The 'sovegna vos' of the fourth section, from the 'Ara vos prec' passage in Canto xxvi, explains the use of the word 'dolour' a few lines before ('Sovegna vos a temps de ma *dolor*'), while 'Our peace in His will' translates the famous line of the *Paradiso* 'E 'n la sua volontade è nostra pace'. Definite suggestions from the *Purgatory* are not only the stairs in the third section, as has been already noticed,[30] but also the landscape dimly seen at the end of the second: 'in the cool of the day, with the blessing of sand . . . the quiet of the desert' (*Purgatory*, I: 'ora mattutina', 'lito deserto').

The pattern of the images in *Ash-Wednesday* seems thus suggested by Dante, but in a very peculiar way. It is as if Eliot had been reading Dante without giving much heed to the meaning, but letting himself be impressed by a few clear visual images: these he rearranges in his own mind just as in a kaleidoscope the same coloured glasses can give a no less harmonious (though different) design than the previous one.

Now this kind of influence fits singularly well what Eliot says of the first impression made on him by Dante (pp. 22–23): 'It is really better, at the start, not to know or care what they do mean . . . clear visual images are given much more intensity by having a meaning—we do not need to know what the meaning is, but in our awareness of the image we must be aware that the meaning is there too'. Thus the influence of Dante's allegory on Eliot consists in producing what Matthiessen has called a 'paradoxical precision in vagueness': the faces and shapes the poet sees on the stairway (*Ash-Wednesday*, iii) have a distant resemblance to those which Dante beholds in ecstatic vision while on his way on the stairs of *Purgatory* (Canto xv); but Eliot's images convey a sense of foreboding which is hardly found in Dante. Indeed Eliot achieves in that section of *Ash-Wednesday* an effect at which

[30] Matthiessen, p. 117.

the French symbolists of the *fin de siècle* are seen striving
in their too frequently disappointing poems: to conjure up
a haunting presence by partly very vivid, partly elusive, traits.
A similar effect is attempted in the fifth section of *The Waste
Land*.[31] Apart from the allegory, *Ash-Wednesday* reveals a
Dantesque influence also in the laboured cadences of many
lines.[32] Of course repetitions and assonances like:

> I no longer strive to strive towards such things. . . .
> Because I know I shall not know . . .
> Blown hair is sweet, brown hair over the mouth blown . . .
> . . . stops and steps of the mind over the third stair . . .
> Against the Word the unstilled world still whirled . . .
> . . . though I do not wish to wish these things . . .

and even more, passages like:

> Both in the day time and in the night time
> The right time and the right place are not here

[31]
> What is the city over the mountains
> Cracks and reforms and bursts in the violet air
>
> . . . .
> A woman drew her long black hair out tight
> And fiddled whisper music on those strings
> And bats with baby faces in the violet light
> Whistled, and beat their wings
> And crawled head downward down a blackened wall
> And upside down in air were towers . . .

The vision recalls to me the apocalyptical one of the Canzone ii of
the *Vita Nuova*, which Pound (p. 111) quotes in Rossetti's translation:

> Then saw I many broken hinted sights,
> In the uncertain state I stepped into.
> Meseem'd to be I know not in what place,
> Where ladies through the streets, like mournful lights,
> Ran with loose hair, and eyes that frighten'd you
> By their own terror, and a pale amaze
>
> . . . .
> And birds dropp'd in mid-flight out of the sky;
> And earth shook suddenly . . .

[32] The beginning of the poem is a literal rendering of Guido
Cavalcanti's famous *ballata*: 'Perch'i' non spero di tornar giammai.'
An echo of the words of this poem: 'la Donna mia Che per sua
cortesia Ti farà molto onore' may be found in the passage: 'Because of the goodness of this Lady . . .'

The place of grace for those who avoid the face
No time to rejoice for those who walk among noise and
    deny the voice— [33]

recall first of all the technique of G. M. Hopkins to an English reader.[34] But Hopkins's technique appears the more legitimate in a piece where the influence of Dante is so strong, in that Dante himself had delighted in the *bisticci* which Hopkins only revived, but did not invent (the vogue was mainly started by Guittone d'Arezzo). Readers of Dante are familiar with such lines as:

> ch'i' fui per ritornar più volte volto
> > (*Inferno*, i, 36)
> Fuor sei dell' erte vie, fuor sei dell' arte
> > (*Purgatory*, xxvii, 132)
> Per grazia fa noi grazia che disvele
> > (*Purgatory*, xxxi, 136)
> > fur negletti
> li nostri vóti, e vòti in alcun canto
> > (*Paradise*, iii, 57)
> Cred'io ch'ei credette ch'io credesse
> > (*Inferno*, xiii, 25)
> infiammò contra me gli animi tutti
> e gl' infiammati infiammâr sì Augusto . . .
> > (*Inferno*, xiii, 67–68)
> > assai ton prego
> e riprego che il prego vaglia mille
> > (*Inferno*, xxvi, 65–66)
> > come piante novelle
> rinnovellate di novella fronda
> > (*Purgatory*, xxxiii, 143–144)
> > ella che vedea il tacer mio
> nel veder di colui che tutto vede
> > (*Paradise*, xxi, 49–50)

[33] See also *Burnt Norton,* iii: 'Distracted from distraction by distraction.'

[34] Cf. Hopkins, *Poems,* 1918: p. 12: 'I am soft sift/In an hourglass': p. 13: 'glow, glory in thunder'; p. 29: 'I caught this morning morning's minion'; p. 35: 'of the best we boast'; p. 44: 'deserve to and do serve God to serve to . . .'; and chiefly *The Leaden Echo and the Golden Echo.*

To come back to the use of images in Eliot: apropos of *Gerontion* Matthiessen writes (p. 62; 1947 ed., p. 63):

As he [Eliot] said once in conversation, the images here are 'consciously concrete'; they correspond as closely as possible to something he has actually seen and remembered. But he also believes that if they are clearly rendered, they will stand for something larger than themselves; they will not depend for their apprehension upon any private reference, but will become 'unconsciously general'.

References in this poem to Mr. Silvero, Hakagawa, Madame de Tornquist, Fräulein von Kulp, De Bailhache, etc.; prayers 'for Guiterriez, avid of speed and power', for Boudin 'blown to pieces' in *Animula*, and similar allusions throughout Eliot's verse to definite people, and to significant details of scenery (for instance in *The Journey of the Magi*: 'and three trees on the low sky,/And an old white horse galloped away in the meadow, etc.'), may be said also to partake of Dante's method, which Professor Grandgent describes thus (p. 272–273), contrasting it with Bunyan's:

The one starts from an abstract concept and gives it a semblance of material form; the other takes something real and makes it stand for the quality it exemplifies. . . . One begets a character called Arrogancy; the other, to embody that vice, introduces an arrogant Florentine, Filippo Argenti, notorious for his unbridled temper. . . . In non-dramatic literature . . . the difference between the two is noteworthy, the second offering far better opportunities for vividness and illusion. Had Dante been a symbolist of the same kind as Bunyan, he would not have told his story in the first person; the hero would have been a shadowy Christian . . . he would have been obstructed, not by a leopard, a lion and a wolf, but by three monsters called, perhaps, Immoderateness, Violence, and Deceit. . . .

After what Pound says (p. 161) of the *Divina Commedia*, that it is 'in fact, a great Mystery Play, or better, a cycle of mystery plays', one turns to Eliot's mystery plays, *The Rock* and *Murder in the Cathedral*, expecting to find in them a Dantesque influence. This, however, if it can be said to exist at all, is put into the shade by the strong and evident Greek influence. The Greek chorus and the Bible are the models of Eliot in his dramas, as they were for authors with whom he does not claim kinship: Milton and Swinburne. No wonder then if some passages of those dramas have an odd Swinburnian ring. Is it again the case of an unsought-for return to an early favourite (we know that Swinburne, no less than Rossetti, influenced the formative years of Eliot's adolescence) [35] through a devious path?

Eliot's most sustained effort in imitating Dante is to be found in the second section of *Little Gidding*, which contains a long composition in unrhymed triplets, where rhythms, images, and ratiocinative passages, are strongly reminiscent of Dante:

> In the uncertain hour before the morning
> Near the ending of interminable night
> At the recurrent end of the unending
> After the dark dove with the flickering tongue
> Had passed below the horizon of his homing
> While the dead leaves still rattled on like tin
> Over the asphalt where no other sound was
> Between three districts whence the smoke arose
> I met one walking, loitering and hurried
> As if blown towards me like the metal leaves
> Before the urban dawn wind unresisting. . . .

Raymond Preston in his valuable commentary, '*Four Quartets* rehearsed', has traced some precise reminiscences of Dantesque passages in this part of the poem, though he has failed to notice that the very first line

> In the uncertain hour before the morning

echoes Dante's (*Purgatory*, ix, 53):

> Dianzi, ne l'alba che precede al giorno,

and he has failed to notice, too, that occasionally a modern influence blends with Dante's, as in the line:

> To purify the dialect of the tribe

[35] See Matthiessen, p. 21 (1947 ed., p. 23).

which is modelled on Mallermé's, *Le Tombeau d'Edgar Poe*:

Donner un sense plus pur aux mots de la tribu.[36]

In *The Dry Salvages* Eliot repeats in Italian the epithet of the Virgin from *Paradise*, xxxiii, 1: 'Figlia del tuo figlio'. But more than individual passages, it is important to stress the Dantesque spirit that permeates the whole, particularly the attempt to reproduce the plain, lucid statements of Dante: as in:

> yet the words sufficed
> To compel the recognition they preceded.
> And so, compliant to the common wind,
> Too strange to each other for misunderstanding,
> In concord at this intersection time
> Of meeting nowhere, no before and after,
> We trod the pavement in a dead patrol.
> I said: 'The wonder that I feel is easy,
> Yet ease is cause of wonder. Therefore speak:
> I may not comprehend, may not remember.'
> And he: 'I am not eager to rehearse
> My thoughts and theory which you have forgotten.
> These things have served their purpose: let them be.
> So with your own, and pray they be forgiven
> By others, as I pray you to forgive
> Both bad and good.'

The episodes of Francesca, of Brunetto Latini, of Cacciaguida, flash before our memory while reading these lines and those which follow in Eliot's poem. Still there is nothing archaic or mannered in this performance; so that while Eliot, before writing the *Four Quartets,* could declare that in twenty years he had written only about a dozen lines in Dante's style successfully, after that poem he can boast of having written at least two pages which, compared not to the dullest, but to any average passage in the *Divina Commedia,* are not 'as straw'.

[36] This influence has been noticed by Prof. Matthiessen, p. 192 (1947 ed.).

INDEX

n. indicates footnote

Abelard, Peter, 341
Accetto, Torquato, 205n.
Achillini, Claudio, 17, 245
Adams, J. Q., 183n.
Adamson, Archbishop, 94
Addison, Joseph 20, 21, 334, 335, 340
Aeschylus, 120n., 314
Alabaster, William, 13
Alanus de Insulis (Alain de Lisle), 30
Albertano da Brescia, 6
Alcaeus, 317
Alciat, 7, 11
Alençon, Duke of, 300
Alexander VI (Pope), *see* Borgia
Alexander, Sir William, 104, 105
Alfieri, Vittorio, 26, 84
Algarotti, Francesco, 23
Allegory, 353 ff., 365, 369
Allen, D. Cameron, 95n.
Allston, Washington, 352n.
Alphonsus, Emperor of Germany, 121, 128
Altichiero da Verona, 61n.
Anabaptist Washt and Washt, The, 134
Anacreon, 267
Andreini, Giovambattista, 19
Andrew, Thomas, 143n.
Anthology, Greek, 207, 208, 267, 270, 279
Antonio, Nicolas, 217n.
Arabian Nights, 74
Arden of Feversham, 118, 146
Aretino, Pietro, 131, 139, 141, 176, 182, 183, 184, 185, 289
Arguzia, 206 ff.
Ariosto, Ludovico, 12, 22, 62, 65, 117, 147, 148, 169, 176, 287–307, 311, 331, 333, 334, 336, 338, 339, 342, 343

Aristotle, 13, 96, 97, 117
Armi, Anna Maria, 286
Armstrong, W. A., 109n.
Ascham, Roger, 9, 10
Assimilation, in what cases it is possible, 5
Auden, Wystan Hugh, 346
Axon, E. A., 65n.
Ayres, Philip, 17

Bachelet, Th., 150
Bacon, Francis, 100, 101, 102, 103
Baddeley, St. Clair, 72
Baïf, Antoine de, 287
Bandello, Matteo, 8
Bang, W., 169
Banking system, introduced into England, 4–5
Barclay, John, 244
Baretti, Giuseppe, 21, 22, 306, 336, 339
Barnes, Barnabe, 127
Baroque culture and art, 16, 211, 247, 251, 252; cult of female saints and martyrs, 204 ff.; partiality for symbols and emblems, 206
Bartoli, Daniello, 27
Basile, Giambattista, 166
Baskerville, John, 307
Battenhouse, R. W., 118n.
Baudelaire, Charles, 191, 192
Baudoin, Jean, 318n.
Bauhusius, Bernardus, 218n.
Beall, C. B., 308n.
Beaumont, Francis, 120, 186
Beauveau, Louis de, 66
Beckford, William, 305
Bedford, Countess of, 193
Bell, Charles G., 315n.
Belleforest, François de, 8
Bembo, Pietro, 270, 271, 272, 277, 278, 282
Benedetti, Anna, 288, 292